Henry Hart Milman

The history of the Jews from the earliest period down to modern times

Henry Hart Milman

The history of the Jews from the earliest period down to modern times

ISBN/EAN: 9783741163432

Manufactured in Europe, USA, Canada, Australia, Japa

Cover: Foto ©ninafisch / pixelio.de

Manufactured and distributed by brebook publishing software (www.brebook.com)

Henry Hart Milman

The history of the Jews from the earliest period down to modern times

THE

HISTORY OF THE JEWS.

FROM THE EARLIEST PERIOD DOWN TO MODERN TIMES.

By HENRY HART MILMAN, D.D.,
DEAN OF ST. PAUL'S.

THREE VOLUMES.—Vol. III.

FOURTH EDITION, REVISED AND EXTENDED.

LONDON:
JOHN MURRAY, ALBEMARLE STREET.
1866.

The right of Translation is reserved.

CONTENTS OF VOL. III.

BOOK XX.

JUDAISM AND CHRISTIANITY.

Effects of the Great Revolutions in the World, from the fourth to the eighth Century — Restoration of the Persian Kingdom and Magian Religion — Jews of Mesopotamia — Babylonian Talmud — Establishment of Christianity — Attempts at Conversion — Constantine — Julian — Rebuilding the Temple of Jerusalem — Theodosius and St. Ambrose — Conflicts between Jews and Christians — Conversions in Minorca and Crete — Tumults in Alexandria — Fall of the Patriarchate.. .. .. Page 1

BOOK XXI.

THE JEWS UNDER THE BARBARIAN KINGS AND THE BYZANTINE EMPERORS.

Irruption and Conquests of the Barbarians — Trade of the Jews — Slave Trade — Decrees of Councils — Of Pope Gregory the First — Conduct of the Christians to the Jews — Arian Kings of Italy — Pope Gregory the First — State anterior to the Rise of Mohammedanism in the Eastern Empire — Insurrections of the Samaritans — Laws of Justinian — Dispute about the Language in which the Law was to be read — State of the Jews in the Persian Dominions — Persecutions — Civil Contests — Conquest of Syria and Jerusalem by the Persians — Reconquest by the Emperor Heraclius 44

BOOK XXII.

JUDAISM AND MOHAMMEDANISM.

Jews in Arabia — Jewish Kingdom in Homeritis — Rise of Mohammed — Wars against the Arabian Jews — Progress of Mohammedanism — State of Spain — Cruel Laws of the Visigothic Kings — Conquest of Spain by the Moors — Persecuting Laws in France 89

BOOK XXIII.

GOLDEN AGE OF JUDAISM.

The Jews under the Caliphs — Rise of Karaism — Kingdom of Khosar — Jews under the Byzantine Empire — Jews breakers of Images — Jews of Italy — Jews under Charlemagne and Louis Debonnaire — Agobard, Bishop of Lyons — Jews in Spain — High state of Literature — Moses Maimonides.. .. .. Page 117

BOOK XXIV.

IRON AGE OF JUDAISM.

Persecutions in the East — Extinction of the Princes of the Captivity — Jews in Palestine — In the Byzantine Empire — Feudal System — Chivalry — Power of the Church — Usury — Persecutions in Spain — Massacres by the Crusaders — Persecutions in France — Philip Augustus — Saint Louis — Spain — France — Philip the Fair — War of the Shepherds — Pestilence — Poisoning of the Fountains — Charles the Fourth — Charles the Fifth — Charles the Sixth — Final Expulsion from France — Germany — The Flagellants — Miracle of the Host at Brussels 154

BOOK XXV.

JEWS IN ENGLAND.

First Settlement — William Rufus — Henry II. — Coronation of Richard I. — Massacre at York — King John — Spoliations of the Jews — Henry III. — Jewish Parliament — Edward I. — Statute of Judaism — Final Expulsion from the Realm 229

BOOK XXVI.

JEWS EXPELLED FROM SPAIN.

Superiority of the Jews of Spain — Early period — Alfonso VIII. — Ferdinand III. — Alfonso X., the Wise — Siete Partidas — Attempt at Conversion — Ferdinand IV. — Alfonso XI. — Pedro of Castile and Henry of Transtamare — Zeal of the Clergy — Pope Benedict XIII. — Conversions — Vincent Ferrer — New Christians — The Inquisition — Ferdinand and Isabella — Expulsion of the Jews from Spain — Sufferings in Italy — In Morocco — In Portugal — Their subsequent History in the two kingdoms 204

BOOK XXVII.

JEWS OF ITALY.

Early Period — The Popes — The family of Peter Leonis — Martin V
Page 325

BOOK XXVIII.

Jews in Turkey — In Italy — In Germany before the Reformation — Invention of Printing — Reformation — Luther — Holland — Negotiation with Cromwell — False Messiahs — Sabbathai Sevi — Frank, &c. — Spinoza 337

BOOK XXIX.

MODERN JUDAISM.

Change in the relative State of the Jews to the rest of Mankind — Jews in Poland — In Germany — Frederick the Great — Naturalization Bill in England — Toleration Edict of Joseph II. — Jews of France — Petition to Louis XVI. — Revolution — Bonaparte — More recent Acts for the Amelioration of the Civil State of the Jews — General Estimate of the number of Jews in Africa, Asia, Europe, America — Conclusion 384

BOOK XXX.

Survey of Influence of the Jews on Philosophy, Poetry, History, &c. 426

INDEX 457

HISTORY OF THE JEWS.

BOOK XX.

JUDAISM AND CHRISTIANITY.

Effects of the Great Revolutions in the World, from the fourth to the eighth Century — Restoration of the Persian Kingdom and Magian Religion — Jews of Mesopotamia — Babylonian Talmud — Establishment of Christianity — Attempts at Conversion — Constantine — Julian — Rebuilding the Temple of Jerusalem — — Theodosius and St. Ambrose — Conflicts between Jews and Christians — Conversions in Minorca and Crete — Tumults in Alexandria — Fall of the Patriarchate.

THE middle of the third century beheld all Israel thus incorporated into their two communities, under their Papacy and their Caliphate. The great events which succeeded during the five following centuries, to the end of the seventh or the middle of the eighth, which operated so powerfully on the destinies of the whole world, in the East as well as in the West, could not but exercise an important influence over the condition, and, in some respects, the national character of the Jews. Our History will assume, perhaps, its most intelligible form, if we depart in some degree from a dry chronological narrative, and survey it in relation to the more important of these revolutions in the history of mankind. 1st, The restoration of the Magian religion in the East, under the great Persian monarchy which arose on the ruins of the Parthian empire. 2ndly, The establishment of Christianity as the religion of the Roman empire. 3rdly, The invasion of the Barbarians. 4thly, The rise and progress of Mohammedanism.

I. The first of these points we have in some degree anticipated. The Prince of the Captivity probably rose to power in the interval between the abandonment of the Mesopotamian provinces by Hadrian, about 118 A.C., and the final decay of the Parthian kingdom, about 229 A.C., when that empire, enfeebled by the conquests of Trajan, and by the assumption of independence in the Persian province, held, but with a feeble hand, the sovereignty over its frontier districts. But his more splendid state seems to have been assumed after the accession of the Persian dynasty.

The reappearance of the Magian religion as the dominant faith of the East, after having lain hid, as it were, for centuries among the mountains of Iran, is an event so singular, that it has scarcely received the notice which it deserves in history. It arrested at once the progress of Christianity in the East, which was thrown back upon the western provinces of Asia and upon Europe, not without having received a strong though partial tinge from its approximation to that remarkable faith. The great Heresiarch Manes attempted to blend the two systems of belief—an attempt the less difficult, as many among the more successful of the early heretics had already admitted into their creed the rudiments of Oriental philosophy, which formed the groundwork of Magianism. But Manes met the fate of most conciliators; he was rejected, and probably both himself and his proselytes violently persecuted by both parties.[*] In

---

[*] Compare Hist. of Christianity, II. 322, &c.

what manner the sovereigns of Persia, and their triumphant priesthood, conducted themselves at first towards their Jewish subjects in Babylonia, we have little certain intelligence. Under Ardeschir Fire Temples arose in all quarters. A new or a revived religion is never wanting in zeal, and zealous religionists are rarely tolerant. Collision was inevitable. Some stories, which bear the stamp of authenticity, appear to intimate persecution. The usage of the Jews in *burying* the dead was offensive to the Magians; and there were certain days in which no light was permitted to be burning, excepting in the Fire Temples.[b] The Jews were unwillingly constrained to pay this homage to the Guebre ceremonial.[c] It is said that a fire-worshipper came into a room in Pumbeditha, where Abba Bar Hona lay ill, and took away the light. R. Jehuda cried out, "Oh, merciful Father! take us under thy protection, or lead us rather into the hands of the children of Esau" (the Romans).[d]

But on the whole their condition must have been favourable, as the pomp of their Prince, the wealth of his subjects, and the flourishing condition of the Mesopotamian schools,[e] are strong testimonies to the equitable and tolerant government of their Persian

---

[b] Jost, Judenthum, ii. 141. When R. Jochanan, in Tiberias, heard of the establishment of the religion of the Guebres, he fell to the earth in grief and dismay.

[c] Jost, Geschichte, iv. 308.

[d] Another saying is not so intelligible; it is a Babylonian saying, "Rather under the Arabs than under the Romans, rather under the Romans than under the Guebres, rather under the Guebres than under the learned Jews

(the learned were very bothheaded in those regions), rather under the learned than under widows and orphans." God severely visited any offence against widows or orphans. Jost, Judenthum, ii. 142.

[e] Jost, Geschichte, iv. 305. See on the schools and succession of teachers at Pumbeditha, which threw into the shade Naharden and Sura, Jost, iv. 310 et seqq.

rulers.[f] The Oriental cast, which many of their opinions had assumed as early as the Babylonian Captivity, and the prevalence of the cabalistic philosophy, which, in its wild genealogy of many distinct œons or intelligences, emanating from the pure and uncreated light, bore a close analogy to the Dualism of the Magians; and its subordinate hierarchy of immaterial and spiritual beings, angels, or genii; would harmonize more easily with, or at least be less abhorrent from, the prevailing tenets of the Magians, than the more inflexible Christianity, which rejected the innovations of Manes.

The compilation of the Babylonian Talmud,[g] as it shows the industry of its compilers, seems to indicate likewise the profound peace enjoyed by the Jewish masters of the schools. This great work was commenced and finished under the superintendence of Rabbi Asche.[h] This celebrated Head of the schools introduced

---

[f] In some instances they introduced slight deviations from the Law, or rather from the Mischna, in favour of their new masters. The rule to abstain from all intercourse with the heathen for three days before each of their holy days, was limited in the case of the fireworshipping to the holy day itself. Though Rab declared it a sin to learn anything of a Magian, yet the Jews studied astronomy in common with them. Jost, p. 143.

[g] The Abbé Chiarini, an Italian, proposed to publish a French translation of the whole Jerusalem and Babylonian Talmuds (p. 52). In his Théorie du Judaïsme, and in his Talmud de Babylone, Leipsic, 1831, he explained his views and intentions.

He met with strong opposition. His death however, while tending the sick of the cholera, in 1832, unhappily cut short his labours.

[h] Chiarini assigns the date of the Talmud of Babylon to the fifth and beginning of the sixth century. R. Asche died A.D. 427. It was finished seventy-three years after the death of Asche by R. Jose (p. 35). It is anterior to the Koran, which borrows from, perhaps quotes it. Chiarini says that it has three characteristics which distinguish it from that of Jerusalem: I. The confusion with which it envelopes the doctrines. II. The subtlety and suppleness which its teachers display in their unequal contest with violence and hard necessity. III. The bitterness

a new mode of teaching; his scholars met twice in the year, and received each time two portions of the Law and of the Mischna, the whole circle of Jewish study, which had been divided into sixty parts. Their comments on their appointed task were brought back on the next day of meeting, the best were selected and harmonized, and from these in thirty years[1] grew the Gemara, which, with the Mischna, forms the Babylonian Talmud,[a] that wonderful monument of human industry, human wisdom, and human folly. The reader at each successive extract from this extraordinary compilation hesitates whether to admire the vein of profound allegorical truth, and the pleasing moral apologue, to smile at the monstrous extravagance,[1] or to shudder at the

---

* and hatred with which they look on all who have contributed to the servitude of the Jews, especially the Christians. Each Talmud has books and chapters wanting in the other. On the borrowing of the Koran from the Talmud, read the excellent treatise of Geiger, Was hat Mohammed aus den Judenthum genommen.[b]

[1] Chiarini makes it about a century or more in its full growth.

[a] Chiarini points out one more remarkable distinction between the Babylonian and Jerusalem Talmuds— the substitution in the Babylonian of commerce in the place of agriculture. p. 57.

[1] There is undeniable truth and justice in the severe words of Edzard, quoted by Chiarini, i. 277 :—" Credat Judæus Apella ista impia atque blasphema de Deo asserta, crebras Rabbinorum contradictiones, innumeras absurditates et falsitates, plusquam aniles fabulas, pessimas et ut plurimum ridiculas Scripturæ sacræ detorsiones, ineptas argumentationes, abjectas de verbo divino locutiones; evidentissima mendacia, plusquam ethnicas superstitiones, ipsum deniqne ad magiam et varii generis peccata alia multiplicem instructionem quæ singulis Gemaræ paginis maximo numero occurrunt . . . esse divina oracula Moisi in Monte Sinai tradita, ut ad posteros propagerentur." But may it not be well to look at the same time to the beam in our own eye? If the Chris-

[b] The first edition, I., of the Babylonian Talmud is that of Bomberg, Venice, 1520. II. Justiniani, Venice, 1546-50. III. Frobenius, Basil. 1578-9-80. (But the passages hostile to Christianity were expunged by order of the Council of Trent.) IV. Cracow, 1603-5. V. Lublin, 1617-22. VI. Amsterdam, in 4to., 1644. VII., VIII. Frankfort on the Oder, 1697, 1715-21. IX. Amsterdam or Frankfort on the Maine, 1714, 1721. There are other later editions. On the translations of separate Treatises and Chapters, see Wolf and Chiarini, p. 45 et sqq.

daring blasphemy. The influence of the Talmud on European superstitions, opinions, and even literature, remains to be traced; to the Jew the Talmud became the magic circle, within which the national mind patiently laboured for ages in performing the bidding of the ancient and mighty enchanters, who drew the sacred line, beyond which it might not venture to pass."

II. The Western Jews must have beheld with deeper dismay, and more profound astonishment at the mysterious dispensations of Providence, the rival religion of Christianity (that apostasy, as they esteemed it, from

---

tianity of the Middle Ages were systematised and cast into one great authoritative book (that Christianity which, as sanctioned and maintained by the Infallible Church, is virtually attributed to the Holy Spirit of God), would there be not found the same conflict between the most exalted and the most debasing notions of the Godhead; the same profound piety and the same gross superstition; the same pure morality and the same doubtful moral chicanery; the same solemn trifling; the same occasional wisdom, the same folly and the same fraud; the same miserable devilry ("chacun de nous en a mille à gauche et dix mille à droite;" so says R. Huna —Chiarini, p. 289); the same trust in the providence and presence of God; the same irreconcileable and remorseless hatred of men of other faith (only that in the Jews, being few and feeble, these passions mostly evaporated in idle curses, in the Christians led to acts of merciless massacre); and the same purity, love, and charity? If on the one hand the gleams of light, wisdom, humanity, love of God, are more rare and feeble in the Talmud (take such a precept as this, "One touch of compunction in the heart of man is worth many and many flagellations"—Chiarini, p.303—compared with the monkish manuals of self-scourging); on the other hand apply the great principle, "pessimi est corruptio optimi;" how much more natural, more pardonable, is this jealous hedge drawn around the imperfect Law, than the engrafting of such low and darkling, if not barbarous and wicked precepts, on the peaceful, pure, simple, and beneficent Gospel! See further on the Talmud, the close of this Book.

" "Depuis la naissance jusqu'à la mort, depuis la pointe du jour jusqu' au lever des étoiles, dans leurs maisons ainsi que dans la Synagogue, leur vie privée et publique n'est qu'une suite de cérémonies minutieuses et des pratiques légales qui se trouvent consignées dans le Talmud." Chiarini, p. 181.

the worship of Jehovah), gradually extending over the whole of Europe, till at length, under Constantine, it ascended the imperial throne, and became the established religion of the Roman world. The period between the death of the Patriarch, R. Jehuda the Holy, and the accession of Constantine to the empire, had been barren of important incidents in Jewish history. The Patriarchate of Tiberias seems gradually to have sunk in estimation. This small spiritual court fell, like more splendid and worldly thrones, through the struggles of the sovereign for unlimited sway, and the unwillingness of the people to submit even to constitutional authority. The exactions of the pontiff, and of the spiritual aristocracy—the Rabbins—became more and more burthensome to the people. The people were impatient even of the customary taxation.[a] Gamaliel succeeded Jehuda, Jehuda the Second, Gamaliel. This pontiff was of an imperious character; he surrounded himself with a sort of body-guard; at the same time he was outshone by his competitors in learning, Simon ben Laches and R. Jochanan, whose acknowledged superiority tended still farther to invalidate the supremacy of the Patriarch.[b]

A temporary splendour was thrown around the Jew-

---

[a] At a period considerably later, the Apostles of the Patriarch are called in a law of Honorius *devastators*. It is asserted in the life of Chrysostom, that the heads of the synagogues were displaced if they did not send in enough money.

[b] Whoever wishes for a more full account of these rivalries, jealousies, and feuds in the school of Tiberias, may read the sixth chapter of Jost's iv^th Book. There is one striking saying of R. Jochanan, showing the Rabbinical character: "A learned Bastard is to be preferred to an ignorant High Priest," p. 162. For other sayings of R. Jochanan, see Jost, Judenthum, ii. 147. The teachings of the Sopherim are intimately interwoven with the Law, and to be held in equal, if not higher estimation. On Simon ben Laches—his reproof of the pomp and pride of his Nasi, p. 150.

iah name by the celebrity of Zenobia, the famous Queen of Palmyra, who was of Israelitish descent. But the Jews of Palestine neither derived much advantage from the prosperity, nor suffered in the fall of that extraordinary woman.[b] Her favourite, Paul of Samosata, seems to have entertained some views of attempting an union between Judaism and Christianity; both parties rejected the unnatural alliance. The Jews spoke contemptuously of the wise men who came from Tadmor, and Paul of Samosata was rejected by the orthodox church as an intractable heretic.[q]

On the formal establishment of Christianity, under Constantine the Great, the more zealous Jews might tremble lest the Synagogue should be dazzled by the splendour of its triumphant competitor, and, recognizing the manifest favour of the Divinity in its success, refuse any longer to adhere to a humiliated and hopeless cause; while the Christians, after having gained this acknowledged victory over Paganism, might not unreasonably expect that Judaism, less strongly opposed to its principles, would relax its obstinate resistance, and yield at length to the universally acknowledged dominion of the new faith.

But the Rabbinical authority had raised an insurmountable barrier around the Synagogue. Masters of the education, exercising, as we have shown, an unceasing and vigilant watchfulness, and mingling in every

---

[b] Jost, Geschichte, iv. 167 : " Von dem angeblichen Judenthum dieser so genannten Kaiserin von Palmyra wissen die Rabbiner nichts." Judenthum, ii. 155.

[q] Euseb. Hist. Ecc. vii. 27 ; Milman, Hist. of Christianity, ii. p. 256.

The Jews repudiated with equal determination this attempt to reconcile the two religions. R. Jochanan refused to receive Palmyrenian proselytes. The Rabbis, like the Christians, reprove the irreligious pomp and luxury of the Palmyrene Court. Jost, ii. 157.

transaction during the whole life of each individual;—still treating their present humiliation merely as a preparatory trial from the over-faithful God of their fathers, and feeding their flock with hopes of a future deliverance, when they should trample under foot the enemy and oppressor;—enlisting every passion and every prejudice in their cause; occupying the studious and inquisitive in the interminable study of their Mischna and Talmuds;*—alarming the vulgar with the terrors of their interdict; while they still promised temporal grandeur as the inalienable, though perhaps late heritage of the people of Israel; consoling them for its tardy approach by the promise of the equally inalienable and equally exclusive privilege of the children of Israel—everlasting life in the world to come;†—these spiritual leaders of the Jews still repelled, with no great loss, the aggressions of their opponents. At the same time unhappily the Church had lost entirely, or in great degree, its most effective means of conversion—its miraculous powers, the simple truth of its doctrines, and the blameless lives of its believers. It substituted authority, and a regular system of wonder-working, which the Jews, who had been less affected than might have been supposed by the miracles of our Lord and his Apostles, had no difficulty in rejecting, either as mani-

---

* Chiarini states, with some truth, that it was one of the objects of the Talmud "d'élever une muraille de séparation entre les Juifs et les autres peuples de la terre, en présentant à ses compagnons d'infortune des remparts plus solides dans la haine et dans l'orgueil que ceux des villes dont ils venaient d'être dépouillés." p. 21.

† It is a curious illustration of the growing alienation between the Jews and the Christians that Origen seems to have kept up an amicable intercourse with many Jews. Jerome, a century later, was obliged to submit to a secret and nocturnal intercourse with his teacher. Epist. ad Pamm. Compare Vitringa, De Syn. Vet.

fest impostures, or works of malignant and hostile spirits. In fact, the Rabbins were equal adepts in these pious frauds with the Christian clergy, and their people, no less superstitious, listened with the same avidity, or gazed with the same credulity, on the supernatural wonders wrought by their own Wise Men, which obscured, at all events neutralized, the effects of the miracles ascribed to the Christian saints. Magical arts were weapons handled, as all acknowledged, with equal skill by both parties. The invisible world was a province where, though each claimed the advantage in the contest, neither thought of denying the power of his adversary. A scene characteristic of the times is reported to have taken place in Rome; the legend, it will easily be credited, rests on Christian authority.[t] A conference took place in the presence of Constantine and the devout empress-mother, Helena, between the Jews and the Christians. Pope Sylvester, then at the height of his wonder-working glory, had already triumphed in argument over his infatuated opponents, when the Jews had recourse to magic. A noted enchanter commanded an ox to be brought forward; he whispered into the ear of the animal, which instantly fell dead at the feet of Constantine. The Jews shouted in triumph, for it was the Ham-semphorash, the ineffable name of God, at the sound of which the awe-struck beast had expired. Sylvester observed with some shrewdness, "As he who whispered the name must be well acquainted with it, why does he not fall dead in like manner?" The Jews answered with con-

---

[t] Even Baronius doubts the authority of this legend. It appears first in the later Byzantines, Zonaras, t. iii. in init.; Simeon Metaphrastes, pars ii.; Glycas, p. 491 (edit. Bonn); Nicephorus, vii. 36; Cedren. t. i. p. 491 (edit. Bonn).

temptuous acclamations—"Let us have no more verbal disputations, let us come to acts." "So be it," said Sylvester, "and if this ox comes to life at the name of Christ, will ye believe?" They all unanimously assented. Sylvester raised his eyes to heaven, and said with a loud voice—"If *he* be the true God whom I preach, in the name of Christ, arise, O ox! and stand on thy feet." The ox sprang up, and began to move and feed. The legend proceeds, that the whole assembly was baptized.

The Christians, by their own account, carried on the contest in a less favourable field than the city of Rome, and urged their conquests into the heart of the enemy's country. Constantine, by the advice of his mother Helena, adorned with great magnificence the city which had risen on the ruins of Jerusalem. It had become a place of such splendour, that Eusebius, in a transport of holy triumph, declared that it was the New Jerusalem foretold by the prophets. The Jews were probably still interdicted from disturbing the peace or profaning the soil of the Christian city, by entering its walls. They revenged themselves by rigidly excluding every stranger from the four great cities which they occupied—Dio Cæsarea (Sepphoris), Nazareth, Capernaum, and Tiberias. As it was the ambition of the Jews to regain a footing in the Holy City, so it was that of the Christians to establish a church among the dwellings of the circumcised. This was brought about by a singular adventure. Hillel had succeeded his father, Judah the Second, in the patriarchate. If we are to believe Epiphanius, the Patriarch himself had embraced Christianity, and had been secretly baptized on his death-bed by a bishop. Joseph, his physician, had witnessed the scene, which wrought strongly upon his mind.[a] The house of Hillel, after his death, was kept closely shut up by his suspicious countrymen. Joseph obtained entrance, and found there the Gospel of St. John, the Gospel of St. Matthew, and the Acts, in a Hebrew translation. He read and believed. When the young Patriarch, another Judah (the Third), grew up, Joseph was appointed an apostle, or collector of the patriarchal revenue. It seems that Christian meekness had not been imbibed with Christian faith, for he discharged his function with unpopular severity. He was detected reading the Gospel, hurried to the synagogue, and scourged. The bishop of the town (in Cilicia) interfered. But Joseph was afterwards seized again and thrown into the Cydnus, from which he hardly escaped with his life. This was not the wisest means of recovering a renegade; Joseph was publicly baptized, rose high in the favour of Constantine, and attained the dignity of Count of the Empire. Burning with zeal—it is to be hoped not with revenge—he turned all his thoughts to the establishment of Christian churches in the great Jewish cities. He succeeded under the protection of the government, and with the aid of a miracle. As he commenced an edifice on the site of a heathen temple in Tiberias, the Jews enchanted the lime which was to be used for mortar—it would not burn. But Joseph having sanctified some water with the sign of the cross, the spell was dissolved, and the building arose to the discomfiture and dismay of his opponents.

The laws of Constantine, with regard to the Jews, throw more real light on their character and condition.[z]

---

[a] Epiphanii Hæres, c. 30. Epiphanius asserts that he heard the whole of this from Joseph himself when 70 years old.

[z] Constantine in a public document declared that it was not for the dignity of the Church to follow that most hateful of all people, the Jews, in the

The first of these statutes appears to authenticate the early part of the history of Joseph, and was, no doubt, framed in allusion to his case.[r] It enacted, that if the Jews should stone, or endanger the life of, a Christian convert, all who were concerned should be burned alive. This statute shows the still fiery zeal of the Jews, and their authority within the walls of their own synagogue; nor had they any right to complain, if proselytes to the established faith should be protected from their violence under the severest penalties. The second more intolerant clause of this statute prohibited all Christians from becoming Jews, under the pain of an arbitrary punishment; and, six months before his death, a third decree was issued by Constantine, prohibiting Jews from possessing Christian slaves.[s] The reason assigned for this

---

celebration of the Passover.

See the Apostolic Canon: Εἴ τις ἐπίσκοπος ἢ ἄλλος κληρικὸς νηστεύει μετὰ Ἰουδαίων, ἢ ἑορτάζει μετ' αὐτῶν, δέχεται αὐτῶν τὰ τῆς ἑορτῆς ξένια οἷον ἄζυμα, ἢ τι τοιοῦτον, καθαιρείσθω· εἰ δὲ λαϊκὸς ᾖ, ἀφοριζέσθω. LXII. apud Cotelcr. Pat. Apost. ii. 451.

[r] "Judæis et majoribus eorum et Patriarchis volumus intimari: quod si quis post hanc legem aliquem, qui eorum feralem fugerit sectam, et ad Dei cultum respexerit, saxis aut alio furoris genere (quod nunc fieri cognovimus) ausus fuerit adtentare, mox flammis dedendus est, et cum omnibus suis participibus concremandus. Si quis vero ei populo ad eorum nefariam sectam accesserit, et conciliabulis eorum se applicaverit, cum ipsis pœnas meritas sustinebit." Cod. Theodos. Tit. xvi. viii.

[s] There is some doubt whether this law was so early as Constantine, and whether Constantine did more than prohibit the circumcision of slaves. The law stands thus in Ritter. Cod. Theodos.: " Si quis Judæorum Christianum mancipium, vel cujuslibet alterius sectæ, mercatus circumciderit, minime in servitute retinent circumcisum, sed libertatis privilegiis, qui hoc sustinuerit, potiatur." If the Jews were altogether prohibited from buying such slaves, the prohibition to circumcise them would seem superfluous. Later statutes show that they had many Christian slaves. Eusebius, however, writes thus, as in the text: Ἀλλὰ καὶ Ἰουδαίοις μηδένα Χριστιανὸν ἀνωμοθέτει δουλεύειν· μὴ γὰρ θεμιτὸν εἶναι προφητοφόντοις καὶ κυριοκτόνοις, τοὺς ὑπὸ τοῦ σωτῆρος λελυτρωμένους ζυγῷ δουλείας ὑπάγεσθαι· εἰ δ' εὑρεθείη τις τοιοῦτος τὸν μὲν ἀπείσθαι ἐλεύθερον, τὸν δὲ ζημίᾳ χρημάτων κολάζεσθαι. Euseb. Vit. Const. iv. 27.

law was, that it was unjust that those who had been made free by the blood of Christ, should be slaves to the murderers of the Prophets and of the Son of God. There was another civil law, of great importance, affecting the Jews; they were constrained to take upon themselves certain public offices, particularly the decurionate, which, from the facility with which the Emperor and his predecessors had granted exemptions, had become burdensome. The law, however, shows, that the right of the Jews to Roman citizenship was fully recognized. The Patriarchs and the Rabbins had the same exemption from all civil and military offices as the Christian clergy. In the markets the Jews had their own officers to regulate the price of things sold among themselves, and were not subject to the ordinary discursor or moderator.*

But still earlier than these statutes of Constantine, Spain, the fruitful mother and nurse of religious persecution, had given the signal for hostility towards the Jews, in a decree passed at the Council of Elvira (Illiberis), which is curious, as proving that the Jews were, to a great extent, the cultivators of the soil in that country. It was a custom for the Jewish and Christian farmers and peasants to mingle together at the festive entertainments given at the harvest-home, or at other periods of rural rejoicing. The Jews were wont in

---

* Cod. Theodos. xii. viii. 3-4.
Chrysostom records a revolt of the Jews in the reign of Constantine, an attempt to rebuild their Temple, and to violate the laws which prohibited their entrance into the Holy City; and that the insurgents were punished by having their ears cut off, branded as slaves, and sold in great numbers. Le

Beau (Bas Empire, i. 167) ventures to date this insurrection in the year A.C. 315. I am inclined to hesitate as to receiving, on the authority of an oration, or rather invective, of Chrysostom, a fact so important, of which there is no other trace in history, or, as I believe, in Jewish tradition. S. Chrys. Hom. 2 in Judæos.

devout humility to utter their accustomed grace before the feast, that the Almighty would, even in the land of the stranger, permit his rains, and dews, and sunshine, to fertilize the harvests. The Christians appear to have been offended at this, apparently very innocent, supplication. The decree of the Council proscribed the meeting of the two races at these festivals, and prohibited the blessings of the Jew, lest, perhaps, they might render unavailing the otherwise powerful benedictions of the Church.[b]

It is said that the Jews in the East revenged themselves for these oppressive laws against their brethren, by exciting a furious persecution against the Christians, in which the Jews and Magians vied with each other in violence.[c]

The increased severity of the laws enacted by Constantius, the son and successor of Constantine, indicates the still darkening spirit of hostility,[d] but the Jews, unhappily, gave ample provocation to the authorities. The hotheaded Israelites of Alexandria mingled themselves in the factions of Arians and Athanasians, which distracted that restless city. They joined with the Pagans, on the side of the Arian Bishop, and committed frightful excesses, burning churches, profaning them with outrages which Athanasius shrinks from relating,

---

[b] "Admoneri placuit possessores, ut non patiantur fructus suos quos a Deo percipiunt cum gratiarum actione a Judæis benedici; ne nostram irritam et infirmam faciant benedictionem. Si quis post interdictum facere usurpaverit, penitus ab ecclesia abjiciatur." c. 49, Concil. Illibent. A.D. 305.

"Si vero aliquis clericus sive fidelis fuerit, qui cum Judæis cibum sumpserit, placuit eum a communione abstinere." c. 50. I have connected the two statutes together, as explanatory of each other.

[c] Sozomen. II. E. li. 9: ἐλέγει δὲ καὶ 'Ιουδαίους τρόπον τινὰ φύσει ὑπὸ βασκανίας πρὸς τὸ δόγμα τῶν Χριστιανῶν ἀπολεμεμέρους.

[d] Cod. Theodos. xvi. 7.

and violating consecrated virgins. An insurrection in Judæa, which terminated in the destruction of Dio Cæsarea, gave another pretext for exaction and oppression.* The Jews were heavily burthened and taxed: forbidden, under pain of death, from possessing Christian slaves, or marrying Christian women; and the interdict of Hadrian, which prohibited their approach to the Holy City, was formally renewed.ᶠ These laws likewise throw light on their condition. Their heavy burthens may indicate that the Jews possessed considerable wealth; the possession of Christian slaves leads to the same conclusion; and the necessity of the enactment against marrying Christian women shows, that, in some ranks at least, the animosity between the two races had considerably worn away. But the prohibition against entering Jerusalem was still further embittered by the distant view of the splendour which the new city had assumed. Christian pilgrims crowded the ways which led to the Holy City,⁸ where the wood of the true cross —the discovery of which by a singular chance is ascribed to a Jew—began to disseminate its inexhaustible splinters through the Christian world. The church of the Holy Sepulchre, built by the Empress Helena, rose in lofty state, and crowned the supposed hill of Calvary, on which their ancestors had crucified Jesus of Nazareth; while the hill of Moriah lay desecrated and desolate, as it had been left by the plough of the insulting conqueror.

---

* Socrates, H. E. II. 33: " Et interea Judæorum seditio qui Patricium nefarie in regul specie sustulerunt." Aurel. Victor in Constant. This evidently means that they had set up their Prince as an independent sovereign.

ᶠ Sozomen. II. E. III. 17.

⁸ Compare the Itinerary from Bourdeaux to Jerusalem, and Wesseling's notes; Hieronym. Oper. I. 103; the famous passage in Greg. Nyssen on the abuse of pilgrimage. The fullest account of these early pilgrimages is in Wilken, Geschichte der Kreuzzüge, c. I.

If then the Jews beheld with jealous alarm the rival religion seated on the imperial throne, and the votaries of Jesus clothed in the royal purple; if they felt their condition gradually becoming worse under the statutes of the new emperors; if they dreaded still further aggressions on their prosperity; they must have looked with no secret triumph to the accession of Julian, the apostate from Christianity. Before long their elation was still further excited by a letter written from the Emperor, addressed to "his brother,"[h] the Patriarch, and the commonalty of the Jews. Julian seemed to recognise the Unity of God, in terms which might satisfy the most zealous follower of Moses.[i] He proceeded to denounce their oppressors, condescended to excuse his brother, annulled the unequal taxes with which they were loaded, and expressed his earnest hope that, on his return from the Persian war, the great designs he had formed for their welfare might be fully accomplished. The temporal as well as the religious policy of Julian advised his conciliation of the Jews. Could they be lured by his splendid promises to embrace his party, the Jews in Mesopotamia would have thrown great weight into his scale in his campaign against the Persians; and in his design of depressing Christianity, it was important to secure the support of every opposite sect. Probably with these views the memorable edict was issued for the rebuilding of the Temple on Mount Moriah, and the restoration of the Jewish worship in its original splendour.[k] The execu-

---

[h] τὸν ἀδελφὸν Ἰουλον τὸν αἰδεσιμώτατον Πατριάρχην.

[i] ἔτι μείζονας εὐχὰς ποιῆτε τῆς ἐμῆς βασιλείας τῷ πάντων κρείττονι καὶ δημιουργῷ Θεῷ. Julian.

[k] Epist. xxv.

[k] Theodoret assigns the following reason for Julian's design to rebuild the Temple. He sent to inquire of the Jews why they had ceased to offer

tion of this project was entrusted, while Julian advanced with his ill-fated army to the East, to the care of his favourite, Alypius.

The whole Jewish world was in commotion; they crowded from the most distant quarters to be present and assist in the great national work. Those who were unable to come envied their more fortunate brethren, and waited in anxious hope for the intelligence that they might again send their offerings, or make their pilgrimage, to the Temple of the God of Abraham, in His holy place. Their wealth was poured forth in lavish profusion; and all who were near the spot, and could not contribute so amply, offered their personal exertions. Blessed were the hands that toiled in such a work; and unworthy was he of the blood of Israel who would not unlock, at such a call, his most secret hoards.[1] Men cheerfully surrendered the hard-won treasures of their avarice; women offered up the ornaments of their vanity. The very tools which were to be employed, were, as it were, sanctified by the service, and were made of the most costly materials: some had shovels, mallets, and baskets of silver; and women were seen carrying rubbish in robes and mantles of silk.[m] Men, blind from the womb, came forward to lend their embarrassing aid; and the aged tottered along the ways, bowed beneath the weight of some burthen which they seemed to acquire new strength to support. The confidence and triumph of the Jews was unbounded:

---

sacrifice. They replied, that it was not lawful for them to sacrifice but in one place, the site of their Temple. Julian, who looked on sacrifice as the one sign of true religion, and that which distinguished the rest of mankind from the Christians, immediately gave orders for the restoration of the Temple. Theodoret's is one of the earliest and most graphic descriptions of the whole transaction. H. E. iii. 20.

[1] Greg. Naz. iv. lii.; Theodoret, iv. 20.

[m] Sozomen, v. 22.

some went so far in their profane adulation as to style Julian the Messiah. The Christians looked on in consternation and amazement. Would the murderers of the Son of God be permitted to rebuild their devoted city, and the Temple arise again from "the abomination of desolation"? Materials had now accumulated from all quarters, some say at the expense of the Emperor, but that is not probable, considering the costly war in which he was engaged. Nor were the Jews wanting in ample resources: timber, stones, lime, burnt brick, clay, were heaped together in abundant quantities.[a] Already was the work commenced; already had they dug down to a considerable depth, and were preparing to lay the foundations, when suddenly flames of fire came bursting from the centre of the hill, accompanied with terrific explosions. The affrighted workmen fled on all sides; and the labours were suspended at once by this unforeseen and awful sign. Other circumstances are said to have accompanied this event; an earthquake shook the hill;[b] flakes of fire, which took the form of crosses, settled on the dresses of the workmen and spectators; and the fire consumed even the tools of iron.[c] It was even added that a horseman was seen careering among the flames, and that the workmen having fled to a neighbouring church, its doors, fastened by some preternatural force within, refused to admit them.[d] These, however, may be embellishments, and are found only in later and rhetorical writers; but the main fact of the interruption of the work by some extraordinary, and, as it was supposed, preternatural

---

[a] Socrates, H. E. III. 20.
[b] Socrates, H. E. III. 20; Theodoret, III. 20; Sozomen, v. 22.
[c] Socrates, ibid.; Theodoret, who adds that a fiery cross appeared in the heavens. The crosses on the Jews' dresses were dark, not light.
[d] Greg. Naz. in Judaeos. iv.

interference, rests on the clear and unsuspicious testimony of the heathen Ammianus Marcellinus.[r] But, in candour, one local circumstance must be mentioned, overlooked by those who impugn, as well as by those who maintain, the miracle—by Gibbon, Basnage, and Lardner—as well as by Warburton. It will be remembered that the hills on which Jerusalem stood were deeply and extensively undermined by subterranean passages. On the surprise of the Temple by John of Gischala, the whole party of Eleazar took refuge in

---

[r] The growth of the story is curious. Ammianus is simple, natural, and credible: "Cum itaque rei idem fortiter instaret Alipius, juvaretque provinciæ rector, metuendi globi flammarum prope fundamenta crebris adsultibus erumpentes fecere locum, exustis aliquoties operantibus, inaccessum; hocque modo elemento destinatius repellente, cessant inceptum." Chrysostom, Adv. Jud., is still modest: ἀλλὰ πῦρ ἀπὸ τῶν θεμελίων ἀναπηδῆσαν πάντας αὐτοὺς διήλασεν; he adds, that the foundations which were laid bare remained so at his time: καὶ τούτου ἐστιν ἕως τοῦ νῦν, τὰ θεμέλια γυμνωθέντα, καὶ αὐτὸν τὲ τὸν χοῦν, ὁπου ἤρξαντο κενοῦν. Orat. de S. Babylon.

Gregory Nazianzen, in his invective against Julian, with a few bold strokes heightens the effect. The Jews of all ages and both sexes were at work, when, alarmed by a hurricane and an earthquake, they fled to a neighbouring temple, the gates of which were closed against them by an invisible power. The Jews endeavouring to force an entrance, a fire broke out and consumed them, as it did Sodom, Nadab, and Abihu. Some Jews, only partially burned, bore on their bodies the marks of the Divine wrath. Of the less modest historians the embellishments are given, with references, in the text. The rubbish, according to Theodoret, moved by night of its own accord: νύκτωρ δὲ ὁ χοῦς αὐτομάτως ἀπὸ τῆς φάραγγος μετετίθετο; violent winds dispersed the vast mass of materials prepared, many thousand measures (modii) of gypsum and chalk. For Gregory Nazianzen's story of the Temple, we read that a number of Jews had taken refuge and fallen asleep in the portico of a neighbouring temple, which fell upon them and crushed them all to death. Sozomen admits that different stories were current. The silence of Cyril, Bishop of Jerusalem, on all these miracles, often alleged, is significant. Jost asserts that there is no allusion in the Talmudic writings to this third building of the Temple; all the quotations about it are from later Jewish writers. Iv. 257. See, however, note *. Those (I suspect, most modern readers) who are not convinced by, will read not without admiration, Warburton's dexterous and bold defence of the miracle. Compare Milman's note on Gibbon in loc.

these underground chambers. Numbers of the Zealots lay hid in similar caverns under Sion after the capture of the city by Titus; and the sudden rising of Simon on the hill of the Temple, after having descended on that of Sion, sufficiently proves the vast range of these mines, which communicated with each other under both the hills over which the city spread. The falling-in of the tomb of Solomon, during the rebellion under Bar-cochab, may also be adduced. In the long period of desolation, during which the hill of the Temple, especially, lay waste, the outlets of these caverns would be choked with rubbish and ruin; and the air within become foul and inflammable. That the vapours, thus fermenting under the whole depth of the hill, should, as is often the case in mines, become accidentally ignited during the work, kindle, and explode with violent combustion and terrific noise resembling an earthquake, was by no means beyond the ordinary course of nature; though it might be far beyond the philosophy of a people excited to the highest pitch of religious enthusiasm, and already predisposed to consider the place as the chosen scene of miraculous interference. Even the fiery crosses on the garments might have been phosphoric exhalations, really seen, and easily wrought into that form by the awe-struck imagination of the Christians: and preternatural interference would hardly be called for to close the doors of a church against fugitives thus under the visible malediction of the Deity.*

Nor, indeed, does the miracle, if we may presume so

* There is a very confused, and probably late, notice of this extraordinary event in the Talmudic writings. It is thrown back to the time of R. Joshua ben Chananiah, who lived during the reign of Hadrian,—a very wild anachronism. The writer adds, that the rebuilding was suspended on account of a change in the mind of the Emperor, and the hatred of the Samaritans! Zunz, Vorfrage, p. 175.

to speak, appear necessary for its end; for, according to the will of the Divine Ruler of the world, a more appalling and insuperable obstacle interrupted the unhallowed work. The discomfiture of the Jews was completed; and the resumption of their labours, could they have recovered from their panic, was for ever broken off by the death of Julian. The Emperor seems not to have reaped the advantages he expected from his attempt to conciliate the race of Israel.[1] The Mesopotamian Jews, instead of joining his army, remained faithful to their Persian masters, and abandoned such of their cities as were not defensible. On his approach, one of these, Dithra, situated among the branches of the Euphrates, was set on fire by his soldiers, and burned to ashes. The apostate himself fell: the Christian world beheld the vengeance of God—the Jew the extinction of all his hopes—in the early fate of this extraordinary man.[2]

The short reign of Jovian, whose policy it was to reverse all the acts of his predecessor, was oppressive to the Jews; but it was only a passing cloud. Valens and Valentinian reinstated the Jews and their Patriarch in their former rights;[v] yet the state of the empire demanded the repeal of their most valuable privilege—exemption from the public services. "Even the clergy," such is the curious argument of this edict, "are not permitted to consecrate themselves to the service of God, without having previously discharged their duty

---

[1] Amm. Marc. xxiv. 3. Compare Le Beau, with S. Martin's Note, iii. 93.

[2] Basnage, viii. 5. The Rabbins, as has been said, are altogether silent about Julian. "Ihre Quellen schweigen von Julian und seinen unternehmung, was auch in der Erfolglosigkeit seinem Grund haben kann." Jost, Judenthum, ii. 470.

[v] The Law of Valens and Valentinian is not extant; but their equity to the Jews and respect for their Patriarchs is clearly shown by a Law of Arcadius, in which their authority is appealed to. Cod. Theodos. xvi. 13.

to their country. He who would devote himself to God, must first find a substitute to undertake his share in the public offices."[x] The Jews could not complain, if, admitted to the protection and rights of Roman citizenship, they were constrained to perform its duties.[y]

During the declining days of the Roman Empire, Christianity assumed a more commanding influence, and the Jews sometimes became a subject of contention between the Church and the Throne.[z] Protected by the Emperor as useful and profitable subjects, they were beheld by the more intemperate churchmen with still-increasing animosity. Maximus, an usurper, during his short reign, had commanded a synagogue, which had been wantonly burned in Rome, to be rebuilt at the expense of the community. Theodosius the Great renewed a similar edict, on a like occasion, and commanded the Bishop of Callinicum, in Osrhoene, to see the work carried into effect. The fiery zeal of Ambrose, Bishop of Milan, broke out into a flame of indignation.[a] In a letter to the Emperor, he declares his disapproba-

---

[x] Cod. Theodos. xii. 1. 99.

[y] It is in curious contrast with later times, that these duties having become onerous, the Jews were compelled by law to undertake them; when they became again posts of profit and honour, the Jews were excluded from them, till very recent days, by common consent.

[z] It is curious that in the Itinerary of Rutilius, who wrote in the reign of Honorius, there is still a confusion between the Jews and Christians, whom Rutilius hates with Pagan impartiality. He lands near Faleria, where the Jews were in a kind of authority:—

Namque loci querulus curam Judæus
agebat,
Humanis animal dissociale cibis;
Reddimus obscœnæ convicia debita genti,
Quæ genitale caput propudiosa metit.
Radix stultitiæ, cui frigida Sabbata cordi
Sed cor frigidius religione sua est.
Septima quæque dies turpi damnata
veterno,
Tanquam lassati mollis imago Dei.
Cetera mendacis deliramenta catastæ
Nec pueros omnes credere posse reor.
Atque utinam nunquam Judæa subacta
fuisset,
Pompeii bellis imperioque Titi.
Latius excisæ pestis contagia serpunt
Victoresque suos natio victa premit.

The allusion to the origin of the Sabbath shows more than usual knowledge of Judaism, but the victory must be that which Christianity was achieving.

[a] Ambros. Epist. xxix.

tion of such outrages as burning synagogues: for priests ought to be the quellers of turbulence, and strive to promote peace, unless, he added, moved by injuries against their God, or contumelies against His Church. At the same time he asserts that no Christian bishop could conscientiously assist in building a temple for the circumcised. "Either the bishop will resist or comply: he must be a sinner or a martyr. Perhaps he may be tempted, by the hopes of martyrdom, falsely to assert his concurrence in the destruction of the synagogue. Noble falsehood! I, myself, would willingly assume the guilt,—I, I say, have set this synagogue in flames, at least in so far that I have urged on all—that there should be no place left in which Christ is denied." The Bishop designated a synagogue as a dwelling of perfidy—a house of impiety—a receptacle of insanity—and concluded, in a tone of mingled pathetic expostulation and bitter invective, "This shall be the inscription of the edifice—'A Temple of Ungodliness, built from the plunder of the Christians.'" Not content with addressing this letter to the Emperor, who was then in Milan, he thundered against him from the pulpit. Theodosius had the weakness to yield to the daring churchman; the edict was recalled, and the Jews remained without a synagogue in that city, which, it may be observed, was divided by half the empire from the diocese of Ambrose. Theodosius, when removed from the influence of Ambrose, and brought by the approach of death to higher notions of Christian justice, issued an edict, which secured perfect toleration to the Jews, and condemned to an arbitrary punishment all who should burn or plunder their synagogues.[b]

---

[b] "Judæorum sectam nullâ lege prohibitam, satis constat: unde graviter commovemur interdictos quibusdam locis eorum fuisse conventus. Sub-

In the mean time the Patriarchate began to display manifest signs of decay. The Jews were seen before heathen tribunals—not only to decide their litigations with Christians, but as a court of appeal against the injustice of their own judicial authorities. Men excommunicated had recourse to pagan judges, not always inaccessible to bribery, to enforce their reinstatement in the rights of the synagogue.[c] A law of Theodosius was passed, which recognized the power of the Patriarchs to punish the refractory members of their own community. This law was confirmed under Arcadius and Honorius: the prefects were forbidden from interfering with the judicial courts of the Jewish primate. The same privileges were assigned to Jewish rulers of synagogues Patriarchs, and Elders, which had been granted to the higher orders of the Christian clergy.[d] They were exempted from attendance on the courts of law on the Sabbath or other holy days. In all causes which did not relate to their religion, they were amenable to the common courts.[e] If the parties agreed to compromise

---

limis igitur Magnitudo tua, hac jussione suscepta, simuletatem eorum qui, sub Christianae religionis nomine, illicita quaeque praesumunt, et destruere synagogas atque expoliare conantur, congrua severitate cohibebit. Dat. iii. Kalend. Octob. Constantinopoli. Theodos. A. et Abundantio Coss. (A.D. 398)." Cod. Theodos. xvi. 1. 9. This was confirmed by Arcadius and Honorius in a special law providing against the forcible entrance of strangers into the synagogues, which were to be held in peace and security. Cod. Theod. xvi. 1. 12.

[c] Cod. Theodos. xvi. 4-8.

[d] Cod. Theodos. ii. viii. 3, a law of Arcadius and Honorius. Compare

viii. 8. 8.

A law of Arcadius prohibits a discreditable practice of certain Jews who took refuge in the churches from their creditors, or tried to escape punishment for their crimes by embracing Christianity. They were not to be admitted as converts till acquitted of their crimes, or till they had paid their debts.

[e] " Judaei, Romano et communi jure viventes de his causis, quae non tam ad superstitionem eorum, quam ad forum et leges ac jura pertinent, adeant solenni jure judicia, omnesque Romanis legibus inferant et excipiant actiones." Cod. Theodos. ii. 1. 10.

and arbitration, and the arbitrators were the Jewish Patriarchs, the provincial judges were to carry the sentence into execution, as of that of arbitrators appointed in the usual way. It would seem that, in disputes with Christians, both parties were expected to appear before the ordinary tribunals.[f] Another law was passed at this period characteristic of the times. It enacted that no Jew should be baptized without strict inquiry, and a sort of previous noviciate of good conduct.[g] Some of the more worthless Jews had played upon the eagerness of the Church to obtain proselytes, and had made a regular trade of submitting to baptism in different places—by which they, in general, contrived to obtain handsome remuneration.[h] This was facilitated by the numerous sects which distracted the Church, who vied with each other in the success of their proselytism, and rendered detection difficult. A miracle came to the assistance of the law in checking this nefarious traffic; unfortunately it was wrought in a Novatian, not in an orthodox congregation. When one of these unworthy proselytes presented himself, the indignant water flowed away, and refused to rebaptize one who had been so frequently baptized before with so little advantage.[i]

The clouds of ignorance and barbarism, which were darkening over the world, could not but spread a deeper gloom over the sullen national character of the Jews. The manner in which the contest was carried on with the Church was not calculated to enlighten their fanaticism; nor was it likely that, while the world around

---

[f] Cod. Theodos. xvi. 1. 13.
[g] Cod. Theodos. ix. 45. 2: "De his qui ad ecclesiam confugient."
[h] Cod. Theodos. xvi. 23. Insincere converts, who had not been baptized, were to be allowed to return to their former faith, it being very wisely judged that this was for the interest of Christianity: "Ad legem propriam (quia magis Christianitati consuletur) liceat remeare."
[i] Socrat. H. E. vii. 17.

them was sinking fast into unsocial ferocity of manners, they should acquire the gentleness and humanity of civilization. No doubt the more intemperate members of the synagogue, when they might do it securely, would revenge themselves, by insult or any other means of hostility in their power, against the aggressions of the Church. Though probably much would be construed into insult, which was not intended to give offence, it argues no great knowledge of Jewish character, or indeed of human nature, to doubt but that great provocation was given by the turbulent disposition of the Israelites.[k] It is a curious fact, and must have tended greatly to darken the spirit of animosity in the dominant Church against the Jews, that, whenever occasion offered, they sided with the Arian faction; while the Arians were in general more tolerant towards the worshippers of the undivided Unity of God, than the Catholic Church. In the religious factions in Alexandria, we have seen them espousing the part of the Arian bishop against Athanasius; and of all the sovereigns during this period, none were more friendly to the Jews than the Arian Gothic kings of Italy. It was about the commencement of the fifth century, that great, and probably not groundless, offence was taken at the public and tumultuous manner in which the Jews celebrated the feast of Purim, and their deliverance under Esther. Not content with beating the benches of the synagogue with stones and mallets, and uttering the most dissonant cries each time that the execrated name of Haman was pronounced, they proceeded to make a public exhibition of the manner in which the enemies of their nation might expect to be treated. They erected a gibbet, on which

---

[k] Cod. Theodos. xvi. De Hæreticis, xliv. They are accused of joining with the Donatists in their tumults, of course in Africa.

a figure, representing Haman, was suspended, and treated with every kind of indignity. Probably blasphemous expressions against all other Hamans might occasionally break forth. The Christians looked with jealous horror on that which they construed into a profane, though covert, representation of the Crucifixion. Sometimes, indeed, it is said, the gibbet was made in the form of a cross, with the body suspended upon it in like manner to that which was now becoming the universal object of adoration. No wonder if the two parties met in furious collision, and if the peace of the empire demanded the intervention of authority to put an end to these indecent scenes. By a law of Theodosius the Second, these festivals were prohibited.[1] In Macedonia, Dacia, and Illyria, these or similar causes of contention gave rise to violent tumults between the Jews and Christians. The synagogues were burned in many places. Theodosius commanded the prefect, Philip, to execute the law with the strictest impartiality: not to suffer the Jews to insult or show disrespect to the Christian religion, yet by no means to interfere with the free exercise of their own faith.[m] In Syria these animosities led to still worse consequences. At a place called Inmestar, between Chalcis and Antioch, some drunken Jews began, in the public streets, to mock and blaspheme the name of Christ. They went so far as to erect a cross, and fastened a Christian boy to it, whom they scourged so unmercifully that he died. The offenders were justly punished with exemplary rigour; but the feud left a rankling hatred in the hearts of the Christians.[n] Some years after, they rose and plundered a synagogue in Antioch. The Roman governor

---

[1] Cod. Theodos. xvi. De Judæis, l. 18.
[m] Cod. Theodos. xvi. l. 21.
[n] Socrates, H. E. vii. 16.

espoused the cause of the Jews, this time the unoffending victims of wanton animosity; and, by an ordinance of the Emperor, the clergy were commanded to make restitution. But the clergy found an advocate in the celebrated Simon Stylites, so called from his passing his life on the top of a slender column, sixty feet high. Theodosius could not resist the intercession of this saintly personage, to whom he wrote under the title of the "Holy Martyr in the Air"—earnestly soliciting his prayers. The order of restitution was annulled—the just prefect recalled.[o] It is possible, however, that the synagogue in question may have been built in violation of a law of the empire, which prohibited the erecting any new edifices for Jewish worship.[p]

Perhaps unfortunately, as encouraging them to pursue such violent means of conversion, the Christians in the island of Minorca, by means of the conflagration of a synagogue, obtained a signal triumph—the baptism of all the Jews in the island.[q] We have the account of this transaction on the authority of the Bishop himself, and it presents a singular picture of the times. The pious Severus was sorely grieved, that in an island where, though more useful animals abounded, wolves and foxes were not permitted to exist—where, though snakes and scorpions were found, yet, miraculously he would suppose, they were deprived of their venom—the Jews should be so numerous and wealthy in the two largest towns of the island, particularly in Magona, now Mahon. Long had he desired to engage in a holy warfare against this unbelieving race. He was at length encouraged to hope for victory by the arrival of the

[o] Evagrius, H. E. i. 13.

[p] Cod. Theod. xvi. 27.

[q] The Letter of Severus in Baronius, sub ann. 418.

relics of the martyr Stephen,[1] which were left in the island by the celebrated Orosius. In a short time the conflict began, and perpetual disputations took place. The Christians were headed by their Bishop, the Jews by a certain Theodorus, a man of acknowledged eminence in Rabbinical learning, and of such consequence in the place as to have filled the office of defender of the city.

The Christians, if we are to believe the Bishop, thought only of spiritual means of attack, persuasion, argument, with whatever miracles the relics of St. Stephen might vouchsafe to throw into their scale. The Jews had laid up in their synagogue more carnal weapons, stones, clubs, arrows, and other arms. Encouraged by two visions, the Bishop set off at the head of all his flock from Immona, and marched in the highest spirits to Magona, where he sent a summons of defiance to Theodorus and the Jews to meet him at the church. The Jews excused themselves because it was the Sabbath—and they could not enter an unclean place on that day. The Bishop immediately offered to meet them on their own ground, the synagogue. They still declined the contest, but surrounded the house in which the Bishop was, in great numbers. The Bishop mildly expostulated with them for having laid up arms in their synagogue. They denied the fact, and offered to confirm their assertion with an oath. "No need of oaths," replied the Bishop; "let us satisfy our own eyes;" and immediately he set forward with his whole troop, singing a verse of the Ninth Psalm, "Their memory hath

---

[1] A Jew plays a conspicuous part in the discovery of these relics—no less a person than Gamaliel himself, the teacher of St. Paul, who appeared in a vision to Lucian, head of a monastery, at Caphargamala in Palestine. These relics were of sovereign efficacy in checking the Pelagian heresy.

perished *with a loud noise*:* but the Lord endureth for ever." The Jews gladly joined in the Psalm, applying it, no doubt, with a very different meaning. A fray began in the streets through some Jewish women throwing stones from the windows. The Bishop could not restrain his flock, who rushed furiously in. The fury of the assailants is directly attributed to Christ himself! No blood was shed on either side, except of an Achan in the Christian party, who endeavoured to purloin some valuable effects, and had his head broken by a stone from his own friends; but the Christians became masters of the synagogue, and set it on fire, with all its furniture, except the books of the Law and the articles of silver. There is no mention of arms having been discovered. The books were carried in reverential triumph to the church; the silver restored. The Christians returned, singing Psalms of thanksgiving, to their church. Three days after, the Jews assembled within the melancholy ruins of their religious house: the Christians also crowded in, and Theodorus began an eloquent vindication of the Law. He argued, he confuted all objections; he poured contempt on his opponents, who, by the confession of their Bishop, were so utterly discomfited as to look for help to heaven alone against this obstinate gainsayer. No miracle, however, was vouchsafed, and they owed their triumph to pure accident. They all began to cry with one voice, "Theodorus, believe in Christ!" The Jews mistook the words, and thought it was a shout of triumph, "Theodorus believes in Christ!" They dispersed on all sides. Women tore their hair, and cried in bitter desperation, "Oh, Theodorus, what hast thou done!" The men fled

---
* These words will not be found in the English translation; they appear in the Vulgate.

away to the woods and rocks. Theodorus, entirely deserted and left alone, had not strength of mind to resist. Reuben, the first of the Jews who had been converted, argued with him, and laid before him the advantages which might attend his becoming a Christian. The Rabbi yielded to these unworthy motives. The example of his defection was followed, and the Jews were generally baptized. The triumphant Bishop strongly recommended to his brethren the laudable example of his own zeal and success—an example which, as far as burning the synagogues, they seem to have been apt enough to adopt; for an express law appears to have been required from Honorius to prohibit these acts of violence.

The conversion of many Jews in Crete[1] reflects more credit on the humanity of the Christians, while it shows the wild and feverish fanaticism which still lay deep within the hearts of the Jews, ready to break forth at the first excitement of those unextinguishable hopes which were alike their pride, their consolation, and their ruin. Among the numerous and wealthy Israelites who inhabited that fertile island, an impostor appeared, who either bore or assumed the name of Moses. He announced himself as the successor of the great Lawgiver, and for a whole year travelled about the island, persuading his credulous countrymen to abandon their possessions and their farms to follow his guidance. They listened; they relaxed their usual industry, and neglected their labours, under the fond hope of speedily obtaining possession of a more fertile land, that of milk and honey. The appointed time came, and at the call of Moses they crowded forth by thousands; for he had proclaimed that, like the Red Sea of old, the deep

[1] Socrates, vii. 38; Nicephorus, xiv. 40.

Mediterranean would be turned to dry land before them. At the dawn of day they followed him blindly to the top of a lofty promontory, from whence he commanded them to throw themselves down. The foremost obeyed; they were dashed to pieces against the rocks, or sank into the unobedient waves. Many perished; more would have shared their fate, but for some fishing craft and merchant vessels belonging to the Christians, who showed the utmost activity in saving the lives of their deluded countrymen, and, by holding up the bodies of the drowned, prevented the rest from following their fatal example. The Jews, at length disabused, turned to revenge themselves on their leader. But he had disappeared; no doubt he had secured a place of retreat, probably with some of the fruits of his imposture. Socrates, the ecclesiastical historian, cannot disguise his suspicion that he was a devil who assumed a human form for the destruction of those unhappy people. But many of the Jews, heartily ashamed of their own credulity, and struck with the brotherly kindness of the Christians, adopted the faith of love and charity.

We must revert to Alexandria, ever the most fatal scene of Jewish turbulence and Jewish calamity. Yet no calamity could induce this gainloving people to abandon that great emporium of commerce. Rarely have we directed our attention to the city of Alexandria but we have seen its streets flowing with the blood of thousands of Jews; at our next view we always find them re-established in immense numbers, and in inexhaustible opulence. To the old feuds between Greeks and Jews in this city, noted at all times for its fierce and mutinous spirit, had succeeded those of the different sects of Christians, and of the Christians, Pagans, and Jews. Even holy bishops were not superior to the violence which the fiery climate seemed to infuse into the veins of these "children of the Sun." The records of the Alexandrian Church present, perhaps, the most un-Christian page in Christian history.* At this period the city was rent into factions on a subject, all-important in those days, the merits of the dancers in the public exhibitions.* These entertainments usually took place on the Jewish Sabbath, and on that idle day the theatre was thronged with Jews, who preferred this profane amusement to the holy worship of their synagogue.ʸ Violent collisions of the different factions perpetually took place, which rarely terminated without bloodshed. Orestes, Prefect of Alexandria, determined to repress these sanguinary tumults, and ordered his police regulations to be suspended in the theatre.* Certain partizans of Cyril, the Archbishop, entered the theatre with the innocent design, according to Socrates, on whose partial authority the whole affair rests, of reading these ordinances. Among the rest was one Hierax, a low schoolmaster, a man conspicuous as an adherent of the Archbishop, whom he was wont frequently to applaud by clapping his hands (the usual custom in the Church) whenever he preached. From

---

* Socrates, H. E. vii. 13. Socrates says of the Alexandrian seditions, δίχα γὰρ αἵματος οὐ παύεται τῆς ὁρμῆς. They always ended in bloodshed.

* The severer Rabbins prohibited the theatre. "Iis denique, qui a ludis abstinuerunt, multi Judæorum accesserunt, qui a Rabbinis sæpius admoniti, coronam theatralem, veluti cœtum irrisorum, quem ingredi Psalmista prohibuerat, suscitatis audio fugerunt." Müller, De Genio Ævi Theodosiani, p. 60, with note. The Rabbinical authority was at its weakest in Greek Alexandria.

ʸ The Jews and Christians, like the Blues and Greens in Constantinople, seem to have espoused the cause of different actors, ὅτι δὲ πλέον διὰ τοὺς ὀρχηστὰς ἐπεπολέμωντο καθ' ἑαυτῶν.

* Perhaps these regulations might appoint different days for the different classes of the people to attend the theatre: this supposition would make the story more clear.

what cause does not appear, but the Jews considered themselves insulted by his presence, and raised an outcry that the man was there only to stir up a tumult. Orestes, jealous of the Archbishop, who had usurped on the civil authority, ordered Hierax to be seized and scourged. Cyril sent for the principal Jews, and threatened them with exemplary vengeance if they did not cause all tumults against the Christians to cease. The Jews determined to anticipate their adversaries. Having put on rings of palm-bark that they might distinguish each other in the dark, they suddenly, at the dead of night, raised a cry of fire about the great church, called that of Alexander. The Christians rose, and rushed from all quarters to save the church. The Jews fell on them, and massacred on all sides. When day dawned, the cause of the uproar was manifest. The militant Archbishop instantly took arms, attacked with a formidable force the synagogues of the Jews, slew many, drove the rest out of the city, and plundered their property.*

The strong part which Orestes took against the Archbishop, and his regret at the expulsion of the thriving and industrious Jews from the city, seem to warrant a suspicion that the latter were not so entirely without provocation. Both, however, sent representations to the Emperor; but, probably before he could interfere, the feud between the implacable Prefect and the Archbishop had grown to a greater height. Cyril, it is said, on one occasion advanced to meet his adversary, with the Gospel in his hand, as a sign of peace; but Orestes,

---

* Baronius relates this act of the Archbishop with characteristic coolness: " Ex Judæis nonnullos neci dat, alios expellit e civitate, eorumque fortunas a multitudine diripi permittit." Sub ann. 415.

suspecting probably that he had not much of its spirit in his heart, refused this offer of conciliation. There were certain monks who lived in the mountains of Nitria. These fiery champions of the Church seized their arms, and poured into the city to strengthen the faction of the Patriarch. Emboldened by their presence, Cyril openly insulted Orestes—called him heathen, idolater, and many other opprobrious names. In vain the Prefect protested that he had been baptized by Atticus, a bishop in Constantinople. A man, named Ammonius, hurled a great stone at his head: the blood gushed forth, and his affrighted attendants dispersed on all sides. But the character of Orestes stood high with the inhabitants. The Alexandrian populace rose in defence of their Prefect; the monks were driven from the city, Ammonius tortured, and put to death. Cyril commanded his body to be taken up, paid him all the honours of a martyr, and declared that he had fallen a victim to his righteous zeal in defence of the Church. Even Socrates seems to shrink from relating this unchristian conduct of the Patriarch. Cyril himself was ashamed, and glad to bury the transaction in oblivion. Before long, however, his adherents perpetrated a more inhuman deed even than the plunder and expulsion of the Jews: it must be related, to show the ferocious character of their antagonists. There was a woman, named Hypatia, of extraordinary learning, and deeply versed in the Platonic philosophy. She lived in great intimacy with Orestes, and was suspected of encouraging him in his hostility to the Patriarch. This woman they seized, dragged her from her chariot, and, with the most revolting indecency, tore her clothes off, and then rent her limb from limb. By another account Cyril himself is accused as having instigated, from jealousy of the fair Platonist's numerous hearers, this horrible act. It is grievous to add, that, through bribes and interest at the imperial court, the affair remained unpunished: nor do we hear that the Jews obtained either redress or restoration to their homes and property.

We gladly avert our eyes to catch a few occasional gleams of better feeling among the Christian hierarchy towards the subjects of our History. The history and the laws of the Empire thus show the Jews in almost every province, not of the East alone, but of Greece, the Islands, Italy, Gaul, Africa, and Spain.[b] It is related that such was the spirit of love produced by the example of the good Hilary, in his diocese of Poitiers in Gaul, that at his funeral the Israelites were heard chanting in Hebrew their mournful psalms of lamentation for the Christian Bishop.[c] Some traits of friendly feeling, and of amicable correspondence with respectable Jews, occur in the elegant works of Sidonius Apollinaris.[d]

In the mean time the Jewish Patriarchate, after having exercised its authority for nearly three centuries, expired in the person of Gamaliel. Its fall had been prognosticated by many visible signs of decay and dissolution. The Jews, ever more and more dispersed, became probably a less influential part of the population in Palestine; at least, those in the Holy Land bore a less proportion to the numbers scattered throughout the world; and thus the bonds of authority over the

---

[b] Socrates, H. E., lil. 13.
[c] Honorat, Vit. S. Hilarii.
[d] Yet Sidonius must apologise for his favourable disposition to a Jew: "Gozolas natione Judæus . . . cujus mihi quoque esset personæ cordi, si non esset certa desperta . ." Ep. ill. 4, and iv. 5. "Judæum prævens charta commendat, non quod mihi placeat error, per quem pereunt involuti. . . . Sed quia neminem ipsorum non decet ea æse damnabilem pronunciam, dum vivit. In spe enim adhuc absolutionis est, cui suppetit posse converti." vi. 11. See also Greg. Tur. il. c. 21.

more remote communities gradually relaxed. A law of Honorius gave a signal blow to its opulence: it prohibited the exportation of the annual tribute* which the collectors of the Patriarch levied on the Jews throughout the Empire, from Rome,' probably from the Western Empire. Five years after, it is true, this law was repealed, and the Patriarch resumed his rights; but the Jews were deprived, by another statute, of the agency—an office, now apparently become lucrative, which their active habits of trade enabled them to fill with great advantage to themselves. At length a law of Theodosius,⁸ which has been differently understood, either stripped the Patriarch of the honorary title of Prefect, which had been assigned to him by former emperors, and thus virtually destroyed his authority; or as some—inaccurately, I conceive—suppose, expressly abolished the office. The crime imputed to the Patriarch was his erecting new synagogues, in defiance of the imperial laws. At all events, Gamaliel—even if after this statute he maintained the empty name of Patriarch—at his death had no successor; and this spiritual monarchy of the West was for ever dissolved.ʰ It may

---

* Jost attributes the gradual decline of the Patriarchate (at an earlier period) to the falling-off of its revenues: "Wenn wir nicht irren, so hatte die Schwäche des Patriarchats ihren Grund im Versiegen der Einnahmen, die ihm in früherer Zeit zugeflossen waren." Judenthum, II. 159. They then began to send out their collectors: ". . . quos ipsi Apostolos vocant, qui ad exigendum aurum atque argentum a Patriarchâ certo tempore diriguntur, e singulis Synagogis exactam summam atque susceptam ad eundem reportent." Cod. Theodos. xvi. 14. Compare, on the title ἀπόστολος, Julian. Epist. xxv. Epiphanius de Hæres. 30, and the note on this law in Ritter's Cod. Theodos.

ᶠ Cod. Theod. xvi. 15.

ᵍ Cod. Theodos. xvi. On the title of Agentes in Rebus, compare note on Law 24.

ʰ Cod. Theodos. xvi. 22:—

"Quoniam Gamalielus existimavit se posse impune delinquere, quod magis est erectus fastigio dignitatum." He was ordered to surrender his pa-

be said that the dominion passed into the hands of the Rabbinical aristocracy. The Jerusalem Talmud had already been compiled, as a new code: it embodied and preserved the learning of the schools in Palestine, which, before the fall of the Patriarchate, had almost come to an end. But the later compilation, the Talmud of Babylon, eclipsed the more obscure and less perfect work of the Palestinian Jews, and became the law and the religion of the whole race of Israel.

The Talmud remains as a whole secluded in its mysteries, except to those who are not only Hebrew scholars, but who have mastered the later and less classical Hebrew (if it may be so said) of the Rabbins.[1] In our days perhaps the Talmud, revealed in all its secret lore, might obtain a fair hearing and a dis-

---

tent (codicillum) of office as honorary Prefect, "Ita ut is eo sit honore in quo ante Præfecturam fuerat constitutus, ac deinceps nullas condi faciat Synagogas; et si quæ sint in solitudine, si sine seditione possent deponi, perficiat." The same edict prohibited the circumcision, by him or any other Jew, of any Christian. Christian slaves were to be emancipated according to the law of Constantine. Compare Law 28.

On the other hand, a law of Theodosius the younger prohibited the depriving the Jews of their synagogues, and burning them. If any synagogues, since the passing of the law, had been consecrated as churches, or for Christian uses, altars were to be given of equal dimensions. Any offerings (donativa) which had not been consecrated to Christian uses were to be restored; if consecrated, an adequate price was to be paid. But while the old syna-

gogues were permitted to stand, no new ones were to be built. Cod. Theod. xvi. 25.

[1] Some separate treatises may be read translated into Latin or into modern languages, a few in the great Thesaurus of Ugolini. The vast scheme of Chiarini, who proposed to publish the whole Babylonian Talmud, translated into French (his single volume contains only the first treatise, the Berscoth), was cut off by his untimely death, in 1832. M. Pinner of Berlin issued proposals even on a larger scale for the publication of the whole Talmud with a German translation and copious notes and illustrations. Only the first volume appeared (at least I, as a subscriber to the work, have received but one, in folio, Berlin, A.D. 1842). I presume that the work has been discontinued, for what reason I know not.

passionate judgement. But immediately after, or indeed before its final compilation had begun, three ages of intense, bitter, unforgiving hatred between Jew and Christian had intervened—ages of division too natural, too inevitable, when Christians hated each other for far less glaring differences, and with even more implacable cordiality, than they did the Jews. During this period the Christian considered himself involved in an inextinguishable blood-feud with the Jew, the murderer as he was esteemed of the Saviour; and the Jew, scattered, despised, downtrodden, could not but look with the gloomiest envy on the Christian, who had succeeded in conquering the world to his faith, an achievement which, in his high days of hope, he had thought to have been his own glorious destiny. He therefore shut himself up in his pride, as if his race were still the chosen, though as yet sorely tried and heavily burthened, people of God. In later times, when the schism grew wider and wider, the only way (as we shall find, it was proposed in the middle ages) to extirpate obstinate Judaism, was to burn and destroy, and utterly root out the Talmud. The Talmud therefore became more dear to the Jew, who was little inclined to unfold its lore to the blind, prejudiced Christians, unable to comprehend, and unworthy of being enlightened by its wisdom. As better times came on, Christian scholars, Lightfoot, Selden, the Buxtorffs, Meuschen, Wolf, Bartolocci, dug into those hidden mines, from the love of knowledge and the desire of illustrating the origin of their own religion. Eisenmenger undertook the hateful task of disclosing all the mysteries of Rabbinical learning, only to make the Jews more detestable to the Christian world, and to expose them to more merciless persecution. The title page of his work is Judaism Exposed (Entdecktes Judenthum).

It is, according to Eisenmenger, a profound and true statement of the frightful manner in which the obdurate Jews curse and scoff at the Holy Trinity, God the Father, the Son, and the Holy Ghost, mock at the Holy Mother of Christ, throughout insult the New Testament, the Apostles and Evangelists, the whole religion of Christ. Odious as was the spirit and intention of Eisenmenger, his reading was vast, his industry indefatigable (two enormously thick quarto volumes are crowded with citations in the original, and with translations). I have never heard his accuracy seriously impeached. But the grave defect of the book is, that passages from the Talmud are heaped together indiscriminately with passages from the modern writings, writings of times when cruel persecution, as well as contempt, had for centuries goaded the miserable Jews to the only vengeance in which, besides overreaching in trade, they could indulge,—writings in their own secret unintelligible language, such as the Toldoth Jesu, and the other "fiery weapons of Satan," published later, to the horror and detestation of Christian Europe, by Wagenseil.[b] Of all the Jewish books, early and late, the extracts in Eisenmenger, read with this caution and in the more generous spirit of our times, form certainly a most curious and instructive collection. Take the strange, monstrous Oriental hyperboles, in which the barbarized Jews endeavoured to describe the Undescribable, to represent under imagery the Inconceivable Godhead and His

---

[b] The 'Tela Ignea Satanæ.' Wagenseil himself admits the wretched trash about the birth and early life of the Saviour, in the Toldoth Jesu, to be very modern: "nam est omnino recens seu abortus," p. 25. I apprehend that it was crushed out of the maddened hearts of the Jews by the Inquisition—a miserable revenge, but still revenge! It first appeared in the Pugio Fidei of the Spanish monk Raymond Martin.

attributes; the wild, sometimes profound, and almost sublime allegories, which Eisenmenger, and probably the more ignorant Jews themselves, understood literally, as they did the strange apologues and parables. Consider the philosophy of the Talmud without the apologetic reserve and prudent suppression of the modern Jewish writers, or without the remorseless literalness of most Christian expositors; without receiving it as altogether a mystery of esoteric wisdom, skilfully and subtly couched in language only really intelligible to the initiate, but as the growth of the human mind in a very peculiar condition, a legendary and a scholasticism, and a mysticism of half-European, half-Asiatic cast. But this would require a perfect mastery of Rabbinical Hebrew in its gradual development and expansion, as well as a calm and subtle, and penetrating, I would almost say, considering the subjects often in discussion, a reverential judgement—the gift of few men, of still fewer who are likely to devote their minds to what after all might prove but a barren study. So alone should we know what the Jews have been, what they may be; and fully understand their writings, and their later history. A religious mind would be above all indispensable; but the combination of religious zeal with respect for the religion of others is the last and tardiest growth in the inexhaustible soil of Christian virtue.[1]

[1] The calm and sober chapters of Jost, in his Judenthum, on the Talmud (Judenthum, II. pp. 202-222), deserve to be read and studied. See his distinction between the Halacha and the Midrasch, p. 213. "While, as the Halacha was the very life of the religion, it rigorously enforced the Law in all its strictest observances, with all the subtlety and ingenuity by which its provisions had been fenced about, and guarded by the most minute definitions, so the Midrasch was the element of the most boundless intellectual activity, or of thought and opinion, 'des Denkens und Meinens.' All which did not belong to the Law it assumed as its province; the conceptions of God,

of angels and spirits; notions of the being and destiny of man in this world and the next; the moral law in all its bearings; the treatment of the historical events in the Jewish annals; the possible meaning of every expression in the Holy Scriptures; the reconcilement of seemingly contradictory characters of Biblical persons; popular traditions and proverbs; popular belief and superstition, even particular observances of the Law, as far as they could be brought into relation with such inquiries,—in short, an endless world of actual life and creative imagination was contained in the Agada or Midrasch." The Agada ". . represents God as acting and speaking as appears to the writers necessary for His purposes; it brings forward holy men and women of the old times before the eyes of its hearers as conversing with God and with spirits; it permits God and the angels to mingle in the commerce and strife of men, often to act according to their wish; on the holy it bestows miraculous powers of the most extraordinary kind. They heal the sick of whom art has despaired, kill with a word or a look . . . . all nature is under their command. . . . . . They have unlimited power over evil spirits. The Agada seizes all sorts of tenets and opinions, which are not accordant with Jewish language and views, to mould them after its own fashion; it takes up Pythagorean and Platonic, Alexandrian and Gnostic, Persian and other Oriental notions, and turns them into Jewish. Hence the infinite charm of variety, and the delight of the Jews to wander in this wild garden; hence the acknowledged impossibility to introduce anything like tenets, or even to lay down principles of tenets."

This fertile imagination of the Jews had already allowed itself free play in the apocryphal books, such as the ivth (so called) Esdras, the Ascension of Isaiah, the Book of Enoch; to say nothing of the *Jewish* part of the Oracula Sibyllina. Compare Ewald, especially on the ivth book of Esdras, xvii. 63, &c.; Hilgenfeld, Die Judische Apocalyptik.

Pinner, in his preface, has cited the opinions of many other learned men as to the real character and contents of the genuine Talmud. See, too, Salvador (Jésus Christ et sa Doctrine) for a defence of the Talmud.

BOOK XXI.

THE JEWS UNDER THE BARBARIAN KINGS AND THE BYZANTINE EMPERORS.

Irruption and Conquests of the Barbarians — Trade of the Jews — Slave Trade — Decrees of Councils — Of Pope Gregory the First — Conduct of the Christians to the Jews — Arian Kings of Italy — Pope Gregory the First — State anterior to the Rise of Mohammedanism in the Eastern Empire — Insurrections of the Samaritans — Laws of Justinian — Dispute about the Language in which the Law was to be read — State of the Jews in the Persian Dominions — Persecutions — Civil Contests — Conquest of Syria and Jerusalem by the Persians — Reconquest by the Emperor Heraclius.

THE irruption of the Northern Barbarians during the latter half of the fourth to about the end of the fifth century so completely disorganised the whole frame of society, that the condition of its humblest members could not but be powerfully influenced by the total revolution in the government, in the possession of the soil, and in the social character of all those countries which were exposed to their inroads. The Jews were widely dispersed in all the provinces on which the storm fell—in Belgium, along the course of the Rhine —in such parts of Germany as were civilized—in Gaul, Italy, and Spain. An early law of Constantine[*] shows them as settled at Colonia Agrippina (Cologne),

---

[*] Cod. Theodos. xvi. 8. 12.

another in Macedonia and Illyricum. The Western
Emperors legislate concerning the Jews as frequently
as the Eastern. In Gaul, Council after Council, not only
those which denounce their commerce in slaves, but
others in every part, in Bretagne, at Agde, in the South,
show them as living on terms of free intercourse with
the Christians; the clergy alone were forbidden to share
in their feasts, or to admit them to their own hospitable
boards.[b] We have seen them mourning over a humane
Bishop of Poitiers; so too over another Bishop, Gallus of
Clermont, whose bier they followed weeping, with lighted
torches.[c] They are employed by another Bishop of Clermont (Sidonius Apollinaris) in offices of trust. The laws
of the Burgundians define the mulct for a Jew who
shall strike a Christian with fist or cudgel or whip
or stone, or pull his hair.[d] If he lifted his hand against
the sacred person of a priest, the penalty was death
and confiscation of goods.[e] In Italy we shall have full
account of their state and condition. The decrees of
the Council of Elvira have already recognised them as
landowners and cultivators of the soil in Spain. Of the
original progress of the Jews into these countries, history
takes no notice; for they did not migrate in swarms, or
settle in large bodies, but sometimes as slaves, following
the fortunes of their masters; sometimes as single
enterprising traders, they travelled on and advanced
as convenience or profit tempted, till they reached the
verge of civilization. On them the successive inroads
and conquests of the Barbarians fell much more lightly

---

[b] Concil. Venet. (Vannes, can. 21); Agathensis (Agde). The Council of Elvira did not confine this prohibition to the clergy.

[c] Gregor. Tur. Vit. Patr. c. vii.

[d] Baronius, Ann. A.D. 445-9, 449-61.

[e] Leg. Burgund. (apud Canciani, xis.). De Judæis qui in Christianum manum præsumerint mittere.

than on the native inhabitants. Attached to no fixed
residence, with little interest in the laws and usages of
the different provinces; rarely encumbered with landed
property or with immoveable effects; sojourners, not
settlers, denizens rather than citizens, they could retreat, before the cloud burst, to the more secure and
peaceful dwellings of their brethren, and bear with
them the most valuable portion of their goods. True
citizens of the world, they shifted their quarters, and
found new channels for their trade as fast as the old
were closed. But the watchful son of Israel fled to
return again, in order that he might share in the plunder of the uncircumcised. Through burning towns and
ravaged fields he travelled, regardless of the surrounding misery which enveloped those with whom he had
no ties of attachment. If splendid cities became a
prey to the flames, or magnificent churches lay in ashes,
his meaner dwelling was abandoned without much
regret, and with no serious loss; and even his synagogue might perish in the common ruin, without either
deeply wounding the religious feelings of the worshippers, who had no peculiar local attachment to the spot,
or inflicting any very grievous loss on a community
who could re-establish, at no great expense, their humble edifice. If, indeed, individuals experienced considerable losses, their whole trading community had
great opportunities of reimbursement, which they were
not likely to overlook or neglect in the wild confusion
of property which attended the conquests of the invaders. Where battles were fought, and immense plunder
fell into the power of the wandering Barbarians, the
Jews were still at hand to traffic the worthless and
glittering baubles with which ignorant savages are
delighted, or the more useful, but comparatively cheap

instruments and weapons of iron and brass, for the more valuable commodities, of which the vendors knew not the price or the use. These, by the rapid and secret correspondence which, no doubt, the Israelites had already established with their brethren in every quarter of the world, were transported into more peaceful and unplundered regions, which still afforded a market for the luxuries and ornaments of life. Already in the time of Gregory the First, a more perilous traffic had begun. Some of the clergy had dared, or had been compelled by want, to alienate the sacred vessels and furniture of their churches to the profane hands of the Jew merchant. Gregory declares with horror[f] that the clergy of Venafro had sold to a Jew two silver cups, two crowns with dolphins, the lilies of two others, six larger and seven smaller pallia.[g] It seems that the sale was illegal, and the Jew could be forced to regorge his prey. Gregory, as we shall hereafter see, was generally just and humane to the Jews. As to the particulars of this commerce, we have no certain information, as, in truth, the fact rests rather on inference than on positive data; but if it existed to the extent we believe, it must have been highly lucrative, when the vendors were ignorant barbarians, and the purchasers intelligent, and, probably, not over-scrupulous traders, well acquainted with the price which every article would bear in the different markets of the civilized world. Nor is it improbable that, by keeping alive the spirit of commerce, which might otherwise have become utterly extinct amid the general insecurity, the interruption of the usual means of communication, and the occupation of the roads by wild marauders, the Jews conferred a great advantage on

---

[f] "Quod dici nefas est." [g] S. Greg. Epist. l. 55.

society, by promoting the civilization of these wild and warlike hordes. But we have ample evidence that one great branch of commerce fell almost entirely into the hands of the Jews—the internal slave-trade of Europe. It is impossible to suppose but that this strange state of things must have inspired a sort of revengeful satisfaction into the mind of the zealous Israelite. While his former masters, or, at least, his rulers, the Christians, were wailing over their desolate fields, their ruined churches, their pillaged monasteries, their violated convents, he was growing rich amid the general ruin; and, perhaps, either purchasing for his own domestic service, at the cheapest price, the fairest youths, and even high-born maidens, or driving his gangs of slaves to the different markets, where they still bore a price. The Church beheld this evil with avowed grief and indignation. In vain Popes issued their rescripts, and Councils uttered their interdicts; the necessity for the perpetual renewal both of the admonitions of the former, and the laws of the latter, show that they had not the power to repress a practice which they abhorred. The language of these edicts was, at first, just and moderate. The Christians had, probably, the wisdom to perceive that, however apparently disgraceful to their cause, and productive of much misery, this trade had also its advantages, in mitigating the horrors and atrocities of war. Servitude was an evil, particularly when the Christian was enslaved to an Infidel or Jew, but it was the only alternative to avoid massacre. Conquering savages will respect human life only where it is of value as a disposable article—they will make captives only where captives are useful and saleable. In the interior of Africa, it may be questionable how far the slave-trade increases or allays the barbarity of warlike tribes. No doubt many marauding expeditions are undertaken, and even wars between different tribes and nations entered into, with no other motive or object of plunder except the miserable beings which supply the slave-marts; but where the war arises from other causes, it would probably terminate in the relentless extermination of the conquered party, if they were not spared, some may say, and with justice, for the more pitiable fate of being carried across the desert as a marketable commodity. But with the northern tribes, the capture of slaves was never the primary object of their invasions; they moved onward either in search of new settlements, or propelled by the vast mass of increasing population among the tribes beyond them: at this period, therefore, this odious commerce must have greatly tended to mitigate the horrors of war, which the state of society rendered inevitable.

From the earliest period after Christianity assumed the reins of the Empire, the possession of Christian slaves by the circumcised had offended the dominant party. Constantine issued a severe law, which prohibited the Jew, under pain of confiscation of property, from buying a Christian slave; but this law was either never executed, or fell into disuse.[b] It was re-enacted by Theodosius, with the addition, that such as were slaves before the issue of the decree were to be redeemed by the Christians.[i] A law of Honorius[k] only prohibited the conversion of Christian slaves to Judaism, not interfering with, or rather fully recognising, the

---

[b] 1 Cod. Theodos. xvi. Sozomen. Ἰουδαῖος δὲ ἀνομοθέτησαν μηδένα δοῦλον ποιεῖσθαι τῶν ἐξ ἑτέρας αἱρέσεως. The slave was confiscated to the public treasury. H. E. iii. 19.

[i] Cod. Theodos. iii. 1. 5. The date is A.C. 384.

[k] 1 Cod. Theodos. xvi. 8. 3. The law is dated A.C. 415.

Jews' right of property in their bondsmen.[1] After the evil had grown, through the incessant barbaric wars, to a much greater magnitude, the Council of Orleans [m] (A.C. 540) took the lead, but with great fairness and moderation, in the laudable attempt to alleviate its baneful effects on the religious as well as the temporal state of the slave. That assembly enacted, "That if a slave was commanded to perform any service incompatible with his religion, and the master proceeded to punish him for disobedience, he might find an asylum in any church: the clergy of that church were on no account to give him up, but to pay his full value to the master." The fourth Council of the same place (A.C. 541) goes further: "If a slave under such circumstances should claim the protection of any Christian, he is bound to afford it, and to redeem the slave at a fair price." Further: "Any Jew who makes a proselyte to Judaism, or takes a Christian slave to himself (probably as wife or concubine), or by the promise of freedom bribes one born a Christian to forswear his faith, and embrace Judaism, loses his property in the slave. The Christian who has accepted his freedom on such terms shall not presume to fulfil the condition, for a born Christian who embraces Judaism is unworthy of liberty." The first Council of Macon (A.C. 582) enacts, "That according to the laws, both ecclesiastical and civil, the conditions by which a Christian, either as a captive in war or by purchase, has become slave to a Jew, must be respected.

---

[1] Jost, Judenthum, ii. 156, mentions Absalus, a wealthy and enlightened Jew of Caesarea, who was on friendly and familiar terms with the Roman proconsul, and though he conversed in Greek with the proconsul, and allowed his daughters to be taught Greek, still lived in amity with the Rabbins, and even lectured in the synagogue. He was served by Gothic slaves, and had an ivory chair.

[m] Labbe. Concil. sub ann.

But since complaints have arisen that Jews living in the great and small towns have been so shameless as to refuse a fair price for the redemption of such bondsmen, no Christian can be compelled to remain in slavery; but every Christian has a right to redeem Christian slaves at the price of twelve solidi,* (to such a price had human life fallen,) either to restore them to freedom, or to retain them as his own slaves; for it were unjust that those whom our Saviour has redeemed by his blood, should groan in the fetters of unchristian persecutors." These laws produced little effect; for in the first place they calculated, far beyond the character of the age, on the predominance of Christian charity over the love of lucre, both in the clergy and the laity. Besides, the whole administration of law had fallen into the worst disorder. Every kingdom, province, or district had its separate jurisdiction; no uniformity of system could prevail; and where the commonalty, many of the administrators of the law, and even the clergy, could neither write nor read, the written rescripts of councils were often but a dead letter. The Fourth Council of Toledo (A.C. 633) recognised the practice of Jewish slave-dealing as in full force. The Tenth at the same place (A.C. 655) complains that "even the clergy, in defiance of the law, sold captives to Jews and heathens." At the close of the sixth century, one of the wisest and most humane Pontiffs filled the Papal chair, Gregory the First. The Pope in his pastoral letters alternately denounces, bewails, and, by authoritative rebuke and appeal to the better feelings, endeavours to suppress, this "cruel and impious" traffic, which still existed in Italy, Sicily, and the South of France. He

---

* According to the calculation adopted by Gibbon for this period, about 36s. of our money.

writes to Fortunatus, Bishop of Naples, "that he has received an account that a Jewish miscreant has built an altar, and forced or bribed his Christian slaves to worship upon it."° The prefect was directed to inflict corporal chastisement on the offender, and to cause all the slaves to receive their freedom. The next year he writes to Venantius, Bishop of Luna in Tuscany, rebuking him for permitting Christian slaves to come into the power of Jewish masters, contrary to his duty. Those who had been long in the possession of such masters, were to be considered as villains attached to the soil (the Jews, it should seem, were considerable landed proprietors or cultivators of the land in Italy). But if the Jew resisted, or abused his seignorial right to transplant the slave ᴾ from the soil to which he belonged, he was to lose his lease of land, as well as his right over the slave. Gregory distinguishes between the possession of and the trade in slaves. No Jew or heathen, who was desirous of becoming a Christian, was to be retained in slavery. Lest the Jew should complain that he is robbed of his property, this rule is to be observed: if a heathen slave, bought as an article of trade, within three months after the sale, and before he finds another purchaser, shall wish to embrace Christianity, the Jew shall receive the full price from a Christian slave-purchaser; if after that time, he shall immediately obtain his freedom, as it is evident that

---

° The altar was dedicated to the blessed *Elias*: a singular circumstance, if true, as it should seem that the Jew tempted other Christians besides slaves to this "saint-worship," so contrary to the spirit of his own religion. The Jew, it is insinuated in the charge, had bribed the Bishop to connivance.

Greg. Epist. lib. ii. ep. 37.

ᴾ "Quod si quispiam de his vel ad alium locum migrare, vel in obsequio suo retinere voluerit, ipse sibi reputet qui jus colonarium temeritate suâ, jus vero juris dominii sui severitate damnavit." Lib. iii. epist. 21.

the Jew keeps him not for sale, but for service.⁴ This was, as it were, within the dominions of the Papacy, at least, almost bordering on the Pope's own particular diocese. In the Gallic provinces, as probably his power was less implicitly acknowledged, so his tone is less peremptory. The slaves in such cases were to be repurchased out of the goods of the Church. Gregory writes to Candidus, a presbyter in Gaul:—"Dominic, the bearer of this letter, has with tears made known to us, that his four brothers have been bought by the Jews, and are at present their slaves at Narbonne. We direct you to make inquiry into the transaction, and, if it be true, to redeem them at a proper price, which you will charge in your accounts, *i. e.* deduct from the annual payment made to Rome."ᶠ Three years earlier he had written to Januarius, Bishop of Cagliari, in Sardinia, rebuking him, because certain slaves, belonging to Jews, who had taken refuge in a church, had been given up to the unbelievers. He here declares "that every slave so seeking baptism becomes free, and the treasures of the poor (*i. e.* the goods of the Church) are not to suffer loss for their redemption."ᵍ

There is in his very curious letter to Fortunatus, Bishop of Naples, an approval of his ardent zeal in favour of Christian slaves bought by the Jews in the Gallic provinces. The Pontiff had intended entirely to interdict the trade. But a certain Jew, Basilius, with several others, had waited upon him, and stated

---

⁴ This appears from a second letter to Fortunatus, Bishop of Naples, lib. v. ep. 31. The Pagan or Jewish slave who wished to embrace Christianity "in libertatem modis omnibus vindicetur."

ᶠ Lib. vi. epist. xxi.

ᵍ "Sive olim Christianus, sive nunc fuerit baptizatus, sine ullo Christianorum pauperum damno religioso ecclesiasticæ pietatis patrocinio in libertatem modis omnibus vindicetur." Epist. lib. iii. 9.

that this traffic was recognized by the judicial authorities, and that it was only by accident that Christian slaves were bought among the heathen.[1] In a solemn tone, the Pontiff thus writes to Thierri and Theodebert, Kings of the Franks, and to Queen Brunehaut:—"We are in amazement that, in your kingdom, Jews are permitted to possess Christian slaves. For, what are Christians but members of Christ's body, who, as ye know, as we all know, is their Head? Is it not most inconsistent to honour the Head, and to allow the members to be trampled on by His enemies? We entreat your Majesties to expel this baneful traffic from your dominions: so will ye show yourselves true worshippers of Almighty God, by delivering His faithful from the hands of their adversaries."[2] Another letter of Gregory, to Leo, Bishop of Catania in Sicily, establishes the curious fact that the Samaritans were likewise widely dispersed, and shared this traffic with the Jews:— "A circumstance, both revolting and contrary to the law, hath been made known to us—a circumstance, if true, worthy of the strongest reprobation and the heaviest punishment. We understand that certain Samaritans resident at Catania buy heathen slaves, whom they are so daring as to circumcise. You must investigate this affair with impartial zeal, take such slaves under the protection of the Church, and not suffer these men to receive any repayment. Besides this loss, they must be punished to the utmost extremity of the law."[3] According to the Roman law, which still prevailed in Sicily, the penalty of circumcising slaves was death and confiscation of property.

---

[1] Lib. vii. 2. 35.
[2] Lib. vii. 2. 115, 116.
[3] Lib. v. epist. 32. Compare lib. vii. epist. 22.

In all other respects, this wise and virtuous Pontiff religiously maintained that tolerance towards the Jews which they enjoyed, with few exceptions, during this period of confusion, and even for some time after the conversion of the Barbarian monarchs to Christianity.[7]

For all this time the Church was either sadly occupied in mourning over the ravages which enveloped the clergy and people in common ruin, or more nobly, in imparting to the fierce conquerors the humanizing and civilizing knowledge of Christianity. It had not the power—we trust, in those times of adversity, that best school of Christian virtue, not the will—to persecute. There is a remarkable picture of the state of the Jews in Africa, in a tract printed among the works of St. Augustine, called the 'Altercation between the Synagogue and the Church.'[8] The date of this record is uncertain; but it seems earlier, rather than later, as Basnage supposes, than the Vandal conquest of that region. The Synagogue maintains that "she is neither the slave nor the servant of the Church, since her sons are free, and, instead of being constrained to wear fetters and other marks of servitude, have full liberty of navigation and of commerce." This seems to indicate considerable extent of trade. On the other hand, the Church rejoins that the Synagogue is obliged to pay tribute to the Christians; that a Jew cannot pretend to the Empire, or to become a count (comes) or governor of a province; that he cannot enter into the senate or the army; that he is not even received at the tables of men of rank; and that if he is allowed the means of obtaining a livelihood, it is only to prevent his perishing of hunger.

[7] See a letter to the Bishop of Palermo, lib. vii. epist. 26. Compare vii. 2. 59.

[8] Augustin. Oper. 'Altercatio Ecclesiæ et Synagogæ.'

Theodoric, the Arian Gothic king of Italy, it has already been observed, openly protected the Jews.[a] His secretary, Cassiodorus, prompted and encouraged this enlightened policy. The king lost no opportunity of expressing his opinion, that the Israelites showed an excessive zeal for the goods and for the peace of this world, while they lost all thought of immortality; but he discountenanced and repressed all insult and violence. He reproved the senate of Rome, because on account of some private quarrel the synagogue had been burned. He strongly rebuked the clergy of Milan, who had endeavoured to make themselves masters of a synagogue and all its property.[b] He repressed the people of Genoa, who had abrogated all the privileges of the Jews, long resident among them; had risen, pillaged, and unroofed the synagogue.[c] He directed that the Israelites should be reinstated in their privileges, and permitted to rebuild their synagogue, provided that it was a plain building, and covered no larger space of ground than their former one. This was at the end of the fifth century. It was about the end of the sixth that the Pope himself assumed the saintly office of protector of the oppressed. From several of the letters of Gregory the First, it appears that the Jews had laid their grievances before him in person, and obtained redress.[d] He severely rebuked those whose intemperate zeal had led them

---

[a] Theodoric. Edict. 143.
[b] Cassiodor. Var. v. 37.
[c] Cassiod. Var. ii. 27, and iv. 33.
[d] Gregory reproves the Bishop of Terracina for having driven the Jews from certain places where they were accustomed to hold their festivities: "Eos enim, qui a Christianâ religione discordant, mansuetudine, benignitate, admonendo, suadendo, ad unitatem fidei necesse est congregare; ne quos dulcedo prædicationis, et prætensus futuri judicii terror ad credendum invitare poterat, minis et terroribus repellantur." Epist. lib. i. 84.

to insult the synagogues by placing the images of the Virgin and the crucified Redeemer within their walls;* yet he was by no means remiss in his attempts to convert these unbelievers; but they were to be won by tenderness, by gentleness, not by threats, terrors, and unjust usage.† The Pope stands in amiable contrast to other potentates of his time. The tyrannical and bloody Chilperic, the contemporary king of Paris and Soissons, with the fierce and ignorant ardour of a man who hoped by his savage zeal for the Christian faith to obtain remission for his dreadful violations of every Christian virtue, compelled the Jews, who seem to have been numerous and wealthy, to receive baptism. But it was remarked that these compulsory converts were but doubtful believers; they observed their own Sabbath as strictly as that of the Church. Chilperic, whom Gregory of Tours calls the Nero of France, was a theologian, in his own estimation, of the highest authority. He wrote on the Trinity and the Incarnation. The orthodox detected manifest Sabellianism in the royal tract, which, nevertheless, the king would impose by summary edicts on his subjects. Chilperic would personally convince the Jews of their blind error. There was a certain Priscus, a vender of ornaments, perhaps a jeweller, in his court. The king one day, pulling the Jew gently by the beard, ordered the good Bishop of

---

* Epist. vii. 11. 5. This crime had been committed by a Jewish convert at Cagliari, who had insulted the synagogue which he had abandoned, by attacking it on the day of the Passover, and placing an image of the Virgin within it. "The Jews," observes the Pope, "are forbidden to build new synagogues, but we have no right to deprive them of the old."

† There is a letter of Gregory appointing a provision for certain converted Jewish females, " rationabili moderatione concurrere, ne victûs, quod absit, inopiam patiantur." Epist. iii. 31. The Jews on the farms of the Church in Sicily were to have their payments lightened. Epist. iv. 6. Compare vii. 33.

Tours, Gregory, the historian, to lay his episcopal hands upon him—the sign of proselytism. The Jew resisted. "O stubborn soul and incredulous race!" said the king, and proceeded to ply the Jew with theological arguments. Priscus resolutely asserted the Unity of God, averred that He neither had nor could have a Son, a consort in his power. The king argued in vain; the bishop tried his skill with gentler and better reasoning, but with as little effect. The Jew stood firm; the king tried blandishments, but with no greater result. He then took to more powerful reasoning; he threw the obstinate unbeliever into prison. The Jew sought to gain time, promised, after he had married his son to a Jewish maiden at Marseilles, to consider, of course to yield to the royal teacher. But the king had more convincing allies than the good bishop. Phatir, a Christian proselyte, at whose baptism the king had been sponsor—thus his son by a closer tie than birth—perhaps from some old grudge, rushed into the synagogue with his armed followers and murdered the defenceless Priscus. The murderers took refuge in the Church of St. Julian. The king, to do him justice, sent troops to seize and execute them. Phatir fought his way through (his accomplices killed each other), and found an asylum in the kingdom of Burgundy, where he was afterwards killed. Some of the Gallic prelates, Virgilius of Arles, and Theodore of Marseilles, followed the example of Chilperic's zeal. They compelled the Jews in their respective dioceses to submit to baptism. But there were merchants among them, it would seem, of wealth and widespread connexions; these men appealed to Pope Gregory. Gregory in his letter* positively prohibits all force. He argues

---

* Epist. l. 45. Compare ii. 15.

with simple good sense, that, however the bishops may have been moved by love for the Redeemer, the compulsory convert will no doubt revert to his former belief; gentle persuasion is the only sure means of changing the heart. The Pope himself, as we have seen, employed these more Christian, though occasionally more politic, and doubtless more effective, means of conversion. He forbade, as we have said, all outrage or insult; but, as we have also seen, he executed rigidly the Laws of Asylum, by which the Jews daily lost their slaves; and while by his protection he appealed to their better feelings, he laid a temptation in the way of their avarice, by offering remission of taxes to all converted Jews. We shall hereafter see the manner in which Spain maintained its dark distinction of being the first as well as the most ardent votary of religious persecution, and the fatal consequences of her implacable intolerance.

Scarcely had the world begun to breathe after the successive shocks which its social state had received from the inroads of the Northern barbarians—scarcely had it begun to assume some appearance of order, as the kingdoms of the Goths, the Vandals, the Lombards, and the Franks, successively arose upon the broken ruins of the Roman Empire—when Mohammedanism suddenly broke forth, and, spreading with irresistible rapidity over great part of Asia, the north of Africa, and Spain, effected a complete revolution in the government, the manners, and the religion of half the world. The Persian kingdom fell at once, and the Magian religion was almost extinguished. In the Asiatic provinces, Christianity, excepting in Armenia, was reduced to an inconsiderable and persecuted sect. A magnificent mosque took the place of the Jewish Temple on the summit of Moriah. The flourishing churches of Africa, the dioceses of Cyprian and Augustine, were yielded up to the interpreters of the Koran, and the Cross found a precarious refuge among the mountains of the Asturias, while the Crescent shone over the rich valleys of Spain and the splendid palaces of Grenada and Cordova. Such a revolution, as it submitted them to new masters, could not but materially affect the condition of the Jews. In most respects, the change was highly favourable; for, though sometimes despised and persecuted by the Saracenic emperors and caliphs, in general their state was far less precarious and depressed than under the Christians; and they rose to their great era of distinction in wealth, cultivation, and in letters, under the mild dominion of the Arabian dynasty in Spain.

In order to trace the influence of this great revolution, we return to the East, and survey the state of the Jews—I. Under the Byzantine empire—II. Under the later Persian monarchs—and III. In Arabia. The Greek empire was rapidly verging to decay; the imperial court was a scene of intrigue and licentiousness, more like that of an Asiatic sultan than of the heir of the Roman name. The capital was distracted by factions, not set in arms in support of any of those great principles which dignify, if they do not vindicate, the violence of human passions, but in assertion of the superior skill of dancers and charioteers. The circus, not the senate, was the scene of their turbulence; the actor, not the orator, was the object of popular excitement. An eunuch, Narses, and a Thracian peasant, Belisarius, alone maintained the fame of Rome for valour and ability in war. The Church was rapidly increasing in power, but by no means, notwithstanding the virtues and talents of men like Chrysostom, in the great attributes of the Christian religion—wisdom, holiness, and mercy. The Jews, probably by their industry as traders and their connexion with their brethren in the East, ministered considerably to the splendour and luxury of the imperial court. But the fall of the Patriarchate, and the dispersion of the community in Palestine, which seems entirely to have lost the centre of unity with the religious capital, Tiberias, lowered the whole race in general estimation. They were no longer a native community, or, it might almost be said, a state, whose existence was recognized by the supreme power, and which possessed an ostensible head, through whom the will of the sovereign might be communicated, or who might act as the representative of the nation. They sank into a sect, little differing from other religious communities which refused to acknowledge the supremacy of the established Church. In this light they are now considered in the imperial laws.[b] Hitherto they had enjoyed the rights of Roman citizenship; but the Emperors now began to exclude from offices of honour and dignity all who did not conform to the dominant faith. This was the great revolution in their state: from followers of a different religion they were degraded into heretics; and the name of heretic implied all that was odious and execrable to the popular ear; all that was rebellious to civil and ecclesiastical authority. It was a crime to be put down by the rigour of the law—and the law put forth its utmost rigour at the hands of the ruling power. In the sixth year of Justin the Elder, a law was promulgated to the following effect:—Unbelievers, heathens, Jews, and Samaritans,

---

[b] Cod. J. de Hær. et Manich. c. 12.

shall henceforth undertake no office of magistracy, nor be invested with any dignity in the state; neither be judges, nor prefects, nor guardians of cities, lest they may have an opportunity of punishing or judging Christians and even bishops. They must be likewise excluded from all military functions. In case of the breach of this law, all their acts are null and void, and the offender shall be punished by a fine of twenty pounds of gold. This law, which comprehends Samaritans as well as Jews, leads us to the curious fact of the importance attained by that people during the reigns of Justin and Justinian.[1] Hitherto their petty religious republic seems to have lurked in peaceful insignificance. Now, not only do its members appear dispersed along the shores of the Mediterranean, sharing the commerce with their Jewish brethren in Egypt, Italy, and Sicily, but the peace of the empire was disturbed by their fierce and frequent insurrections in Palestine. Already in the preceding reign, that of Zeno, their city of Sichem, which had now assumed the name of Neapolis (Naplous), had been the scene of a sanguinary tumult, of which we have only the Christian narrative—the rest must be made up, in some degree, from conjecture. The Samaritans still possessed their sacred mountain of Gerizim, on which they duly paid their devotions. No stately Temple rose on the summit of the hill, but the lofty height was consecrated by the

---

[1] A curious law (Cod. Theodos. xiii. v. 18) had united the Jews and Samaritans in the privilege or the exemption from serving in the corn-ships which supplied Constantinople. This seems to have been the function of the Navicularii in question in this law, and probably applied to the Jews and Samaritans in Alexandria, where they coexisted in the time of Hadrian. The greater part, as poor and employed in petty trade (inopes, vilibusque commerciis occupati), were to be exempt; the men of substance (idonei facultatibus) were not to be excused from this public duty.

veneration of ages.[1] It is not improbable that the Christians, who were always zealously disposed to invade the sanctuary of unbelief, and to purify, by the erection of a church, every spot which had been long profaned by any other form of worship, might look with holy impatience for the period when a fane in honour of Christ should rise on the top of Mount Gerizim. The language of our Lord to the woman of Samaria, according to their interpretation, prophetically foreshowed the dedication of that holy mountain to a purer worship. No motive can be suggested so probable as the apprehension of such a design, for the furious, and, as we are told, unprovoked attack of the Samaritans on the Christian church in Naplous. They broke in on Whit Sunday—slew great numbers—seized the Bishop Terebinthus in the act of celebrating the Holy Eucharist—wounded him—cut off several of his fingers, as they clung with pious tenacity to the consecrated emblems, which the invaders misused with such sacrilegious and shameless fury as a Christian dare not describe. The bishop fled to Constantinople, appeared before the Emperor, showed his mutilated hands, and at the same time reminded him of our Lord's prophecy. Zeno commanded the offenders to be severely punished, expelled the Samaritans from Gerizim; and the Christians had at length the satisfaction of beholding a chapel to the Virgin on the peak of the holy mountain, surrounded by a strong wall of brick, where, however, a watch was constantly kept to guard it from the Sama-

---

[1] Procopius, De Ædificiis, v. 7.

Procopius ignorantly asserts that there never had been a Temple on Gerizim. He also strangely misrepresents the words of Christ, which he cites as if predicting that the true worshippers (the Christians) should worship on Gerizim. This leads to the notion that the Christians were contemplating the building a church there.

ritans. During the reign of Anastasius, some Zealots, led by a woman, clambered up the steep side of the precipice, reached the church, and cut the guard to pieces. They then cried out to their countrymen below to join them; but the timid Samaritans refused to hearken to their call; and Procopius of Edessa, the governor, a man of prudence and decision, allayed the tumult by the punishment of the offenders. This chapel was still further strengthened by Justinian; and five other churches, destroyed by the Samaritans, rebuilt.[1]

The rankling animosity between the two religions—aggravated, no doubt, by the intolerant laws of Justinian, hereafter to be noticed—broke out in a ferocious, though desperate insurrection. It originated in a collision between the Jews and Samaritans, and the Christians; many houses were burned by the Samaritans. Justinian, enraged at the misconduct of the Prefect Bassus, deposed him, and ordered his head to be cut off on the spot. A certain Julian, by some reported to have been a robber chieftain, appeared at the head of the Samaritans. He assumed, it is averred, the title of King, and even had some pretensions to the character of a Messiah. All around Naplous they wasted the possessions of the Christians with fire and sword, burned the churches, and treated the priests with the most shameless indignities. By one account Julian is said to have entered Naplous while the games were celebrating. The victor was named Nicias; he had won the prize from the Jewish and Samaritan charioteers. Julian demanded his religion, and on his reply that he was a

---

[1] Vit. S. Sabæ. Joann. Malala, p. 448, Edit. Bonn.; Theophan. l. p. 274. Compare Le Beau, viiL 118.

Christian, instead of conferring the crown upon him, had his head struck off. The whole district was a desert; one bishop had fallen in the massacre, and many priests were thrown into prison or torn in pieces. A great force was sent into the province; and, after a bloody battle, the Samaritans were defeated, Julian slain, and Silvanus, the most barbarous enemy of the Christians, taken, and put to death. One, however, of the insurgents, named Arsenius, found his way to Constantinople. He was a man of great eloquence and ability, and succeeded in convincing the Emperor, who was usually entirely under the priestly influence, as well as the Empress, that the Christians were the real authors of this insurrection. The ecclesiastics of Palestine were seized with amazement and terror at the progress of this man—whom they characterize as "a crafty and wicked liar"—in the favour of the Emperor. They had recourse to St. Sabas, and induced him to undertake a mission to Constantinople in their defence. The venerable age (he was ninety years old) and the sanctity of Sabas triumphed over, it may be feared, the reason and justice of Arsenius. The Samaritans were condemned; the leaders of the insurrection adjudged to death; the rest of the people expelled, and interdicted from settling again in Naplous; and, by a strange edict, the Samaritans were no longer to inherit the property of their fathers. Arsenius himself bowed to the storm, and embraced Christianity: many of the Samaritans, at the preaching of Sabas, or more probably to secure their property to their children, followed his example, or pretended to do so, with hypocrisy which may offend, but cannot surprise. The Emperor offered magnificent presents to Sabas; the holy man rejected every personal advantage; but requested a remission of taxes for his brethren, whose fields had been wasted, and property burned, in the recent tumults.

This apparent success in converting the great part of an obstinate race of unbelievers to the true faith, with some other events of the same nature, no doubt encouraged Justinian in his severe legislative enactments against the Jews and Samaritans. These nations were confounded with the recreant or disobedient sons of the Church, the heretics: they were deprived of all civil dignities, and at the same time compelled to undertake the offices attached to those dignities. Every burthen of society was laid upon them; but the honour and distinction which should be the inseparable rewards of such public services were sternly denied. They might be of the Curia, but the law which made sacred the person of the Curiales, and made it a crime to strike them, to put them to the torture, to exile them, had no application to the Jew, the Samaritan, or the heretic.[m] The proselyting zeal which dictated the constitutions of Justinian entered into the bosom of families, under the specious pretext of securing Christian converts from the unwarrantable exercise of the parental authority. Either supposing that the law which forbade the intermarriages of Samaritans or Jews with Christians was perpetually eluded, or providing for the case of one party becoming a convert while the other adhered to his faith, Justinian enacted that among parents of different religions, the chief authority should rest with the true religion. In defiance of the father, the children were to be under the care of the mother; and the father could not, on the ground of religion, refuse either a maintenance or

---

[m] Nov. Constit. 45, c. 1.

his necessary expenses to the child.ᵃ "Unbelieving parents, who have no other well-grounded cause of complaint against their believing children, are bound to leave them their property, to afford them a maintenance, to provide them with all necessaries, to marry them to true believers, to bestow on them dowries and bridal presents according to the decree of the prefect or the bishop." Further, the true believing children of unbelieving parents, if those children have been guilty of no act of delinquency towards their parents, shall receive that share of their inheritance, undiminished, which would have fallen to them if their parents had died intestate; and every will made in contravention of this regulation is declared null and void. If they have been guilty of any delinquency, they may be indicted and punished; but even then they have a right to a fourth part of the property.ᵇ

The above edict included both Jews and Samaritans: in the following, an invidious distinction was made. In litigations between Christians and Jews, or Christians among each other, the testimony of a Jew or a Samaritan was inadmissible: in the litigations of Jews among each other, the Jew's testimony was valid; that of a Samaritan as of a Manichean of no value. Another statute enacted that the synagogues of the Samaritans should be destroyed, and that whoever attempted to rebuild them should be severely punished. The Samaritans were entirely deprived of the right of bequeathing their property: only true believers might presume to administer to the effects of a heretic, whether he died with or without a will. Thus no Samaritan had more than a life interest in his property; unless his son was

---

ᵃ Cod. Just. i, v. 12. 1.   ᵇ Ibid. 13, 1.

an apostate, it was for ever alienated, and went to a stranger, or to the imperial treasury. No Samaritan might bear any office, neither teach nor plead in courts of law: impediments were even placed in the way of his conversion; if he conformed in order to obtain an office, he was obliged to bring his wife and children with him to the church. Not merely could he not bequeath, he could not convey property to an unbeliever; if he did so, it was confiscated to the treasury. The children of mixed marriages must be believers, or forfeit their inheritance; or where this was partly the case, the unbelieving children were excluded. "The true believers alone inherit: if none are members of the Church, it passes to the nearest relations; in default of these, to the treasury. The Prefects and Bishops are to enforce these statutes in their respective districts, and the infringement of them is to be punished by the severest penalties." These cruel statutes—which sowed dissension in the bosom of every family, caused endless litigations among the nearest relatives, almost offered a premium on filial disobedience, and enlisted only the basest motives on the side of true religion—were either too flagrantly iniquitous to be put in execution, or shocked the cooler judgement of the Imperial legislator.

A decree was issued a few years after, modifying these enactments, but in such a manner as perhaps might tempt the sufferers to quote, if they had dared, the sentence of their own wise king, "The tender mercies of wicked men are cruel." In this edict, after some pompous self-adulation on his own clemency, Justinian declared, that on account of the good conduct of the Samaritans, attested by Sergius, Bishop of Cæsarea, who, to his honour, seems to have interposed in their behalf, the rigour of the former laws was mitigated. The Samaritans were permitted to make wills, to convey property, to manumit slaves, to transact all business with each other. It abandoned all claims of the treasury upon their property; but it retained the following limitation, "because it was just that Christian heirs should have some advantage over unbelievers." Where part of the family had embraced Christianity, and the father died intestate, the children who were true believers inherited to the exclusion of the rest. But in case the latter, at a subsequent period, were converted, they were reinstated in their inheritance, with the loss only of the interest of those years during which they remained obstinate. Where the father made a will, the unbelieving heirs could not claim more than a sixth part; the rest could only be obtained, as above, by the change of their religion. A deceitful peace, maintained by the establishment of a proconsul in Syria, with a considerable body of troops, lasted for about twenty-five years. At the end of that time a new insurrection took place in Cæsarea. The Jews and Samaritans rose, attacked the Christians, demolished the churches, surprised and massacred the Prefect Stephanus in his palace, and plundered the building. The wife of Stephanus fled to Constantinople. Adamantius was commissioned to inquire into the origin of the tumult, and to proceed against the guilty with the utmost rigour. Of the real cause we know nothing. Adamantius condemned the insurgents, executed many, confiscated the property of the most wealthy, probably for the restoration of the churches, and reduced the whole province to peace.

As the Samaritans will appear no more in this History, I pursue, to its termination, the account of this people.

The Samaritans found means to elude these laws, by submitting to baptism, resuming their property, and then quietly falling back to their ancient faith. A law of Justin, the son of Justinian, denounces this practice, and re-enacts almost the whole iniquitous statute of his father.[p] How far these measures tended to the comparative extinction of the Samaritan race, we cannot ascertain; but, at this time, they had so almost entirely in their hands the trade of money-changing, that a money-changer and a Samaritan, as, afterwards, a Jew and an usurer, were equivalent terms. Yet, after this period, few and faint traces of their existence, as a separate people, appear in history. In the seventeenth century, it was discovered that a small community still dwelt in the neighbourhood of their holy mountain, and had survived all the vicissitudes of ages, in a country remarkable for its perpetual revolutions; that they still possessed the copy of the Law in the old Samaritan character;[q] and even to this day their descendants, a

---

[p] This singular law exempted the Samaritan peasants and husbandmen from its harsh provisions. Their cultivation of the soil did not concern themselves alone, but the welfare of the state, and especially the power of paying taxes to the state. Besides, the labouring on the soil presupposes a want of higher knowledge, which may naturally keep husbandmen from discovering the superiority of the Christian religion. Keeping the Sabbath, or performing any act which might throw suspicion on the sincerity of his conversion, subjected the Samaritan to exile or other punishment. No one was to be baptized until properly instructed. No Samaritan might have a Christian slave; a Samaritan captive, on turning Christian, acquired his freedom.

[q] I do not remember that they attracted much notice among the earlier pilgrims or crusaders. The Samaritans were found by the traveller Pietro della Valle, in Cairo, Jerusalem, Gaza, Damascus, and Aleppo. Benjamin of Tudela speaks of one hundred Samaritan families in Sichem. After the Reformation the learned world were interested with a correspondence entered into with them by the famous Joseph Scaliger. R. Huntingdon, chaplain to the British Factory of Aleppo, sent to Europe more copious information. Their copy of the Old Testament was brought to Europe, and assumed great importance in Biblical criticism.

feeble remnant of this once numerous people, are visited with interest by the traveller to the Holy Land.*

The zeal of the Emperor, while it burned more fiercely against the turbulent and disaffected Samaritans, in whose insurrections the Jews of Palestine seemed to have shared both the guilt and the calamities, did not neglect any opportunity of attempting either by force, or, we can scarcely hesitate to add, fraud, the proselytism of the Jews dispersed throughout the Eastern empire. The two great means of conversion were penal laws and miracles—sometimes compulsion. Among the boasted triumphs of the reconquest of Africa from the Vandals, was the reduction to the true faith of Borium, a town on the borders of Mauritania, where the Jews are said to have had a splendid temple, no doubt a synagogue more costly than usual.* The miracles indeed of this age are almost too puerile to relate; we give one specimen as characteristic of the times. It was the custom of the Church to distribute the crumbs of the consecrated Host which might remain, to children, summoned for that purpose from their schools. While Mennas was Bishop of Constantinople, the child of a Jewish glass-blower went to the church with the rest, and partook of the sacred elements. The father, inquiring the cause of his delay, discovered what he had done. In his fury he seized the child, and shut him up in the blazing furnace. The mother went wandering about the city, wailing and seeking her lost offspring.

---

* The Samaritans have in modern times been visited over and over again by curious travellers. Their numbers seem at last to be dwindling away, so as to threaten their total extinction. See the latest, a very interesting account, by Mr. Grove, in a recent volume of Vacation Travels.

* Procop. de Ædif. vi. 2. The temple was said to be of the age of Solomon.

The third day she sat down by the door of the workshop, still weeping, and calling on the name of her child. The child answered from the furnace, the doors were forced open, and the child discovered sitting unhurt amid the red-hot ashes. His account was, that a lady in a purple robe, of course the Blessed Virgin, had appeared and poured water on the coals that were immediately around him. The unnatural father was put to death, the mother and child baptized.[t] Such were the legends which were to convince that people who had rejected the miracles of Christ and his Apostles. The Jews were too wise or too superstitious, too quick and adroit, not to work counter-miracles, too credulous and ignorant not to believe them. In an age of daily wonders, wonders cease to be wonderful: familiarity with such solemn impressions destroys their solemnity and impressiveness; they pass away, and are as rapidly effaced as the ordinary business of life. Good and evil spirits were by common consent invested in powers bordering on omnipotence; each party saw nothing but the works of devils in the alleged miracles of the other.[u]

The laws were probably little more effective, and deeply imbued with the darkness of the age. An Imperial decree, not easily understood, and not worth much pains to understand, was issued, to establish an uniformity in the time at which the Jewish Passover and the Christian Easter were celebrated.[x] The Jews were forbidden, under heavy pecuniary mulcts, from following their own calculations. In the same edict, with singular ignorance of the usages of the people for

---

[t] Evagr. H. E. iv. 36.

[u] "Der Thalmud ist eben so voll kindischer Märchen aus der neuen Zeit, wie die Kirchenschriftsteller der er- wähnten Jahrhunderte." Such is the ingenuous confession of Jost, v. 194.

[x] Prosp. Hist. Anc. c. 28; Basnage, viii. 350.

whom he was legislating, Justinian prohibited the Jews from eating the Paschal Lamb, a practice which they had discontinued for five centuries.[7] But the Emperor had an opportunity of inflicting upon Judaism a more fatal blow, of which, it is probable he himself did not apprehend entirely the important consequences. A schism had arisen in the synagogues, between the teachers and the commonalty, the clergy and the laity of the Jews. With a singular abandonment of their jealousy of all foreign interference in what may be called the domestic concerns of their religion, an appeal was made to the Emperor, and the conflicting parties awaited his mandate on a subject where, one might have supposed, they would rather have looked for the interposition of their God. The great point in dispute was the language in which the Scripture was to be read,[z] and the expositions made, in the synagogue. On the decision the dominion of the Rabbins depended— it trembled to its foundations. With the fall of the Patriarchate, the connexion of the scattered synagogues of the West with Palestine had been interrupted. The schools had likewise been entirely closed, or fallen into disrepute. The Semicha, or ordination by the imposition of hands, formerly received in Palestine, was suspended. The learned youth were obliged to seek their education in the schools of Babylonia. Thus they lost the sanctity which still, in popular opinion, attached to whatever came from the Holy Land. They probably, were strangers, and by no means well acquainted with the Western languages. The people, who had now entirely forgotten both the Hebrew of the Scriptures and the vernacular language of Palestine, began imperiously to demand

---

[7] Basnage, Hist. des Juifs.   [z] See Jost, v. 181, et seqq.

the general use of Greek translations. The craft of the Rabbins was in danger; it rested almost entirely on their knowledge of the original Hebrew writings, still more of the Mischnaioth and Talmudic Comments. Hebrew was the sacred language, and, the language of learning once superseded by Greek, the mystery would be open to profane eyes, and reason and plain common sense, instead of authority, might become the bold interpreters of the written Law, perhaps would dare to reject entirely the dominion of tradition. In vain had been all their painful and reverential labours on the Sacred Books. In vain had they counted every letter, every point, every mark; and found mysteries in the number of times in which each letter occurred in the whole volume, in its position, in its relation to other letters. The deep and hidden things of the Law were inseparable from the Hebrew character. Besides its plain, and obvious meaning every text was significant of higher matters to the ears of the initiate. All the decisions of the schools, all the sayings of the Rabbins, were locked up in that sacred language. The Mischna, and the Talmud itself, might become a dead letter; for if the Scriptures were read in the vernacular tongue, the knowledge of Hebrew might cease to be a necessary qualification of the teacher. The Rabbins had much reason, and more stubborn prejudice, on their side. The elder Wise Men had always looked with jealousy on the encroachment of Greek letters. "Cursed be he that eateth swine's flesh, and teacheth his child Greek," had been an old axiom, perhaps, from the time of the Asmoneans. They were fighting for life and death, and armed themselves with all the spiritual terrors they could assume. They fulminated their anathemas; they branded their opponents as freethinkers and atheists.

At length the affair came before the Emperor. Whether his passion for legislation, which sometimes, even the Christian bishops complained, induced Justinian to intrude into concerns beyond his province, led him to regulate the synagogue; or whether the disputes ran so high as to disturb the public peace, and demand the interference of the supreme authority; or whether the appeal was, in fact, voluntarily made; an edict was issued, which is still extant among the imperial constitutions.[*] It enacted, that no one, who wished to do so, should be prevented from reading the Greek Scriptures in the synagogue; it enjoined those who read Greek to use the Translation of the Seventy, which had been executed under the special, though less manifest, influence of the Holy Ghost, because the prophecies relating to Christianity were most clear in that translation; but it did not prohibit the version of Aquila, or any other. It positively interdicted the use of the Mischna, as the invention of worldly men, which misled the people into miserable superstition. None of the Archiperacitæ, the readers of Peracha, or Extracts of the Talmud, on pain of confiscation of goods, and corporal chastisement, were to forbid the use of other languages, or dare to utter ban or interdict against such practices. On the other hand, freethinking, atheism, and such crimes, were to be severely punished; whoever denied the existence of God, of the angels, the Creation, and final judgement, was condemned to death. The law terminated with a solemn admonition to read the Scriptures, so as to improve their spirits and hearts, and increase in knowledge and morality. The law was wise and moderate; but, as Jost observes, the Emperor

---

[*] Nov. Const. 146.

probably prevented its operation by betraying too openly its object—the conversion of the Jews. The spirit of the age was against him; the Rabbins eventually triumphed—the Talmud maintained its authority.

In his former persecuting edicts, the shortsighted Emperor had alike miscalculated his own strength and the weakness of the Jews. Rome, in the zenith of her power, might despise the discontents of a scattered people, or a mutinous province, but in these disastrous times, it was dangerous for the feeble Eastern empire to alienate the affections of the meanest of its subjects. The Jews had the power, and could not be expected to want the desire of vengeance. Even in the West they were of some importance. During the siege of Naples by Belisarius, the Jews, who loved the milder dominion of the Gothic kings, defended one quarter of the city with obstinate resolution, and yielded only when the conqueror was within the gates.[b] On the eastern frontier, now that the Persian monarchy on the Tigris was an equal match for the wreck of the Roman Empire on the Bosphorus, an oppressed and unruly population, on the accessible frontier of Syria, holding perpetual intercourse with their more favoured, though by no means unpersecuted, brethren in Babylonia, might be suspected of awaiting with ill-suppressed impatience the time when, during some inevitable collision between the two empires, they might find an opportunity of vengeance on masters against whom they had so long an arrear of wrong. The hour at length came; but, as the affairs of the Jews in the Eastern empire, at least in Palestine, are now inseparably moulded up with those of Persia, we turn our attention to the Eastern

---

[b] Procop. de Bello Gothico, L. 10, p. 53, Edit. Bonn.

Jews, briefly trace their history down to the time of Justinian, and then pursue the mingled thread to the appearance of Mohammed.

II. From the death of R. Asche, who commenced the Babylonian Talmud, dark were the days of the children of the Captivity. During the reigns of the Persian kings from Izdigerd to Kobad, from about 430 to 530 (A.C.), the dominant Magian religion oppressed alike the Christian and the Jew. The Sabbath, say the Jewish traditions, was taken away by Izdigerd.[c] Still, however, the Resch-Glutha, or Prince of the Captivity, maintained his state, and the famous schools of Nahardea, Sura, and Pumbeditha, were open. Civil discords had nearly destroyed the enfeebled state; and the house of David, from whose loins the princes of the Captivity deduced their rank, was well nigh extinct. Here, as elsewhere, great jealousies existed between the temporal and spiritual power: the former attempted, the latter would not endure, encroachment. The rupture took place when it might have been expected that they would have lived in the greatest harmony; for the Prince of the Captivity, R. Huna, had married the daughter of R. Chanina, the master of the schools, a grandson or great-grandson of R. Asche, who commenced the Talmud.[d] But ambition listens not to the claims of blood and kindred. The Resch-Glutha, or his judge, attempted to interpret the Talmud in the presence of the Wise Man. Chanina resisted this usurpation of his province. The Resch-Glutha decoyed

---

[c] Jost, v. 222; but Jost is obliged to admit that the history of these Persian persecutions, in which several Resch-Gluthas, Rabbis, and learned men were put to death, is altogether confused and obscure.

[d] Jost, v. 226. There are two versions of the story; I have blended some particulars of both.

Chanina into his power, sat in judgement on him, ordered his beard to be shaved, and cast him forth, interdicting all the inhabitants of the city from affording him shelter, or the necessaries of life. Chanina (we have no better history than this legend to offer) wept and prayed. A pestilence broke out in the royal family, and every soul perished except a child, with which the widowed daughter of Chanina, the Prince's wife, was pregnant. Chanina dreamed a dream: he saw himself in a grove, where he cut down all the stately cedars; one young plant alone remained. He was awakened as by a violent blow on the head; an old man stood by, who said, "I am the lord of this grove, the King David." He reproached the dreamer for having thus cut off all the lofty cedars of the house of David, and forcibly reminded him of his duty to watch over the single scion of the royal stock. Chanina waited night and day by his daughter's door; neither the fiery heat of noon, nor torrents of rain, could induce him to remove till the child was born. He took the infant and superintended his education with the most diligent care. In the mean time a certain Paphra, distantly allied to the royal house, bought, like the Roman Didius, the princely dignity, and enjoyed it for fifteen years. At that convenient time he came to a most ignoble end; a fly flew into his nose, and made him sneeze so violently that he died! The young Zutra ascended the throne. During his reign of twenty years, an enthusiast, named Meir, brought ruin on the whole community. He proclaimed himself, most probably, a Messiah; he pretended that a fiery column preceded his march, and with four hundred desperate followers he laid waste the country. The Persian king, Kobad, speedily suppressed the insurrection. Meir was put to death, and all the heads of the Captivity were involved in his fate. The Prince of the Captivity, Zutra, and R. Chanina his tutor, were hanged. This great insurrection took place in 530 A.C., a year before Nushirvan's accession. At this disastrous period, many of the Babylonian Jews wandered from their afflicted settlements; some, it is believed, found their way to the coast of Malabar. A son of Zutra fled to Tiberias, where he renewed the Semicha, or laying-on of hands; and, it is supposed, contributed to disseminate the Babylonian Talmud among the Jews of the West.

Chosroes the Just, or Nushirvan, who ascended the throne of Persia in the fifth year of Justinian, 531 A.C., was not more favourable to the Jews of Babylonia. Their schools were closed by authority. But so great was the impatience of the Palestinian Israelites under the oppressive laws of Justinian, that they looked with anxious hope to, and are reported by Christian writers to have urged, by an offer of 50,000 men, and by the splendid prospect of the plunder of Christian Jerusalem, the hostile advance of the Persian monarch.[*] These hopes were frustrated by the conclusion of an "everlasting peace" between Justinian and Nushirvan, in which the pride of Rome was obliged to stoop to the payment of a great sum of money. The "everlasting peace" endured barely seven years, and the hopes of the Jews were again excited; but their day of vengeance was not yet come. After extending his conquests to Antioch, Nushirvan was constrained by the ability of Belisarius to retreat. Peace was again con-

---

[*] Theophan. Chronogr. p. 274, Edit. Boun.; but Theophanes has confused the dates, and places this offer at the commencement of the reign of Justinian. See Basnage, and Just.'s criticism on Basnage.

cluded, Jerusalem remained unplundered, and the Jews and Samaritans were abandoned to the vindictive justice of their former masters. Under Hormisdas, the successor of Chosroes Nushirvan, the Babylonian Jews were restored to their prosperity. Their schools in Pumbeditha, Sura, and Nahardea, were reopened. A new order of doctors, the Gaonim, the Illustrious, arose; and their prince resumed his state. After the fall and death of the weak Hormisdas, the Jews espoused the party of the usurper Bharam,[f] or Varanes, against the son of Hormisdas, Chosroes the Second, the rightful heir of the throne, and by no means, I believe with Gibbon, the parricide, who fled to implore, and obtained, the assistance of Maurice, Emperor of the East. Among the executions which followed the triumphant restoration of Chosroes to the throne of his ancestors, the Jews had their full share.[g] There was a new Antioch built by Nushirvan, and peopled with the inhabitants of the old city, whom he transported thither, and who were struck with agreeable astonishment at finding the exact counterpart of every house and street of their former residence. The Jews formed a considerable part of this community, and when the storm first burst on the city, Mebod, the general of Chosroes, inflicted on them the most dreadful penalties for their disloyalty; some were cut off by the sword, others tortured, others reduced to slavery. But this was vengeance, not persecution; the Jews submitted, and made their peace with Chosroes. When that king, summoned alike by gratitude and ambition, prepared to burst on the Byzantine empire, to revenge on the barbarous usurper Phocas the murder of his

---

[f] Theophylact Simocatta, v. 6, 7, p. 218, Edit. Bonn.
[g] Gibbon, c. xlvi. vñi. p. 193, Edit. Milman.

friend and protector Maurice, and that of his five sons, the Palestinian Jews were in a state of frantic excitement, still further aggravated by the persecutions of Phocas, who compelled a great number of their brethren to submit to baptism. Ever rash in their insurrections, they could not wait the appointed time: they rose in Antioch, set the splendid palaces of the principal inhabitants on fire, slew numbers, treated the Patriarch Anastasius with the worst indignity, and dragged him through the streets till he died.[b]

Phocas sent Bonosus and Cotto against the insurgents, who defeated them with great loss, and revenged, as far as they had time, the outrages which had been committed in all quarters. But they were compelled to retreat, and the Jews beheld, in a paroxysm of exultation, the unresisted squadrons of Chosroes pouring over the frontier: Antioch surrendered without a blow.

Chosroes turned towards Constantinople; his general, Carusia, advanced to the conquest of Palestine and Jerusalem.[i] The Jews arose at his approach; from

---

[b] Theoph. Chronog. p. 457, Edit. Bonn. Chronicon Paschale. This brief notice merely says, ἀπῃρέθη ὑπὸ στρατιωτῶν, p. 699, Edit. Bonn.

[i] Theophylact Simocatta, v. 6, 7, p. 216, Edit. Bonn. Simocatta's account of the Babylonian Jews, their commerce, their wealth, their disposition to ally themselves with the Persians to revenge themselves on the Romans, is curious: τῶν γὰρ Ἱεροσολύμων ὑπὸ Οὐεσπασιανοῦ τοῦ αὐτοκράτορος ἁλόντων, τοῦ τε ναοῦ ἐμπεπραμένου ὀρθοδοῦντες πολλοὶ τῶν Ἰουδαίων τὴν Ῥωμαίων ἀλκὴν ἐκ τῆς Παλαιστίνης ὡς τοὺς Μήδους καὶ πρὸς τὴν ἀρχὴν γόνον τιθήνην μετανεστεύουσιν, ἐξ ἧς ὁ προπάτωρ ἐτύγχανεν ἐν 'Αβραάμ· τὰ τιμιώτατα τοίνυν οὗτοι ἐμπορευσάμενοι καὶ τὴν ἐρυθρὰν περαιούμενοι θάλατταν, περιουσίας χρηματίσαντες μεγάλας περιεβάλλοντο· ἐντεῦθεν καὶ πρὸς τὰς στάσεις καὶ τὰς Βαβυλωνίας τῶν δήμων ἐκκαθάρσεις ἑτοιμότατα διωλίσθαινον· ἔστι γὰρ πόνηρον τὸ ἔθνος καὶ ἀπιστότατον· φιλόθρυβόν τε καὶ τύραννον, καὶ φιλίας ἥκιστα μνημονικόν, ζηλότυπόν τε καὶ ὑποβάσκανον, καὶ ἐς ἔχθραν ἀμετάδοτόν τε καὶ ἀδιάλλακτον. p. 218; also Dionys. Patriarcha, apud Asseman. Biblioth. Orient. ii. 102.

Tiberias and Nazareth they joined him in great numbers, till their force amounted, according to report, to 24,000 men. Before the capture of Jerusalem, new causes of exasperation were added to the dreadful arrears of ancient vengeance. In Tyre it is said that the incredible number of 40,000 Jews had taken up their dwelling. They sent secret messengers to all their brethren in Palestine, in Damascus, in Cyprus, in the mountainous districts of Galilee, and in Tiberias, to assemble suddenly before the walls of that city, on the night of the Christian Easter. The conspiracy reached the ears of the Christians. The Bishop and powerful citizens seized the most wealthy of the Jews, threw them into prison, and put the gates and walls in the best possible state of defence. The Jews appeared, and revenged themselves by the destruction of the suburbs for the failure of their surprise; but every time a Christian church, the great object of their animosity, was set on fire, the besieged struck off the heads of a hundred Jewish prisoners, and cast them over the wall. This horrible retaliation produced no effect; twenty churches sank into ashes, and the heads of 2000 Jews lay bleaching on the sand.[k] At length, on a rumour of the advance of the Imperial forces, the Jews retreated to join their brethren in the easier achievement of entering, under the protection of their Persian allies, the streets of Christian Jerusalem.

It had come at length, the long-expected hour of triumph and vengeance; and they did not neglect the opportunity. They washed away the profanation of the Holy City in Christian blood. The Persians are said to have sold the miserable captives for money. The vengeance of the Jews was stronger than their avarice; not

---

[k] Eutychll Ann. II. p. 220-223, from whom the author quoted by | Hottinger (Hist. Orient.) took it, St. Martin, note on Le Beau, sl. 8.

only did they not scruple to sacrifice their treasures in the purchase of these devoted bondsmen, they put to death without remorse all they had purchased at a lavish price.[1] It was a rumour of the time that 90,000 perished. Every Christian church was demolished; that of the Holy Sepulchre was the great object of furious hatred; the stately building of Helena and Constantine was abandoned to the flames; "the devout offerings of three hundred years were rifled in one sacrilegious day."[m] But the dream of Jewish triumph was short; the hope of again possessing, if not in independence, under the mild protection of the Persian monarch, the Holy City of their forefathers, vanished in a few years. The Emperor Heraclius, who seemed to slumber on the throne of Byzantium like another Sardanapalus, allowing the Persians to conquer and even to occupy their conquests, Jerusalem itself, the Sacred City, undisturbed, suddenly broke the bonds of sloth and pleasure. After a few campaigns, conducted by the Roman with equal boldness and ability, the Persian monarch, instead of arraying his victorious troops under the walls of Byzantium, trembled within his own insecure capital; and the provinces which he had overrun, Syria and Egypt, passed quietly under the sway of their former masters. Heraclius himself visited Jerusalem as a pilgrim, where the wood of the true Cross, which had been carried away to Persia, was reinstated with due solemnity, the exiled Bishop Zacharias replaced on his throne, and the Christian churches were restored to their former magni-

---

[1] Theophan. Chronog. p. 463, Edit. Bonn.
Chronicon Paschale, sub ann. 614, p. 704, Edit. Bonn. The chronicler is silent about the sale of the Christians, which rests on a later authority; but the chronicle is as brief on this and event as may be.
[m] Gibbon, viii. 226.

ficence." If the clergy enforced upon the kneeling and penitent Emperor the persecution of the Jews, it must be acknowledged that provocation was not wanting; for how many of them had been eye-witnesses of, perhaps sufferers in, the horrible atrocities committed on the capture of the city! Yet we have no authentic account of great severities exercised by Heraclius.° The law of Hadrian was re-enacted, which prohibited the Jews from approaching within three miles of the city — a law which, in the present exasperated state of the Christians, might be a measure of security or mercy, rather than of oppression.

ⁿ Theophan. Chronograph. p. 504, Edit. Bonn.
° There is one case of conversion, in which no doubt force was used on a certain Benjamin in Tiberias. Theophanes.

BOOK XXII.

JUDAISM AND MOHAMMEDANISM.

Jews in Arabia — Jewish Kingdom in Homeritis — Rise of Mohammed — Wars against the Arabian Jews — Progress of Mohammedanism — State of Spain — Cruel Laws of the Visigothic Kings — Conquest of Spain by the Moors — Persecuting Laws in France.

DURING the conflict between the Persian and Roman Emperors, a power was rapidly growing up in the secret deserts of Arabia, which was to erect its throne upon the ruins of both. Mohammed had already announced his religious doctrine—"There is but one God, and Mohammed is His prophet"—and the valleys of Arabia had echoed with the triumphant battle-cry of his followers, "The Koran or death!" The Jews were among the first of whom Mohammed endeavoured to make proselytes—the first opponents—and the first victims of the sanguinary teaching of the new Apostle. For centuries, a Jewish kingdom[a] or kingdoms, unconnected either with the Jews of Palestine or Babylonia, had existed in that district of Arabia called, in comparison to the stony soil of one part and the sandy waste of the other, Arabia the Happy.[b] Of their origin we have no

---

[a] This kingdom must, of course, be carefully distinguished from the Arabic kingdom conterminous to Palestine, over which Aretas ruled at the time when St. Paul retired into Arabia (Gal. i. 17), and in which no doubt were multitudes of Jews.

[b] Saba, Yemen, Homeritis, were either situated in this region, or were the general name of the whole, or each of

distinct account; but among the various afflictions and dispersions of the Jewish people, it would have been extraordinary if a place of refuge so near, and at the same time so secure, had not tempted them to venture on the perils of the desert—which, once passed, presented an almost insuperable barrier to the pursuit of an enemy. Their mercantile brethren, who visited the ports of the Red Sea, might bring home intelligence of the pleasant valleys which ran down to the coast, and from which gales of aromatic sweetness were wafted to their barks as they passed along. Ancient tradition pointed, and probably with truth, to these regions, as the dwelling of that famous Queen of Sheba who had visited their great king in his splendour; and in the hospitable dominions of her descendants, the race of Solomon's subjects might find refuge. In some respects, the Arabian tribes were their brethren; they seem to have entertained great respect, if they did not learn it from the Jews, for the memory of Abraham. They practised circumcision in Sabæa, like the Jews, on the eighth day, and they abhorred swine's flesh. However they came there, Jewish settlers, at least one hundred and twenty years before Christ, had built cities and castles, and established an independent kingdom.[c] Arabian tradition (we dare not dignify it with the name of history) assigns a Jewish king to the dis-

---

a separate district, of which the limits were not clearly defined.

[c] They had many converts, it is said, among the Arab tribes. "Sozomène remarque, l. vi. c. 38, que par suite des rapports que les Arabes du désert avaient eus avec les Juifs, beaucoup d'entr'eux avaient adopté les usages Judaïques, τῶν 'Ιου- δαίκως ζώσιν. Les auteurs orientaux font la même remarque, et nomment plusieurs des tribus Arabes qui avaient embrassé la religion Juive. Il s'en trouvait beaucoup dans les environs de la Mecque. Elles furent les premiers adversaires de Mahomet." St. Martin, note on Le Beau, iii. p. 449; but compare note viii. p. 47.

trict of Homeritis, about that period, named Abu-Carb-Asaad.⁴ It adds the inconsistent circumstance, that he first strewed with carpets the sacred temple of Mecca called the Caaba. If this be true, Judaism in Arabia must have been more social and tolerant than elsewhere; for the Caaba, before the time of Mohammed, was, undoubtedly, a temple of idolatrous worship; and though the Jew might assert that the God of Israel maintained the first place, many associate or subordinate deities claimed their portion in the sacrifices of Mecca.* The line of Jewish kings in Homeritis is continued, though a broken series; but we have no space for these barren annals, and pass on to the last of these Homeritish kings, who reigned and fell a short time before the rise of Mohammedanism. The feuds of Christians and Jews spread into these retired and fertile valleys, and, connected, perhaps, with political circumstances, inflamed the warlike habits of tribes in which the old Arabian blood was far from extinct. Christianity had first penetrated into Yemen in an Arian form, probably during the reign of Constantius, son of Constantine the Great.ᶠ With the Arians, the Jews, as usual, seem to have lived on terms of amity. The Catholic faith spread from the other side of the Red Sea, under the protecting influence of the powerful kings of Ethiopia or Abyssinia. Eles-baan, the king of that country, had extended his conquests over the opposite shore of the Red Sea; and Dunaan,⁸ the Jewish King of Homeritis, after many defeats, had been obliged to pay tribute to the Ethiopian. But his restless spirit disdained submission;

---

⁴ Compare Jost (Geschichte, v. 241). This king was nearly cotemporary with John Hyrcanus. Jost quotes Michaelis, Orient. et Exeg. Bibl. iv. 157.

* See them in Jost, v. 243, 245.
ᶠ Pagi, Crit. in. Baron. sub ann. 351.
⁸ The name is variously written Dhu Nowas. Jost. According to Le Beau

every defeat only kindled the burning desire of vengeance and independence. The invasions of the Ethiopian, dependent on the precarious navigation of the Red Sea, were often suspended—probably, at certain periods, in winter at least, were entirely cut off. Dunaan resolved on the bold measure of attempting the sudden extermination of the Christian power in Yemen; after the loss of their allies, the Abyssinians would find it difficult to maintain their footing in the country. He seized a favourable opportunity, rose, and executed all the Christians within his power; and appeared before the walls of Nagra, their chief city, at the head of 120,000 men. He summoned the inhabitants to take down the cross, which stood on a height above the city, and to deny the Christian religion. A singular negotiation ensued. The besieger demanded the acknowledgment of the Unity of God, as the supreme Head of the Church, and the denial of a plurality of Persons in the Godhead. The Christians readily acknowledged the Unity, but refused to yield on the other point. On their refusal, Dunaan gave the signal for the execution of many of his Christian captives in the sight of their brethren, and the sale of others as slaves. At length, on a promise of freedom of conscience, the Christians opened their gates, but the perfidious Arab violated the terms—threw Areth and others of the leaders into chains, and then demanded

---

and St. Martin, Elea-baan, then a pagan, to revenge the massacre of a caravan passing through Homeritis to the Red Sea and Ethiopia, had invaded Homeritis, killed the king Dimian or Dimnos or Damianus, established a Christian king on the throne, and had himself been baptized by a bishop sent by order of the Emperor Justin to Axum. The Jews, on the death of the Christian king, revolted, regained the superiority, and set up Dunaan; massacred a great number of Christians, and destroyed the churches. Compare throughout Le Beau, viii. 53, and St. Martin's notes.

Paulus, the bishop, who had formerly been among his most eloquent opponents. The bishop had been for two years in his grave, but Dunaan revenged himself on his lifeless bones, which were disinterred and burned. Many priests, monks, and nuns, as the most active of his adversaries, suffered the same fate; and obtained, in the estimation of their brethren, the honours of martyrdom. Dunaan then tried arguments on Areth and the rest of his prisoners, to convince them of the absurdity of worshipping a crucified God. On the rejection of his arguments, he had recourse to more summary means of conviction — threats of instant death; these likewise were unavailing. Areth and his companions submitted cheerfully to execution. They could not well do otherwise, for their wives and daughters had before crowded forth, as if they were hastening to a bridal, to partake in the glory of suffering for their faith. Such, with many more particulars, is the tenor of a letter ascribed to Dunaan himself,[h] and addressed to Al Mondar, a prince of the Saracens, whose alliance he courted. I confess that I doubt, or rather feel assured, that this letter is either entirely fictitious, or greatly interpolated. The crimes of Dunaan, and the wrongs of the Christians, did not remain long unavenged.[i] With the spring, Elesbaan, and a formidable force of 120,000 men, invaded the region.[k] Dunaan, after an obstinate defence, was defeated, and lost his life;[l] and in his person expired the Jewish kingdom of the Homerites. After his death,

---

[h] It is contained in the Syriac letter of Simeon, Bishop of Beth-Arsam, ap. Asseman. Bibl. Orient. I. 364. Acta of the Arab martyrs in Metaphrastes.

[i] Le Beau, viii. 58. Compare Schultens Hist. Joctan.

[k] The 120,000 men of Metaphrastes are reduced by Hamzah of Ispahan and Nowairi to 10,000. Tabari gives 30,000. St. Martin's note.

[l] The Arab historians agree that after his defeat Dunaan threw himself into the sea.

Abraham, son of Areth, founded a Christian kingdom, which scarcely acknowledged the sovereignty of the feeble son of Eles-baan. The Christian dynasty in its turn was overthrown by the conquering arm of the Persians, and Arabia was reckoned among the subject realms of Chosroes the Second.[m]

But though they had lost their royal state, the Jews were still numerous and powerful in the Arabian peninsula; they formed separate tribes, and maintained the fierce independence of their Ishmaelitish brethren. Mohammed manifestly designed to unite all those tribes under his banner.[n] While his creed declared implacable war against the worshippers of fire, it respected the doctrines of the Jews,[o] and at least of the less orthodox Christians. The Apostle of God was the successor, greater indeed, of the former delegates of heaven Moses and Isha (Jesus).[p] It was only the fire of the Magians which was at once extinguished, and the

---

[m] Procop. de Bell. Pers. I. 20. Abraham, at the instigation of Justinian, had promised to invade the Persian kingdom, but after one feeble effort abstained from all aggression. The whole history of these obscure wars, and the affairs of the Jewish and Christian kings of Homeritis, is well worked out, and the conflicting Oriental authorities cited and balanced, by St. Martin in his notes on the chapter of Le Beau.

[n] "Children of Israel, remember my favour wherewith I have favoured you, and that I have preferred you above all nations." Sale's Koran, Sora, II. The Koran recites all the narratives of the deliverance from Egypt, and in the Desert. Read the whole following passages.

[o] "We gave unto the children of Israel the book of the Law, and wisdom and prophecy; and we fed them with good things, and preferred them above all nations; and we gave them plain ordinances concerning the business of religion; neither did they fall to variance except after the knowledge had come unto them, through envy amongst themselves; but the Lord will decide the controversy between them on the day of resurrection concerning that wherein they disagree." Sale's Koran, c. 45; ii. 368.

[p] "We formerly delivered the book of the Law to Moses, and caused apostles to succeed him, and gave evident miracles to Jesus the son of Mary, and strengthened him with the Holy Spirit." Sora, ii. p. 17.

palace of Chosroes, which shook to its foundations, at his birth.⁴ All the traditions which the old Arabian creed had preserved from immemorial ages, or with which it had been impregnated from the Jews resident in Arabia, still find their place in the Koran; and Abraham, the common father of the two races, holds the most conspicuous rank in their religious history.⁷ Jerusalem was appointed the first kebla of prayer; and in the nocturnal journey, during which the Prophet was transported to the holy city of the Jews, the mysterious winged horse, the Borak, arrested its course to pay homage to Mount Sinai, and to Bethlehem, the birth-place of Jesus. To the first part of the new creed, every Jewish heart would at once respond, "There is but one God"—why should not their enthusiasm, their impatience in awaiting the too-long-delayed Messiah, their ambition, or their avaricious eagerness to be glutted with the plunder of misbelievers, induce them to adopt the latter clause, "and Mohammed is His Prophet"? "We formerly gave unto the family of Abraham a book of revelations and wisdom, and we gave them a great kingdom. There is of them that believe on him, and there is of them who turneth aside from him; but the raging fire of hell is a sufficient punishment. Verily those who disbelieve our

---

⁴ Abulfeda, Vit. Moham. p. 3. Compare the new edition, or rather new Life of Mohammed, by Sprenger: "In der Nacht, in welcher der Prophet geboren wurde, zitterte die Halle des Chosroes, und es fielen vierzehn Coquets (schorfa) herunter, und das Feuer der Magier, welches tausend Jahre vorher sie erlöschen war, erlosch, und der See von Salva trocknete aus." See further the dream of the High Mobed, that he saw camels, followed by Arabian horses, pass the Tigris, and spread over Persia; the terror of the King, and the measures which he adopted to obtain an interpretation of the awful vision which prefigured the Mohammedan conquest, p. 134.

ʳ Sale's note, vol. i. p. 26.

signs, we will surely cast them to be broiled in hell-fire; so often as their skins shall be well burned, we will give them other skins in exchange, that they may taste the sharper torment; *for God is mighty and wise.* But those who believe, and do that which is right, we will bring into gardens watered by rivers: therein shall they remain for ever, and there shall they enjoy wives free from all impurity; and we will lead them into perpetual shades."[a] Such was the alternative offered to the Jews! But the Jews stood aloof in sullen unbelief; they disclaimed a Messiah sprung from the loins of Hagar the bondwoman. Nothing remained but to employ the stern proselytism of the sword.[b] The tone of Mohammed changed at once: the Israelites were taunted with all the obstinacy and rebellion of their forefathers; they were coupled with idolaters as the worst of unbelievers;[c] and the Koran bitterly mocks their vain hope "that the fires of hell shall touch them only for a few days."

The storm fell first on the Kainoka, a tribe who dwelt in Medina. In the peremptory summons to embrace Islamism, were these words:—"Lend to the Lord on good interest?"—"Surely," said the sarcastic Phineas, the son of Aynbah, "the Lord must be poor to require a loan!" The fiery Abubeker struck him a violent blow, and declared that, but for the treaty existing between the tribes, he would have smote off his head. An accidental tumult gave rise to the first open warfare. A Jewish goldsmith insulted an Arabian maiden—the Arabs slew the offender.[d] The Jews, the Beni Kainoka, were in a violent commotion, when Mohammed sent

---

[a] Sura, v. p. 105.
[b] Sale's note on c. lii. vol. I. p. 88.
[c] "Thou shalt surely find the most violent of all men in enmity against the true believers to be the Jews and the idolaters." Sura, v. p. 149.
[d] Vit. Moham. ap. Gagnier, p. 61; Abulfeda, Vit. Abr. Beer.

them the peremptory alternative, "Islamism or war." "We are ignorant of war," answered the Jews; "we would eat our bread in peace; but if you force us to fight, you shall find us men of courage." They fled to a neighbouring citadel, and made a gallant defence for fifteen days, at the end of which they were forced to surrender.² Mohammed issued immediate orders for a general massacre—he was hardly prevailed upon by the powerful Abdollah, son of Obba, to spare their lives— their wealth was pillaged.⁷ Their arms fell to the lot of the conquerors, and Mohammed arrayed himself in a cuirass, which either the Jews or his followers asserted to have belonged to King David;⁸ they added, in defiance of Jewish history, that he had it on when he slew Goliah. The miserable tribe, thus plundered and defenceless, was driven to find a settlement on the frontier of Syria. The turn of the tribe of Nadhir came next,⁹ but they provoked their fate by a treacherous

---

⁶ I rejoice to find in the new Life of Mohammed by Mr. Muir, carefully drawn from the Koran and the most accredited traditions, full agreement with the general views of this chapter. Perhaps Mr. Muir would not accept all the traditions in the text. The scene here briefly related is very strikingly told, lil. p. 135. Mr. Muir gives a curious illustration of the ill-blood between the Moslems and the Jews. "For many months after the arrival of Mohammed [at Medina], it so happened that no children were born to the Moslem women; and the rumours began to spread that their barrenness was occasioned by Jewish sorcery." pp. 60, 61.

⁷ Koran, c. 59: "The spoils of the inhabitants of these people which God hath granted to his Apostle, are due unto God and that Apostle, and him who is of kin to the Apostle, and the orphans, and the poor, and the traveller, that they may not be for ever divided in a circle among such of you as are rich. . . . Like those who lately proceeded them [*the idolaters who were slain at Bedr, or the Jews of Kainoka who were plundered and sent into exile before those of al Nadhir.* Sale's note], they have tasted the evil consequences of their deed, and a painful torment is prepared for them hereafter." li. p. 430.

⁸ Abulfeda, c. 35. Compare Pococke, Hist. Arab. p. 11.

⁹ But see in Muir some treacherous and revolting murders perpetrated on Jews by the express command of Mo-

attempt to assassinate the Prophet at a peaceful banquet.[b] They were besieged in their castle, and constrained to surrender, though with all the honours of war. Their wealth was confiscated, by a special revelation of the Koran, to the sole benefit of Mohammed himself and the poor; while the merciless edict pursues them into the next world, and, for their resistance to the Prophet, condemns them to everlasting hell-fire.[c] The vanquished Nadhirites retreated from the neighbourhood of Medina—they joined the Koreish, the inveterate enemies of Mohammed, and the Jews of Koraidha, in a new war against the Prophet. On the very evening of the day on which Mohammed won the memorable battle of the "Ditch,"[d] against the Koreish, he advanced to extirpate the Jews of Koraidha. His followers even neglected, without rebuke, the evening prayer, in their thoughts of vengeance. The Angel Gabriel, they believed, led the way, and poured terror into the hearts of the Koraidhites. Even Caab, the son of Asad, the brave author of the war, counselled surrender.[e]

---

hammed: "On the morning after the murder of Kab [Kab's chief offence was the publication of amatory sonnets about the Moslemite women]. Mohammed gave a general permission to his followers to slay any Jews whom they might chance to meet." iii. p. 148. The defeat of Mohammed at Ohod took place between these events.

[b] But as his followers saw nothing to excite suspicion, and as the chapter in the Koran specially devoted to the subject does not hint at such perfidy, the charge is open to grave suspicion. Muir, 209.

[c] Compare Muir, p. 209-215, with the extracts from the Sura, III.: "They are like unto Satan, when he said unto man 'Become an infidel;' and when he had become an infidel, the Tempter said, 'Verily I am clear of thee! Verily I fear the Lord of all worlds!' And the end of them both is that they are cast into the fire—dwelling for ever therein! That is the reward of the transgressors."

[d] Or rather the retreat of the Koreish from the Ditch which was the main defence of Medina. The fortress of the Koraid tribes (Muir writes it Coreitza) was two or three miles distant from Medina.

[e] "And he hath caused such of those who have received the Scriptures to come down out of their fortresses, and

A.C. 628.   WAR IN KHAIBAR.   95

They descended from their castle, hoping to obtain
mercy through the intercession of their allies. The
judgement was left to the venerable Saad, the son of
Moadh.[f] Saad was brought, sick and wounded, into the
camp. "Oh, Abu-Amru," (it was the name of Saad,)
cried the Jews, "have mercy upon us!" Saad uttered
his judgement with awful solemnity: "Let all the men
be put to death, and the women and children be
slaves." "A divine judgement!" exclaimed the fierce
Prophet—"a judgement from the highest of the seven
heavens!" Seven[g] hundred Jews were dragged in chains
to the marketplace of Medina—graves were dug—the
unhappy wretches descended into them—the sword did
its office, and the earth was heaped over their remains.
The inflexible Prophet looked on without emotion, and
this horrible butchery is related with triumph in the
Koran. The next Jewish victim was the powerful
Salam; he was assassinated in his bed by order of the
Prophet. The Jews of Khaibar now alone preserved
their independence. Khaibar was a district six days'
journey to the south-east of Medina;[h] rich in palm-
trees, and fertile in pastures, and protected by eight
castles, supposed to be impregnable. The Apostle led
forth to war two hundred horse and fourteen hundred
foot; as he entered the territory of Khaibar he exclaimed to his troops—"On, with redoubled speed!"

---

he cast into their hearts terror and dismay: a part of them ye slew, and a part ye made captives, and God hath caused you to inherit their land and their houses and their wealth." Sale's Koran, xxxiii. p. 275, with his note. The story is more fully told in Abulfeda and in Gagnier.

[f] Compare throughout, Muir, p. 272, &c. Saad had been wounded at the Ditch: "Mohammed knew well the bitter hate into which his former friendship had been turned by the treachery of the Coreitza." Therefore Mohammed chose him as arbiter of their fate.

[g] Eight, according to Muir.

[h] About 100 miles. Muir. Compare throughout, vol. iv. ch. 21.

He then turned to heaven in prayer—" Lord of the Heavens, Lord of the Earths, Lord of the Demons, and all that they lead into evil—Lord of the Winds, and all they disperse and scatter—grant us the spoil of this city, and preserve us from evil."[1] Allah had before promised him great booty: the evil he apprehended was, the poison which was afterwards given to him by a Jewish woman. The prayer ended, he cried again, " Forward, in the name of Allah !" The Jews of Khaibar were slumbering in peaceful repose. Their first castle, Naem, was taken by assault; the second, Natan, the castle of Asad, son of Moad, made a more vigorous defence. The Moslemites were reduced to great extremities, for the country had been wasted, and all the palm-trees destroyed. At length Natan fell, and Mohammed became master of an immense booty in corn, dates, oil, honey, flocks of sheep, cattle, and asses, and armour of all sorts. One author adds, that they brought to the Prophet a camel-skin full of collars, bracelets, garters, ear-rings, and buckles, all of gold, with an immense number of precious stones. Alkamus, the third citadel, made a still more gallant resistance. It was here that Ali distinguished himself. He planted the standard on the walls: he clove the skull of Marhab, the great champion of the Jews, through his buckler, two turbans, and a diamond which he wore in his helmet, till the sword stuck between his jaws.[2] Abu-Rafe, an eye-witness, declares that the " Strong Lion," Ali, seized the gate of the city, which eight men could not lift, and used it as a buckler.[3] On the capture of Alka-

---

[1] Gagnier, ii. 47.
[2] Gagnier, ii. 54, from Gannabi.
[3] " Abu-Rafe," observes Gibbon, in his usual caustic vein, " was an eye-witness—but who will be witness for Abu-Rafe?"

mus, Kenana, the chief, was horribly tortured, to induce him to betray the secret hiding-place of his treasures;[a] but the patient Jew endured to the utmost, and a more merciful Islamite relieved him by striking off his head. Three more of the castles fell. The two last surrendered on the promise that the lives of the besieged should be spared.[b] The inhabitants of the cities of Fadai and Khaibar capitulated on the condition of surrendering, besides all their wealth, which was vast, not merely in the fruits of the earth, sheep, and camels, but in treasure and jewels, half the revenue of their fields and pastures, which they were still to cultivate for the use of the Prophet. But Mohammed reserved the right of exiling them according to his good pleasure—a right which was afterwards exercised by the Caliph Omar, who alleged the dying injunction of the Prophet, that but one faith should be permitted to exist in Arabia. Some of the Jews of Khaibar were transplanted to Syria; yet it is supposed that some vestiges of their creed may still be traced among the Arab tribes of that district.[c]

---

[a] Here, as at Koraidha, Mohammed appropriated to himself the beautiful Jewess Rihâna, who, however, refusing to change her religion, was only his concubine. He cast his mantle over the lovely Safia, the wife of Kenana. Muir adds, "Indeed he is not free from the suspicion of being influenced in the destruction of Kenana by the desire of obtaining his wife."

[b] It was during this war that a Jewish woman made Mohammed a present of a poisoned sheep; he tasted it, but was warned not to eat any more. Still its fatal effects lurked in his constitution. Bishr, a favourite follower of Mohammed, died of partaking more largely of the poisoned shoulder of the kid. The woman, Zeinub, sister of the brave Marhab, avowel her guilt. "I said within myself, If he is a prophet, he will be aware that the shoulder of the kid is poisoned; but if he be a mere pretender, then we shall be rid of him, and the Jews will again prosper."

[c] Gagnier says that they continued to inhabit their former lands on condition of cultivating them, it is presumed for the benefit of their masters, as being better versed in the arts of husbandry. Niebuhr supposed that he discovered traces of Judaism among those tribes.

But the persecution of the Jews by the Mohammedans was confined to the limits of the Arabian peninsula. Under the empire of the Caliphs, which rapidly swallowed up the dominions of Persia, and many provinces of the Eastern empire, though doomed by the haughty spirit of Islamism, perhaps by the legislation of Omar, to perpetual inferiority,* this people might rejoice in the change of masters. Jerusalem yielded an easy conquest to the triumphant Omar, and though the Jews might behold with secret dissatisfaction the magnificent mosque of the conqueror usurping the sacred hill on which the Temple of Solomon had stood, yet still they would find consolation in the degradation of the Christians, and the obscurity into which the Church of the Holy Sepulchre was thrown; and even, perhaps, might cherish the enthusiastic hope that the new Temple might be destined for a holier use. Some Christian writers accuse the Jews of a deep-laid conspiracy to advance the triumph of Mohammedanism; but probably this conspiracy was no more than their united prayers and vows, that their oppressors might fall before a power which ruled them on the easy terms of tribute, the same which they exacted from all their conquered provinces. This union of their hearts was natural; they might well rejoice in the annihilation of the throne of Persia, for Izdigerd, the last of her kings, had commenced a fierce persecution of the Jews in his dominions;⁴ and the Christians could lay little claim to their faithful attachment as subjects. No doubt, as the tide of Moslemite conquest spread along the shores of Africa, the Jews exulted, rather than deplored the change of masters; 40,000 of their race were found by Amrou in Alexandria, at the conquest of that

---

* Comp. in Eroch und Grüller, p. 190. | Epist. R. Scherir ap. Joch, quoted by
⁴ Schevet Jehuda. Persecut. tertia. | Jost, p. 315.

city, and suffered no further oppression than the payment of tribute.¹ In one country alone (we overleap a century) it is probable that they took a more active interest than their secret prayers and thanksgivings in the triumph of the Crescent. Spain had already taken the lead in Jewish persecution. Spain maintained its odious distinction, and Spain had without doubt reason to rue the measures which set a great part of its most industrious population in justifiable hostility to its laws and government, and made them ready to hail the foreign conqueror as a deliverer and benefactor. The lust of Roderick, and his violation of the daughter of Count Julian, led not more directly to the subjugation of his country than the barbarous intolerance of his ancestors towards the Jews. Their wrongs, in the violence done to their consciences, were not less deep than that suffered by the innocent Caava; their vengeance was less guilty than that of the renegade Julian.

For above a century their wrongs had been accumulating. As early as the reign of Recared, the first Catholic king of the Goths, they had attained unexampled prosperity in the Peninsula. They were, to a great extent, the cultivators of the soil, which rewarded their patient industry with the most ample return; and often the administrators of the finances, for which they were well qualified by their knowledge of trade. Bigotry, envy, and avarice, conspired to point them out as objects of persecution.² Laws were passed, of which the spirit

---

¹ Jost, v. 310.
² Even Gregory the Great, so just, almost charitable, to the Jews in other countries, cannot withhold his approbation of the cruel laws of the orthodox Recared. He disguises it, probably disguised it to himself, under admiration for the disinterestedness of Recared, who refused a large sum of money from the Jews to abate his rigour:— "Quod cum vestra Excellentia constitutionem quamdam contra Judæorum perfidiam dedisset, hi de quibus prolata fuerat, rectitudinem vestræ mentis de-

may be comprehended from the preamble and the titles:—"Laws concerning the promulgation and ratification of statutes against Jewish wickedness,^t and for the general extirpation of Jewish errors."^u That the Jews may not celebrate the Passover according to their usage; that the Jews may not contract marriage according to their own customs; that the Jews may not practise circumcision; that the Jews make no distinction of meats; that the Jews bring no action against Christians; that Jews be not permitted to bear witness against Christians: of the time when their converted

---

flectere. peccaniarum summas offerendo molitî sunt, et omnipotentis Dei placere judicio requirens, auro innocentiam prætulit." ix. ii. 122.

^t The modern Spanish writer Amador de los Rios is too good a Roman Catholic not to justify these proceedings, "quand ce peuple (the Goths), après avoir accepté déjà la religion des vaincus, dans le troisième Concile de Tolède, comprit la nécessité de veiller à sa conservation et à son agrandissement, et dut finir en même temps par mettre un terme aux excès des Juifs." These excuses were their superior civilization, and better knowledge of the arts necessary to life. "Enfin leur caractère et leur naturel audacieux et rusé les avaient placés dans une position avantageuse, position qui eût pu, peut-être, les conduire, avec le temps, à être les dominateurs des Goths mêmes." Magnabal's Translation, p. 28.

^u Lex Wisi-Goth. l. xii. t. 11, 12: "De datis et confirmatis leg. super Judæam nequitiam promulgatis."

"Nam cum virtus Dei totum universaliter acie verbi sui hærsium extirpaverit fomitem vel surculum, solâ Judæorum nequitiâ ingemuscimus arva nostra esse polluta regiminis nostri:" A *Catholic* land might not endure Jewish cultivators. Leges Wisi-Gothorum, lib. xii., ap. Canciani, iv. p. 185-6.

The first law is directed against Christian renegades to Judaism. No baptized Jew shall again leave or profane the faith of the holy Christian religion, assail it by act or word, or secretly or openly blaspheme it. These proselytes were to take care not to damage the document which they had signed of their conversion to Christianity.

The laws, however, in the text are expressly directed against all Jews: "De cunctis Judæorum erroribus generaliter extirpandis. Ne Judæi more suo celebrent Pascha. Ne Judæi more suo fœdus copulent nuptiale. Ne Judæi carnis faciant circumcisionem," &c. Their distinction of meats was looked on with special detestation: "Cum beatus Apostolus dicat, omnia munda mundis; coinquinatis autem et infidelibus nihil est mundum ; merito Judæorum detestabilis vita et discretionis horrendæ immunditia, omnium sordium horrore immundior, et refelli oportet et abjici debet."

descendants are admissible as witnesses: of the penalties attached to the transgressions of these statutes by the Jews: against the circumcision of slaves by the Jews." The penalty for these offences was even more extraordinary than the offences themselves: the criminal was to be stoned to death, or burned by the hands of his own people.* These laws, however, do not at first seem to have come into operation.* It is suspected, from a passage in a letter of Pope Gregory, that the Israelites paid a large sum of money for their suspension. Three statutes of Sisebut,* the fourth in succession from Recared, complained of the neglect of Recared's law by his degenerate successors. Sisebut disclaimed their culpable toleration, and sternly re-enacted, with rigid provisions, the prohibition to the Jews to have Christian slaves; such slaves were declared at once free; if after a fixed time any Jew was found in possession of a Christian slave, half his substance was to be forfeited to the Treasury. It was a capital crime for a Jew to circumcise a Christian, man or woman. Children born of Jewish or Christian parents (this law seems to contemplate mixed marriages or concubinage) were to be

---

* "Quicunque aut superioribus vetitis legibus aut suis inouia placitis temerare voluerit, vel frustrare præsumpserit, mox juxta sponsionem eorum gentis suæ manibus aut lapide puniatur, aut igne cremetur." The king had the suspicious power of mercy; he might grant the guilty Jew, with all his confiscated property, as a slave to any of his favourites, "sicque fiat ut nec rem amissam recipiat dominus, nec libertatem reparet servus." L. W. xii. t. xi.

* "Si certe bi, qui in ritum Hebræorum traducti sunt, in eâ perfidiâ stare voluerint." The edict pursues the transgressor of the law beyond this world to the Day of Judgement: " Futuri etiam examinis terribile cum patuerit tempus, et metuendus Domini adventus fuerit reseratus, discretus a Christiano grege perspicue ad lævam cum Hebræis asuretur flammis atrocibus, comitante sibi diabolo ut ultrix flamma in transgressoribus aeternâ pœnâ deserviat, et locuples remuneratio Christianis faventibus hinc in æternum copiosé detur." Leges Wisi-Goth. apud Canciani, iv. 188.

* Sisebut's accession, A.C. 612.

brought up as Christians; at the same time there is a singular provision, that if any convert from Christianity shall obstinately adhere to Judaism, he shall be publicly flogged, shaven, and granted in perpetual servitude to whomsoever the king shall will. The third law seems to imply that the general feeling was not in full accordance with the fierce intolerance of the king: it denounces the penalty of excommunication and fine against any one, even bishop, priest, or monk, who shall in any way patronize or defend the victims of these laws. But the zealous Sisebut was not content with these slow and indulgent measures; he would extirpate the perfidious and detested race from the contaminated land. About four years after, he began his remorseless persecution. The Spanish monarch was excited, it is said, by the Emperor Heraclius,[y] who had found out that his empire was threatened with danger from the circumcised, and, ignorant of the secret growth of Mohammedanism, determined to extirpate the dangerous race throughout the world.[z] Among the smouldering ruins of the Christian churches, and the vestiges of recent Christian massacre in Jerusalem, Heraclius might unhappily have found

---

[y] Basnage is disposed to believe this, as well as Mariana, on whose authority it chiefly rests; but the Spanish historian Ferreras has shown that Sisebut had begun to persecute the Jews before his treaty with Heraclius, ii. p. 340.

The historians of the East are silent about it: it rests on monkish traditions in the West. Compare Schröckh, xi. p. 303. Vit. S. Amandi Trajectensis.

Lafuente, ii. p. 407, fully accepts the story of Heraclius, doubtfully that of the 90,000 converts. But he writes in the nobler spirit of later times: "Los (Judios) que quedaran en nostra peninsula sufrieron todo género de violencias, no habia humiliacion, no habia mal tratamento, no habia amargura, que no se les hiciera probar; y Sisebot aquel prencipe tan compasivo y humano, que vertea lagrimas a la vista de la sangre que se derramaba en los combates, veia impasible las crueldades que con los Judios se cometian. A tanto arrastra el excesivo celo religioso."

[z] See p. 286.

stronger reasons for the persecution of the Jews; but as we have no satisfactory evidence of his having wreaked his vengeance in his own dominions, it may be doubted whether his jealous vigilance extended so far as to the extremity of the West. Sisebut must bear alone the shame, he probably thought, alone inherit the glory of his oppressive measures. The Jews were commanded, at once, either to abandon their religion or to leave the dominions of the Goths. According to their own account, they assembled with tears and groans in the court of the palace, obtained an audience, and held a singular theological debate with their royal antagonist. The king declared that he was constrained by his conscience to force them to receive baptism. They adduced the example of Joshua, who did not, they said, compel the Canaanites to accept the Law of Moses, but allowed them peace on condition of their observing the seven Noachic precepts.[a] The king, perplexed by this daring historical argument, replied that he recognised no authority superior to his own; that it was his bounden duty to enforce his law, because all who were not regenerate in baptism must perish everlastingly.[b] The Jews replied, that as the Israelites, who despised the Holy Land, were sufficiently punished by being excluded from its bless-

---

[a] Damage relates this scene on the authority of Solomon ben Virga, Scheret Juda, p. 93. The Jewish writer has committed an anachronism and fixed the reign of Sisebut as late as 800.

[b] Mariana, lib. vi. Mariana asserts that there were laws inserted in the Fuero Juzgo with this intent. I can find only the three laws above attributed to Sisebut. But of the persecution there can be no doubt, from other sources, especially the noble remonstrance of Isidore of Seville: "In initio regni sui Judæos ad fidem Christianam permovere æmulationem quidem Dei habuit, sed non secundum scientiam. Potestate enim compulit quos provocare fidei ratione oportuit." Isidor. Hisp. in Chronico. Mariana is indignant, not so much at the intolerance of the king, though he acknowledges that it was "cosa illicita y velada entre los Christianos, que a

ings, so they would pay an adequate penalty, by being excluded from eternal life. Sisebut rejoined, that men might be left to themselves to accept or refuse temporal advantages, but that they must be forced to receive spiritual blessings, as a child is forced to learn his lessons. But the king's orders were more effective than his arguments. The Jews were thrown into prison, and treated with the utmost rigour. Some fled into France or Africa, others abandoned their religion, 90,000 are reported to have submitted to baptism: but how far their hearts renounced their creed, or how speedily they relapsed, must remain uncertain.

But Sisebut did not carry out these atrocious acts without one voice of noble Christian remonstrance raised against him, that of Isidore of Seville, who boldly reproved the king's zeal not according to knowledge. In the next reign but one, that of Sisenaud, the Jews obtained a relaxation of the oppressive statutes, probably from an unexpected quarter. The rare example was displayed of a synod of clergy in that age, of Spanish clergy, openly asserting the tenets of reason and Christian charity. The Fourth Council of Toledo, under the Presidency of Isidore of Seville, enacted, "that men ought not to be compelled to believe, because God will have mercy on those on whom He will have mercy, and whom He will He hardeneth. As

---

alguno se haga fuerça para que lo fca contra su voluntad." But no wonder that the king erred, since he presumed to take into his own hands affairs that belong to the ecclesiastical power. Mariana's pity for the terrible sufferings of the Jews, finds easy consolation: "Por esta manera la divina justicia con nuevos castigos trabajava y afligia aquella nacion maltrada, en pena de la sangre de Christo hijo de Dios, que tan sin culpa derramaron." The proceedings of the Fourth Council of Toledo, too, bear witness to the persecution. The doubtful authority for the 90,000 baptized is Aimoin, Hist. Franc. iv. 22. Compare Gibbon, ch. 37.

man fell by his own free will in listening to the wiles of the serpent, so man can only be converted by his free acceptance of the Christian faith." Yet, with remarkable inconsistency, the Council likewise decreed, "that all who had embraced the faith must be constrained to adhere to it, and to remain within the Church. For, as they had received the Blessed Sacrament, the holy name of God would be blasphemed, and the faith disgraced, by their falling off."[c] The Council sadly acknowledges how hollow and insincere had been many of their enforced conversions. Not only did many of these New Christians practise in secret Jewish ceremonies, but they were guilty of performing the abominable rite of circumcision. The children of such parents were to be taken from them, and brought up either in monasteries or under the care of pious men. There is a humiliating confession too: such was still the influence of the wealth of the Jews, that many laymen and clerks, even bishops, were bought to be their protectors. The penalty for this profane and sacrilegious connivance was in some cases not less than excommunication.[d] The prohibitions against the Jews holding civil offices and retaining Christian slaves were renewed. The children of Jews by Christian mothers (this seems to have been not uncommon) were to be brought up as Christians. The gleam of light and mercy was but transient. The Sixth Council of Toledo (the wise and good Isidore of Seville had died in the interval[e]) indignantly disclaimed the tolerant

---

[c] IV. Concil. Tolet. ann. III. Sisenandi, A.C. 633. "Qui autem jampridem ad Christianitatem venire coacti sunt, sicut factum est temporibus religiosissimi principis Sisebuti." Art. lvii.

[d] "Tanta est quorundam cupiditas, ... multi quippe hucusque es sacerdotibus et laicis accipientes a Judæis munera, perfidiam eorum patrocinio suo favebant." Art. lvii.

[e] He died A.C. 636. Life in Smith's Dictionary.

spirit of the former synod. It praised Suintila the Second for his violent proceedings against the Jews, and blessed God that they possessed a prince so full of ardour for the faith.[f] The Council enacted that every king on his accession should take an oath to execute these laws, and passed an anathema on that sovereign who should neglect this indispensable part of his royal duty. Under Recescuinth, the Eighth Council of Toledo, A.C. 653, re-enforced the obligation of the king to execute the laws against the Jews with the utmost severity.[g] To this Council a curious petition was presented. The undersigned baptized Jews expressed their readiness to submit to the law; they acknowledged its justice and wisdom in the humblest language, recited and declared their assent to all its prohibitions: of circumcision, Jewish marriages, distinctions of meats, sabbatical observances. The only indulgence they requested was an exemption from being constrained to eat pork, a food to which they could not habituate themselves; even that they could endure, without disgust and horror, if only used in cookery with other things.[h] But the most extraordinary fact in all this history is, that not only were these laws ineffective in the conversion or extirpation of the Jews,[i] but that there were yet Christians who embraced Judaism. One of the Visigothic laws indignantly

---

[f] The canon of the VI. Council of Toledo, under Suintelle (A.C. 638), confirms more distinctly the persecution of Sisebut. The Most Christian King, by the inspiration of God, had determined, "prævaricationes et superstitiones eorum eradicare funditus, nec sinit degere in regno suo eum qui non sit catholicus." Canon iii.

[g] VIII. Conc. Toletanum, Canon x. xii.

[h] "Ea tamen quæ cum ipsis decocta sunt, absque fastidio ac honore sumamus." VIII. Conc. Tolet. ap. Labbe.

[i] Canon xvii.

enacts the punishment of death for such an offence. "Even many of the clergy," declares the Tenth Council of Toledo, "a fact monstrous and unutterable, pursue an execrable commerce with the ungodly, and do not scruple to sell to them Christian slaves, and thus give Christians up to be converted to Judaism."[k] The Ninth Council had decreed, that all baptized Jews were bound to appear in the church, not only on Christian, but also on Jewish holy days, lest, while professed Christians, they should practise secret Judaism. But the Twelfth Council of Toledo, or rather the Legislature with the full assent and approbation of the Council, in the reign of Ervig, far surpassed its predecessors in the elaborate cruelty of its enactments, even if aimed only at Jews professing Christianity. There is indeed a singular ambiguity in the wording of the law—it appears generally to include all Jews,[m] but most of its provisions seem especially directed against conformists to the Church. Are we to suppose that the Church, only legislating for its members, intended these laws specially for Jews within its pale? or that this conformity had been so general as to comprise nearly all the Jews within the realm?[n] The Jews were assembled in the Church of the Holy Virgin, at Toledo, and the resolutions of

---

[k] Leges Wisi-Goth. xii. li. 27. "De Judaizantibus Christianis: Ut nullus omnino veniam mereatur, qui a meliore proposito ad deterius declinasse convincetur." It proceeds to enact death and confiscation of goods against any one guilty of this cruel and stupendous crime: "Quicunque Christianus, et præsertim a Christianis parentibus ortus, sexûs scilicet utriusque, circumcisionem, vel quæcunque Judaicos ritus, exercuisse repertus est."

[m] Concil. Tolet. ix. A.C. 656, Canon vii.

[n] "Proinde si quis Judæorum de his scilicet qui nondum sunt baptizati, aut se baptizare distulerit, aut filios suos vel famulos nullo modo ad sacerdotem baptizandos remiserit, vel se suosque de baptismo subtraxerit, et vel unius anni spatium post legem hanc editam quispiam illorum sine gratia baptismatis transierit." Lex lii.

this Christian assembly were read aloud.° The preamble complained that the crafty Jews had eluded all former laws, and attributed the failure of these statutes to the severity of the punishment enacted, which was death in all cases—contrary, it was added, to the Holy Scriptures. The penalties of the new statutes were mitigated, but not in mercy. The general punishment was one hundred lashes on the naked body; after that the offender was to be put in chains, banished, and his property confiscated to the lord of the soil.ᵖ This was the penalty for profaning the name of Christ, rejecting the Sacrament of the Lord's Supper, blaspheming the Trinity—for not bringing children or servants, themselves or their dependants, to baptism—for observing the Passover, the New Moon, the feast of Tabernacles (in these cases, on real conversion, the land was restored) for violating the Christian Sabbath, or the great festivals of the Church, either by working in the field, or in manufacture. If these days were desecrated by a servant, the master was liable to a fine. The circumcision of a child was more cruelly visited, on the man, by mutilation—on the woman, by the loss of her nose and

---

° This appears from the subscription to the Laws. Leges Wisi-Goth. xii. iii. Canciani, 190, 201. In fact these were Laws of the Realm enforced by the assent and confirmation of the Council—the whole in Canciani. It was a consolidation of the Statute Laws against the Jews.

ᵖ "Nam quædam leges sicut culparum habent diversitates, non ita discretas in se retinent ultiones, sed permista scelera transgressorum ad unius permittuntur legis pœnale judicium. Nec secundum modum culpæ modus est adhibitus pœnæ, cum major minorque transgressio unius non debent multationis prædampnari supplicio: præsertim cum dominus in lege suâ præcipiat pro mensurâ peccati erit et plagarum modus. Unde lex ipsa quæ miserebitur de pœnâ, quâ perimenda sit transgressio Judæorum, quia Deus mortem non vult, nec lætatur in perditione viorum, pro eo quod in se peremptionem continet mortis, in nullo verâ valetudinis retinebit statum." p. 191.

the seizure of her property. The same penalty was attached to the conversion of a Christian to Judaism. The former punishment — scourging, imprisonment, banishment, and confiscation—was incurred by those who made a difference in meats. An exemption was granted to new converts, who were not constrained to eat swine's flesh if their nature revolted against it. The same penalty fell on all who intermarried within the sixth degree of relationship. Such marriages were declared null; the property was to be divided among the children, if not Jews. If there were no children, or only children educated in Judaism, it fell to the lord of the soil. No marriage was hereafter to be contracted, without a clause in the act of dower that both would become Christians. All who offended against this law, even the parents concerned in such a marriage, were to be fined or scourged. All subjects of the kingdom who harboured, assisted, or concealed the flight of a Jew, were to be scourged, and have their property confiscated. Whoever received bribes from a Jew to conceal his practice of Judaism, was fined thrice the sum he had received. The Jew who read, or allowed his children to read, books written against Christianity, suffered one hundred lashes; on the second offence the lashes were repeated, with banishment and confiscation. Christian slaves of Jews were declared free; the Jews had no right of emancipating them; but a given time was allowed, in which they might sell those of whom they were possessed. As many Jews, in order to retain their Christian slaves, pretended to Christianity, the whole race were commanded, by a given day, to bring their slaves for sale, or publicly to embrace Christianity. If not immediately baptized, they were to lodge a solemn protest of their faith with the bishop; and all converts

were to take an oath, of which the form was subjoined
—an oath of terrific sublimity, which even now makes
the reader shudder, when he remembers that it was
forced upon unwilling consciences, and perhaps taken
by those who secretly renounced its obligations. All
Jewish slaves, by embracing Christianity, obtained their
freedom. No Jew could take any office by which he
might have authority over, or constrain a Christian,
except in certain cases where power might be granted
by the feudal lord. In such a case, if he abused the
law, he was punished by the loss of half his property,
or by stripes. Even the noble who granted such a
power was liable to a fine, or, in default of payment, to
the same ignominious punishment. No Jew might be
intendant, house steward, or overseer. Should a bishop,
priest, or other ecclesiastic, commit the property of the
Church to a Jewish intendant, his property was to be
confiscated—in default, himself burnt. No Jew could
travel from one town or province to another, without
reporting himself to the bishop or judge of the place.
They were forced to eat, drink, and communicate with
Christians; they could not move without a certificate
of good behaviour and a passport. On the Jewish
Sabbath and holy days they were all to assemble before
the bishop. The bishop was to appoint women to overlook their wives and daughters. The spiritual person
who took a bribe to relax his vigilance was to be
degraded and excommunicated.[q] Whoever protected a

---

[q] There is one provision which gives no high notion of the morality of the Christian clergy, who demanded, enforced, and were to execute this atrocious system of persecution: "Id tantum præcipue observandum est, ne quorundam sacerdotum carnalia corda, dum eas libidines execrabili contaminatione exagitant, occasiones quaslibet inquirant, per quas libidinis suæ votum efficiant." Lex xxl.

Jew against his spiritual overseer, was to be excommunicated and pay a heavy fine. No civil judge could act in any case of this kind without the concurrence of the priesthood, if their presence could be procured. The remission of penalties might be granted, on a certificate of Christian behaviour. All spiritual persons were to communicate these statutes to the Jews in their respective dioceses and cures. Such were the acts of the kingdom of Spain, ratified or commanded by the Twelfth Council of Toledo: but happily laws, when they are carried to such an extreme of cruelty as to shock the general feeling, usually prevent their own execution. The Council might enact, but the people would carry into effect but imperfectly these horrible scenes of scourging and confiscation. Wealth, notwithstanding the menaces of the law, would purchase immunity and exemption; and though many fled, and many probably outwardly conformed, the successor of Ervig, Egica, found it expedient to relax the laws, so far as to allow baptized Jews all the privileges of citizens,[r] which before were but jealously or imperfectly bestowed;[s] in all other respects the statutes of Ervig remained in force. Fear may have extorted this concession; but the fear of the monarch shows how ineffective the former laws must have been, if the Jews were still so numerous as to be formidable.

Already the shores of Africa were beginning to gleam

---

[r] XVI. Concil. Tolet. A.C. 693: "Dan por nobles y horros de tributos a todos los Judios que de coraçon abraçasen la religion Christiana." Mariana, vi. c. xviii. The nobles seem to have been exempt from tribute: a privilege of no slight value to the wealthy Jewish Christians. Compare on the reigns of Ervig and Egica, Lafuente.

[s] XVII. Concil. Tolet. A.C. 694: "Tanta foit pro eorum conversione mansuetudinis nostrae intentio." In Præf.

with the camps of the Saracens, who threatened to cross the narrow strait, and overwhelm the trembling Gothic monarchy. No wonder if the impatient Jews hourly uttered vows, or held secret correspondence with their free brethren in Africa, to accelerate the march of the victorious deliverer. The year after the conciliatory edict of Egica, a Council was again held at Toledo: the king denounced a general conspiracy of the Jews (ungrateful as they were for his merciful desire to convert them to Christianity) to massacre the Christians, subdue the land, and overthrow the monarchy. "Already," declared the king, "this people, defiled by the blood of Christ and infamous for the profanation of their oaths, have meditated ruin against the king and kingdom —the supreme dominion of which they would usurp—and, proclaiming that their time is come, have begun the work of slaughter against the Catholics."[1] There was a vast confederacy, it was averred and believed, among the Hebrews, in Spain and beyond the sea, to exterminate the Christian faith. The affrighted and obsequious churchmen instantly passed a decree to confiscate all the property of the Jews to the royal treasury—to disperse the whole race, as slaves, through the country—to seize all their children under seven years of age—to bring them up as Christians, marry them to Christian wives, and to abolish for ever the exercise of the Jewish faith. A great flight of the Jews probably took place; for Witiza,

---

[1] "Ausu tyrannico inferre conati sunt ruinam patriæ ac populo universo . . . sed et regni fastigium sibi 'ut præmissum es) per conspirationem usurpare maluerunt . . . ut suum quasi tempus invenisse gaudentes diversas in catholicos exercerent stragea." The statute (c. viii.) does not alone refer to their foreign connections, but also in the address of the king are these words: "Nuper manifestis confessionibus indubie pervenimus, hos in transmarinis partibus Hebræos alios consuluisse ut unanimiter contra genus Christianum agerent."

the successor of Egica, attempting too late to heal the wounds by conciliation, granted them permission to return into the Gothic states, with full rights of freedom and citizenship." He even compelled or persuaded a Council at Toledo, presided over by the archbishop, to concur in this act of toleration. This Council is indignantly declared illegitimate and heretical by the annalists of the Church of Rome.* But the vows of the Jews had been heard, or their intrigues had been successful. They returned, and to the enjoyment of all rights and privileges of freedom—not indeed under Christian kings, but under the dominion of the Moorish Caliphs, who established their rule over almost the whole of Spain.' The munificence of these sovereigns bears the appearance of gratitude for valuable services, and confirms the suspicion that the Jews were highly instrumental in

---

" Read Mariana (L. vi. c. 19). Witiza began (as Mariana admits) nobly: he recalled from exile many persons whom his father had driven from their homes, restored their confiscated possessions, honours, and dignities. He ordered all the papers relating to charges of treason to be burned. But he soon yielded himself to flatterers, kept many concubines with the pomp of queens; and, a greater crime, he issued an edict permitting the clergy and monks to marry,—an abominable and foul law, which nevertheless found favour with the many, even with most (que a muchos y a los mas dió gusto). He issued another law refusing obedience to the Pope. Finally, *to complete his wickedness, he abrogated the laws against the Jews*, and allowed them to return to Spain.

* The Council is not admitted to the honour of a place in Labbe, who refers to Baronius, sub. ann. 701.

' The Mohammedan historians of the conquest of Spain acknowledge the Jews as their allies. It is probable that in the invasion itself they were deeply involved. Of the Berbers who formed the great mass of Turks a vast number were Jews (Judaism had spread wide in Northern Africa). There can be no doubt that the African Jews were in correspondence with their brethren in Spain. On the capture of Grenada, of Toledo, of Seville, the Jews were entrusted with the occupation of these cities, while the Moslems passed on to other conquests. See Gayangos Hist. of Mohammedan Dynasties of Spain (Orient. Trans. Fund), pp. 280, 284, and Note, p. 531.

advancing the triumph of the Crescent. At all events, when Toledo opened her gates to the Moorish conqueror (whether the Jews were openly or secretly active in the fall of the city), with what infinite satisfaction must they have beheld the capital of the persecuting Visigothic kings, of Reccared, and Sisebut, and Ervig, and the seat of those remorseless Councils which had forcibly baptized, or exiled their devoted ancestors, or deprived them of their children, now become the palace of kings, if not kindred in lineage, yet Monotheists like themselves, under whose rule they knew that their brethren in the East and in Africa were permitted to enjoy their lives and their religion undisturbed, under whom they found equal justice, rose to high honour, at least laboured under no proscription, dreaded no persecution! How much more must they have exulted when they were summoned to assume the command of this great city, and to maintain it for their Moslem deliverers! The reward of their prayers or of their acts for the success of Islamism was a golden age of freedom, of civilization, and of letters. They shared with and emulated their splendid masters in all the luxuries and arts which soften and embellish life, during that era of high, though, if we may so say, somewhat barbaric civilization, under which the southern provinces of Spain became that paradise for which they were designed by nature.

France had obeyed the signal of Spain, and hung out the bloody flag of persecution. But her measures were ill-combined, and probably worse executed; for many of the fugitives from Spain sought and found comparative security among their brethren in Gaul.* Early in

---

* Jost somewhat quaintly complains that they were persecuted with bad sermons: "Von der Geistlichkeit überall mit schlechten Predigten gequält wurden." v. 149. Sulpicius, Bishop of Bourges, a famous preacher, aided the

the seventh century, A.C. 615, Clotaire the Second, in a council of the clergy, issued a decree disqualifying the Jews from all military or civil offices which gave them authority over Christians. But by a strange provision the Jew who should attempt to attain or exercise his power, was to be baptized by the bishop with all his family, as if, instead of suffering a penalty, he was to be graciously admitted to a privilege.[a] The Council of Rheims (627) annulled all bargains entered into by Jews for the purchase of Christian slaves; that of Chalons, on the Marne, prohibited the Jews from selling Christian slaves beyond the frontier of the kingdom.[b] The devout Dagobert, it is said, though probably with as little truth, instigated, like his contemporary Sisebut of Spain, by the Emperor Heraclius, issued an edict commanding all Jews to forswear their religion or leave the kingdom.[c] But in the northern part of France this

---

effect of his sermons by hunting the obstinate Jews out of his diocese.

[a] The whole statute (Concil. Paris. can. xv.) is obscure : "Ut nullus Judæorum qualemcunque militiam aut actionem publicam super Christianos aut petere a principe aut agere præsumat. Quod si tentaverit, ab Episcopo civitatis illius, ubi actionem contra canonum statuta competeret, cum omni familiâ gratiam baptismi consequatur."

[b] Concil. Remense, can. xi.; Concil. Cabill. IX., circiter ann. 650.

[c] See back, p. 102. This tale is thus told in the curious Chronicle of Rabbi Joseph ben Joshua ben Meir, translated for the Oriental Fund by M. Bialloblotski :—" And it came to pass in the twenty-first year of his reign, that Heraclius, being very wise in the knowledge of the planets, saw in his wisdom the kingdom of Rome fall in his days under the soles of the feet of the circumcised. And this Belial said in his heart, 'The Lord will do this glorious thing on behalf of the Jews only, for they are circumcised.' And his wrath was kindled against them; and he commanded in all the cities of his kingdom to kill all the Jews who refused to change their glory for that which doth not profit. And he sent messengers to Dagobert, king of France, that he also might act according to this wicked saying. And Dagobert hearkened unto him; and many Jews changed their glory, and many were slain with the edge of the sword in France in those days. May the Eternal avenge the blood and repay vengeance to his enemies ! Amen and

edict was so little enforced, that a Jew held the office of tax-collector at the Gate of St. Denys in Paris.[d] In the South, where they were far more numerous and wealthy, they carried on their trade with uninterrupted success. In the great rebellion of the Gallic part of the Visigothic kingdom, Paul, who had usurped the throne, and Hilderic Count of Nismes had recalled the Jews into the realm.[e] King Wamba, the predecessor of Ervig, on the suppression of the rebellion took vengeance on the Jews by re-enforcing the persecuting edicts of Sisebut I.; but in later days the wiser monarchs of the Visigothic kingdom in France altogether renounced the intolerant policy of the Merovingian race.

Amen! And Heraclius, the Belial, knew not this word related to the Nazarenes, for like unto us they are circumcised." vol. i. p. 10.

Rabbi Joshua is a late writer, but may have known traditions from earlier documents, which have not been detected in those writings by modern scholars. The Christian authorities are silent on these persecutions.

[d] Gesta Dagoberti.

[e] Archbishop Rodrigues, quoted by Amador de los Rios, p. 31; Mariana vi. 13. King Wamba reigned A.C 672–680.

BOOK XXIII.

GOLDEN AGE OF JUDAISM.

The Jews under the Caliphs — Rise of Karaism — Kingdom of Khosar — Jews under the Byzantine Empire — Jews breakers of Images — Jews of Italy — Jews under Charlemagne and Louis Debonnaire — Agobard, Bishop of Lyons — Jews in Spain — High state of Literature — Moses Maimonides.

WE enter upon a period which I shall venture to denominate the Golden Age of the modern Jews. To them, the Moslem crescent was as a star, which seemed to soothe to peace the troubled waters on which they had been so long agitated. Throughout the dominions of the Caliphs, in the East, in Africa, and in Spain; in the Byzantine empire; in the dominions of those great sovereigns, Charlemagne, his predecessor and his successor, who, under Divine Providence, restored vigour and solidity to the Christian Empire of the West, and enabled it to repel the yet unexhausted inroads of Mohammedanism; everywhere we behold the Jews not only pursuing unmolested their lucrative and enterprising traffic, not merely merchants of splendour and opulence, but suddenly emerging to offices of dignity and trust, administering the finances of Christian and Mohammedan kingdoms, and travelling as ambassadors between mighty sovereigns. This golden age was of very different duration in different parts of the world. In the East it was, before long, interrupted by their own civil dissensions, and by a spirit of persecution which seized the Moslemite sovereigns. In the Byzantine empire, we are greatly in want of authentic information, both concerning the period in question, and that which followed it. In the West of Europe it was soon succeeded by an age of iron. In Spain, the daylight endured the longest—to set in deep and total darkness.

The religious persecutions of the Jews by the Mohammedans were confined within the borders of Arabia. The Prophet was content with enforcing uniformity of worship within the sacred peninsula which gave him birth. The holy cities of Mecca and Medina were not to be profaned by the unclean footstep of an unbeliever. His immediate successors rose (or degenerated, shall we say?) from stern fanatics to ambitious conquerors. "The Koran or the sword" was still the battle-cry; but whoever would submit to the dominion of the triumphant Caliph, or render himself useful in the extension of his conquests, might easily evade the recognition of the Prophet's title. The Jews had little reason to regret, or rather had ample cause to triumph in, the ruin of their former masters. The kings of Persia, who had sometimes vouchsafed to protect, but had sometimes cruelly persecuted the Jews, were now cast from their thrones, without any compassion, or rather with inward feelings of triumph and revenge from their Jewish subjects. Whether they paid tribute to a Magian or Mohammedan sovereign, was to the Jews indifferent. Feeble governments are in general more tyrannical, more iniquitous in the distribution of justice, more rapacious in their taxation, than strong ones. An Islamite sovereign on the throne of Damascus or Bagdad would not be more oppressive than a Byzantine on the throne of Constantinople, or a Persian on the throne of Ctesiphon. The Jew would receive as substantial—and not more capricious—justice from an Islamite Cadi as from a Roman Prefect or Magian Satrap. The capitation tax, or whatever form the new assessment bore, if as inexorably exacted, was more simple, less ingeniously extortionate than that of the Byzantine Exchequer, or the Persian Treasury. His religion the Jew knew too well to be odious, to be despised, often persecuted, by Gueber and Christian. Doomed indeed by the laws of Omar to perpetual inferiority, it might be more respected, it could not be trampled on more contemptuously or more mercilessly than by the Magian or the Christian. Though, doubtless, during the terrible conflict and the general plunder which attended on the Mohammedan conquests, the wealth of the Jews did not escape, yet in the East, as in the North, they would not scruple to make up their losses, by following in the train of the yet fierce and uncivilized conqueror, and by making use of their superior judgement, or command of money, to drive a lucrative bargain with the plunderer. Whenever a commissariat was wanting to the disorganised hordes which followed the Crescent with irresistible valour, the corn-ships or caravans of the Jews would follow in the wake of the fleet or army. At the capture of Rhodes, the celebrated fallen Colossus, which once bestrode the harbour of that city, one of the wonders of the world, was sold to a Jew of Emesa, who is reported to have loaded nine hundred camels with the metal.[*] The greater and more certain emoluments of the mercantile life would lead the Jews to addict themselves more and more to traffic, and to abandon the cultivation of the soil, which they had

---

[*] Theophanes, Chronographia, t. p. 327, Edit. Bonn.

hitherto pursued in many places. For, as the Moslemite sovereigns levied a disproportioned tribute on the believer and the unbeliever, the former paying only a tenth, the latter a fifth, or even a third, of the produce, the Jew would readily cede his land, which remunerated him so ill, for trade which offered, at least, the chance of rapid wealth.[b]

In every respect the Jew, under his Mohammedan rulers, rose in the social scale. The persecution of their Arabian brethren, if known by the Jews scattered over the wide face of the Persian and Roman empires, would be heard almost with indifference. The Arabian Jews, in fact Bedouins like the rest of the Arabs, had no relations with their remote brethren. The bloody scenes at Nadhir, at Koraidha, at Khaibar, were but the collisions of hostile Arab tribes; and beyond the boundaries of Arabia, the sword of religious persecution had been sheathed. The religious sympathies of the Jews would be more disposed towards, at least be less sternly hostile to, the Monotheism of Islam, than to the Fire-worship of Persia, or what they, in common with the Mohammedans, did not scruple to condemn as the Polytheism of the Christians. There was no Mohammedan Priesthood like the Magian and Christian hierarchy, whose pride and duty it was to compel mankind to accept their faith. Proselytism no doubt had its temptations and advantages, and so went on to some extent; but the sincere religious Jew was not searched out, and followed into his privacy, to detect his hateful opinions. He was not proscribed by the law as almost as bad as a heretic. The Caliph, the successor of the Prophet, was content with the submission, something approaching to

---

[b] Jost, vi. 14.

adoration from the true believer, but this was the Moslem's special privilege and distinction. To the rest of the world his toleration might be contemptuous, condescending, but it was still toleration; it was not an active, busy, ubiquitous scrutiny of the faith and opinions of his subjects. Provided they demeaned themselves peaceably, and paid their tribute, they might go to the Synagogue rather than to the Mosque. Mohammedanism had borrowed so much from Judaism, that there was not that constant and flagrant opposition between their habits and modes of life. The circumcised Mohammedan could not object to the circumcised Jew; the aversion to swine's flesh was common; the Koran was full of recognitions of the sanctity of the Mosaic Law; and altogether the Eastern cast of their usages approximated the Mohammedan and the Jew, much more intimately than the Jew and the Christian. The Jew, though usually at this time become monogamous, could hardly, in the face of his patriarchs and kings, hold polygamy to be licentious or unlawful. The wealthy Jews among the Mohammedans sometimes followed the example of their masters. There was another link, which perhaps joined them more closely, at least in aversion to Christianity, the common hatred of images and image-worship.

When the Caliphs began to delegate to others the sword of conquest or extermination, and to establish themselves in the splendid state of peaceful sovereigns, the Jews were equally useful in teaching these stern barbarians the arts and luxuries of civilized life. They spoke a kindred language. Hebrew and Arabic are the two most prolific branches of what are now called the Semitic family of tongues. The Hebrew literature was admirably adapted to the kindred taste of the Arabians.

The extravagant legends of the Talmud would harmonize with their bold poetical spirit; their picturesque apologues were the form of instruction in which the Arab tribes had ever delighted to listen to moral wisdom; even the niceties of their verbal disputes would not be without charm to their masters, who soon began to pay attention to the polish of their own rich and copious language. Already, in the time of Omar, the second Caliph, and his successor Abdalmeleeh, a trust of great importance, the coinage, had been committed to the care of a Jew. Either shocked that faithful Moslemites should use money stamped with an image, or eager to assume that distinction of sovereignty, the uttering coin, the Caliph instructed the Jew to substitute the emphatic sentence, "Say there is one God, one."* The traffic of the Jews would disseminate that coin which their art had enabled them to provide. But it was not by mechanical operations alone, like the coinage, or by traffic, in which, as single traders, or even as mercantile firms, they pervaded the whole East as well as the West, that the Jews rendered invaluable services to the Barbarian conquerors; and aided very powerfully in raising them from the chieftains of wild, marauding tribes into magnificent, in some respects enlightened, sovereigns. In the interworking of European civilization, its knowledge, sciences, and arts, into the Oriental mind, who were so qualified to be the mediate agents as the Jews? Besides the rigid Rabbinical Jews, who formed their constituted communities, there were no doubt a great number who, perhaps, held more loosely to the tenets of their forefathers, and were the descendants and representatives of the Græcised Jews

---

* Al Makrisi, Hist. Mon. Arab. Tychsen, quoted by Jost, vi. 15.

in the time of our Saviour. It is well known that the works of many of the great Greek writers, especially their natural philosophers, writers on medicine (Jewish physicians were in great repute in the East as in the West), metaphysical philosophers, were, sooner or later, translated into the Arabic. And who so likely to be the translators, as the Jews, who stood between the Asiatic and European races? By traffic, residence, perhaps habits, they were familiar with Greek, and acquired Arabic, as a kindred language to their own, with great facility: Arabic, indeed, to a great extent became the vernacular tongue of the Jews.[d] Hebrew, Rabbinical Hebrew, became a sort of sacred language. We know what took place to a great extent under the flourishing dominion of the Mussulmen in Spain; when Europe, seeking her old lost treasures of arts and knowledge among the more enlightened descendants of the Arabs, found the learned Jews of Cordova and Toledo, as it were, halfway between the East and West, and used them as intermediate agents in that intellectual intercourse. So, in all probability, at an earlier period, in Damascus and Bagdad, the Jews were the most active interpreters, not only of the Western languages, but of the Western mind, to the conquerors. The Caliph readily acknowledged as his vassal the Prince of the Captivity, who maintained his state as representative of the Jewish community; probably, through him the tribute was levied on his brethren. A singular story is told of Omar the Second, which illustrates the high degree of credit which the Jews were permitted to attain in the

---

[d] Compare E. Renan, Langues Sémitiques, p. 164. Bassnage claims as a Jew Honain, the famous translator of many works from Greek into Syriac. (D'Herbelot, art. "Honain.") Euclid, and the Almagest of Ptolemy, some works of Hippocrates and Galen, were translated by him and his scholars.

court of the Caliphs. Omar, a secret follower of Ali
whose name was still cursed in the mosques, was anxious
to reconcile his people to the name of the Prophet's
vicar upon earth. An innocent comedy was got up in
his court, in which a Jew played a principal part. The
Jew came boldly forward, while the throne was encircled by the splendid retinue of courtiers and people,
and asked in marriage the daughter of the Caliph.
Omar calmly answered, "How can I give my daughter
in marriage to a man of another faith?" "Did not
Mohammed," rejoined the Jew, "give his daughter in
marriage to Ali?" "That is another case," said the
Caliph, "for Ali was a Moslemite, and the commander
of the faithful." "Why, then," rejoined the Jew, "if
Ali was one of the faithful, do ye curse him in your
mosques?" The Caliph turned to the courtiers and
said, "Answer ye the Jew?" A long silence ensued,
broken at length by the Caliph, who arose, and declared
the curse to be rejected as impious, and ordered these
words to be substituted in the prayer: "Forgive us,
Lord, our sins, and forgive all who have the same faith
with us." At a later period, A.C. 753, under Abu Giafar
Almansor, we find the Jews entrusted with the office of
exacting a heavy mulct laid upon the Christians. It
was a tax which comprehended ecclesiastics, monks,
hermits, those who stood on columns.[e] The sacred vessels of churches were seized, and purchased by the
Jews. Under this fostering government the schools
flourished; those in Sura and Pumbeditha were crowded
with hearers: the Gaonim, or the Illustrious, were at
the height of their fame;[f] they formed a sort of senate,

---

[e] Κιονίτας τῷ Θεῷ εὐαρεστοῦντας.
Theoph. Chronog. 357, p. 663, Edit.
Bonn.
[f] Jost gives a list of these teachers,

and while the Prince of the Captivity maintained the sovereign executive power, they assumed the legislative. Their reign was for the most part undisturbed, though sometimes a rapacious Caliph or an over-zealous Iman might make them feel that the sword of authority still hung over them, and that the fire of zealous Islamism was not yet burned out. Giafar the Great is reported to have framed an edict to force Jews and Christians to embrace Islamism. The Sultan Vathek held them in contempt and dislike. His brother and successor, Motavakel, was a sterner persecutor. He issued an edict that all the Jews and Christians in his empire should wear a leather girdle, to distinguish them from the faithful. He prohibited them from sitting on the Divan of Justice. At first he only forbade their use of iron stirrups; but he degraded them still farther; they were no longer to mount the noble horse, they were only permitted to ride the mule or the ass. This debasing distinction is still put in force by law or by usage, enforced by popular hatred, in many parts of the Turkish dominions.*

On the whole, however, the long and unaccustomed interval of peace, and the free intercourse with their enlightened masters, introduced a spirit of bold inquiry, which threatened, even at this zenith of its power, to shake the dominion of the Rabbins to its basis.[b] The Karaites, the Protestants of Judaism, who perhaps had never entirely been extinct, began to grow again into a formidable sect. The older Karaites (it is quite uncertain when they assumed the name) probably fell

mostly undistinguished men, from the Seder Haddoroth. Anhang. vL p. 354.

* Some add that their houses were marked or defaced by images of swine, apes, or devils. Jost, vl. 85; D'Her-belot, Bibl. Orient. art. "Motavakel."

[b] The great Jewish astronomer Mashalla was held in high honour at the court of the Caliph Almamon, A.C. 831. Basnage, lx. 2.

into disrepute through the abuse of their doctrines by
the unpopular Sadducees. After the fall of Jerusalem,
Pharisaism, under its more regular and organized form
Rabbinism, obscured her once dangerous rival. The
Sadducean doctrine was probably too loosely rooted in
the heart to withstand the hour of trial. The present
world displayed such a scene of interminable dreariness
to those who denied a world to come, that we cannot
wonder if their creed refused to support them when the
first obstinacy of resistance had worn away. The Sadducees dwindled into an unnoticed sect; and, though
the worst part of their doctrines might retain a secret
hold on the hearts of the unprincipled, it could no
longer balance the prevailing power of Pharisaism,
which was the main support both of the spiritual and
temporal throne—the sole acknowledged doctrine of the
national universities. Karaism was now revived in its
purer form, rejecting entirely the authority of tradition,
and resting its whole faith on the letter of the written
Law. The Mischna, the Gemara, the Cabala—all Talmudic lore—the Karaites threw indignantly aside.

The Luther of this Reformation, which perhaps was
not less rapidly diffused for its similarity to the simpler
creed of Islamism, was named Anan, who, with his son
Saul, revolted from Rabbinism. What is known concerning the lives of these men, rests chiefly on the
authority of the Rabbins, and must be received with the
same mistrust as the accounts of our own Reformers
from the writings of their adversaries. In a contest for
the succession to the Princedom of the Captivity, or to
some other high office, Anan was passed by, and his
younger brother appointed. Embittered by the affront,
Anan assembled the wreck of the Sadducean party, so
called probably by contempt, and persuaded them to

name him to the dignity. Tumults arose; the government interfered; and Anan was thrown into prison. He recovered his freedom, some say by a large sum of money, which his followers gladly paid, as he gave out that he had been visited in a dream by the Prophet Elias, who encouraged him in his adherence to the pure Law of Moses. But his success was chiefly owing to an artifice suggested by an Arabian philosopher, whom he met with in the prison. He demanded of the Vizier a public disputation with his adversaries, and represented the only cause of their differences to be a dispute about the period of the new moon. The Caliph was a dabbler in astronomy; and Anan, by dexterously adopting his opinion, obtained a triumph.[1] The Karaites retired to the neighbourhood of Jerusalem, to maintain in peace their simple creed—in their adherence to which, the sight of the Holy City might confirm them. They hoped that thus a pure and righteous people might be ready to hail the accomplishment of its last Article. The following were, and still are, the Articles of the Karaite belief:—I. That the world was created; II. That it had an uncreated Creator; III. That God is without form, and in every sense One; IV. That God sent Moses; V. That God delivered the Law to Moses; VI. That the believer must deduce his creed from the knowledge of the Law in its original language, and from the pure interpretation of it; VII. That God inspired the rest of the prophets; VIII. That God will raise the dead; IX. That God will reward and punish all men

---

[1] Anan the Karaite, according to Scherina Gaon and Abraham ben David, was contemporary with R. Juda Gaon, who died in 763 A.C. Mordecai makes him contemporary with Caliph Abu Giafar, who began to reign 754 A.C.—no great difference. The Karaites have been described in Trigland!us de Karaitis, Woolf, Bibliotheca Hebraica, and 'Mordecai.' Other tracts may be found in Ugolini's Thesaurus.

before His throne; X. That God has not rejected His unhappy people, but is purifying them by affliction, and that they must daily strive to render themselves worthy of redemption through the Messiah, the Son of David. The Karaites formed a regular community, under their Nasi, which name afterwards gave place to that of Hachim; they have since spread into many countries, where they are hated and denounced as heretics by the Rabbins. They found their way from the East into Spain at the height of Jewish prosperity and learning. They made more progress in the Christian states than among the Arabic Jews. They were met with jealous opposition by the Rabbinical authorities; they made proselytes from their familiarity with Arabic, more vernacular with the Jew than the Rabbinical Hebrew. But all intermarriages were forbidden by the dominant party; their trade was discouraged; they had no great or eloquent writers, and had dwindled away almost to nothing before the great expulsion of the Jews from Spain.[j] Their chief settlements in later days have been in Poland and the East of Europe, in the Taurus, and in Tartary.

If their own writers deserve credit, at a period not very distant from this, the Jews in the East attained to a still more eminent height of power and splendour. Judaism ascended the throne of a great kingdom on the west of the Caspian Sea—a kingdom before the strength of which the Persian monarchy trembled, and endeavoured to exclude its inroads by building a vast wall, the remains of which still excite the wonder of the traveller: while the Greek Empire courted its alliance. The name of this realm was Khazar, or Khozar;[k] it

---

[j] There seems likewise to have been a Sadducaic sect in Spain.

[k] Basnage discredited the whole story, as he could not trace the exist-

was inhabited by a Turcoman tribe, who had gradually abandoned their nomadic habits and maintained considerable commerce: their capital, Bilangiar, was situated at the mouth of the Wolga, and a line of cities stretched across from thence to the Don. They exchanged dried fish, the furs of the North, and slaves, for the gold and silver, and the luxuries of southern climates. Merchants of all religions, Jews, Christians, and Mohammedans, were freely admitted, and their superior intelligence over his more barbarous subjects induced one of their kings, Bulan (A.C. 740), to embrace the religion of the strangers. By one account he was admonished by an angel—by another he decided in this singular manner between the conflicting claims of Christianity, Moslemism, and Judaism. He examined the different teachers apart, and asked the Christian if Judaism was not better than Mohammedanism—the Mohammedan whether it was not better than Christianity. Both replied in the affirmative; on which the monarch decided in favour of Judaism. According to one statement secretly, to another openly, he embraced the faith of Moses, and induced learned teachers of the Law to settle in his dominions. Judaism became a necessary condition on the succession to the throne, but there was the most liberal toleration of all other forms of faith. The dynasty lasted for above two centuries and a half; and when R. Hasdai, a learned Jew, was in the highest confidence with Abderrahman, the Caliph of Cordova, he received intelligence of this sovereignty possessed by his brethren, through the ambassadors of the Byzantine Emperor. After considerable difficulty Hasdai succeeded in

---

ence of such a kingdom; but De Guignes, and the more recent accounts | of the Russian Empire, have satisfactorily proved that point.

establishing a correspondence with Joseph, the reigning king. The letter of Hasdai is extant, and an answer of the king, which does not possess equal claims to authenticity. The whole history has been wrought out into a religious romance called Cosri, which has involved the question in great obscurity: Basnage rejected the whole as a fiction of the Rabbins—anxious to prove that "the sceptre had not entirely departed from Israel:" Jost inclines to the opinion that there is a groundwork of truth under the veil of poetic embellishment. More modern writers admit without hesitation, and almost boast of the kingdom of Khosar.[1]

We travel westward, not, as usually, to sadden our eyes and chill our hearts with tales of persecution and misery, but to behold the Jews the companions and confidential ministers of princes. We pause to glean the slight and barren information which we possess of the state of the Jews in the Byzantine Empire. The writers of the opposite party accuse the Jews as instigators and abettors of the iconoclastic Emperors (the destroyers of images); and a fable, equally irreconcileable with chronology and history, has been repeated of their zeal in this, by some called sacrilegious, warfare. It is said that they instigated the Caliph Yezid the Second to order the demolition of images in his dominions.[m] The outraged saints were revenged by the untimely death of Yezid, attributed to their prayers. The successor of Yezid acknowledged, it is added, his father's impiety, and determined to wreak vengeance on his advisers. They fled; but two of them, resting near a fountain in Isauria, beheld a youth, driving an ass laden with petty

---

[1] Cassel, in Ersch and Grüber, p. 21.

[m] Cedrenus, L 789, Edit. Bonn.

With this account Zonaras and Theophanes mainly agree.

merchandize. They looked on him with fixed eyes, saluted him as the future Emperor, but at the same time they strongly urged his compliance with the second commandment of the Law.° Unfortunately, among the few facts which are known of the period is this, that Leo the Isaurian, in the early part of his reign, persecuted the Jews. It is highly probable that, when the Emperors gave the signal for havock, the Jews, stimulated by covetousness as well as religious zeal, would not be the last to strip or break in pieces, or melt the costly ornaments, and even the images themselves, made of the precious metals. We may conceive the religious horror which the devout image-worshipper would feel, when the unclean hands of the circumcised either seized, or bought from authorized plunderers, the object of his profound adoration, and converted it, like any other object of traffic, to profane uses. But, inured to hatred, the Jew would have no fear to encounter it for the gratification at once of his revenge and his avarice. We know little further of their state, but that they were under the avowed protection of some of the succeeding Emperors. Constantine Copronymus, probably on account of his hatred of images, was called a Jew;° and Nicephorus and Michael the Stammerer are named, as extending their paternal care over this usually proscribed race.°

In Italy we know little of the condition of the Israelites; but the silence of history concurs with the single fact with which we are acquainted, to represent those

---

° Enough of Leo's early life is known utterly to confute this fable. Leo, though an Isaurian, left his native country early. The whole family was transported to Thrace by Justinian. Leo was in Justinian's guard in 705. Le Beau, xii. 175, relates these kills fictions.

° Theophanes, Chron. p. 617, Edit. Bonn.

° Michael the Stammerer, perhaps on account of his equal toleration, was called by some a Jew, by others the sink of all religions. Basnage, ix. 9.

days as days of peace. The Pope Zacharias found it necessary to interdict not only the old grievance, the possession of Christian slaves by Jews, but also unlawful sexual intercourse and marriage between the two races.

Whatever guilt, either of secret perfidy[q] or prayer for the success of the invader, might attach to the Jewish inhabitants of the South of France during the invasion of that country by the Moors of Spain; yet when the barrier of the Pyrenees was established by the valour of Charles Martel, and by the ability of the new race of sovereigns who succeeded to the feeble Merovingians, Pepin and Charlemagne, these monarchs not merely refrained from all retribution, but displayed the more enlightened policy of conciliation towards their wealthy and useful subjects.[r] Though even under Charlemagne, at the commencement of his reign, they were treated with the old Roman or religious contempt; they were disqualified like slaves, infamous persons, Pagans, and heretics, from bringing criminal actions;[s] though they were prohibited from hiring the lands of Christians, or letting their lands to Christians (a proof that they were still cultivators of the soil),[t] yet the legislator, as time advanced, seemed to become more liberal. The Jews

---

[q] They are accused of betraying Toulouse to the enemy; but the siege of that city by the Moors appears altogether apocryphal. The singular custom which certainly existed for a considerable period in Toulouse, by which a syndic or representative of the Jews was constrained to appear before the authorities and receive three boxes on the ear, originated no doubt in some other unknown cause. See Hist. de Languedoc, ii. p. 151. See also, infrà, p. 146.

[r] Beugnot, Juifs d'Occident, p. 74.

[s] "Placuit ut omnes servi . . . ad accusationem non admittantur, omnes etiam infamiæ maculis aspersi, et turpitudinibus subjectæ personæ, heretici etiam sive Pagani sive Judæi." Capit. l. 1.

[t] "Non liceat Christianis Judæorum neque Paganorum res emphyteosis vel conductionis titulo habere, neque suorum similiter eis accommodare." Addit. 3, c. xv.

were only restricted in the possession of Christian slaves, subjected to the general marriage law of the empire, commanded to observe the prohibited degrees, and to conform to the general law of dower. The offender was liable to a fine of one hundred sous, and to suffer one hundred stripes.[a] Their commerce was unrestricted, except by a limitation enforced on Charlemagne, rather by the irreverent covetousness of the clergy, than by the misconduct of the Jews. Bishops, abbots, and abbesses were only prevented by a severe inhibition from pledging or selling to the circumcised the costly vestments, rich furniture, and precious vessels of the churches.[x] To the flourishing commerce of the Israelites, the extended dominions of Charlemagne opened a wide field. From the ports of Marseilles and Narbonne their vessels kept up a constant communication with the East. In Narbonne they were so flourishing that, of the two prefects, or mayors of the city, one was always a Jew; and, as we shall presently see, the most regular and stately part of the city of Lyons

---

[a] "Nulli Christianorum vel Judæorum licent matrimonium contrahere nisi præmissâ dotis promissione. Illud tamen fore præcipimus ut si quis Christianus vel Christiana, aut Judæus vel Judæa, nuptiale festum celebrare voluerit, non aliter quam sacerdotali benedictione intra sinum sanctæ ecclesiæ perceptâ, conjugium cuipiam ex iis adire permittimus. Quod si absque benedictione sacerdotis quispiam Christianorum vel Judæorum neviter conjugium duxerit; aut 100 principi solidos exsolvat, aut 100 verberatus publicæ flagellis suscipiat." Was this law really carried into execution? and were the Jews compelled to be married in Christian churches? Did the Jews prefer the payment of the fine? and was it, in so far, a tax on their marriages? If the Jews would scruple to enter the church, many ecclesiastics doubtless would hold their churches desecrated by the presence of Jews, and certainly would not bless an unbaptized Jew.

[x] "Ut singuli, episcopi, abbates, et abbatissæ diligenter considerent thesauros ecclesiasticos ne propter perfidiam aut negligentem custodiam aliquod aut de gemmis aut de vasis reliquo quoque thesauro perditum sit ; quia dictum est nobis quod negotiatores Judæi, necnon et alii, gloriantur, quod quicquid illis placeat, possent ab eis emere." Capit. A.C. 806 ; Bouquet, v. p. 677.

was the Jewish quarter. The superior intelligence and education of the Jews, in a period when nobles and kings, and even the clergy, could not always write their names, pointed them out for offices of trust. They were the physicians, the ministers of finance, to nobles and monarchs. As physicians they alone perhaps (for they had taught the Arabians) kept up the sacred traditions of the art, the knowledge of the properties of drugs, which had come down from the East and from the Greeks. They were in the courts of kings, in the schools of Salerno and Montpellier. It is true that if their medical skill (which all mankind must submit to the necessity of employing) forced them into places of trust and honour, it exposed them to inevitable dangers. If they were successful they were liable to the suspicion of sorcery and unlawful dealing. Knowledge and magic were so closely allied in the popular mind, that a wonderful cure wrought by a Jew could not be wrought by science, still less by divine aid, therefore must be wrought by diabolic aid. If they were unsuccessful, the dying patient must have been the victim, not of incurable malady or even of ignorance; the Jewish physician must knowingly have administered poison, as in the case of Zedekiah, the physician of Louis the Pious, accused of the death of Charles the Bald.

As financiers too we find them in the courts of kings and of the great vassals, encountering all the hatred which attaches to the levying heavy, mostly ill-apportioned, taxation upon an impoverished people. Their wisest measures probably, as beyond the political economy of the age, would be arraigned as the most cruel and iniquitous; yet they were unable or unwilling to decline these perilous dignities, by which, honestly or dishonestly, they obtained great opportunities of advantage, and stored up wealth to themselves, to be the righteous or unrighteous pretext for the plunder by the sovereign whom they served, or the vengeance of the people whom they stripped. In them the possession of wealth was sufficient proof of extortion and iniquity. At all events, they were usurers, and whether they exercised usury, on what might now be called fair or unfair terms, usury was in itself a sin and a crime. They rose even to higher dignities; when Charlemagne, either with some secret political design, or from an ostentatious show of magnificence, determined on sending an ambassador to the splendid Caliph, Haroun al Raschid, Europe and Asia beheld the extraordinary spectacle of a Jew, named Isaac,[7] setting forth on this mission, with two Christian Counts, who died on the road, and conducting the political correspondence between the courts of Aix-la-Chapelle and Bagdad. It cannot be wondered if this embassy gave rise to the wildest speculations in that ignorant age, both as to its objects and its event. It was given out that the Caliph granted Judæa as a free gift to Charlemagne; others limited his generosity to Jerusalem, others to the key of the Holy Sepulchre. The secret objects probably never transpired beyond the councils of Charlemagne; but it was known that Isaac returned with presents of a wonderful nature from the East. Among these was an enormous elephant, of such importance that his death is faithfully chronicled by the monkish annalists; jewels, gold, spices, apes, a clock,

---

[7] His acquaintance with the language and manners of the East no doubt designated the Jew for this mission. One reads in Basnage with surprise:—"On est étonné de ce que l'Empereur choisissait un Juif pour cet emploi, pendant qu'il avoit dans ses états un si grand nombre de sujets capables de le remplir." Charlemagne would have been puzzled to find many subjects capable, without the Jew, of negotiating in the East. Basnage contradicts himself in the next sentence.

and some rich robes, doubtless of silk. To these were added, by universal tradition, the keys of the Holy Sepulchre at Jerusalem.[a] Isaac acquitted himself with such ability, that he was entrusted by his imperial protector with another mission to the same quarter.

The golden age of the Jews endured, in still-increasing prosperity, during the reign of Charlemagne's successor, Louis the Débonnaire, or the Pious. At his court the Jews were so powerful, that their interest was solicited by the presents of nobles and princes. His most confidential adviser was a Jewish physician, named Zedekiah. The wondering people attributed Zedekiah's influence over the Emperor to magic, in which he was considered a profound adept. The monkish historians relate, with awe-struck sincerity, tales of his swallowing a whole cart of hay, horses and all, and flying in the air like Simon Magus of old.[a] A sort of representative of the community, the defender of their privileges, the master of the Jews,[b] resided within the precincts of the court. The general privileges of the race were preserved with rigid equity. They were permitted to build synagogues; their appeals were listened to with equal

---

[a] Eginhard. Vit. Carol. M. This was magnified, in later days, into a grant of Jerusalem and the whole of Judæa, but, according to the quaint speech attributed to Haroun al Raschid, as the Emperor lived so far off, and if he moved his troops to Palestine the provinces of France would revolt, the Caliph therefore would still defend the country, and pay over the revenues to Charlemagne. The grant is affirmed by the monks of St. Gall (apud Pertz, the Annales Fuldenses, ibid.), and by the Saxon poet:—

"..... Pervarum denique princeps Hunc Aaron,idem foerrat cui subditos, India Exceptis, Oriens totus: caraverat ultro Kjus amicitias se fœdere jungere firmo. Nam gemmas, aurum, vestes, et aromata crebro Ac reliquas Orientis opes direxerat illi; Ascribique locum sanctum Hierosolymarum Concessit propria Caroli semper ditioni." Lib. iv. apud Pertz.

The death of the elephant Bubalus is recorded by Eginhart, sub ann. 810. Monach. Engoliam. apud Pertz.

[a] Chronic. Hirsaugen.

[b] This title was borne by Evrard, who appears in the Inquiry on the charges advanced by Bishop Agobard.

—their enemies said, with partial—justice; they had free power to traffic, and to dispose of real or personal property; even their slave-trade was protected.* They had moreover interest enough to procure the alteration of certain markets, which were customarily held on their Sabbath, to another day. They began to be recognised as under the special protection of the Emperor, as in later days in feudal language they were "the men of the Emperor."[d] They were to appear at the court annually, or every two years, to render their accounts in the king's chamber (no doubt they were taxed with rigid impartiality), and to do the Emperor service.[e] Besides this general protection, several charters are extant, granting special privileges to certain Jewish communities and individuals. One to certain Jews of Languedoc, securing to them the right of possessing and holding in perpetual tenure certain hereditaments, of which they had been unjustly despoiled. This showed that they were landowners on a considerable scale. They were to hold these estates, with the houses and other buildings, lands cultivated and uncultivated, vineyards, meadows, pastures, watercourses, mills, rights of way. They held these estates in full right of property, of alienation, gift or exchange, without let or hindrance.[f] Another to a certain Domat

---

[c] "Habeant etiam licentiam mancipia peregrina emere, et intra imperium nostrum vendere, et nemo fidelium nostrorum præsumat eorum mancipia peregrina sine eorum consensu baptisare." Charta Lud. Pii, 32, 33, 34; Bouquet, iv.

[d] The Jews certainly had the power of holding allodial property in the Narbonnese, by the grants of Pepin le Bref, Charlemagne, and Louis the Pious, the historians of Languedoc say, "parce qu'ils y étoient très puissants et en grand nombre." Compare Hist. de Languedoc, I. Notes, p. 739.

[e] See this remarkable charter, Histoire de Languedoc, I, preuve 75, p. 322.

It was, "Actum Francofurdi palatio regis, in Dei nomine feliciter. Amen. Its ut deinceps annis singulis, aut post duorum annorum curriculum, man-

Rabbi, and his grandson Samuel,[e] granting them exemption from various tolls and taxes—permission to hire Christian slaves, who were, however, not to be forced to work on Sundays and holidays—and generally to deal in slaves within the limits of the Empire. Every litigation with a Christian was to be settled by the evidence of three Jews and three Christians. It forbade all persons to encourage their Christian slaves in disobedience under pretence of being Christians and seeking baptism.[h] It took the persons of the abovenamed under imperial protection.[i] Their death was to be punished at the price of ten pounds of gold. They were not to be submitted to the ordeal of fire or water, nor scourged—but allowed in every respect the free observance of their Law.

Agobard, Archbishop of Lyons, beheld with jealous indignation this alien people occupying the fairest part of his city, displaying openly their enviable opulence. Their vessels crowded the ports—their bales encumbered the quays—their slaves thronged the streets. In a Christian city, the Church seemed to vail its head before the Synagogue. He endeavoured, by the exercise

---

dante missionum ministro, ad nostrum veniant palatium, atque ad cameram nostram fideliter, unusquisque ex suo negotio ac nostro deservire student." Charta Lud. Pii, 32, 33, 34; Bouquet, 624.

[e] Charter to Domat Rabbi, apud Bouquet, vi. 649.

[h] "Suggesserunt etiam iidem Judaei Celsitudini nostræ de quibusdam hominibus, qui contra Christianam religionem suadent mancipia Hebræorum sub antentu (obtentu) Christianae religionis contemnere dominos suos et baptizari; vel potius persuadent illis ut baptisentur ut a servitio dominorum suorum liberentur, quod nequaquam sacri canones constituunt, immo talia perpetrantes districtâ anathematis sententiâ puniendos dijudicant." This alludes to a canon of the Council of Gangra. No wonder that the clergy were indignant at the imperial favour towards the Jews. Compare Agobard's Letter. There are two similar precepts in favour of other Jews, p. 650.

[i] "Sub mundeburdo et defensione nostrâ."

of his episcopal authority, to prevent that approximation of the two races which seemed rapidly advancing.[k] He forbade his flock, among other things, to sell Christian slaves to the Jews—to labour for the Jews on Sundays—to eat with them during Lent—to buy the flesh of animals slain by them—or to drink their wine. As far as he could he prohibited all social intercourse, which seems not to have been uncommon.

The Jews considered these laws of Agobard an infringement of their rights; they appealed to their royal protector for redress. A commission of inquiry was issued, a commission which Agobard describes as terrible to the Christians, mild to the Jews,[l] and at the head of it was Count Evrard, called in other places protector of the Jews. The Archbishop was commanded to withdraw his obnoxious edicts. Agobard was at Nantes. He declared himself ready to submit to the royal decree, but proceeded to offer a petition to the king against his adversaries. He accused them (a strange charge!) of selling to the Christians meat unclean to themselves, because the Mosaic law about slaying cattle was not rigidly observed, which, he said, they called Christians' meat, and wine unclean, as partly spilled on the ground. He accused them of cursing daily the Christians and Christ in their synagogues. He accused them of the insufferable pride with which they vaunted the royal favour; that

---

[k] Louis the Pious granted exemptions to Jews, who held his diplomas, from certain tolls and taxes characteristic of the times. 1. Teloneum, tax on goods conveyed by water carriage; Paraverdum, the obligation to furnish post horses for the public use on the military roads; Mansionaticum, free quarters for soldiers; Pulveraticum, tax levied on farmers pro labore et pulvere; Cespitaticum, obligation to make hedges on the roadsides; Ripaticum, duties on landing goods on quays; Portalicium, port dues; Transaticum, toll on sledges, &c.; Cænaticum, provisions for soldiers on march.

[l] "Christianis terribilis, Judæis mitis."

they went freely in and out of the royal palaces; that the highest persons solicited their prayers and blessings; that they boasted of gifts of splendid dresses to their wives and matrons from royal and princely donors.[m] He complained of the bad effects produced by the concession of the change of the market-day from the Jewish Sabbath, the Saturday, and that the Jewish had many more hearers than the Christian preachers, and, indeed, were held by the uninstructed to be the better preachers.[n] He added the more weighty charge, that the Jews frequently stole Christian children to sell them as slaves. This petition was followed by a long theological argument, to prove the wisdom and justice of persecuting the Jews—the most detestable of unbelievers.[o] The Archbishop pressed St. Paul into his service. He cited, with as little justice, the example of many of the most illustrious bishops—Hilary and Sidonius Apollinaris, Ambrose, Cyprian, Athanasius, besides a host of Gallic

---

[m] De insolentia Judæorum, Oper. Agobardi: "Dum enim gloriantur, mentientes simplicibus Christianis, quod cari sint vobis propter Patriarchas; quod honorabiliter ingrediantur in conspectu vestro et egrediantur; quod excellentissimæ personæ cupiant earum orationes et benedictiones; et fateantur talem se legis auctorem habere velle qualem ipsi habent . . . dum ostendunt præcepta ex nomine vestro, aureis sigillis signata, et continentia verba, ut putamus non vera; dum ostendunt vestes muliebres, quasi a consanguineis vestris vel matronis Palatinorum uxoribus eorum directis," &c.

[n] "At dicunt imperiti Christiani melius eis prædicare Judæos quam presbyteros nostros."
M. Bédarride (Les Juifs en France,

en Italie, et en Espagne, Paris, 1859) observes with justice on this fact:—
"Il paraît qu'ils comptaient parmi eux des hommes à qui le talent de la parole n'était pas étranger, puisqu'ils prêchaient publiquement. Il paraît, de plus, que ces prédicateurs parlaient la langue du pays, puisqu'ils étaient à portée de se faire entendre des Chrétiens," p. 85. M. Bédarride mentions conversions from Christianity to Judaism, among which was "un diacre du Palais, nommé Putho."

[o] "Ex quibus demonstratur quam detestabiles habendi sunt inimici veritatis, et quomodo pejores sunt omnibus incredulis, Scripturis divinis hoc docentibus, et quam indigniora omnibus infidelibus de Deo sentiant et rebus cœlestibus." Ibid.

Bishops and Gallic Councils. He entered into long
details of the absurdities taught by the Rabbins, their
anthropomorphic notions of the Deity (among the rest
he charged them with holding the eternity of the
letters of the alphabet, and the assertion that the Mosaic
Law was written many ages before the world began),
and of the blasphemies which they uttered concerning
Christ.[p] It was all in vain: the Court turned a deaf
ear to his complaints, and Agobard set off for Paris, to
try the influence of his personal weight and character
before his sovereign. He was received with cold civility
—constrained to wait in an antechamber while the
councillors of state laid his appeal before the king—and
then received permission to retire to his diocese.[q] He
wrote another despatch, bitterly inveighing against the
influence and conduct of the Grand Master of the Jews.
But his sorrows were poured forth more fully into the
confidential bosom of Nebridius, Bishop of Narbonne,
whom he called upon to co-operate with him in
separating the Christians from a people who, he says,
"are clothed with cursing as with a garment. The
curse penetrates into their bones, their marrow, and

---

[p] Many of these charges are very curious, as showing that some of the stranger notions in the Talmud, of course made infinitely more strange by misconception and misrepresentation, were current concerning the Jews in Europe.

[q] He humbly acknowledges that he was overawed by the manifest favour of the Court towards the Jews: "Nuper' cum in Palatio tempus redeundi nobis jam fuisset indultum, suavissima Dilectio vestra sedit [the councillors were Adalhard Wala, and Elisachar, who then reigned supreme over Louis the Pious], et andivit me mussitantem potius quam loquentem contra eos qui Judæorum querelas astruelant." Adalhard and Wala were of the high ecclesiastical party. Agobard contents himself with urging more justly the protection of certain slaves of the Jews, who desired baptism. But he admits that the Jews ought to be paid for the loss. On Adalhard and Wala, see Latin Christianity, ii. p. 246, &c.

their entrails, as water and oil flow through the human body.' They are accursed in the city and the country, at the beginning and ending of their lives: their flocks, their meat, their granaries, their cellars, their magazines, are accursed." His denunciations were as unavailing as his petitions: while an instance is related of an officer of the palace joining the synagogue, the Archbishop was constrained to complain once more of the violence offered to a Jewess who had embraced Christianity.'

In the reign of Charles the Bald, the Jews maintained their high estate, but dark signs of the approaching Age of Iron began to lower around.' Amilo, Archbishop of Lyons, the successor of Agobard, accuses the Jews, who were tax-gatherers, of forcing the poor peasants in remote districts by the cruelty of their exactions to deny Christ." But the active hostility of the clergy was no longer checked by the stern protection of the royal authority. In Lyons many converts were made, by whose agency so many children were seduced from their parents, that the Jews were obliged to send their offspring for education to the less zealous cities of Vienne, Macon, and Arles. Remigius, later Archbishop of Lyons, announced his triumph to the king, and desired that the Bishop of

---

' "Scientes . . . omnes qui sub lege sunt, sub maledicto esse, et indutos maledictione sicut vestimento, quæ intrat sicut aqua in interiora eorum, et sicut oleum in ossa eorum," &c.

" Agobard of Lyons was a prelate in some respects in advance of his age: he dared to condemn many popular superstitions. On image-worship he adopted the moderate view, nearly that of the Council of Frankfort; above all, he wrote a treatise of great power and strong sense against judicial ordeals.

' Jewish merchants (negotiatores) by a law of Charles the Bald were to pay a tenth in duty, while the Christians paid an eleventh. Cap. Car. Calv. apud Balusium.

" "Quidem ipsorum qui in nonnullis civitatibus inlicitè constituuntur, silent in remotioribus locis Christianos pauperes et ignaros pro eodem teloneo scriter constringere, deinde ut Christum negent persuadere."

Arles might be admonished to follow the example of his zeal. The Councils began again to launch their thunders; that of Meaux (A.C. 845) re-enacted the exclusion of the Jews from all civil offices. This decree was followed up by that of Paris (A.C. 845); but in the distracted state into which the kingdom soon fell, probably these ordinances were not executed. If it be true (but of its truth there is not much probability) that Charles the Bald was poisoned by the famous Jewish physician of his father, Zedekiah, an act, which so weakened the royal authority, was a measure most pernicious to his countrymen. The Jews thenceforth, instead of being under the protection of a powerful monarch, fell rapidly under the dominion of those countless petty independent sovereigns who rose under the feudal system, whose will was law, and whose wants would not submit to the slow process of exaction and tribute, but preferred the raising more expeditious supplies by plunder and massacre. An edict of Charles the Simple, among other gifts, bestows on the Archbishop of Narbonne all the lands and vineyards possessed by the Jews, however acquired, in the whole county (A.C. 897). The King seems to have had no doubt of his right to give, the Archbishop no doubt of the justice of receiving, this donation; these properties had before belonged to them. It would seem that the Jews were no longer to hold real property.

Still commerce, even in the rudest and most anarchical times, is a necessity of mankind. But in all these Germanic kingdoms in general, the kings, princes, warriors, were too proud to engage in what they held to be base and degrading occupations; the serfs were too indigent and down-trodden to rise above daily labour. The cities with their guilds had not yet risen to, or recovered, their mercantile importance. Yet the interchange of commodities between remote countries was never entirely broken off; foreign wares found their way from one region to another; the diffusion of articles of necessity or of luxury might be precarious, interrupted, irregular, yet it never entirely ceased. Europe was never without some of the precious treasures, the stuffs, the spices, of Asia; queens and high-born ladies must be decked with jewels; rich stuffs were demanded for the array of knights, for the housings of their coursers.[a] The Church above all, from her own wealth or the wealth of her votaries, must have gold and velvet and precious stones for her vessels and monstrances; her censers must be filled with frankincense. Spices for banquets, or even for more common use, were still supplied; medicinal drugs, many of which came from the East, were furnished, it is probable, as well as administered by Jewish physicians, who were everywhere: above all, the slave-trade, the traffic in captives taken in war, was still active. The inroads of the Northmen, and later of the Hungarians, no doubt gave it new life. The constant legislation on that subject, even to a late period, shows how deeply the Jews were concerned in this traffic, which in those days brought much property and little discredit to the Jew,' thus dealing to Christians some revengeful satisfaction for their insults and wrongs. The Jews probably alone, the wealthier of them, had capital; they alone had mutual intelligence and correspondence; they frequented every fair and market; they knew and communicated to each

---

[a] The monk of St. Gall mentions a Jewish merchant, a favourite of Charlemagne, "qui terram repromissionis sæpius adire, et inde ad cismarinas provincias multa pretiosa et incognita solitus erat afferre." De Gest. C. M. i. 18.

other the prices of commodities; they were a vast mercantile firm spread through Europe, and having some, it might be precarious, connexion with their brethren in the East, in Africa, in Spain, in most Mohammedan countries. Trade alone, active prosperous trade, will account for their vast numbers, their dangerous wealth, even their rising intellectual importance. There was silent continued intercommunication of thoughts and ideas between the East and West, as well as constant traffic in material things. In the North of Germany and in Northern France their position and influence were seemingly not so high; they were, however, already in a certain sense under special imperial protection. But the vast numbers which were found in all the flourishing German cities on the Rhine, and their great and tempting wealth before the Crusades, must have been the growth of previous centuries. Their relation to the Christian merchant-citizens till that outburst of fanaticism seems in general to have been amicable. In the South of France we hear of Jewish fleets on the Mediterranean. The Norman piracies probably, making peaceful navigation next to impossible, rather than want of capital or activity, put an end to these enterprises. We may safely therefore dismiss as an unhistoric legend their betrayal of Bordeaux to the Normans,[y] whom they must have been wise enough to know to be their most fatal enemies. The incessant and increasing hostility of the bishops in Languedoc and Dauphiny betrays the jealousy as well as the aversion of these prelates. Towards the end of the ninth century (A.C. 889), the Archbishop of Sens, from some motive

---

[y] This accusation is found in the Ann. Berlin. sub ann. 847. They are also accused of betraying Barcelona to the Moors, A.C. 853.

which the monk Oleron thinks fit not to reveal, expelled the Jews from his diocese.[a]

Even the strange usage that the Syndic of the Jews in Toulouse presented himself three times a year to receive a box on the ear from the Christian mayor, shows at once their importance and their odiousness to the Christians; an usage of which the well-attested barbarous close seems to prove the historic truth, though its origin is lost in obscurity.[a] A stern, iron-handed magistrate struck the poor Syndic with such force as to scatter the brains of the unfortunate unbeliever. But even the title of Syndic implied the regular and organized community. The Jews appealed to the king against this and other acts of oppression. The king answered that "they only suffered the penalties due to their sins."[b]

It was in Spain that the golden age of the Jews shone with the brightest and most enduring splendour. Yet, during its earlier period, from the conquest by the Moors till towards the end of the tenth century, when, while Christian Europe lay in darkness, Mohammedan Cordova might be considered the centre of civilization, of arts, and of letters, though we are certain that the Jews, under the enjoyment of equal rights and privileges, rivalled their masters, or rather their compatriots, in their advancement to wealth, splendour, and cultiva-

---

[a] "Judæos certâ de causâ, ab urbe expulit." Apud Bouquet, viii. 237.

[a] It is attributed to the betrayal of Toulouse by the Jews to the Saracens, and its recapture by Charlemagne, who punished their treachery by this ignominious ordinance, and with a fine of a certain number of pounds of wax, no doubt for religious uses. But Basnage has well exposed the anachronisms and want of historic truth in the whole story of the capture (not the siege, which is confounded with that of Toulouse by the Saracens), and its recovery by Charlemagne. Hist. des Juifs, tom. ix. ch. 3.

[b] Vit. S. Theodardi, apud Bouquet, vii.

tion; though they had their full share, or, perhaps, as more intelligent, a disproportionate share, in the high ministerial and confidential offices of the court; though by the perpetual intercourse kept up with their brethren in the East, we may safely infer that by land along the North of Africa,[c] and by sea along the course of the Mediterranean, their commerce was pursued with industry and success; yet we have not much distinct information concerning their state and proceedings. In fact, it is difficult to discriminate them from the race among whom they lived on terms of the closest amity during these halcyon days. In emulation of their Moslemite brethren, they began to cultivate their long disused and neglected poetry; the harp of Judah was heard to sound again, though with something of a foreign tone—for they borrowed the rhythm peculiar to the Arabic verse. Yet, though but a feeble echo of their better days, we would gladly explore this almost hidden source of Jewish poetry. There too Rabbinism, while its throne was tottering to decay in the East, found a refuge, and commenced a new era of power and authority. The Talmud was translated into Arabic, under the auspices of Moses "clad in sackcloth." Moses was one of the most learned men of the East. A singular adventure cast him upon the hospitable shore of Spain, and through him the light of learning, which, by the rapid progress of the iron age of Judaism in Babylonia, by the extinction of the authority of the Prince of the Captivity, the dispersion of the illustrious teachers, and the final closing of the great schools, seemed to have set for ever, suddenly rose again in the West, in renewed and

---

[c] According to Condé, Hist. des Arabes, i. 144, the Jews were very numerous and prosperous at Tunis and in Morocco, ii. 234.

undiminished splendour. Four Babylonian Rabbins, of great distinction, of whom R. Moses was one, fell into the hands of a Spanish pirate.[d] The wife of Moses accompanied him in his voyage; the high-minded woman, dreading defilement, looked to her husband for advice; Moses uttered the verse of the Psalm: "The Lord said, I will bring again from Bashan, I will bring again from the depths of the sea." She plunged at once into the ocean, and perished.[e] Moses was brought as a slave to Cordova, and redeemed, though his quality was unknown, by a Jew. One day he entered the synagogue, clad as a slave in a scanty sackcloth. Nathan, the judge of the Jews in Cordova, presided. In the course of the debate the slave displayed such knowledge, that Nathan exclaimed, "I am no more judge; yon slave in sackcloth is my master, and I am his scholar." Moses was installed by acclamation as head of the community. Moses, and his son and successor, Enoch, enjoyed the protection of Hasdai, the son of Isaac, the minister of the Caliph; and though the learned pre-eminence of this family was disturbed by the rivalry of R. Joseph, to whom the task of translating the Talmud had been committed, yet such was the popularity of his grandson, Nathan, and such the wealth of his compatriots, that as often as the head of the Jewish community went forth to enjoy the delicious refreshment of the groves and gardens near Cordova, he was attended by his admiring disciples in immense numbers, and in most

---

[d] A.C. 990. The name of one of these Rabbins has not been preserved. One was R. Shemariah ben Elchanan, who was bought by the Jews of Alexandria, ignorant of his learning. He became head of the community at Alexandria. The third was R. Husshiel, who was bought at Tunis. He became head of the community at Kairouan. The fourth was R. Moses.

[e] Compare Damage, ix. 130, and Jost. vi. 107.

sumptuous apparel. It is said that seven hundred chariots swelled his pomp.

The long line of learned descendants, which formed the great school of Arabico-Jewish learning, belongs to the history of their literature, for which our work has not space. This line stretched away to the end of the twelfth century, when it produced its greatest ornament —the wise Maimonides, the first who, instead of gazing with blind adoration and unintelligent wonder at the great fabric of the Mosaic Law, dared to survey it with the searching eye of reason, and was rewarded by discovering the indelible marks of the Divine wisdom and goodness.[f] The life of Maimonides marks an epoch in the civil as well as in the literary and philosophic history of Judaism; and that life is a most instructive exposition of the extent and influence of Judaism, of the state and condition of the Jews at that eventful period. He was born at Cordova, March 30th, 1135. His father, a distinguished Talmudist, was the author of a Commentary on the Astronomic Treatise of Alfarghani. His father was his first instructor; but in the Arabian schools he was a disciple of Aben Pace. The youth of Maimonides witnessed the great revolution in the relation between Islamism and Judaism. To the

---

[f] There are many Lives of Maimonides.

I would venture to recommend a singularly clear and fair statement of his life and his opinions in the Etudes Orientales of M. Franck, author of an excellent book (La Kabbale, Paris, 1861). I subjoin the concluding sentences on the More Nevochim: "Ce livre, comme nous l'avons déjà dit, peut être considéré comme la première tentative du Rationalisme, et par cette qualité seule, de quelque manière qu'on le juge, il acquiert dans l'histoire générale des idées une incontestable importance. Mais il inspire également le respect par les puissantes facultés de l'auteur, la prodigieuse souplesse de son esprit, la variété de ses connaissances, l'élévation de son spiritualisme, enfin par la lumière qu'il répand sur quelques-uns des points les plus obscurs de l'histoire de l'esprit humain." p. 360.

wise tolerance, the peaceful harmony, which had raised the Ommyad Caliphs to their height of splendour, succeeded, when Maimonides was thirteen years old, the fanatic dynasty of the Almohades. Abd-el-Mouhmen, the founder of the dynasty, was a predecessor of Philip II., rather than a successor of the Abderrahmans. The fanatic Caliph issued a decree that, on pain of exile, the Jews and the Christians must alike embrace Islamism. Many Jewish families, as in the later days of the Inquisition, made a base and hypocritical profession of Mohammedanism. Among these was the family of Maimonides, and, at sixteen years old, the great doctor of the synagogue, the glory of Israel, the second Moses, was a professed Mohammedan. But the profound study of the religious writings of his people wrought conviction in the mind of the youth. Before the age of twenty-three he had composed a treatise on the Calendar, commented certain parts of the Talmud, and begun his great work on the Mischna (the Porta Mosis, translated by Pococke). Maimonides with his father and his family determined to leave the inhospitable shores of Spain. Africa was under the dominion of the Almohades; but the persecuting laws were executed with less severity. He passed to Morocco, dwelt some time at Fez, and then embarked for the Holy Land. He reached St. Jean d'Acre, and from thence made a pilgrimage to Jerusalem. He finally settled at Fostat, the port of Cairo. The famous Saladin had founded the Fatimite Empire. The Vizier of Saladin, the Kadhi al Fâdhel, took the learned Jew under his protection; and at Fostat the fame of Maimonides, as the most skilful physician, as the most profound philosopher, and the oracle of the religious belief among the most enlightened Jews and Arabians, grew to its height. At the early down Maimonides used to pass over to Cairo to transact his business in the capital; he was the Court physician. On his return, such were the crowds of all classes and orders who came to consult him on all questions, medical, philosophical, religious, that he had hardly time to snatch a hasty meal: he was compelled to intrude on the night for his profounder studies. Thus oppressed with business, Maimonides found time to complete his voluminous medical, philosophical, and theological writings.* His fame chiefly rests on the More Novochim, "the guide to those who have lost their way." Maimonides may be held as the founder of Rationalism; the first who endeavoured on broad principles to establish the harmony of reason and religion. He was the speculative parent of Spinoza and of Mendelssohn. His knowledge was vast; he was master not only of the Bible, but of all the Talmudic writings, of the genuine Aristotle, and of the Aristotelian Arabic philosophies; he had read earlier Eastern writings, with how severe a

---

* Maimonides was probably one of the first of his nation, notwithstanding their study in Spain and elsewhere of astronomy, who anticipated most Christians in the bold assert on that the heavenly bodies were not created for the sole use of man. The assertion itself, and the arguments by which it is maintained, are equally remarkable. "It is shown by demonstration that the distance from the centre of the earth to the supreme altitude of the planet Saturn is a journey of nearly 8700 years, reckoning 365 days in the year, and forty miles for each day's journey, according to the mile in the Law, which is of a thousand cubits." Maimonides deduces from this the insignificance of the earth as compared to all the celestial spheres, of man as compared to the earth: "and from the height of the heavens do not we learn how limited is our apprehension of Almighty God?" (Lib. lii. cap. xiv.) The chapters on the Origin of Evil, in which he urges and expands the notion, much received in later times, that it is the privation of Good, are very curious, and deserve the study of the philosopher and divine. Like all Jewish philosophers, his great tenet is the absolute Incorporeity of God (lib. l. cap. xxvi., &c.) On the meaning of the Law being written by the finger of God, see lib. l. cap. lxvi. His favourite phrase is that the Law "speaks the language of the sons of men."

critical spirit remains to be determined. He was a profoundly religious man. On such subjects as the Unity of the Godhead, the Creation, the Providence of God, on Foreknowledge and Free-will, while he asserts the power and authority of Reason, he limits its range with calm severity. He discusses all these questions with the freedom and fulness of the best Christian schoolmen, but without their arid logic and cold, subtle dialectics. To my judgement his spiritualism is more pure and lofty. During his life, such was the awe of his name that men hardly dared to reprove the fearless reasoner. After his death he was anathematized by the more superstitious of his brethren. But in later ages, the more enlightened the race of Israel, the higher has stood the fame of him whom his ardent admirers proclaimed a second Moses.[h]

We revert to a sadder spectacle—the rapid progress of the Iron Age of Judaism, which, in the East and in the West, gradually spread over the Jewish communities, till they sank again to their bitter, and, it might almost seem indefeasible, inheritance of hatred and contempt. They had risen but to be trampled down by the fiercer and more unrelenting tread of oppression and persecution. The world, which before seemed to have made a sort of tacit agreement to allow them time to regain wealth that might be plundered and blood that might be poured forth like water, now seems to have entered into a conspiracy as extensive, to drain the treasures and the blood of this devoted race.

Kingdom after kingdom, and people after people,

---

[h] The More Nevochim I only knew with the aid of Bustorf's translation. A large part, however, may now be read in the French of M. Munk, whose profound Hebrew learning, wide range of philosophical inquiry, and perspicuous language, are full guarantees for the trustworthiness of his translation.

followed the dreadful example, and strove to peal the knell of the descendants of Israel; till at length, what we blush to call Christianity, with the Inquisition in its train, cleared the fair and smiling provinces of Spain of this industrious part of its population, and self-inflicted a curse of barrenness upon the benighted land.[1]

[1] By far the most complete, I fear the most veracious, account of the persecutions of the Jews during the Middle Ages, has been collected, with his indefatigable industry, by Dr. Zunz in the preliminary chapters to his Synagogal Poesie des Mittelalters, Berlin, 1855. It fills about forty-three pages, from pp. 15 to 58. It is interspersed with extracts from Hebrew poetry translated into German. In some parts it rests on Jewish authorities, occasionally manuscript. It is a most hideous chronicle of human cruelty (as far as my researches have gone, fearfully true). Of the number of victims of course I cannot speak with full reliance. Perhaps it is the more hideous, because the most continuous, to be found among nations above the state of savages. Alas! that it should be among nations called Christian, though occasionally the Mohammedan persecutor vied with the Christian in barbarity.

BOOK XXIV.

IRON AGE OF JUDAISM.

Persecutions in the East — Extinction of the Princes of the Captivity — Jews in Palestine — In the Byzantine Empire — Feudal System — Chivalry — Power of the Church — Usury — Persecutions in Spain — Massacres by the Crusaders — Persecutions in France — Philip Augustus — Saint Louis — Spain — France — Philip the Fair — War of the Shepherds — Pestilence — Poisoning of the Fountains — Charles the Fourth — Charles the Fifth — Charles the Sixth — Final Expulsion from France — Germany — The Flagellants — Miracle of the Host at Brussels.

Our Iron Age commences in the East, where it witnessed the extinction of the Princes of the Captivity by the ignominious death of the last sovereign, the downfall of the schools, and the dispersion of the community, which from that period remained an abject and degraded part of the population. Pride and civil dissension, as well as the tyranny of a feeble despot, led to their fall. About the middle of the ninth century, both the Jews and Christians suffered some persecution under the Sultan Motavakel, A.C. 847. His edict was issued prohibiting their riding on lordly horses; they were to aspire no higher than humble asses and mules; they were forbidden to have an iron stirrup, and commanded to wear a leather girdle. They were to be distinguished from the faithful by a brand-mark, and their houses were defaced by figures of swine, devils, or apes. The latter addition throws some improbability on the story.* After

---
* See ante, p. 125.

the reign of Motavakel, the Caliphate in the East fell into confusion, split up into separate kingdoms under conflicting sovereigns.[b] About this time Saccai was Prince of the Captivity. Towards the middle of the tenth century (A.C. 934), David ben Saccai held that high office. Under David ben Saccai the Resch-Glutha resumed the pomp, title, and independence of a king. The Jews boast that, while his weaker ancestors had condescended to pay tribute, David refused that humiliating act of submission. But it was the feebleness of the Caliphate under Muctador, rather than the power of the Resch-Glutha, which encouraged this contumacy.[c] It has been conjectured that the interval during both these periods,[d] from A.C. 817 to about A.C. 916, was filled by a line of hereditary princes. The learned aristocracy, the Heads of the Schools of Sura and Pumbeditha, by whom the power of the Resch-Glutha, which sometimes aspired to tyranny, was limited,[e] seem likewise to have been hereditary. The race of that of Sura expired, and the Resch-Glutha, David ben Saccai, took upon himself to name an obscure successor called Om. Tob.[f] Om. Tob's incompetency became apparent, and R. Saadiah was summoned from Egypt. Saadiah was a great opponent of the doctrine of the transmigration of the soul, then a received article of the Jewish creed. Perpetual feuds distracted this singular state. The tribunals of the Resch-Glutha and of the Masters of the Schools, the civil and spiritual powers, were in perpetual collision. David, the Prince, on some

---

[b] Jost, vi. 84, 85.
[c] The obscure intrigues which led to the elevation of David ben Saccai may be read in Jost, vi. 96.
[d] Gans, Tsemach David, p. 130; Basnage, iv. 4; Jost, vi. p. 77, &c.
[e] David ben Saccai attempted also to nominate the chief of the School of Pumbeditha. This caused great discord and confusion.
[f] In Jost, the rival of Saadiah, Om. Tob, is R. Semaiah.

dispute about money, laid his ban on Saadiah. Saadiah hurled back the ban upon the Prince, and transferred the sovereignty to his brother. For seven years this strife lasted, till at length peace was restored, and the whole community beheld, with the utmost satisfaction, the Prince of the Captivity, who, on the death of his brother, regained his uncontested authority, entering the house of the Master of the School to celebrate together the joyful feast of Purim. The peace remained unbroken till the death of the Prince of the Captivity and that of his son. Saadiah became the guardian of his grandson. Saadiah was a man noted for the strictest justice, and his literary works were esteemed of the highest value.

Both the great dignities seem to have been united in the person of Scherira, who ruled and taught with universal admiration in the School of Pherutz Schabur from 967 to 997 A.C. Pherutz Schabur was a city five miles from Babylon. It is asserted, no doubt with the usual Jewish exaggeration, that this city was inhabited by 900,000 Jews. At the end of thirty years Scherira felt the approach of age, and associated his son Hai in the supremacy. But the term of this high office drew near. A violent and rapacious sovereign, Ahmed Kader, filled the throne of the Caliphs. He cast a jealous look upon the powers and wealth of this vassal sovereign. Scherira, now one hundred years old, and his son Hai, were seized either with or without pretext, their riches confiscated, and the old man hung up by the hand. Hai escaped to resume his office, and to transmit its honours and its dangers to Hezekiah, who was elected Chief of the Captivity. But, after a reign of two years, Hezekiah was arrested with his whole family by the order of the Caliph, Abdallah Kaim ben Marillah (A.C. 1036). The Schools were closed. Many of the learned fled to Egypt or Spain (the revulsion in Spain under the Almohades had not yet taken place); all were dispersed. Among the rest two sons of the unfortunate Prince of the Captivity effected their escape to Spain, while the last of the House of David (for of that lineage they fondly boasted), who reigned over the Jews of the Dispersion in Babylonia, perished on an ignominious scaffold.

The Jewish communities in Palestine suffered a slower but more complete dissolution. If credit is to be given to the facts relating to the revolutions in the East, in that singular compilation, the Travels of Benjamin of Tudela, which bears the date of the following century, from A.D. 1160 to 1173,[a] we may safely select his humiliating account of the few brethren who still clung, in poverty and meanness, to their native land.[b] There is an air of sad truth about the statement, which seems to indicate some better information on this subject than on some others. In Tyre Benjamin found 400 Jews, glass-blowers. The Samaritans still occupied Sichem; but in Jerusalem there were only 200 descendants of Abraham, almost all dyers of wool, who had bought a monopoly of that trade. Ascalon contained

[a] The object of this author seems to have been not unlike that of the celebrated Sir John Mandeville, besides the account, seemingly credible, of the countries which he really visited, to throw together all he had ever heard or read of the strange and unvisited regions of the farther East.— *Original Note.*

[b] Much light has been thrown on the Travels of Benjamin of Tudela by the new edition and English translation, with valuable Notes and Essays, especially by Dr. Zunz, published by Asher, Berlin, 1840. It seems clear that Benjamin of Tudela, probably as a merchant, travelled as far eastward as Bagdad. So far his descriptions are perfectly trustworthy. Dr. Zunz has traced the names of many of the Rabbins and distinguished men of whom Benjamin writes, and vouches for their accuracy. Beyond Bagdad Benjamin writes from hearsay, with a large admixture of fable, in parts curiously resembling Marco Polo. See Asher's Preface; and Dr. Zunz, in his valuable Essay on the contributions of the Hebrews to the science of geography, vol. ii.

153 Jews; Tiberias, the seat of learning and of the kingly patriarchate, but fifty. This account of Benjamin is confirmed by the unfrequent mention of the Jews in the histories of the later Crusades in the Holy Land, and may, perhaps, be ascribed in great measure to the devastations committed in the first of these depopulating expeditions. It is curious, after surveying this almost total desertion of Palestine, to read the indications of fond attachment to its very air and soil, scattered about in the Jewish writings. Still it is said, that man is esteemed most blessed, who, even after his death, shall reach the land of Palestine and be buried there, or even shall have his ashes sprinkled by a handful of its sacred dust. "The air of the land of Israel," says one, "makes a man wise;"[1] another writes, "He who walks four cubits in the land of Israel is sure of being a son of the life that is to come." "The great Wise Men are wont to kiss the borders of the Holy Land, to embrace its ruins, and roll themselves in its dust." "The sins of all those are forgiven who inhabit the land of Israel." He who is buried there is reconciled with God as though he were buried under the altar. The dead buried in the land of Canaan come first to life in the days of the Messiah. He who dies out of the Holy Land dies a double death. Rabbi Simeon said,[j] "All they who are buried out of the land of Canaan must perish everlastingly; but for the just, God will make deep caverns beneath the earth, by which they will work their way till they come to the land of Israel; when they are there, God will breathe the breath of life into their nostrils, and they will rise again."[k]

---

[1] Bara Bathra.
[j] Ketuboth.
[k] "Postquam Judæi patriâ pulsi, et exterres facti sunt, amant terræ ejus cineres tam impotenter ut miræ felicitatis loco habeant, si cui contigit

In the Byzantine Empire, if we may place any reliance, as we surely may, on the same authority, the numbers of the Jews had greatly diminished. Corinth contained 300 Jews; Thebes, 2000 silk-workers and dyers. Two hundred cultivated gardens at the foot of Parnassus. Patras and Lepanto contained a small number; Constantinople, 2000 silk-workers and merchants, with 500 Karaites. They inhabited part of Pera, were subject to the ordinary tribunals, and were often treated with great insult and outrage by the fanatic Greeks.

We pursue our dark progress to the West, where we find all orders gradually arrayed in fierce and implacable animosity against the race of Israel. Every passion was in arms against them. The monarchs were instigated by avarice; the nobility by the warlike spirit generated by chivalry; the clergy by bigotry; the people by all these concurrent motives. Each of the great changes which were gradually taking place in the state of the world seemed to darken the condition of this unhappy people, till the outward degradation worked inward upon their own minds. Confined to base and sordid occupations, they contracted their thoughts and feelings to their station. Individual and national character must be endowed with more than ordinary greatness if it can long maintain self-estimation after it has totally lost the esteem of mankind; the despised will usually become despicable. I proceed in a few brief sentences (all my limits will allow) to explain the effects of the more remarkable changes in society which developed

---

vel mortuo ibidem sepeliri, vel pugillo illius pulveris post fata conspergere, vel viventi ibidem degere." From the Dissertation of John a Lent de Pseudo- | Messiis, apud Ugolini, Thesaurus—a melancholy picture of wretched depression and frantic hope.

themselves during these dark ages, as far as they affect the character and condition of the Jewish people: 1st. The feudal system; 2nd. Chivalry; 3rd. The power of the clergy; 4th. The almost general adoption of the trade of money-lending and usury by the Jews themselves. I shall then pursue the course of time, which will lead us successively to the different countries in which the Jews were domiciliated.

I. In that singular structure, the feudal system, which rose like a pyramid from the villains or slaves attached to the soil to the monarch who crowned the edifice, the Jews alone found no proper place. They were a sort of outlying caste in the midst of society, yet scarcely forming part of it; recognised by the constitution, but not belonging to it; a kind of perpetual anomaly in the polity.[1] Their condition varied according to the different form which the feudal system assumed in different countries. In that part of Germany which constituted the Empire, the Jews, who were always of a lower order than their brethren in Spain and in the South of France, were in some respects under the old Roman law. By this law their existence was recognised, freedom of worship in their synagogues was permitted, and they were exempted from all military service. The last was a privilege not likely to be extorted from them. The noble profession of arms would have been profaned by such votaries.

The whole Jewish community were considered as

---

[1] Comp. Bengnot. Juifs d'Occident, Introduction, pp. 58, 59: "Quiconque ne trouvait pas sa place dans la hiérarchie féodale n'était rien.... Tels ont été les Juifs au sein de la féodalité, privés de tout espèce de droits quand chacun venait d'en acquérir; isolés au milieu d'une société qui avait réglé ses rangs à manière à n'oublier personne, partout ils s'taient traités comme étrangers, et dans ce temps l'étranger etait un ennemi."

special servants of the imperial chamber, *i.e.*, the Emperor alone could make ordinances affecting the whole body, and the whole body could demand justice or make appeal to their liege-lord. But this imperial right would not have been recognised by the great vassals as allowing the Emperor to seize, punish, plunder, or in any manner to interfere with the Jews domiciliated in their several feuds. In fact, while the community was subject to the liege-lord, the great feudatories and the free cities either obtained by charter, of which there are numerous instances, or assumed with a strong hand, or were persuaded by the Jews themselves to accept, dominion over the Israelitish inhabitants of their domains. The high and remote tribunal of the Emperor would afford inadequate protection for any oppressed Jew; he was glad to have a nearer and more immediate court of appeal. Travelling, as the Israelites perpetually did, from town to town, from province to province, the fierce baron might respect the passport, which was always absolutely necessary, of some powerful noble, some princely bishop, or some wealthy community of free burghers, while he would have smiled in scorn at the general imperial edict for allowing Jews to pass unmolested. In some cities, as in Worms, there were regular officers appointed to protect the Jews, who could not perform any of their ceremonies or processions in public without these guardians to shield them from the violence of the populace. In France and in England they were the property of the king. It will appear hereafter how the kings granted them to favourites, like lands, resumed them, and treated them altogether as goods pertaining to the Crown.[m]

[m] In France, according to Gul Brito, King Philip Augustus (see hereafter), who at one time only demanded for himself a fifth part of the debts due to

In Italy, at least in the South, besides the doubtful protection of the Emperor, they acknowledged the more powerful authority of the Pope. They were supposed to be in some manner under the special jurisdiction of the See of Rome.[n] In the Norman kingdom of Naples the feudal system soon makes its appearance. Sichelgaite, wife of Roger Duke of Apulia (son of Robert Guiscard), bequeaths the revenue of the Jews in the city of Salerno to the Church of Our Lady.[o] Duke Roger makes over the Jewry and all the Jews, except those of his proper domain, to the Archbishop of Salerno.[p] In the South of France they seem to have been considered as a kind of foreign vassals of the great feudatories; in the North, of the king. For while the edicts of the sovereign for their expulsion and readmission into the land were recognised in the North, they seem to have been executed either imperfectly or not at all in the South. The general

---

the Jews, might legally have taken the whole:—

"Et poterat totum sibi tollere si voluisset. Nec prejudicium super hoc fecissent eisdem, Tanquam servorum res et catalla suorum." Lib. 1.

[n] Thomas Aquinas (Summa 22, a. 10) lays down the axiom that the Jews are slaves of the Church (the Church in its widest sense), "quia cum ipsi Judæi sint servi Ecclesiæ." He proceeds to the question, whether if the slave of a Jew becomes Christian he becomes free without any price being paid for his redemption? It is answered in the affirmative, because the Jews themselves being slaves of the Church, the Church can dispose at her will of the property of her slaves. This applies to persons born in slavery,

or if, being infidels, they had been bought for the purpose of domestic slavery. If the slaves had been bought merely for the purpose of sale, they were to be brought to market in three months. This clause (if it does not refer to former times) seems to imply an active slave-trade still going on in Europe and in the hands of the Jews. I may take the opportunity of adding that Thomas Aquinas takes the milder view (that of Pope Gregory the Great), as to tolerating the religious rites of the Jews, and condemns the forcible baptism of Jewish infants against the will of their parents.

[o] Charter quoted from Pirrus, Sicilia Sacra.

[p] Charter of Duke Roger, Muratori, Antiq., vol. i.; Depping, p. 150.

effect of the feudal system was to detach the Jews entirely from the cultivation of the soil, though it worked more slowly in some countries—in the South of France and in Spain—than in others. They could not be lords, they were not serfs—they would not serve, or by the older law were exempted from military service to their lords. But this almost extra-legal protection under the great vassals was of course subject to every caprice of the lawless and ignorant petty chieftains who exercised these local sovereignties.[q] It was obtained only by proving to the liege-lord that it was his interest to protect; and his eyes, blinded by ignorance and perhaps bigotry, could only be opened to his real interests by immediate and palpable advantages. The Jew must pay largely for precarious protection; he was only tolerated as a source of revenue, and till almost his life-blood was drawn, it would be difficult to satisfy the inevitable demands of a needy and rapacious master. The Jew thus often became a valuable property; he was granted away, he was named in a marriage settlement,[r] he was bequeathed,[s] in fact he was pawned,[t]

---

[q] "A l'exemple des Rois, les Barons s'étalent appropriés les Juifs. Un Baron disait 'mes Juifs' comme il disait 'mes terres,' quand il énumérait ses revenues." Depping, p. 174.

[r] In a contract of marriage between Rostang de Pasquier and the daughter of Bernard Atto, Viscount of Nismes, Agde, and Beziers, "damus tibi et filiæ nostræ unum Judæum et unum burgensem in Biterris, Burgensem, Raymondum Durante, Judæum Benjamin, ambo cum tenazonibus eorum, et succersores eisdem, et cum eisdem tenemonibus." Here the Burgher and the Jew were granted in the same manner. Histoire de Languedoc, ii.; Preuves, 419. William of Montpellier adds to her dower all his Jews of Montpellier. Ibid. 476. Aymeric, Viscount of Narbonne, endowed his wife, A.C. 1087, with the city of Narbonne and the taxes on the Jews therein. Ibid. ii. 266; Preuves, p. 557.

[s] Raymond of Trincavel in his will bequeaths a Jew. Ibid. 550.

[t] The same Raymond of Trincavel pawns all his customary rights to payments in kind, of honey, canelle, and pepper, from the Jews on feast-days. It

he was sold, he was stolen.* Permission to the Jew to employ his industry for his own profit implied a share in that profit to the lord.* Even churchmen of the highest rank did not disdain such lucrative property. Louis, King of Provence, grants to the Archbishop of Arles all the possessions which his predecessors have held of former kings, including the Jews. Philip the Fair, after contesting the property of forty-three Jews, bought of his brother, Charles of Valois, all the Jews of his dominions and lordships. These Jews produced four hundred and thirty francs six sous every quarter; a Jew of Rouen, Samuel Viola, brought in to the same king three hundred livres a quarter.'

II. Chivalry, the parent of so much good and evil, both in its own age and in the spirit which has descended from it and has become infused into the institutions and character of modern Europe, was a source of almost unmitigated wretchedness to the Jew, unless in so far as the splendour which the knight might display in his arms and accoutrements was a lucrative source of traffic. The enterprising Jew often probably made a considerable

---

* Thibault, Count of Champagne, made a treaty with King Philip that neither should retain the Jews of the other. Some of Thibault's Jews had taken refuge from his oppressions in the territory of the King. His widow reclaimed them. There was a long negotiation about the property of Cresselin, a very rich Jew. Ibid.

* A modern writer has well expressed this: "Ils pouvaient donner un libre cours à leur industrie commerciale à la charge de partager de gré ou de force avec les Seigneurs les profits qu'ils en avaient retirés. C'est ce qui explique pourquoi les Seigneurs étaient si soigneux de conserver les Juifs qui leurs appartenaient. C'était la portion la plus productive de leur Seigneurie. Aussi la personne des Juifs était elle un objet de commerce: on se les vendait, on se les donnait, quelquefois les Seigneurs se les volaient les uns les autres, et ne permettaient plus au Juif qui se trouvait sur leurs terres de retourner dans celles de leurs maîtres." Bédarride, Les Juifs en Italie, en France, et en Espagne, p. 103.

' Other instances in Depping.

commission on the Milan corslet, the Damascus or
Toledo blade, the gorgeous attire which the knight
wore, or the jewels in which his lady glittered in the
tournament.* Magnificence was the fashion of the
times, and magnificence would often throw the impoverished noble into the power of the lowly man of
traffic. But the knight was bound by the tenure of his
rank to hate and despise the Jew. Religious fanaticism
was inseparable from chivalry. When Clovis, the King
of the Franks, embraced Christianity, while the pious
preacher was dilating on the sufferings of the crucified
Redeemer, the fiery convert sprang up and exclaimed,
"Had I and my brave Franks been there, they dared
not to have done it." The spirit of this speech was
that of the knighthood of the Middle Ages. What they
could not prevent they could revenge. The knight was
the servant of God, bound with his good sword to
protect His honour, and to extirpate all the enemies of
Christ and His Virgin Mother. Those enemies were all
unbelievers, more particularly the Jew, whose stiffnecked
obstinacy still condemned him; every Jew was as deadly
a foe as if he had joined in the frantic cry of *Crucify
Him! Crucify Him!* The only refuge of the Jew from the
hatred of the knight was in his contempt. The knight
was not suffered to profane his sword with such vile
blood; it was loftier revenge to trample him under foot.
But the animosity without the pride of this chivalrous
feeling descended to the lower orders; he who could
not presume to show his zeal for his Redeemer on the
person of a Moslemite unbeliever, contented himself

---

* This has not escaped the author of that noblest of historical romances, Ivanhoe, who on this point is as true to history as in the rest of the work he is full of the loftiest spirit of poetry.

with the humbler satisfaction of persecuting a Jew. In awful disregard of the one great Atonement, it was a prevailing feeling that men might wash away their sins by the blood of their infidel fellow-creatures. We shall see this inhuman sentiment dreadfully exemplified in the history of the Crusaders.

III. The power of the clergy, no doubt, tended greatly to increase this general detestation against the unhappy Jew. Their breath was never wanting to fan the embers of persecution. In that age of darkness, hatred of heresy and unbelief was the first article in the creed of him who taught the religion of love. But it is remarkable that not only were there splendid and redeeming instances of superiority to this unchristian spirit (they will hereafter be noticed), but it was only in the dark and remote parts of the Christian world that this total gloom prevailed. Light still shone in the centre. Of all European sovereigns, the Popes, with some exceptions, have pursued the most generous policy towards the Jews. Among the exceptions it is melancholy not to be able to inscribe the great name of Innocent III. without some reservation. Innocent's first edict about the Jews is one of calm and enlightened humanity. Though it opens with the usual ill-omened phrase concerning Jewish perfidy, yet it confirms all the favourable statutes of his predecessors, protects their synagogues, their cemeteries, their festivals from insult; condemns in strong terms compulsory baptism, and places their persons and property under the safeguard of the law.[a] But in later days Innocent could not behold their wealth, their power, their influence in France, without jealousy. In a letter to the Count of Nevers, with words tending to inflame

---

[a] Innocent. Epist. ii. 302

the worst passions, he declared them to be under the wrath of God, branded with the curse of Cain, guilty of the blood of the Redeemer.[b] He is indignant that they should be employed in finance and in the collection of taxes; imputes to the French nobles that they render more than equal justice to the Jews in their litigations with Christians about debts; he threatens the Count with the severest chastisement as guilty of this favour towards the enemies of God.[c] But if there be a shade of darkness on the bright fame of Innocent III., there is a gleam of light thrown on the dark character of Innocent IV., by his remarkable enactment in favour of the Jews of Germany.[d] In Italy, and even in Rome, the Jews have been more rarely molested than in other countries. They have long inhabited in Rome a separate quarter of the city, but this might have been originally a measure at least as much of kindness as contempt—a remedy against insult rather than an exclusion from society.[e] The adversaries of the Roman Church may ascribe this

---

[b] "Quanto magis ergo divinam formidare potes offensam quod faverem præstare non metuis, qui unigenitum Dei filium cruci affigere præsumpserunt, et adhuc a blasphemiis non quiescunt." Innocent III., Epist. x. 190.

[c] Among the strange charges brought by Innocent III. against the Jews is that they sell the milk of women for ordinary milk to nourish Christian children: "Itu similia Judæis mulieribus facientibus de lacte quod publice venditur pro parvulis nutriendis." They trampled the wine-presses in linen stockings, drew out the best wine for themselves, and sold the refuse to the Christians, even though that wine might be used for the Holy Eucharist.

[d] This calm, firm, enlightened edict will shortly appear at full length.

[e] The Ghetto, Judæa, Jodaica, Judæaria; hence the Venetian Giudecca; in Verona, La Zuecca. Muratori, Antiq. Ital. Dissert., &c. See the curious grant, quoted above, from Roger Duke of Apulia to the Archbishop of Salerno and his successors (A.D. 1090) of all the Judæa and Jews of that city, excepting those of his own domain or those whom he may have brought with him, "quod hoc ego tantum conduxero." There was a Giudecca in Constantinople. See the curious grant of the Doge of Venice, ibid.

to "the wisdom of the serpent," which discovered the advantages to be derived from the industry of the Jews, rather than to "the gentleness of the dove;" but where humanity is the result, let us not too invidiously explore its motives. Since the reign of Innocent II. (1130), at the accession of the Pope, the Jews have been permitted to approach the presence of the Pontiff, and to offer a copy of their Law.[f] The Pontiff receives their homage, and mildly expresses his desire that their understandings may be enlightened to perceive the hidden meaning of their own sacred volume. In the remote provinces it is to be feared that religious animosity was often aggravated by that hatred which unprincipled men feel towards those who possess the secret of their crimes. The sacred property of the Church was still often pawned by the licentious monks or clergy. No one would dare to receive the sacred pledge but a Jew, who thus frequently became odious, not only as an importunate creditor, but as exposing, by clamorous and public demands of payment, transactions never meant to meet the light. As early as the reign of the Emperor Henry I., among the pious Emperor's gifts to the Monastery of Monte Casino was a vest or altar-cloth, which he redeemed from a Jew, to whom it had been pledged for fifty gold pieces.[g] Guifred, Archbishop of Narbonne, in order to raise money to buy the Bishopric of Urgel for his brother, sold the crosses, the reliquaries, the vessels and all the plate of the Church of Narbonne to certain Jewish goldsmiths, who trafficked with them in Spain.[h] The Chapter

---

[f] The first act of this kind took place on the visit of Innocent II. to Paris. The Pope replies, "May God remove the veil which is now over your eyes!" Sugerii Ablat. Vit. Ludovic. Grossi; Bouquet, xii. 58.

The Jews had also a place at the coronation of the Emperors at Rome. Pertz, Leges, II. 192.

[g] Leo Ostiensis, II. 43.

[h] Hist. de Languedoc, II. p. 184.

of Strasburg complain that the Abbot Godfrey, of the Monastery of St. Leonard, had pledged the Missal, Mornlia Job (St. Gregory's book), a gilded cross and chandeliers, two altar-cloths, three copes, and a chasuble for five marks to the Jews of Einheim; a chalice, three chasubles, and four books for nine marks and twenty deniers to the Jews of Rodesheim.[1]

In many cases it was religion itself which seemed to the Christian clergy to impose the duty of persecution. In Beziers, at the beginning of the Holy Week (of the week during which the sufferings of the Redeemer on the cross and his divine patience were represented, in symbol and in language, to the eyes and to the heart of the believer, not forgetting his sublime words of prayer for his enemies, even the Jews), it was an ancient usage to pelt the Jews with stones—a perilous licence for a fierce rabble. The preacher mounted the pulpit, "You have around you," he said, "those who crucified the Messiah, who deny Mary the Mother of God. Now is the time when you should feel most deeply the iniquity of which Christ was the victim. This is the day on which our Prince has graciously given us permission to avenge this crime. Like your pious ancestors, hurl stones at the Jews, and show your sense of His wrongs by the vigour with which you resent them."[k] The bishop who put down this practice, Raymond of Trincavel, was accused of having been bribed: no other motive could be suggested for this act of humanity, justice, and piety.[l]

---

[1] Schoefflet, Alsatia Diplomatica, Note sub ann. 1215. Compare for England, Madox, Hist. of the Exchequer, p. 153.

[k] Ex Chronic. Gaufredi Vosiensis.

Apud Bouquet, xii. 194.

[l] Hist. de Languedoc, B. 488. The Jews of Beziers then lived in a separate quarter surrounded with walls.

IV. But avarice and usurious practices were doubtless charged, not without justice, against the race of Israel. In the nation and in the individual, the pursuit of gain as the sole object of life, must give a mean and sordid cast to the character. To acquire largely, whether fairly or not, was the highest ambition of the Jew, who rarely dared or wished to spend liberally. All the circumstances of the times contributed to this debasing change. The more extended branches of commerce, were almost entirely cut off. Their brethren in the East had lost their wealth; the navigation of the Mediterranean was interrupted by the Norman pirates; the slave-trade had entirely ceased or was prohibited, as well by the habits of the times as by law. In the cities and free towns they were excluded by the jealous corporate spirit from all share in the burghers' privileges. The spirit of the age despised traffic, and the merchant is honourable only where he is held in honour. The Jews no doubt possessed great wealth; what was extorted from them is ample proof of the fact, and some of them by stealth enjoyed it; but even the wealthiest and most liberal were often obliged to put on the sordid demeanour and affect the miserable poverty of the poor pedler of their own nation, whose whole stock consisted in his pack of the cheapest portable articles.

This necessity of perpetual deception could not but have a baneful effect on the manners and mind of the people. Their chief trade seems to have been moneylending, of which, till they were rivalled and driven out of the open market by the Lombards, they were the sole possessors. This occupation was not likely to diminish either their own sordid meanness or their unpopularity. The ignorance of the age denounced all interest for money alike as usury. The Jew was judged out of his own Law, and all the Scriptural denunciations against usury were brought forward, especially by the clergy, to condemn a traffic of which they felt and submitted to the necessity. The condemnation of usury by the Church, as unlawful, contributed, with the violence of the times, to render the payment of the usurer's bond extremely insecure. He argued, not unfairly, that the more precarious, the greater ought to be his gains: he took refuge in fraud from violence and injustice. Society was at war with the Jew. Some sudden demand of tribute, or some lawless plunderer, would sweep away at once the hard-wrung earnings of years;[*] the Jew, therefore, still practised slow and perpetual reprisals, and reimbursed himself from the wants of the needy, for his losses from the violent. Demolish his secret hive, like the ant, the model suggested by his wise king, he would reconstruct it again, and ever at the expense of his enemy. It was, generally throughout the world, the Christian, who, according to our universal Master of nature, would spit upon and spurn the Jew; and the Jew, who, when he found his advantage, would have the pound of flesh nearest the heart of his bondsman. It was a contest of religious zeal which had degenerated into the blindest bigotry, and associated itself with the most ferocious and unchristian passions, against industry and patience, which had made a forced but intimate alliance with the most sordid craft and the most unfeeling avarice, to the utter extinction of every lofty principle of integrity and honour.

---

[*] Montesquieu thus observes of the Middle Ages: "Le commerce passa à une nation pour lors couverte d'infamie, et bientôt il ne fut distingué des usures les plus affreuses, des monopoles, de la levée des subsides, et de toutes les manières malhonnêtes d'acquérir de l'argent. Les Juifs, enrichis par leurs exactions, étaient pillés par les princes avec la même tyrannie: chose qui consoloit le peuple, et ne les soulageoit pas." Esprit des Lois, xxi. 20.

Attempts were constantly made to restrict the exactions of the Jews from the poor: they were prohibited from taking in pawn the tools of the artisan and the implements of husbandry. By a law of Philip Augustus the interest on loans was limited to two deniers per week on the livre: this would amount to above forty per cent. Later the rate of interest was doubled, for it was found that the debtor was compelled by the Jew to inscribe a larger sum than he actually borrowed. Interest on debts was generally limited to the year, to prevent, —which it did not do—all accumulation. The weekly interest was manifestly intended for the debts of the poor. There is a very curious parchment roll in the French royal archives,[a] according to which (probably during one of the expulsions of the Jews) certain inhabitants of the small town of Vitry, about five hundred, claimed sums said to have been extorted from them by the Jews to the amount of eight hundred and forty-four livres nine sous. This may show how widely these exactions spread, and how they affected the poorest classes of society. It shows, too, the utter insecurity of all these debts, and that the Jews, almost the only holders of that rare commodity, money, could hardly be expected to refrain from making as rich a harvest as possible during their short gleam of broken sunshine.

It is time to proceed to our melancholy task, the rapid picture of the Iron Age of Judaism in the West. The first dark scene in our tragic drama is laid in a country where we should least expect to find it, the Arabian kingdom of Grenada. It took place when the Golden Age was in all its brightness, a foreshadowing of darkness to come. It was brought on by the imprudent

---

[a] Cited by M. Depping. Compare his book, p. 180.

zeal of the Jews. The nation was in the highest degree of prosperity and esteem: R. Samuel Levi was at once prince of his own nation and vizier of the king, Mohammed ben Gehwar, when one of the Wise Men, Joseph Hallevi, attempted to make converts among the Moslemites. The stern orthodoxy of Islamism took fire, the rash teachers were hanged, the race persecuted, and fifteen hundred families, of whom it was said that he who had not heard of their splendour, their glory, and their prosperity, had heard nothing, sank into disgrace and destitution.[o]

A few years after, the Christian monarch, Ferdinand the Great, as though determined not to be outdone in religious zeal by his rival, the Moslemite king, before he undertook a war against the Moors, determined to let loose the sword against the Jews in his own territories. To their honour, the clergy interfered, prevented the massacre, and secured not only the approval of their own consciences, but likewise that of the Pope, Alexander the Second, who, citing the example of his predecessor, Gregory the Great, highly commended their humanity.[p] The sterner Hildebrand assumed a different tone; he rebuked Alfonso the Sixth for having made laws restoring to the Jews certain rights, submitting, as the Pontiff declared, the Church to the synagogue of devils.[q] During this whole period of contest between the

---

[o] Basnage, ix. 5. This was near a century before the persecution from which Maimonides took refuge in Egypt.

[p] "Noverit prudentia vestra nobis placuisse quod Judæos qui sub vestra potestate habitant, tutati estis ne occiderentur: non enim gaudet Deus effusione sanguinis, neque lætatur perditione malorum." Alexander II. Berengario, Vice-Comiti Narbonensi (circa 1061).

[q] "Dilectionem tuam monemus ut in terrâ tuâ Judæos Christianis dominari, vel supra eos potestatem exercere, ulterius nullatenus sinas. Quid est enim Judæis Christianos supponere vel hos eorum judicio subjicere, nisi ecclesiam

Christians for the recovery of Spain and the Mussulmen in their desperate defence of their conquests, the Jews stood on a perilous neutral ground. Their creed was obnoxious in different degrees to both. If they could have lived a peaceful life, they were disposed to submit quietly to the conqueror: but their wealth tempted the cupidity of both; both were inclined to employ them in the unpopular but lucrative functions of financiers and tax-gatherers; and their own propensities to gain induced them to undertake these offices under Christian or Mohammedan rulers.

Of all people the zealous Jews must have beheld with the greatest amazement the preparations for the Crusades, when the whole Christian world, from the king to the peasant, was suddenly seized with a resolution to conquer the Holy Land of *their* fathers, in order that they might be masters of the sepulchre of the crucified Nazarene. Though they had been so long exiled from that holy soil, though the few Jews who dwelt in Palestine were but as strangers in the land, Jewish tradition had still clung, as has been said, with undying fondness to their rightful ownership, to the hopes of returning to that blessed country. Their restoration to Judæa, to Jerusalem, was to be the great work—the final triumph of the Messiah, whensoever or wheresoever He should appear. And now of that land to breathe the air of which was wisdom, to tread the soil of which seemed to the living happiness, to the buried a share in the first resurrection, the Christians were about to usurp the lordship. The followers of Jesus,

---

Dei supprimere et Satanæ synagogam exaltare, et dum inimicis Christi velis placere, ipsum Christum contemnere." | Greg. VII. Epist., apud Baronius, sub. ann. 1080.

the false Messiah, were to take possession of the realm which awaited the coming of the true Messiah.

But the times must have opened a most extensive field for traffic and usury; and no doubt the Jews, suppressing their astonishment, did not scruple to avail themselves of such a golden opportunity of gain. Nothing was too valuable, too dear, or too sacred, but that it might be parted with to equip the soldier of the Cross. If the more prudent and less zealous monarchs, like our William the Second, or nobles or churchmen, profited by the reckless ardour of their compatriots to appropriate, at the lowest prices, their fair fields and goodly inheritances, no doubt the Jews wrung no unprofitable bargains from the lower class of more needy and as reckless adventurers. Arms and money must be had;[r] and the merchant or usurer might dictate his own terms.

But little did this prudent people foresee the storm which impended over them.[s] The nation was widely

---

[r] Even towards the close of the Crusades the princes, knights, even the clergy, were dependent on Jewish money-lenders for the sums requisite for their own equipment and that of their followers. The Lateran Council, which is the fullest exposition of the privileges of the Crusaders, contains the following canon:—"Judæos vero ad remittendas usuras per sæcularem compelli præcipimus potestatem, et donec illis remiserint ab universis Christi fidelibus per excommunicationis sententiam eis omnino communio denegetur. His autem qui Judæis debita solvere nequeunt in præsenti, sic Principes sæculares utili dilatione provideant: quod post iter arreptum, usquequo de eorum obitu vel reditu certissime cognoscatur, usurarum incommoda non incurrant, compulsis Judæis proventus pignorum, quos interim ipsi perceperint in sortem, expensis deductis necessariis, computare, cum hujusmodi beneficium non multum videatur habere dispendii, quod solutionem sic prorogat, quod debitum non absorbet." Manal, Concil. xril. p. 1097, et seqq.

[s] The Jews had been accused, at an earlier period, the beginning of the 11th century, of stimulating the persecutions of the Christian pilgrims to Jerusalem by the Mohammedan Sultans Azed and Hakim in Egypt. These sovereigns had destroyed the

dispersed in Germany; some statutes of King Ladislaus show their existence in Hungary; in Bohemia they had rendered good service, and lived on amicable terms with the Christians; in Franconia they were numerous; but their chief numbers and wealth were found in the flourishing cities along the banks of the Moselle and the Rhine. When the first immense horde of undisciplined fanatics of the lowest order, under the command of Peter the Hermit and Walter the Penniless, and under the guidance of a goose and a goat, assembled near the city of Treves, a murmur rapidly spread through the camp, that while they were advancing to recover the sepulchre of their Redeemer from the Infidels, they were leaving behind worse unbelievers, the murderers of the Lord.[1] In the words of Jewish tradition, no doubt generally faithful in its record of their calamities, "the abominable Germans and French rose up against them, people of a fierce countenance that have no respect to the persons of the old, neither have they mercy upon the young, and they said, 'Let us be revenged for our Messiah upon the Jews that are among us, and let us destroy them from being a nation, that the name of Israel may be had no more in remembrance; so shall they change their glory and be like unto us; then will we go to the East.'"[2] With one impulse the Crusaders rushed to the city, and began a relentless pillage, violation, and

Christian temple over the Holy Sepulchre. Cedrenus, II. 486 (Edit. Bonn); Zonaras. Radulph Glaber has a story of the persecutions of the Jews at Orleans on account of (premature) information given to the Mussulmen of an intended crusade. Compare Le Beau, Hist. du Bas Empire, xiv. p. 202.

[2] "Nos Dei hostes, inquiunt, Orientem versus, longis terrarum tractibus transmissis, desideramus aggredi, cum ante oculos sint Judæi, quibus inimicitior extitit gens nulla Dei." Guibert Abbas, ad ann. 1095.

massacre of every Jew they could find. In this horrible day men were seen to slay their own children, to save them from the worse usage of these savages. Women, having deliberately tied stones round themselves that they might sink, plunged from the bridge, to save their honour and escape baptism. Their husbands had rather send them to the bosom of Abraham than leave them to the mercy, or rather the lustful cruelties, of the Christians." The rest fled to the bishop's palace as a place of refuge. They were received by the bishop, Engelbert, with these words:—" Wretches, your sins have come upon you; ye who have blasphemed the Son of God and calumniated His Mother. This is the cause of your present miseries—this, if ye persist in your obduracy, will destroy you body and soul for ever." He reproached them with their disregard of Daniel's prophecy of our Lord's coming, and promised protection to their persons, and respect to their property, on their conversion and baptism. Micha, the head of the Jews, mildly requested instruction in the Christian tenets; the bishop repeated a short creed; the Jews, in the agony of terror, assented. The same bloody scenes were repeated in Metz, in Spiers, in Worms, in Mentz, in Cologne. It was the Sabbath in Spiers; ten were slain, a woman killed herself to escape pollution. The bishop (all bishops were not like Engelbert of Treves) saved the rest, for, says Jewish tradition, "he had compassion on them, and he delivered

---

* Brower, Ann. Trevirensis, l. p. 571, describes this scene, and would persuade his readers that the Jews were driven to desperation only by their fears. He says nothing of the previous massacre. The Jews "non parcerent ætati, cui etiam Christiani pepercissent." The affair at the bridge he turns against the Jews: "Liberos parentes letho ipsi potius quam offerri baptismo vellent stolidè jactitabant."

them out of the power of the enemy." The bishop is accused, not by the Jews, of having received a large bribe for his mercy. Did his Christian flock suppose that his humanity could not be accounted for but by his venality? In Worms the Jews took refuge in the bishop's palace; all their houses were pulled down; all that had not escaped were put to the sword. The books of the Law were trampled under foot; none were spared but children and sucklings, who were forcibly baptized, in Jewish language, "defiled with the proud water." Many killed themselves; the brother slew his brother, the neighbour his neighbour, the father his sons and daughters, the bridegroom his bride, the husband the wife of his bosom. The bishop's house was surprised; all, except a very small remnant, fell by the hands of the murderers or their own. About eight hundred perished; a young Levite stabbed a noble kinsman of the bishop, and of course was cut to pieces. In Mentz again they fled to the bishop's palace, but in vain; a massacre of 1300 took place; the women killed themselves, and some of the old men covered themselves with their praying garments, and said, "He is the Rock; his works are perfect." Sixty lay concealed in the bishop's treasure-house; they fled to the Rheingau to their brethren there, were pursued and slain, all but two, Uri and Isaac, who were forcibly baptized. Isaac's two daughters were also forcibly baptized. Isaac slew his polluted daughters, lit a fire in his house, and offered a burnt offering as an atonement; then the two went into the synagogue, and, as they saw the flame arise, slew themselves. In Cologne the terror was overwhelming, but here the power of the bishop, again the protector of the Jews, was more equal to his humanity. The synagogues were sacked, the books of the Law trampled in the dust; but the bishop sent them into the neighbouring villages with directions that they should be well treated. One obstinate man, probably a Rabbi, Isaac, refused to fly; he was dragged into the church, where he spat upon and blasphemed the Image; he was put to death, and his death, with that of a woman, are the only murders recorded at Cologne in the Jewish Chronicle.[x] The locust band passed on;[y] everywhere the tracks of the Crusaders were deeply marked with Jewish blood. A troop, under Count Emico, offered the same horrid sacrifices to the God of Mercy, in the cities on the Maine and the Danube, even as far as Hungary, where the in-

---

[x] Many of these incidents are from the very curious Chronicle of Rabbi Joseph ben Joshua ben Meir, the Sphardi, translated from the Hebrew for the Oriental Fund by C. H. F. Bialloblotsky, London, 1835. The names of other cities and towns in the book of R. Joshua are so disguised that it is impossible to make them out. Some of the scenes, especially that in Mirah, are very striking. It is curious to compare the general tone of the monkish annalists of the Crusades: "Per orbem universum omnium Christianorum consensu decretum est, ut omnes Judæi ab illorum terris vel civitatibus funditus pellerentur. Hique universi odio habiti, expulsi de civitatibus, alii gladiis trucidati, alii fluminibus necati, diversisque mortium generibus interempti. Nonnulli etiam sese diversâ clade interemerunt." Itadulph. The Chronicon Virdun. says, "Quanquam a multis improbetur factum et religioni adversari judicetur." Apud Bouquet, xiii. That they sent all these Jews to hell (ad Tartara demittunt) is a common phrase. The number of the Jews massacred is of course variously stated. Some Jewish accounts give only 5000, seemingly heads of families. Aventinus (Annal. Bohem.) gives 12,000 in Bavaria and the cities on the Danube. The Add. to Lambert of Aschaffenborg thus relates the massacre at Mentz: "Apud Moguntiam vero utriusque sexus Judæi numero mille et quatuor decem interfecti sunt, et maxima pars civitatis arsâ est. Judæi qui per diversas provincias, metu compellente, Christiani facti sunt, iterum a Christianitate paulatim recesserunt." Sub ann. 1097. Compare Sig. Gembl. sub ann. 1096.

[y] It is curious that R. Joshua (my book was written before the appearance of the translation) uses the same image "The locusts have no honey, and yet go they forth, all of them, by bands." Prov. xxx. 27, p. 30.

fluence of the king, Coloman, could not arrest his violence.* . How little horror these massacres excited may be judged from the coolness with which they are related by the faithful representatives of the spirit of the times, the monkish historians. The Emperor Henry the Fourth alone saw their atrocity; in an edict issued from Ratisbon, he permitted such Jews as had been baptized by force to resume their religion, and ordered their property to be restored. At this period many took refuge in Silesia and Poland.

Nor were the persecutions of the Jews in the First Crusade confined to Europe. On the capture of Jerusalem by Godfrey of Boulogne, all the Jews in the Holy City—so reports Jewish tradition—were put to the sword by the devout worshippers of Him who wept over the foreseen doom of the children of Jerusalem on its first capture.*

Half a century elapsed for the Jews to multiply again their devoted race, and to heap up new treasures to undergo their inalienable doom of pillage and massacre. A second storm was seen gathering in the distance; and, like a bird of evil omen, which predicts the tempest, the monk Rodolph passed through the cities of Germany to preach the duty of wreaking vengeance on all the enemies of God. The terrible cry of "HEP," the signal for the massacre of the Jews (supposed to be an abbreviation of "Hierosolyma est perdita"—*Jerusalem is lost*) ran through the cities of the Rhine. The Jews knew who were included under the fatal designation of Christ's enemies; some made a timely retreat, but

---

* Maclus represents less favourably the conduct of the King of Hungary. "Resque Ungarorum, persuasus principibus hoc facere, non restituit." c. xv.
* Dr. Zunz, Notes to Benjamin of Tudela, pp. 89 and 896.

frightful havoc took place in Cologne, Mentz, Worms, Spiers, and Strasburg. They found an unexpected protector, the holy St. Bernard,[b] who openly reprobated these barbarities, and, in a letter to the Bishop of Spiers, declared that the Jews were neither to be persecuted nor put to death, nor even driven into exile. Jewish tradition does justice to St. Bernard: "And he [God] sent after this Belial [Rodolph the Monk] the Abbot St. Bernard from Clairvaux, a city that is in Tzarphath [France]. And he called also after their manner, saying, 'Let us go up into Zion, to the sepulchre of the Messiah. But take thou heed that thou speak to the Jews neither good nor bad, for whosoever toucheth them is like as if he had touched the apple of the eye of Jesus; for they are His flesh and bone; and my disciple Rodolph has not spoken aright— for of them it is said in the Psalms, "Slay them not, lest my people forget."' . . . . And he took no ransom of the Jews, for he spake good of Israel from his heart. . . . . If it had not been for the compassion of the Lord that He had sent this priest, there would have none escaped or remained of these. Blessed be he that ransometh and delivereth!" In other places, to which St. Bernard's influence did not extend, the Jews bought security at a heavy price.[c] If in truth St. Bernard was

---

[b] I have elsewhere observed the curious fact, that of the biographers of St. Bernard among the moderns are two converted Jews, Neander and the Père Ravaignan.

[c] "And in other places the Jews gave their silver and their gold to deliver their lives from destruction; they withheld nothing from them of all they demanded, and the Lord delivered them." R. Joshua, p. 119. In Cologne an aged Jew refused to submit to baptism. A fierce Crusader struck off his head, placed it on the roof of a house, and trampled the body under foot. The Jews appealed to the mayor; the body was removed and buried in their cemetery. They purchased of the bishop, by pledging their houses and all their property in the

disposed to mercy, other churchmen, who approached the nearest to St. Bernard in influence and authority, spoke a different language. Peter the Venerable, the Abbot of Clugny, addressed a letter to the King of France, denouncing the wickedness of sparing the most detestable and impious Jews, while they wage war on the less detestable and impious Saracens.[d] He would not condemn them to a general massacre (such was his mercy), but in pure charity only to general pillage. For their great crime, according to Peter the Venerable, besides their obduracy and blindness to the Saviour, was not their cruel and grinding usury, but the receiving of stolen goods, the furniture and sacred vessels of the Church, which they treated with contumely so dreadful that it might not be thought of, much less described in words.[e] Peter arraigns a royal statute, an antiquated

---

city, the strong castle of Wolkenberg, in which they defied the wild assaults of the rabble. A murder was committed on two young Jews near Wolkenberg. The Jews bought of the bishop the surrender of the murderer. They put out his eyes; he died in three days. The Jews' fierce exultation of triumph was, "Thus may all thy enemies be destroyed, O Lord!" p. 121.

[d] "Sed quid proderit inimicos Christianae spei in exteris aut remotis finibus insequi ac persequi, si nequam blasphemi, *longè Saracenis deteriores* Judæi, non longè a nobis, sed in medio nostro, tam libere, tam audacter, Christum, cunctaque Christiana Sacramenta, impune blasphemaverint, conculcaverint, deturpaverint.... Si detestandi sunt Saraceni (quia quamvis Christum de Virgine, ut nos, na-

tum fatentur, multaque nobiscum de ipso sentiunt, tamen Deum, Deique filium quod magis est, negant, mortemque ipsius ac resurrectionem, in quibus tota summa salutis nostra est, diffitentur), quantum execrandi et odio habendi sunt Judæi, qui nihil prorsus de Christo vel fide Christianâ sentientes, Ipsum virgineum partum, cunctaque redemptionis humanæ sacramenta abjiciunt, blasphemant, subsannant!"

[e] "Non inquam ut occidantur admoneo, sed ut congruente sequitiæ suæ modo puniantur, exhortor. Et quid congruentius ad puniendos illos impios modus, quam ille quo et damnatur iniquitas, et *adjuvatur charitas*. Quid justius quam ut his quæ fraudulenter lucrati sunt, destituantur; quæ nequiter furati sunt, ut furibus, et quod pejus est, hucusque audacibus et im-

and diabolic statute,' which secured the Jews in the possession of such property, and did not compel them to declare from whence they had obtained it. The Abbot forgot the ordinances which had so frequently prohibited the clergy from selling or pawning the sacred treasures. The law may have been intended to shield such ecclesiastics from shame and punishment. With the zealous Peter these men perhaps were no better than thieves, thus alienating the inalienable property of their churches. His conclusion is⁵ that it was just that the Jews should be plundered without scruple or remorse, in order that the expense of a war against one race of Infidels should be maintained by the ill-gotten and justly confiscated wealth of another race

punitis, auferantur! Quod loquor omnibus notum est; non enim de simplici agricultura, non de legali militia, non de quolibet honesto et utili officio, horrea sua frugibus, cellaria vino, marsupia nummis, arcas auro vel argento cumulant, quantum de his, quæ ut dixi dolose Christicolis subtrahunt; de his quæ furtim furibus empta vili pretio res carissimas comparant." He goes on to say that the Jews bought of thieves censers, crosses, consecrated challices; that they insulted these holy vessels. ". . . . quia, ut a veracibus viris audivi, eis uthbus cœlestis illa vasa ad ejusdem Christi nostrumque dedecus nefandum illi applicant, quos horrendum est cogitare, et detestandum dicere." Petri Venerab. Epist.

ᶠ " Insuper ut tam nefarium furum Judæorumque commercium tutius esset, lex jam vetusta, sed vere diabolica, ab ipsis Christianis principibus procuratit, ut si res ecclesiastica, vel quod deterius aliquod sacrum vas apud Judæum repertum fuerit, nec rem sacrilego furto possessam reddere, nec usquam furem Judæus prodere compellatur. Manet inultum scelus detestabile in Judæo, quod horrida morte suspendii ponitur in Christiano. Pinguescit deinde et deliciis affluit Judæus, unde laqueo suspenditur Christianus."

ᵍ Auferatur ergo vel ex maxima parte imminuatur Judækarum divitiarum male parta pinguedo; et Christianos excercitus, qui ut Saracenos expugnet, pecuniis vel terris propriis Christi Domini sui amore non parcit, Judæorum thesauris tam male acquisitis non parcat. Reservetur eis vita, auferatur pecunia, ut per dextras Christianorum adjutas pecunia blasphemantium Judæorum expugnetur infidelium audacia Saracenorum. Hæc tibi, benigne Rex, scripsi, amore Christi, tuique atque exercitus Christiani." Epist. Petri Venerab. apud Bouquet, xv. p. 641.

of Infidels. Throughout this Crusade the absence of the Emperor Conrad in the Holy Land deprived the Jews of their legal protector, so that many cruel acts of individual murder took place, despite the merciful intervention of St. Bernard and the Pope, at Mentz, at Bacharach, at Aschaffenburg (where a woman drowned herself to avoid baptism), at Wurtzburg, where the rabble accused them of drowning a young man who was made a martyr. The army passed on, as the Jews record with triumph, to perish by plague, famine, and the sword. "The Jews returned to dwell in quiet throughout the land of Ashkinaz [Germany]." An attempt to raise the old terrible cry of Hep, before the Crusade of Frederick Barbarossa, was put down by the stern vigour of the Emperor. The Jews testified their gratitude by lavish presents.[b] The Pope, Eugenius the Third, espoused the same humane part, and it has been conjectured that his release of all debts due to Jewish usurers, was a kind of charitable injustice, to diminish the general odium against this unhappy people. The turbulent Rodolph was shut up in his cloister.

These atrocities, however (and I cannot lament my want of space, which prevents me from entering more at large into such and similar crimes), were the acts of a fanatic mob in the highest state of religious intoxication. We must now behold a mighty sovereign and his barons uniting in deeds, if less sanguinary, not less unjust. Both in the North and South of France, the Jews were numerous and wealthy.[i] They boast that

---

[b] R. Joshua, 186.

[i] See the payments made by the Jews to the Bishop of Beziers, Hist. de Languedoc, ii. 293 (Preuves, 209). William, Viscount of Montpellier, grants the appointment of a Jew (or Saracen) as Bayle in Montpellier, p. 442 (A.C. 1146). Preuves, p. 46. Lands pledged to Jews, ib. (Preuves, p. 101).

they were as numerous as when they went forth from Egypt.[k] In the South they were the most flourishing, they were more mingled with the people, were not entirely dispossessed of their landed property, and were sometimes called to manage the finances of the great feudatories. In Narbonne, according to Benjamin of Tudela, who visited them, they held great domains under the protection of the princes of the land. In Beziers, in Montpellier, they still drove a most prosperous traffic. They had great establishments in Lunel, where there was a famous synagogue, in St. Gilles, in Arles, in Carcassonne. In Toulouse, Roger, Viscount of Carcassonne, had a Jew for his minister of finance. In these, and other southern cities, lived their most distinguished Rabbis, and flourished their most prosperous schools. In the North they were spread throughout the country; hardly a large city or town was without them. Their synagogues in Troyes, Dijon, Macon, vied in the learning of their Rabbis, and in the wealth of the communities, with Beziers, Montpellier, and Marseilles. While the Christians were but scantily instructed in the cathedral schools, the Jewish seminaries of learning flourished in many cities. But Paris was their head-quarters. Jewish tradition and the monkish Christian annals agree in their numbers, their wealth, their luxury; they had numerous households, domestic servants, "worshippers of strange gods;" the Christianity of those days was idolatry to the Jews. That they possessed, in Paris and its neighbourhood, lands, houses, meadows, vineyards, barns, and other immoveable property, was sadly

---

[k] "Tantus vero tamque innumerabilis in illis regnis propemodum Judæorum numerus fuit ut altero tanto plures fuisse diseris quam olim ex Egypto egressi sunt." Schevet Judah, 156.

shown when the edict for the confiscation of all these possessions was issued. It is said by the monkish writers that they owned half Paris.[1]

But public detestation lowered upon them with a threatening aspect. Stories were now propagated, and found an easy belief among ignorant and prejudiced minds, of the most blasphemous and sanguinary crimes perpetrated by the Jews. A renegade monk accused them of intelligence with the infidel sovereigns of Palestine. No deaths could take place under mysterious circumstances but, if Jews were to be found, the Jews were guilty of the murder. It was generally believed that they often decoyed Christian children into their houses, and crucified them alive;[m] that, by bribery or

---

[1] "And the Jews multiplied in Paris in those days, and waxed very mighty in riches and goods, and they took unto themselves man-servants and maid-servants, the daughters of strange gods, from every one whom they chose." R. Joseph, p. 191.

"Siquidem .... multitudo maxima Judæorum Parisiis habitabat, quæ de diversis orbis partibus ob pacis diuturnitatem illuc convenerat." Vincent de Beauvais, quoted in the Fortalitium Fidei, p. 193. "Ubi lougam habentes conversationem in tantum ditati sunt quod fere meditatem totius civitatis sibi vindicaverant." Vincent de Beauvais and Rigord (Bouquet, xvii.) use the same words.

[m] It was the same in Germany. See in R. Joshua, where they are accused of throwing a child into the water (in that case there was no child), and of having drowned a Gentile girl who had fallen into the Rhine near Biberich.

When they arrived at Cologne all who were in the Jewish barges were thrown into the river, and there was a general cry to force the Jews to be baptised. It must be added that the Emperor Frederick Barbarossa seized the opportunity of fining the city of Cologne 500 pieces of gold, the bishop 4200. p. 178.

"Cartissimè enim" (so writes an author quoted in the Fortalitium Fidei) "compartum est quod omni anno in qualibet provincia sortes nittuntur, quæ civitas vel oppidum Christianorum sanguinem aliis civitatibus tradat." "And they began to hate them more, and found false accusations against them, saying that every year they nailed a Gentile on the cross in a cave; and so they embittered their lives." R. Joshua. The monk Rigord is even more minute and particular. He says that the Jews every year, at Easter, descended into their caves, and

theft, they would obtain possession of the consecrated Host, and submit it to every kind of insult. Yet both king and nobles felt that to this odious race they stood in the humiliating relation of debtors. The lavish expenditure caused by the Crusades, and the heavy exactions of the government, made it necessary to raise money on any terms.* Their only alternative lay between the Jews and the few Lombard money-lenders, whom St. Bernard seems to mean when he denounces certain Christians as more extortionate usurers than the Jews. Thus the Jews had a hold upon almost all the estates of the country; they had mortgages on half Paris—this perhaps was their ownership—and scarcely any one but had some article in pawn; even the clergy, whose pleasures were not without expense, had still committed vessels, reliquaries, even reliques, to the profane hands of these relentless extortioners, who probably scrupled little to wring the greatest profit from the general distress.* These vessels they were charged with misusing in the most revolting and contemptuous

---

perpetrated the cruel and impious rite. Rigord, in Bouquet, or in Guizot, Coll. des Mémoires.

* See the remarkable letter of Innocent III., quoted above, to the Count of Nevers. Not only were the widows and orphans despoiled of their inheritance, but the Church of her tithes, "Cum Judæi castella et villas detineant occupata, qui ecclesiarum prælatis de parochiali jure contemnant penitus respondere." Epist. x. 190. Also to the Bishop of Auxerre, "Judæi qui cum villas, prædia et vineas emerant decimas ex eisdem ecclesiis et personis ecclesiasticis debitas reddere contradicunt." Epist. x. 61.

* "Sed et vasa sacra pro instante ecclesiæ necessitate sibi nomine vadei supposita tam viliter tractabant, quod eorum infantes in calicibus oflas in vino fartas comedebant, et cum eis bibebant." Quoted in Fortalitium Fidei. "And they laid against them false accusations, saying, "Ye take the silver vessels and the goblets which are in the churches as a pledge, and despise them, and give to drink out of them unto your sons and your daughters for the sake of displaying them."" R. Joshua, p. 191.

manner; they made the chalices serve as porringers for their children. The Jews stood to the rest of society something in the relation of the patricians in early Rome and in Athens to the impoverished commonalty, but without their power; it is said, indeed, that they imprisoned their debtors in their own houses.[p] Such was the state of affairs on the accession of the ambitious Philip Augustus. The predecessor of Philip Augustus, Louis VII., though he had passed a severe law against Jewish converts to Christianity who had relapsed to Judaism, punishing them with death and mutilation, yet had been so mild to the Jews as to merit a rebuke from Pope Alexander III. It is his reproach by a historian of the day, that, though a defender of the Church, yet from excessive cupidity he had favoured the Jews too much, and given them privileges contrary to the laws of God and of the realm.[q] During the youth of Philip Augustus, it is said that a Jew (whether, as is often the case, the frequent mention of a crime had excited some man of disordered imagination to perpetrate it) had crucified a youth named Richard at Pontoise;[r] the body was

---

[p] "Alii Parisiis in domibus Judæorum sub juramento adstricto, quasi in carcere tenebantur captivi." Rigord, apud Bouquet, xvii.

[q] Apud Bouquet, xii. p. 186.

[r] "Saint Richard, dont le corps repose dans l'Eglise de S. Innocent des Champeaux à Paris, fut ainsi égorgé et crucifié par les Juifs, et merité par ce martyre de monter dans le royaume des cieux." Rigord, in Guizot, p. 15.

Just seems to admit the truth of the crucifixion of Richard of Pontoise, I know not on what grounds. I can conceive such things at a later period of the persecutions. At such later period Rabbi Joseph acknowledges that in the city of Nons (?) in Germany, a Hebrew, a foolish man, met a Gentile girl, and slaughtered her and cast her into the midst of a well, before the face of the sun, *for he raved with madness*. The result was a rising of the people, in which the murderer was killed; many Jews were broken on the wheel, among them the brothers of the murderer. His mother

brought to Paris, and wrought many miracles. No sooner had Philip ascended the throne, than he took a short way to relieve his burthened subjects, by an edict which confiscated all debts due to the Jews, and commanded them to surrender all pledges in their hands.[*] Among the effects a golden crucifix, and a Gospel, adorned with precious stones, were found. Soon after this the Jews were peacefully assembled in their synagogues on the Sabbath (February 14),[1] when suddenly all these buildings were surrounded by the royal troops, the Jews dragged to prison, while the officers took possession of their houses. A new edict followed (April), which confiscated all their unmoveable goods, houses, vineyards, fields, barns, wine-presses, to the use

---

was buried alive. The bishop exacted a heavy fine from all the Jews. p. 219.

[*] The hatred of the Jews to Philip Augustus was indelible. R. Joseph thus announces his birth: "And in his old age he [Louis VII.] begat a son, and he called his name Philip, and by surname Deodatus, and others called him Augustus; and he was an oppressor of the Jews from his birth, and from the womb, and from his conception." p. 141.

"And Philip (he came to the throne at fifteen) was pleasing in the sight of his servants, because he was an oppressor of the Jews. And when he was chosen, he executed judgements among them, for they accused them wrongfully; but every year they shed innocent blood, and Israel was brought very low." p. 170.

[1] "Venerabilis ergo Philippus rex und vivente patre dio mente clausum gestaverat et ob patris reverentiam perficere formidaverat, in ipso regni initio zelo Dei flammatus, aggressus est. Nam ad ipsius mandatum capti sunt Judæi per totam Franciam in Synagogis suis in Sabbato." Vincent. Bellov. in Fortalit. Fidei. As Philip's accession was at the age of fifteen, he must have been a precocious persecutor. Alberic des Trois Fontaines thus relates the act of Philip, sub ann. 1182: "Et quia Judæos odio habebat et multos in eis de nomine Jesu Christi blasphemare audebat, omnes eorum debitores a debitis absolvit, quintâ parte summæ fisco retentâ, et eodem anno omnes de regno ejecit, datis prius induciis vendendi supellectiles suas, et paramli ea quæ necessaria sunt egressui, antequam eos omnino ejiceret. Domos autem et vineas et alias possessiones retinuit fisco."

of the king and his successors,[n] and commanded them instantly to sell their moveables and to depart from the kingdom. As they had in vain appealed to the king, who was as hard as a rock or as iron,[x] so in vain they appealed to the nobles and to the ministers of the Gospel. Holy bishops as well as fierce barons closed their ears against the supplications of unfortunate creditors and obstinate unbelievers. Obliged to part with their effects at the lowest prices, the Jews sadly departed, amid the execrations of the people, and bearing away little but their destitute wives and children, from the scenes of their birth and infancy. Some submitted to conversion; some offered, in vain, splendid presents to the king and to the nobles. The decree was rigidly executed in the royal domains;[y] in the South of France the great vassals paid less respect

---

[n] "Quant à leurs domaines tels que maisons, champs, vignes, granges, pressoirs, et autres immeubles, il (le Roi) s'en reserve la propriété pour ses successeurs en trône de France et pour lui." Rigord.

[x] "Il eut été plus facile d'attendrir ses rochers, et changer le fer en plomb, que de faire renoncer l'âme du Roi très Crétien, à la resolution que Dieu lui avait inspiré." Rigord.

[y] In 1181, when Philip Augustus banished the Jews from his kingdom, they had two synagogues in Paris; one in the City, Rue de la Juiverie, was, after their expulsion, turned into a church, by the name of S. Mary Magdalene in the City; the other was in the Rue de la Tacherie, which formerly had the name of La Juiverie. In 1198, when recalled into France by the same king, they repaired the syna- gogue in the Rue de la Tacherie and established a second in an ancient tower of one of the walls of Paris, near the cloister of S. Jean de Grève. This tower and the adjacent street were called "Pet au Diable," in mockery, it is said, of this synagogue. They had two cemeteries, one in the Rue Galande, the other at the bottom of the Rue de la Harpe, near the banks of the Seine; lower down on the river was a mill for their exclusive use. They had afterwards establishments in the Cul de Sac de S. Faron, Rue de la Tissanderie, hence called Cul de Sac des Juifs, in the Rue de Judas, Mont S. Geneviève, in the Rue des Lombards, in the Rue Quincampoix in the City, and in the Enceinte du Palais. From Dulaure, Hist. de Paris, t. p. 526.

to the royal edict, even where it had authority, and the Jews were still found in those provinces, sometimes in offices of trust.

But, strange as it might appear to them, the nation was neither more wealthy nor the public burthens less grievous, after this summary mode of wiping off the national debt. Before twenty years had elapsed, France beheld her haughty monarch bargaining with this detested race for their readmission into the country, and, what is no less extraordinary,* the Jews, forgetting all past injustice, in the steady pursuit of gain, on the faith of such a king, settling again in this inhospitable kingdom,* and filling many streets of Paris which were assigned for their residence. It was not till twenty years after, that an edict was issued to regulate their usurious exactions and the persons to whom it might be lawful to lend money. This ordinance, by tacitly sanctioning all transactions but those inhibited, recognised at once the extent, the legality, and the importance of these affairs. The Jews became as it were the standing and authorized money-lenders of the realm. They were forbidden to lend to those who lived by daily labour, and therefore had nothing to pledge for their debts; to any

---

* Ordonnance des Rois, 1188. "And in the year 4958 Philip, the king of Tzarpath (France) allowed the Jews to dwell in Paris *against the will of the nation*, but they did not lengthen out their days there, for they cast them out a second time into another country." R. Joseph, p. 220.

* Jost is almost as indignant against his forefathers as against the king: "Beide Theile machten sich keine Erklärungen, keine Ehrenrettungsversuche, keine Versprechungen: Beide Theile waren geldgierig, und beide schlossen den Vergleich, jeder in der Absicht den andern zu berücken: die Juden wollten, durch Wücher die alten Verlüste ersetzen; der König hoffte durch sie seinen Schatz zu füllen; wenigstens nahm er vorher so viel das er dem andern Theile Zeit lassen könnte sich zu erholen." vi. p. 272.

Monk or Regular Canon without consent of the Abbot or his Chapter, signified in their letters patent. They were forbidden to take in pawn any church ornaments, any vestment stained with blood, any ploughshare, any animal used in husbandry, or unwinnowed corn. Knight, burgess, or merchant must give an assignment of some hereditament, tenement, or rent, with consent of the lord. The Jew was rescued from violence in enforcing his just demands. The interest was limited to two deniers on the livre per week (more than 40 per cent.). The other articles of this decree regulated the payment of existing debts. Philip Augustus and some of his barons made another ordinance for the regulation of debts to Jews. It enforced their having a common seal as the register of their debts under appointed officers. This ordinance limited the interest to the same amount; all old debts were to be re-scaled on a stated day. If the debtor was on his travels, the debt was to be officially recorded and the interest due thereon. No Church property was to be pledged without the assent of the Count or Baron. As soon as a loan is paid over to a debtor, both parties shall swear that the sum received is in accordance with the agreement; if this is not done, the creditor loses his right, the debtor is liable to punishment by the king. No debt is good without the signature and seal of the parties, unless the Jew has some gold, silver, or valuable article in pawn. Two substantial men in each city shall keep, one the seal, the other the roll of the debt. These men must take an oath not to affix the seal without having carefully investigated the transaction; every town shall keep a notary for Jewish business, and give security for the accuracy of all the legal instruments. In the South the condition of the Jews was still comparatively prosperous; it was among the bitter charges of Pope Innocent the Third against Raymond, the heretical Count of Toulouse, that he employed Jews in high official situations.

On the accession of Louis VIII., A.C. 1223, he gratified his impoverished barons with a new decree, which at once annulled all future interest on debts due to the Jews, and commanded the payment of the capital within three years, at three separate instalments.[b] The Jews were declared attached to the soil, and assigned as property to the feudatories,[c] or rather recognised as property belonging to them of right; no one might receive or retain the Jew of another. In the crusade against Raymond, the seventh Count of Toulouse, it was among the terms of his submission, that he should no longer employ Jewish officers.

Louis IX. ascended the throne A.C. 1226; a man whose greatness and whose weakness make us alternately applaud and reprobate his claim to the designation of Saint. But his greatness was his own, his weakness that of his age. Unhappily it was this darker part of his

---

[b] Ordonnances des Rois, A.C. 1296. Second Ordinance, Sept. 1.

[c] Ordonnances des Rois, t. 47. See the words of the statute in Hallam, Middle Ages, i. p. 107. The preamble is declared to be enacted, "per assensum Archiepiscoporum, Episcoporum, Comitum, Baronum et Militum regni Franciæ qui Judæos habent et qui non habent," A.C. 1223. "Ordinavimus de statu Judæorum quod nullus nostrum alterius Judæos recipere potest vel retinere." It was renewed with some alterations in 1230.

In 1278 the seneschal of Carcassonne is ordered to compel the Jews, who had transferred themselves from the Jewry of the king (the king had by this time acquired greater power in the South) in Beziers to that of the bishop, to return to their former synagogue. The bishop was fined and ordered to destroy the new synagogue which he had built for them. Hist. de Languedoc, iv. p. 27. They are said to be "taillables à la volonté" of their lords. iv. 75-98.

character which necessarily predominated in his transactions with the Jews. Already during his minority an edict had been passed, again prohibiting all future interest on debts due to Jews. Louis himself entered into the policy of forcing them to give up what was considered the nefarious trade of usury. Another law (soon after his accession) recognised the property of each baron in his Jews, whom he might seize by force on the estate of another.[4] In 1234, Louis, for the welfare of his soul, the souls of his father and all his ancestors, annulled one-third of all debts due to Jews.[e] No bailiff might arrest or maltreat a Christian for any debt due to a Jew, or force him to sell his hereditaments. The populace readily concurred with their devout monarch in the persecution of their creditors. Louis was actuated by two motives, both grounded on religion: one, implacable hatred towards the enemies of Christ;[f] the other, a conscientious conviction of the unlawfulness of usury.[g] The Lombards and Cahorsins shared in the devout abhorrence of the

---

[4] "Ubicunque aliquis invenerit Judæum suum licitè capere poterit tanquam proprium servum." On this M. Depping justly observes, "C'est ainsi que les planteurs d'Amérique réclament leurs nègres partoût où ceux-ci se sont réfugiés. Les Juifs soumis aux Barons n'étaient donc guère meilleurs que les esclaves dans les colonies, si n'est qu'on les laissait exercer leur industrie," the gains of which they claimed to share, and often confiscated. Depping, p. 190.

[e] "Quietavit . . . tertiam partem totius debiti quod debebant Judæos."

[f] "Aussi vous dis je, me dist le roy, que nul si n'est grand clerc et théo- logien parfait ne doit disputer aux Juifs, mais doit l'omme lay, quand il oit mesdire à la foy Chretienne, defendre la chose non pas seulement des paroles, mais à bonne espée tranchant, et en frappant les mélisans et mescréans à travers le corps, tant qu'il put le faire entrer." Joinville, Vie de S. Louis.

[g] The Marquis Pastoret observes, "Les mesures que prit Louis IX. contre les Juifs eurent bien plus pour objet de garantir ou de protéger des Français tourmentés par leurs usures, que d'en enrichir par les confiscations le trésor de l'état." Préface, xv., Ordonnances des Rois.

saintly monarch, but the Christians were left to the
tender mercies of the Church; the king took upon
himself the duty of repressing the usuries of the
Jews, at least those which were his own (it may be
doubtful how far he interfered with those of his feudatories), or preventing their poison from infecting
his realm.[h] Much of his injustice may be traced to
a desire of converting the Jews from usurious money-
lenders into laborious artisans. It may be observed,
too, that even the pious king, in his zeal for the
Crusades, had been obliged to borrow of the Jews,
even on usurious terms. There is a singular struggle
between conscience and bigotry in the good king, and
conscience gets the upper hand. He orders that measures
be taken by trustworthy persons to make restitution
even to the heirs of those usurers to whom debts are due.
There is, too, a singular conflict between the intolerance
and the piety of the Saint. Though in one place the
law states that the Jews are to be expelled from the
realm and their property sold, yet their synagogues
with their cemeteries are to be restored, as though he
would not cut them off from the worship of God.[i] But
policy or justice entered little into the minds of the

---

[h] "De Christianis fœneratoribus et usuris eorum ad prælatos ecclesiæ pertinere videtur, ad me vero pertinet de Judæis, qui jugo servitutis mihi subjecti sunt ne scilicet per usuras Christianos opprimant .... et veneno suo inficiant terram meam." Gul. Carnot, quoted by Ducange, Sur les Établissements.

[i] So I understand the Ordinance of 1257-8, though it is not quite clear: "Cum antequam iter arripuissemus transmarinum quædam bona percepimus a Judæis, non tamen animo retinendi. Et postmodum cum Judæos ipsos de terrâ nostrâ mandavissemus espelli, aliqua percepimus quæ habebant; insuper et de bonis quorundam usurariorum in Normanniâ defunctorum invenerimus aliqua percepisse ...... Restituantur usuræ his a quibus habitæ fuerunt, vel eorum hæredibus, si possunt inveniri." Ordonnances des Rois, sub ann.

populace. In 1239, they rose upon the Jewish quarter in Paris, and committed frightful ravages. Their example was followed in Orleans and many other considerable cities. The great vassals were not behind in lawless barbarity. The Assize of Brittany surpassed the worst fanaticism or injustice of sovereign or people.[k] It was held by John the Red, at Ploermel. It complained that husbandry was ruined by the usurious exactions of the Jews. It banished them from the country, annulled all their debts, gave permission to those who possessed their property to retain it; it prohibited any molestation or information against a Christian who might kill a Jew; in other words, it licensed general pillage and murder.

The next ordinance of the pious Louis was aimed not only at the usuries, but also at the religion of the Jews. Something of awe mingled with the general feeling of detestation against this devoted race. The Jews were suspected of possessing much dark knowledge which they employed to wreak their revenge on Christians. They were in alliance with the evil spirits. They were the masters of many fearful secrets and cabalistic spells. A Council prohibited their practising as physicians; for who knew by what assistance they might heal? The great source as well of their blasphemies against Christ as of these dangerous and mysterious secrets, was their dark and unintelligible Talmud. An edict was issued for the destruction of these volumes. Four-and-twenty carts full of ponderous tomes were committed to the flames in Paris.[l]

---

[k] Compare Beugnot, Juifs d'Occident, p. 99.

[l] "Cæterum ordinationem factam in perpetuum de Judæis observari districtè præcipimus quæ talis est : Judæl cessent ab usuris, et blasphemiis, sorti-

Could St. Louis have completed his task, and eradicated the Talmud from the hearts of the Jewish people, he might have shaken· the Rabbinical power, and inflicted a fatal blow upon the religion. Many of the Wise Men fled, to secure their treasures of knowledge. The emigration was well timed for St. Louis, who wanted money for his Crusade. The goods of the emigrants and their debts were seized for the Crown. One thing was yet wanting to fill the cup of misery. Notwithstanding his marked and indelible features, in the common dress of the country, the Israelite might escape the blind fury of the populace. To complete his outlawry, and to mark him out as an object of inevitable persecution, it was ordained that he should wear a sort of conspicuous outward brand upon his dress; this was called the Rouelle. It was to be worn by both sexes, and consisted of a piece of blue cloth on the front and on the back of the garment. This device originated in the clergy. It was enacted as a general usage throughout Christendom by the Council of Lateran, under Innocent the Third—a pontiff in his later days more hostile than his predecessors to the Jews.[m] It was enforced by other councils, as at Rouen and at Arles. It was finally made a law of the realm by St. Louis, in the year before his death,[n] who thus bequeathed to the miserable subjects, whom he had oppressed during his life, a new legacy of shame and calamity.

We are fatigued, our readers also are perhaps equally

---

legis et characteribus, et tam Talibus [the Talmud] quam alii libri, in quibus loveniuntur blasphemiæ, comburantur, et Judæi qui hæc observare noluerunt appellantur et transgressores legitimè puniantur. Et vivant omnes Judæi de laboribus manuum suarum, vel negociationibus sine terminis vel usuris." Ordonnance, sub ann. 1254, c. 32.

[m] See above, p. 187, note ª.
[n] Bouquet, xii. 238.

so, with the dreary prospect, which, like the desert wilderness, still spreads before us. We know not where to look for gleams of Christian mercy through these clouds of fanaticism and injustice. In Germany, indeed, the Emperors strove against the spirit of the age; Frederick Barbarossa was accused of too great leniency to the Jews. The Archbishop of Cologne, it has appeared, was called to account by the Emperor for arbitrary maltreatment of the Jews.[o] That most extraordinary man, Frederick the Second, aggravated the suspicions which attached to his Christianity on account of his high-minded resistance to the Papal power, by extending what was deemed unchristian protection over this proscribed race. They brought him intelligence that three Christian children had been found dead, at the time of the Passover, in the house of a Jew. "Let them be buried then," coolly replied the philosophic Emperor.[p] But the Emperor rendered the Jews a more effectual service, by instituting an investigation of the fact whether Jews were bound to murder children on that day. The cause was decided by grave theologians by the acquittal of the Jews from this monstrous charge. But our astonishment is great (our History has already dwelt on this strange fact) on finding Frederick's mortal antagonist, Innocent IV., one of the haughtiest bigots who ever sat on the Papal throne, issuing a Bull to the archbishops, bishops, and nobles of Germany, in which he treats with scorn the figments of murders charged against the Jews, and brands as crimes the cruelties exercised against them.[q] Of all the Bulls issued from the

---

See above, p. 187.
[p] Zemach David, quoted by Jost,
vii. p. 242.
[q] I cannot refrain from quoting

Vatican this is one of the most extraordinary (I would fain suppress the suspicion that there was temptation to usurp authority and display his supremacy over the subjects of the Emperor). Among the thunders of terrible excommunications, the strong winds of ambitious usurpation, it is something to hear the "still small voice" of humanity, justice, and charity. As to Frederick II, wherever there was learning there was sure to be

this remarkable Bull, from which extracts have been given, at full length: "Archiepiscopis et Episcopis per Alemanniam constitutis lachrymabilem Judæorum Alemanniæ recepimus quæstionem, quod nonnulli tam ecclesiastici quam seculares principes, ac alii nobiles et potentes vestrarum civitatum et diœcesum, ut eorum bona injuste diripiant et usurpent, adversus illos impia consilia cogitantes et fingentes occasiones varias et diversas; hoc considerato prudenter, quod quasi ex archivis eorum Christianæ fidei testimonia prodierunt, Scripturâ divinâ inter alia mandata legis dicentis 'Non occides,' ac prohibente illos in solemnitate paschali, quicquam morticinum non contingere, falso imponant eisdem, quod in ipsâ solemnitate se corde pueri communicant interfecti, credendo id ipsam legem præcipere cum sit legi manifestè contrarium; ac eis malitiosè objiciunt hominis cadaver mortui, si contigerit illud alicubi reperiri. Et per hoc et alia quamplurima figmenta sævientes in ipsis, eos super his non accusatos, non confessos nec convictos contra privilegia illis ab Apostolicâ Sede clementer indulta spoliant contra Deum et justitiam omnibus bonis suis; et inediâ, carceribus, ac tot molestiis, tantisque gravaminibus premunt ipsos, diversis pœnarum affligendo generibus, et morte turpissimâ eorum quamplurimos condemnando, quod ildem Judæi quasi existentes sub prædictorum nobilium et potentium dominio, deterioris conditionis, quam eorum patres sub Pharaone fuerunt in Ægypto, coguntur de locis inhabitatis ab eis et suis antecessoribus, a tempore cujus non extat memoria, miserabiliter exulare: unde hoc exterminium metuentes duxerunt ad Apostolicæ Sedis prudentiam recurrendum. Nolentes igitur præfatos Judæos injuste vexari, quorum conversionem Dominus misericorditer expectat; cum testante Prophetâ, credantur reliquiæ salvæ fieri eorundem; mandamus quatenus eis vos exhibentes favorabiles et benignos, quicquid super præmissis contra eosdem Judæos per prædictos prælatos, nobiles, et fideles inveneritis temere intentatum, instatum debitum legitimè revocato, non permittatis ipsos de cetero super iis, vel simillibus indebite molestari." Raynold. Ann., sub ann. 1241, c. lxxxiv. Notwithstanding this Bull, the Cardinal Raynaldus relates the story of Hugh of Lincoln as an undoubted historical fact (1255); also another case in London, on the authority of M. Paris, 12, 1244.

the patronage of the enlightened Emperor.' The Jews contributed their share to the cultivation of Oriental learning, which Frederick had so much at heart. A grateful pensioner gives him the praise of loving knowledge, and those who made it their occupation.*

We pass over many similar incidents, which show the barbarous credulity of the Christians, and pause only to relate the most extravagant of all. When the victorious hordes of the Mongolian Tartars threatened to overrun the whole of Europe, the Jews are said to have held a meeting, to have solemnly recognised this wild people as brethren, descendants of their own ancestors, and determined to assist their plans of conquest over their Christian oppressors. For this purpose they made proposals to the Emperor to enter into a feigned league with the fierce savages to supply them with the rich wine of the country, which they promised to mingle with poison. The waggons set forth with their freight; they were stopped on a bridge over the Danube by a collector of tolls; they insisted on passing free, as being employed on a service of vital interest to the Empire. The toll-collector suspected their truth, and forced open one of the casks—which was found to contain arms. Yet even this tale was received with ready credulity.¹

---

* On the manner in which the legislation of Frederick II. affected the Jews of Sicily compare Von Raumer, Die Hohenstauffen, iii. 486, 498, 540, and more hereafter.

* " L'Empereur Frederick II. encourages les travaux des Juifs. Jacob ben Abba Mar-l-ben-Anxoll, qui vivait à Naples, dit, à la fin de sa traduction du Commentaire d'Ibn Rosch sur l'Organon, achevée en 1232, qu'il avait une pension de l'Empereur, qui, ajoute il, ' alma la science et ceux qui s'en occupent.'" Munk, Mélanges, p. 335.

¹ This strange, wild story is told, as if he believed it, by Matthew Paris, sub ann. 1241. The Tartars were the descendants of those Jews who were shut up by God, at the prayer

The Council of Vienna, A.C. 1267, urged still farther that most dangerous plan of persecution, the total separation of the Jews from the society, and consequently from the sympathies, of their fellow-men. The canons of this Council are a singular record of the relation in which the two races stood to each other at this time. The canons were not only addressed to the prelates of Vienna, but also to the Archbishops of Salzburg and Prague, and to their suffragans. So great was the insolence of the Jew, that he presumed to pass himself off as a Christian, and so escape contempt, if not insult; Christian holiness was in danger of infection by this audacious familiarity.[a] The Jew was ordered to wear the high horned cap,[b] under pain of an arbitrary fine by his liege-lord. The Jew was to pay to the parish priest not only tithes, but all dues which might have been demanded if his house had been occupied by a Christian. The Jews were not to frequent the stoves, the baths, or the shops of the Christians; they were not to have any Christian servants, man or maid, especially not nurses. Sexual intercourse with a Christian woman was severely punished, in the man with imprisonment, the woman was to be flogged out of the town. No Christian might receive a Jew at a banquet, or eat and drink with Jews, or dance at their weddings, or buy meat of them, lest

---

of Alexander the Great, within the Caspian Gates. The Christians were persuaded, it is said, that the Tartars were Jews, and would only drink wine made by Jews. The ungrateful Jews had rather succour the enemies of the human race than the Christians who allowed them to live and to conduct their commerce among themselves, and even to practise, according to their Law, usury among the Christians as strangers and Egyptians.

[a] "Cum in tantum insolentia Judæorum excreverit ut per eos in quamplurimis Christianis jam dicatur infici puritas Christianæ sanctitatis."

[b] "Cornutum pileum."

it should be poisoned.⁷ Strange contradiction! showing at once the intimacy which had grown up between both the rich and the poor of both races, and the aversion instilled into their heart, as if the Jew would inevitably poison the Christian if he could. The attempt to suppress extravagant usury, according to one canon, is more intelligible; such bargains came under the cognisance of the Ecclesiastical Courts. When the Host was carried through the streets the Jews, at the sound of the bell, were to shut themselves up in their houses, and to close their doors and windows. Yet there was a singular dread that this hated race was by no means so despicable, or rather had, in some respects, a dangerous superiority. Not only was there a prohibition against disputing on religious subjects, not only were the Jews not to prevent their wives and children from becoming converts to Christianity, but a prohibition was thought necessary against alluring Christians to Judaism, a prohibition against circumcising Christian proselytes. Their increasing wealth and prosperity, too, was acknowledged by the inhibition to build new synagogues; they might repair, but neither make them larger, nor more costly, above all, not of a greater height.⁸

In Spain, the darkness gathered more slowly; as the Christian kingdoms gradually encroached on the still-retreating Mohammedans, the Jews seem to have changed their masters with no great reluctance, and the moderation or the policy of the sovereigns of Castile and Arragon usually refrained from any act which might

---

⁷ "Ne forte Judæi per hoc Christianos quos hostes reputant fraudulenter machinentur venenatum."

⁸ Concil. Vienn., apud Labbe, sub ann. 1267.

array these useful subjects against them. It has been seen* that the later Islamite sovereigns departed from the lofty policy of the great founders and monarchs of Mohammedan Spain; as though the atmosphere of Spain was fatal to that rare virtue, the King of Grenada had renounced toleration. These petty sovereigns had degenerated from the magnificent Abder-rahmans. The persecution which compelled the young Maimonides to dissemble or deny his faith, and drove him to the more hospitable court of the Sultan in Cairo, could not but leave at least apathy among the Jews towards the progress of the Christians. They remained in their neutral position. The first Christian monarchs, who, in general, allowed the conquered Moors to dwell in peace in their dominions, would hardly proscribe the less hostile Jews. No doubt at first they retained possession of their wealth, their synagogues were unviolated, they might even dare to appear wealthy. What commerce there was, was in their hands, and was enjoyed without rivalry in the kingdoms hardly won and hardly maintained by the swords of the Christians; such occupation was beneath the warriors of the Cross, even if they had had time, leisure, or capital, to devote to mercantile pursuits. The Jews were still frequently entrusted by Christian and Moorish kings with the administration of the finances, and, as they were permitted to maintain a loftier rank in society, so they did not disgrace that rank by those base and extortionate practices to which they sank or were reduced under less generous masters; they were respected, and respected themselves. Thus, on the surrender of Toledo (May, 25, 1085) to Alfonso, King of Castile, according to

---

* See back, p. 173.

the terms of the capitulation,[b] the Moorish inhabitants retained their houses, their property, and one mosque for their worship; no doubt the Jews, then at least less obnoxious, were included under the same favourable terms. It would be curious to inquire whether they then retained the magnificent synagogue, resembling in its architecture the famous mosque of Cordova, which afterwards became the Church of S. Benet, a surprising monument of their wealth, their splendour, and their Asiatic taste for gorgeousness.[c] It is said that seventeen years after the capitulation and reconciling edict there was a furious insurrection of the Christians, whom Alfonso had induced in great numbers to people the conquered city, and a massacre of the Jews from religious hatred, and perhaps even stronger jealousy of their wealth. The streets of Toledo ran with blood; fires consumed a vast mass of wealth, and saved it from the hands of the plunderers. The synagogues were

---

[b] "Les Capitulaires signées et jurées par le Roi Alphonse [the VI.], at Toledo] accordaient aux Maures le droit de rester dans leurs foyers, de se gouverner par leurs propres lois, de conserver les rites de leur religion. Les Juifs obtinrent le même privilége, et dans la culte Chrétiènne on vit continuer de vivre en même temps les trois populations, qui avoient vécu pendant leur esclavage." Amador de los Rios (Magnabal), p. 42. The extracts from the Fueros, cited by Amador de los Rios, are not quite intelligible, and seemingly contradictory. The fine in one for the death of a Jew seems to have been very light. In another, the Christian who struck a Jew, on conviction paid four maravedis; the Jew who struck a Christian, ten. If the Christian killed the Jew, he paid 100 maravedis; if a Jew a Christian, he suffered death and forfeited all his property, in kind, to the Alcaldes. This Fuero is not of unquestioned authenticity. But in the Fuero of Najara (A.D. 1076) the murder of a gentleman, a monk, and a Jew, were ranked together. The fine was inflicted on the inhabitants of the town.

[c] See the print of the church, with its fine Moorish horseshoe arches, in the España artística y monumental, por D. Gennaro Perez de Villa Amil. Paris, 1702. There is a second synagogue, now S. Maria la Buena, more Moorish and fantastic.

pillaged, the Rabbins murdered in their seats. The king in vain attempted to allay the tumult; law and authority were feeble against bigotry and rapacity.[d]

Nearly a century passed, in which the almost total silence of history, Jewish and Christian, is the best proof of the peace and prosperity of the Jews under the Christian sovereigns. No doubt they were made to contribute from their wealth to the Christian conquests, a subsidy readily paid for protection. The persecutions by the Mohammedan kings of Morocco drove multitudes of Jews into the rising kingdom of Portugal, where they bore a large proportion to the Christians.[e] It is a singular admission of the Jewish historian that the period of advancing civilization, and it may be added of Christian amity, facilitated the conversion of Jews to Christianity. Even as early as 1106 a famous physician of Alfonso VI. (the conqueror of Toledo), after careful study of the Jewish writings, at the age of twenty-four embraced the faith of the Gospel. The king was his sponsor; he was named Petrus Alphonsi. The proselyte endeavoured, in writings yet extant, to convert his brethren.[f]

We return to France to witness a repetition of the same extraordinary proceedings which signalized the reign of Philip Augustus; the monarch oppressing, and finally expelling the Jews; Philip Augustus himself, and his successor,[g] reduced by his poverty to enter into an ignominious treaty with these exiles, and the indefatigable Jews as readily returning to undergo the same

---

[d] Mariana, iv. c. 16.
[e] Amador de los Rios, p. 44, with authorities.
[f] Jost, ix. 249: "Die fortschreitende Bildung erleichtete den Juden den Übertritt zur Kirche."
[g] Ordonnance du Roi (Philip le Hardi), without date.

or worse calamities. Philip III. enforced and increased the severity of the laws of Louis IX.[b] During his wars in Languedoc, in 1296, Philip had extorted large sums from the Jews on the charge of immoderate usury.[i]

Philip IV. (the Fair) was the most rapacious, perhaps the most cruel, sovereign who ever sat on the throne of France. His whole reign was a period of financial difficulty. He resorted to every measure, however unscrupulous, which could fill his still-craving coffers. He was constantly tampering with the coin of the realm. He plundered though he employed the Italian usurers. His primary quarrel with the Pope, Boniface VIII., whom he persecuted to madness and to death, was about money matters. His chief motive in the suppression of the Templars was the hope, baffled by the subtlety of another Pope, of the confiscation of their vast estates to his own use. Such a king was not likely to leave the rich Jews in peace. Among his first acts was the expulsion of the Jews, who had fled from England to Gascony (they had been already plundered), from his realm: they were too poor to be received as subjects. Now, however, Philip the Fair, after some vain attempts to wean the Jews from their usurious dealings, and to enforce their adoption of commercial habits, after selling his protection to individuals, and even limiting the power of the clergy over their persons, and prohibiting the Inquisition from proceeding against them, adopted the policy of Philip Augustus, the total expulsion of the race. It might seem as if by his former indulgence and protection he had fed them up to be more secure

---

[b] Ordonnance, A.C. 1290; Ordonnance, 1299; Ordonnance, 1302. The clergy might inflict canonical punishment.

[i] Hist. le Languedoc, iv. p. 83.

and richer victims of his avarice. In one day (the 22nd July, 1306) the most wealthy Jews of Languedoc were seized, their goods sold, and their debts confiscated to the Crown.[k] The establishments of greater or less splendour which they had held for centuries in Toulouse, Carcassonne, Beziers, Narbonne, Pamiers, Montpellier, Nismes, Lunel, Beaucaire, were at once to be abandoned, were broken up and pillaged.[m] Gerard of Cortona, Canon of Pisa, with two others, were sent to sell all their goods for the king's benefit, especially at Narbonne, Pamiers, and Capestang.[n] The same scene took place in Paris; their synagogues were converted into churches, their cemeteries desecrated, their grave-stones torn up and used for building. Five years after, whether the law of expulsion had been imperfectly executed, or many of them had stolen back to the place of their former abode, or whether, as the king declared, they had been allowed to return to prove their own debts for the advantage of the Crown, a second total expulsion took place, and the soil of France was for a time secured from the profanation of the feet of the circumcised.[o]

---

[k] "Et le secret fut si bien gardé qu'il n'en échappa aucun." Hist. de Languedoc, iv. 135. Philip was a consummate adept in these summary and well-organised arrests. He practised them even more successfully against the Templars. See Hist. of Latin Christianity.

[m] Ordonnance, 1306, to the Seneschals of Toulouse and Bigorre.

[n] Hist. de Languedoc, iv. 138.

[o] For the first expulsion and plunder in 1306, no reason is assigned but the King's will. In 1311 Philip the Fair is become piously jealous about the morals and religion of his Christian subjects, as well as their oppression by usury: "Ex multiplici fide dignorum clamor auribus nostris insonuit, quod Judæi, quos, quamvis eorum migratibus nephandis sceleribus, de regno nostro expuleos pro *declarationes veritatis debitorum ipsorum toleranus recovari ad tempus*." The edict goes on first to accuse them of making, though some just, many false demands on Christians, of cruelly vexing and oppressing widows and orphans, of compelling innocent persons to fraudulent and extortionate bargains, of making

Yet scarcely had the son of Philip the Fair, Louis X. (Hutin), ascended the throne, than the disordered state of the royal finances, and the common clamour of the people (so states the royal ordinance), constrained the submission of the king and all his nobles[p] to the re-admission of the Jews, and the Jews without hesitation consented to purchase, at a considerable price, the happiness of inhabiting a land where they had already been thus plundered and maltreated.[q] Unhappy race—the earth perhaps offered them no safer asylum! They were permitted to settle in the kingdom of France for twelve years; their cemeteries, their synagogues, and their sacred books were restored, except the Talmud; they were encouraged to reclaim before the tribunals such debts as had not been recovered by the royal commissioners, of which they were to receive one-third; the other two-thirds went to the king.[r] The secret motive

---

usurious and intolerable contracts (gestus intolerabiles docuat), and then, "moresque et actus fidelium quos alias exprimere fas prohibet, illicitis modis et variis dehonestant, et tot mala etiam pollulant et divulgant, quod ex eorum morâ, si protrahatur amplius, sequeretur errore priore novissimas longè pejor." Ordonnance, 1311.

[p] It is remarkable that R. Joshua preserves no tradition of the cruel persecutions under Philip the Fair. He records the hatred of the King for Pope Boniface VIII., the outrage of Sciarra Colonna at Anagni; as if this event had absorbed the awe of the world. But on the milder edicts of Louis X. he has this grateful sentence: "And he allowed the Jews to live in the cities of his kingdom, for they found favour in his eyes, and he accepted their persons and made a covenant with them." p. 236. The ordonnance says: "Comme nous avons pris les dis Juifs en notre espécial protection." They were still under most of the restrictions of the law of St. Louis.

[q] Ordonnance du Roi, July, 1315. The sort of apologetic preamble to this ordinance is curious: "Since our Holy Mother, the Church of Rome, tolerates them in memory of the Passion of our Lord, and for their conversion to Christianity by conversation with Christians."

[r] Louis grants the petition of the nobles of Provence, that the property of their Jews seized by the Crown, by himself, or his father, be restored to them.

of this mercy is sufficiently clear. But dearly did they purchase the precarious life which they led in this unsettled land.* The next king, Philip the Long, issued an ordinance, in some degree favourable to the Jews on the royal domains. The king's Jews were not to be challenged by Christians to wager of battle, except in case of murder. Their taxes were to be regulated; such taxes were to be levied on the Jews of Champagne and other royal domains according to their property. They were excused, when on journeys, from wearing their distinguishing mark. They ceased to be serfs as they had been. Their property was no longer held in mortmain, but passed to the nearest relatives. Another ordinance renewed the prohibition to lend money to daily labourers, or take tools or instruments of husbandry in pledge, or church ornaments, or unthreshed corn; to lend to monks without consent of their superiors. If any knight would pawn his horse, his clothes, or other moveables, the Jew might receive them in pledge without the interference of the lord. The debtor was not bound to sell his hereditament or rent to pay his debts; but two-thirds were to be assigned to the Jew; the third he was to retain to live upon.† Thus the Jews seem again to acquire a legal state and position

---

* There is a curious ordinance of this time, addressed to certain commissioners in the Bailiwick of Bourges, concerning the affairs of Jews expelled from the realm. Their confiscated wealth no doubt consisted in considerable part of debts due from Christians. The Crown must lay down rules for the recovery of these debts. It was assumed that debts not claimed by Jews for twenty years could not be valid, as no Jew would have refrained so long from claiming them. If a debtor could be proved from Jewish cartularies to have paid his debt, he was to be held free. On the other hand, the debts only were to be exacted without usurious interest; and no one was to be imprisoned for a debt due to a Jew. The Crown was content to get possession of the goods volentes credere bonis.

† Ordonnances, February, 1318.

in society. They might live by manual labour, by merchandise, and acquire property in houses and lands. But of all strange laws (its meaning is obvious, and will hereafter be explained) was one, abrogated only in 1381, which confiscated the whole property of the Jew converted to Christianity.⁰ Still, however, despite of these tolerant edicts, besides that the king himself on one occasion extorted from them a fine of 150,000 livres,ˣ they were exposed to the tyranny of their lords the Barons, to the jealousy of the clergy, and to the usurpations of the Inquisition, eagerly watching an opportunity to comprehend them within its fatal sphere.ʸ

But these evils, through strong faith,—it may be feared, through far stronger avarice,—might have been endured. A worse and more unforeseen devastation burst upon their heads. This was the rising of the peasants. Long before, during the captivity of Saint Louis, a multitude of the lowest orders had assembled, and announced their intention, or rather their Divine commission, to rescue their beloved saint and king.

ʷ There is an account of the goods of the Jews in the Bailiwick of Orleans, in Depping, quoted from Broussel, Usage des Fiefs. The sale of their property, not reckoning merchandise, jewels, and plate, amounted to 33,700 livres 46 sous 5 deniers. A building, their great school, brought 340 livres. Another school in the city, 140. Depping, p. 219.

ˣ Hist. de Languedoc, iv. 190, with the assessment on the different cities in Languedoc. Preuves, 164.

ʸ In the reign of Philip the Long (A.C. 1319) an inquest was held on certain Jews of Lunel, accused of having performed what seems to have been a kind of mock Mystery of the Saviour's Passion. A crucifix was carried in public procession, the Jews, dancing and shouting (tripudiantes) dragging it through the mire, treating it with the utmost derision, and even striking the sacred image. The offenders were found guilty, and were to be amerced in person and property. Hist. de Languedoc (Preuves, p. 161). In the same year Bernard Guido, the Inquisitor of Toulouse, burned two cartloads of Talmuds, "pour les impiétés et les blasphèmes qui étaient dans ce livre contre Jésus Christ et la Sainte Vierge." iv. p. 181.

They had signalized their zeal by great barbarities against the Jews. Now a more general commotion took place; under the guidance of a priest and a monk the peasants and shepherds drew together from all quarters. Their design they probably knew not themselves. Some vague prophecies were said to be received among them, that the Holy Land was to be conquered only by shepherds and by the poor in spirit. They travelled in still-increasing masses, committing no violence or outrage, entreating bread at the gates of the wondering cities for the love of God. They had neither arms nor discipline; many were without shoes. The flocks, the labours of the field, were abandoned as they passed; young and old fell into their ranks. They marched in a kind of order behind a banner with a white cross. So they traversed the kingdom from Bourges, one party northward to Paris, where the government was appalled by their appearance; the greatest number spread into Languedoc.* They were driven only by famine to excesses against their Christian brethren, but by the sternest fanaticism to the most relentless barbarities against the Jews. The plunder of the defenceless, feeble, and wealthy Jews, would enable them to purchase arms, and all they wanted. They might then war on the Saracens. In their agony of distress, the Jews appealed to the king. He sent an idle monition, and a few horsemen to their defence. The Shepherds laughed to scorn their feeble aid. They appealed to the Pope, at Avignon, who issued an anathema, equally ineffectual. Everywhere this unhappy race, which the government could not perhaps have protected

---

* For the Pastoureaux compare Latin Christianity, v. p. 280; Hist. de Languedoc, iv. 228 et seqq.

if it would, were pillaged, massacred, or put to the torture. Where they could, they fled to the fortified places; five hundred made their escape to Verdun, on the Garonne; the governor gave them a tower to defend; the Shepherds assailed them, set fire to the gates; the desperate Jews threw their children, in hopes of mercy, down to the besiegers, and slew each other to a man.[a]

In almost all the cities of Languedoc these frightful scenes took place. At Angoulême, at Bordeaux, at Agen. At Castel Sarasin they were persuaded to be so merciful as to allow the alternative of baptism or death. All but one woman yielded. As it appears from a commission issued by the new king, Charles IV., there had been indiscriminate massacre in Auch, Gimont, Verdun, Toulouse, Rabenstein, Guillan, and many other cities.[b] This, however, was but the beginning of sorrows. An epidemic pestilence followed in the ensuing years. But a people in such a state of excitement could not look to the natural causes of such a visitation, the universal distress and famine consequent on the general abandonment of labour, and the widespread devastation. Dark rumours were propagated that the fountains, and even the rivers, of the kingdom had been poisoned.

---

[a] The Schevet Judah (Historia Judaica), as translated by Gentius, now begins to be historical; it contains one curious and not improbable circumstance concerning this outbreak. It originated in a vision seen by a boy, confirmed by the sign of a miraculous cross upon his arm. There were 300,000 in the host. Some one (quidam) suggested, " primum aggrediamur Judæos, populum imbellem, fractum, omnique destitutum auxilio, quem vel uno etiam digitulo sternere poterimus. Victores Judæorum, qui divitiis abundant, spoliis potiti, bellica arma comparabimus, et multis augebimur divitiis. Tunc Saracenis bellum inferre." p. 8 et seqq.

[b] Continuator Naugis. These persecutions are related in the Schevet Judah, Persecutio xiv.

Public detestation pointed at once to the authors of this dire crime, the Lepers and the Jews; the Lepers as the agents, the Jews as the principals. A correspondence was said to have been detected between the King of Tunis and other Infidel kings and the Jews, offering them large rewards for their co-operation in this diabolic scheme. The poor Lepers were first tortured to confess, and on their confession condemned. The Jews' turn came next, for the partial plague seemed to give them comparative exemption from its ravages, whether from the cleanliness of their habits from frequent ablutions, possibly better food, or from constitutional causes. This was enough to designate them as accomplices in some dark way with the dire pestilence. The Pope, John XXII., had seized the opportunity of their misery, during the preceding year, to aggravate it, by denouncing their detestable sorceries and magic, and by commanding their Talmuds to be burned.[c] The Papal sanction was thus given to the atrocities which followed. In many provinces, says a chronicler, especially in Aquitaine, the Jews were burned without distinction. At Chinon a deep ditch was dug, an enormous pile raised, and 160 of both sexes burned together. Many of them plunged into the ditch of their own accord, singing hymns, as though they were going to a wedding. Many women with their children threw themselves in to escape forcible baptism.[d] At Paris, those alone were

---

[c] It is just to add, in favour of John XXII., the following sentence from the Abbas Uspergensis: "De hac peste infamati Judæi, quod fontibus infectis promoverint et propterea combusti fuerunt a mari usque ad Alemanniam, præter civitatem Avinionem, ubi Papa eos tutatus fuit." Sub ann. 1334.

[d] The description of the later Plague, the Black Plague, the Plague of Boccaccio, in Rabbi Joshua is striking:—"In the second year of King Philip there was a great plague, from the rising of the sun to the going down

burned who confessed their crimes, but the richest were detained in prison to verify their confiscated debts. The king received from their spoils 150,000 livres.

In the midst of this, Philip V. died A.D. 1322, and the heir, King Charles IV., graciously pardoned the survivors, on condition of a large payment: 57,000 livres were assessed on the Jews of Languedoc; they were permitted to leave their prisons to collect the sum required, and then, as the height of mercy, allowed to gather together the rest of their effects and leave the kingdom. A third time the same strange scene was enacted.

A second pestilence, in 1348, completed the wretchedness of the few Jews that remained in this desolated country: while themselves were perishing by hundreds, the old accusation of poisoning the wells was renewed, and the sword of vengeance let loose to waste what the plague had spared.[*]

---

thereof, and there was no city that was too high for it. And there was a great cry from one end of the world to the other, the like whereof never was. In the city which went out by a thousand there were but one hundred left, and of that which went out by one hundred only ten were left at that time; and for one that died or was sick, of the Jews, there died and sickened one hundred of the people of the land, and they clothed themselves with jealousy." R. Joshua chiefly dwells on the persecutions in Arragon and Catalonia, especially in Barcelona and Tarigah (Tarragona). He adds, "Also in the kingdom of Provence the Jews drank the cup of astonishment in those days. . . . And in Ashkenaz [Germany] they accused them of casting poison into the wells. And they chastened them with rods and with thorns, and burned them with fire. May the Lord avenge the blood of his servants that was shed. Amen! amen!" pp. 239-243. Compare Schevet Judah, p. 151.

[*] Trithemius (Chron. Hirsaug et Sponheim) thus describes the plague, the rumours about poisoning the fountains, the horrible massacre of the Jews, which was by no means confined to France, sub ann. 1348: "Hujus calamitatis causa Judæis fuit imposita, quod fontes et aerem intoxicassent, unde persequutio in eos Christianorum gravissima fuit subsequuta. Nam in diversis mundi partibus cum talis in eos æstimatio Christianorum fuisset publicata, alii fuerunt miserabiliter

JEWS EJECTED FROM FRANCE.

The Jews, driven in this merciless manner from the country where their portion had been the unrestrained excesses of the boors, and legal punishment as authors of a great national calamity, the pestilence, by which they as well as the Christians had suffered so dreadfully'—

---

suffocati, alii præcipitati in aquam, alii submersi, alii capitibus truncati, alii combusti, alii gladiis et lanceis perfossi, atque alii vario tormentorum genere interempti. Nonnulli vero illorum cementes in malo se positos, necatis liberis primùm cum uxoribus, ne in manus crudeliter sævientium Christianorum devenirent, se cum domibus et mansionibus, igne apposito, incendio perennerunt. Hæc autem in Judæos persequutio prænotato anno incipiens, biennio duravit; quæ utrum jure an injuriâ peracta sit non est nostrum judicare, quamvis non nobis videtur verisimile, *quod omnes totius orbis fontes, etiam si voluissent*, veneno inficere potuissent."

They were received with kindness by Clement VI., in the territory of Avignon.

' As late as Velly and Villaret this monstrous story retained its place in what were considered the authoritative histories of France. It is worth while to transcribe the narrative: "Les Infidèles en furent alarmés, et pour rompre ce dessein [a new Crusade] prirent les mesures les plus abominables. Le Roi de Grénade, animé sans doute par les Mahométans d'Asie, excita les Juifs à empoisonner tous les puits, et toutes les fontaines. Souvent chassés, quelquefois massacrés, toujours persécutés en France, nourrissant dans leur cœur une haine secrète, mais implacable, contre la nation, les Juifs acceptent la proposition; mais surveillés de près, ils jugent prudent de charger les lépreux de l'exécution; et pour les y déterminer, ils leurs donnent de l'argent et leurs font croire que ceux qui ne mourront pas du poison deviendront lépreux. Ceux-ci, rebut de la société à cause de leur mal, cédant à cette double tentation, empoisonnent toutes les eaux de la Haute Guienne et du Poitou, suivant les uns *avec du sang humain, de l'urine, trois sortes d'herbes, et des hosties consacrées:* tout cela desséché, mis en poudre dans un sachet, était jeté dans les puits et dans les fontaines; suivant d'autres, on employait *la tête d'une couleuvre, des pattes de crapaud, et des cheveux de femmes*, souillés d'une liqueur noire et puante, le tout à preuve des flammes. Le complot fut découvert par deux lettres Arabes, interceptées, et que l'on conserve, avec la traduction, dans le Trésor des Chartes. Des lépreux et des Juifs, *mis à la torture*, s'avouent coupables de la plus horrible conspiration qui eut jamais été tramée. Ils sont brulés vifs et leurs biens confisqués. A Paris on livre aux flammes les Juifs coupables; on bannit les autres en *retenant les biens des plus riches*, qui fournirent au Roi la somme alors énorme de 150,000 livres. Ailleurs, coupables ou non, on les brula indistinctement. Quant aux lépreux,

loaded, in short, with every popular outrage and calumny, began nevertheless to steal back into a land where their sordid industry still found a harvest. And no sooner were the distresses of the kingdom at their height, through the civil wars, the conquests of the English, and the captivity of the king (John), than they opened a negotiation with the Regent to purchase the privilege of returning to this land of lawlessness and blood. Miserable truly was the condition of the kingdom which led to the peace of Bretigny, A.C. May 8, 1360; there seemed to be no resource but to acknowledge the dependence of France on Jewish industry and wealth. In these times the Dauphin, as Regent, had debased the coin; the Jacquerie suppressed only by horrible massacres, the licence of the disbanded soldiery, which ravaged almost the whole country; the intolerable taxation, had reduced France to the lowest extremity.[e] It was a strange event, the capitulation of a great kingdom with subjects despised with ineffable scorn, but recently persecuted without remorse and forced to fly the realm, yet who dictated terms, if not honourable, yet advantageous to themselves. And on these terms, outcasts, indeed, equally in the rest of the world, the Jews were content to purchase a limited period of residence, precarious safety, with the chance of gain among a people who, from the king in his palace, the noble in his castle, to the insurgent peasant, looked on them

---

on les enferma tous à perpétuité." Velly or Villaret, Hist. de France, Philip V., A.C. 1321. Are these letters still in the Trésor des Chartes? This account, in substance the same, varies much in different copies. In the modern reprint of Velly by Desodoards the crime as against the Jews and lepers is declared to be inadmissible.

[e] See the state of the kingdom in Sismondi, 'Hist. des Français,' lx. c. 25.

with undisguised hatred, and were ready, on the first impulse, to renew all the horrors of former massacres, plunder, and exile. Before the conclusion of the treaty they were already in the kingdom, as appears by the appointment, during the Regency (March, 1361), of Louis Count d'Etampes, as guardian of the Jews. In Languedoc they were in great numbers; in Nismes one large street, and several smaller ones, were assigned for their occupation; in Toulouse, in the absence of Louis d'Etampes, the royal Protector, Robert of Outre Eau, was appointed as their guardian, to defend them against the insults and injuries of the populace.

Menecier (Manasseh) of Vesoul, and Jacob of Pont St. Maxime, conducted the treaty on the part of the Jews. The price of admission into the kingdom was fixed at fourteen florins for a man and his wife; for children and servants one florin two tournois; the price of residence at seven florins annually for man and wife; children and servants, one florin. The treaty was for twenty years. The Jews might buy houses, possess synagogues, cemeteries, and their sacred books. They were no longer under baronial jurisdiction, but under the king,[h] represented by his officer, the guardian of the Jews. They were free from all other taxes, except land tax. They might trade in money as in other merchandise.[i] They might take in pawn anything except religious books, church furniture or ornaments, or church vessels,[j] agricultural implements and tools.

---

[h] See the extraordinary oath imposed by Eliezer of Villeneuve on a Jew bearing witness in a court of justice in his domains (A.D. 1337) in Beugnot, p. 112.

[i] "Ils paissent marchander tant de leurs deniers comme de leurs autres marchandises et denrées quelconques." Art. 8.

[j] "Saints reliques, calices, sanctuaires, livres, aournements, ou autres biens d'église dediés à Dieu." Art. 10.

The interest of money was fixed at four deniers the livre weekly, double the former standard. They might defend their houses and property from unlawful attacks. They could not be challenged to trial by battle. They were not to be compelled to hear Christian sermons. Finally, all their former privileges were confirmed. They were free if they could find bail. They were pardoned all crimes charged against them, even robbery and murder, if committed before they left France.[k]

For some time the position of the Jews seemed materially improved; though still pursued by the clergy and the people with unmitigated hatred, they had detached the Crown from the hostile confederacy.[l] In Languedoc the clergy published an excommunication against all who should furnish the Jews with fire, water, bread, or wine.[m] In Languedoc, too, the zeal of some Jewish converts would force their former brethren to attend the churches to hear sermons, amidst the mockery and insults of the Christians. They appealed to the king, Charles V., who issued an ordinance inhibiting all compulsion, not only as unjust, but as irreverent to the Church and to the Holy Sacrament.[n] The civil power, the Marshal d'Audenham, interposed and repressed the fiery zeal of the Church. The Jews obtained a prolongation of the term of sufferance in the land for ten years; they paid

---

[k] The whole in the Ordonnances, especially Ordonnance v. (p. 491), recited under the date of its confirmation, Bois de Vincennes, May, 1370; July, 1372.

[l] The abbot of St. Denys had an especial privilege from the king to possess as many as five families of Jews. No doubt he protected them.

Ordonnances, iv. p. 139.

[m] Ordonnances, iv. p. 339 (Aug. 1378).

[n] Ordonnances, v. p. 167 (March, 1368). In 1360 powers were given to certain commissioners to redress all wrongs perpetrated against the Jews in Languedoc by their guardians. Ordonnances, vi. p. 407.

for this privilege 3000 livres in gold. Charles the Fifth renewed the treaty first for six, afterwards for ten years. The Crown began to have open dealings with, and to raise loans from, the Jews. In 1378 they lent the king 20,000 livres, and covenanted to furnish 200 per week." It was from the wealth of the Jews that Paris began to rear her fortresses and lofty edifices. The prudent Menecier de Vesoul, their acknowledged representative, appears to have conducted their affairs with great address; the worst grievance must have been their being still compelled to wear a distinguishing mark upon their dress; but even this they obtained permission to lay aside on a journey. Menecier de Vesoul, his wife and children, John his son-in-law, Master Matathias and his mother, and Abraham his son, alone had the privilege of exemption from the penalty of twenty sous if they should appear without the mark, the ensign of the Jews.ᵖ But with their wealth their danger inevitably increased. Whether honest or usurious, their gains were wrung from an impoverished nobility and people. During the administration of the Duke of Anjou (1380), who had confirmed the privileges of the Jews granted by John ᑫ and Charles V.,ʳ a tumult took place, arising, it was said, out of the heavy burthens of the people. The nobles cried aloud for the expulsion of the Jews; the people at their instigation wreaked their rage partly on the archives where their debts, or rather the debts of the nobles, were registered, partly on the Jews, who were pillaged and slain, their children torn from their mothers' arms,

---

* Hist. de Languedoc, iv. p. 325.
ᵖ Ordonnances, v. p. 498.
ᑫ King John openly avowed the principle of his indulgence : " The more privileges the Jews possess, the better will they be able to bear taxation."
ʳ Ordonnances, vi. p. 521.

and carried to the churches to be baptized. The strong arm of authority allayed for a time, but could not suppress, the brooding storm of popular emotion.* The Duke of Anjou published a proclamation on all the crossways, with sound of trumpet, that all persons should restore, on pain of death, the plunder of which they had robbed the Jews; very few obeyed the order.

During the early part of the reign of Charles the Sixth, the Jews were treated with equity and consideration;¹ in the frequent disputes which arose about the registering and recovery of their debts, they obtained equal justice; in one respect alone they were unfortunate—they were withdrawn from the special jurisdiction of the king, and submitted to the ordinary tribunals.² But the distresses of the country still increased; with the distresses, the difficulty of obtaining money: every order lay at the mercy of the moneylender. But former calamities did not teach the Jews moderation; regardless that they were arraying against themselves both nobles and people, they went on accumulating their perilous riches, till, like a thunderclap, the fatal edict (Sept. 7, 1394) burst upon them, commanding them once more to evacuate the kingdom, though on milder terms, with the liberty of receiving

---

* Anonyme de S. Denys; Juvenal des Ursins, 27; Sismondi, Hist. des Français, xi. 818.

¹ Peter Aymeric, Doctor of Laws, was appointed guardian of their privileges in the three seneschalties (Beaucaire, Carcassonne, Toulouse). Hist. de Languedoc, iv. 366. In 1387 the Duc de Berri granted remission to the Jews of the three seneschalties of their usuries and other crimes, on the payment of 5000 francs in gold, with a promise only to demand the ordinary tax. This tax was 10,000 francs a year, in half-yearly payments. Ibid. iv. 390. Their usurious practices were pardoned. iv. 396.

² Ordon. des Rois, vii. 648. Comp. Beugnot, Juifs d'Occident, p. 130.

all debts due to them, and of selling their property.[x] The cause of this change in the royal policy is probably to be sought in the malady of the unhappy king.[y] His confessor was perpetually at his ear, urging to the disordered and melancholy monarch the sin of thus protecting an accursed people from the miseries to which they were deservedly doomed by the wrath of God. The nobles hated them as debtors, the people as fanatics. The queen was won over,[z] and the advice of those few wise counsellors who represented the danger of depriving the country of the industry of such a thriving and laborious community, was overborne by more stern advisers.[a] An accusation made without proof against the Jews of Paris, of the murder of converts to the Church, aggravated the popular fury. Four of the most wealthy were scourged two successive Sundays in all the cross roads of Paris, and bought their lives at the price of 18,000 francs. The rest were allowed a month to wind up their affairs, and the whole Jewish community crossed for the last time the borders of France, for a long and an indefinite period of banishment.[b]

---

[x] "Doresnevant nul Juif ou Jouifve ne habitent, ou converseut en nostre dit royaume, ni en aucune partie d'icelluy en Langualoc." Juvenal des Ursins.

[y] Lobineau, Hist. de Bretagne, p. 407.

[z] Juvenal des Ursins, Hist. de Charles VI., pp. 129-675.

[a] The edict was published at Toulouse, 1394. Ordonnances, vii. 675. There remained twelve families of Jews in Toulouse, seven in the rest of the Seneschalty. The Count of Foix endeavoured to prevent the expulsion of the Jews from Pamiers. But the officers of the Seneschalty compelled them to depart, fifty-six in number, men and women. It was probably the influence of the lords which protected the few who lingered behind in Provence and Languedoc.

[b] I must doubt the justice of M. Beugnot's remarks on this final expulsion of the Jews from France. Though perhaps they had ceased to be absolutely necessary to the commerce of the kingdom, commercial ri-

The history of the German Jews during the thirteenth and fourteenth centuries displays the same dreary picture of a people, generally sordid, sometimes opulent, holding their wealth and their lives on the most precarious tenure. No fanatic monk set the populace in commotion, no public calamity took place, no atrocious or extravagant report was propagated, but it fell upon the heads of this unhappy caste. In Germany the Black Plague raged in all its fury, and wild superstition charged the Jews, as elsewhere, with causing and aggravating the misery and themselves enjoying a guilty comparative security amid the universal desolation.[c] Fatal tumults were caused by the march of the Flagellants,[d] a host of mad enthusiasts, who passed through the cities of Germany, preceded by a crucifix, and scourging their naked and bleeding backs as they went, as a punishment for their own offences and those of the Christian world. These fanatics atoned, as they supposed, rather than

---

valry may to a certain extent have conspired with intolerance: "Soyons assurés que ce ne fut pas l'intolérance religieuse qui fit chasser les Juifs de France. On proscrivit en eux ces audacieux usuriers, qui, par leurs complaisances financières, mettaient le désordre dans les deniers publics, rendaient vaines les garanties accordées aux peuples par les rois, et ruinaient l'état en le désorganisant." Poor Jews! even history written by enlightened men in modern days is still darkened by the old prejudices. Sismondi's account of this final expulsion of the Jews is far more wise, just, and true. xxii. p. 52.

[c] Compare the History of the Epidemics in the Middle Ages, by Dr. Hecker, translated by C. Babington, London, 1859, and the account of the Black Plague, the persecutions of the Jews, above all the remarkable confessions wrung from them by torture at Chillon and elsewhere, p. 70 et seqq.

[d] On the Flagellants compare Hist. of Latin Christianity, iv. 396. "Surrexit secta Poenitentium seu Flagellatorum, Teutonicâ Crucebröder, in Alemannia; et anno sequente, scilicet MCCCL., qui fuit Jubilæus, magna persecutio Judæorum, ut fere ubique cremarentur. Tanquam morte rei tunc cruciabantur Hebræi."— Engelhus. Chron. apud Leibnitz, ii. 1128.

aggravated, their sins against the God of Mercy, by plundering and murdering the Jews in Frankfort and other places.* The same dark stories were industriously propagated, readily believed, and ferociously avenged, of fountains poisoned, children crucified, the Host stolen and outraged. The power of their liege-lord and Emperor ᶠ recognised by the law of the empire, even when exerted for their protection, was but slightly respected and feebly enforced, especially where every province and almost every city had or claimed an independent jurisdiction. Still, persecuted in one city they fled to another, and thus spread over the whole of Germany, Brunswick, Austria,ᴱ Franconia, the Rhine Provinces, Silesia, Brandenberg, Bohemia, Lithuania, and Poland. Oppressed by the nobles, anathematized by the clergy, hated as rivals in trade by the burghers in the commercial cities, despised and abhorred by the populace, their existence is known by the chronicle, rarely of protective edicts, more often of their massacres.ʰ In Prague,

---

* The chapter in Raumer's Hohenstaffen, v. 381, Die Juden, may be consulted with advantage.

ᶠ "Imperialis auctoritas in priscis temporibus ad perpetuam Judaici sceleris ultionem, Judæis induxerit perpetuam servitutem." Lunig Reichs' Archiv, quoted by Von Raumer, p. 312. The harsh language of the law would intimate that the Emperor was invested with this power solely that he might wreak vengeance on the Jews, and keep them in perpetual slavery.

ᴱ In the middle of the thirteenth century there were Jews in Austria, generally farmers of the royal domains, entitled Counts of the Donau. Depping, p. 236, with authorities. See the grant of the Emperor Frederick I. to the Duke of Austria. "Et potest in terris suis omnibus tenere Judæos et usurarios publicos, quos vulgus vocat gewerttshin sine imperii molestia et offensa." Pertz, Leges II. 101. In the year 1335 Ernest Duke of Brunswick, in his grant of privileges to the city of Hameln, enacts, "Quicunque Judæus moratur vel morabitur in civitate, nobis ad nullum servitium tenebitur, sed civitati tenetur ad jura civilia." Apud Leibnitz, Script. Brunsw. II. 513.

ʰ "Item primo Alberti Imperatoris anno (1298) Judæorum aliquot millia Norimbergæ, Hertzpell, Rot-

where no doubt their wild old cemetery, if its legends were carefully deciphered, would tell terrible stories;[1] in Nuremberg, Wurzburg, and Rottenberg.

Of the means by which the general hatred was exasperated and kept alive, none was so universal, none so deeply stirred the passions of the Christian's breast, sunk into the popular belief, none, therefore, was so fatal to the Jews in all lands, as the tales of the crucifixion of Christians, certainly of children, and usually at Easter. It would be curious to inquire how many saints the Jews have thus undesignedly added to the Calendar,[J] saints famous for the miracles wrought by their bodies and by their

---

tenburga et in albis terris ob malefacta combusti fuerunt, infantibus aliquot ad baptismum reservatis:" so coolly writes the Abbas Uspergensis, p. 204.

[1] " Pragæ comburebantur Judæi, ad tria millia, Die Paschæ, quia blasphemabant Sacramentum Eucharistiæ in bonâ feriâ quintâ, et Sabbatho Sancto precedentibus. Versum.

M simul et tria C.L.X.LI. removete, Paerbs luce reus Pragæ perit esse Judæus. De quorum strage prædictus Wencealaus Rex recepit v. tunnas plenas argento, ut fumabatur." Chronic. Engelhus. Leibnitz, ii. 1134. There is a very curious passage, De Reformatione Monasteriorum (written about 1470), Leibnitz, ii. p. 818. The writer asserts that the Jews were settled in Halle before the birth of Christ, as is certified by inscriptions on the tombstones in their cemetery. Were these Spanish Jews, who had imported from Spain the fictions so constantly pleaded in that country as exempting them from the guilt of Christ's crucifixion? It appears that

a popular preacher (a monk) so stirred up the shopkeepers of Halle by denouncing the usuries of the Jews (a graphic passage of one of his sermons is cited) that they refused all dealings with the race. A signal was given when a Jew appeared in the streets, and all the shops were shut. The preacher returned to the charge, "'How then are the Jews to live if not by usury?' Let them take to husbandry or mechanical employments, dig gardens, cleanse the streets, or work like labourers." The Jews refused to do this; the people were obstinate; the consulate of Halle, therefore, by the advice of the preacher, and with the approbation of the archbishop, drove them out of the town (of their long immemorial residence no notice was taken), refused to readmit them, and turned their synagogue into a chapel dedicated to the Virgin Mary.

[J] In the Fortalitium Fidei the Consideratio Septima begins with the cruelty of the Jews to the Messiah, their cruelty to themselves, as en-

reliques;[k] saints who were the object of devout worship, and to whose shrines men gathered by thousands. Each country has added to this holy host;[l] France (to name but a few), St. Robert of Pontoise; England, St. Hugh of Lincoln, St. William of Norwich; Germany, St. Wernher of Bacharach, St. Simon of Trent;[m] Spain, S. Juan Passamente, the Martyr of Granada. Christian poetry abused its magic power, seizing on these fables, and melting them into the hearts of the people. Of all Chaucer's Tales none is so exquisitely pathetic as that of the lost child, whose mother had taught it to repeat, with infantine fondness, the "Alma Redemptoris Mater."[n] The mother sought the missing child, and wandered in her search into the Jews' quarter. She

---

tailing on their own heads perpetual captivity and eternal damnation, and their cruelty to Christians. These chapters give a succession of all the monstrous and frightful stories of this kind current in the Middle Ages.

[k] See Trithemius, Chron. Hirsaug, et Sponhelm. The following may be found: A.C. 1236, several Christians murdered in a mill. Jews burned for this offence in Haguenau, 1207. The boy Wernher pricked to death with needles; worshipped as a martyr at Bacharach, 1432. A boy murdered in the village of Weiler. The Jews burned at Kreuznach. As late as 1510 the Margrave of Brandenburg burned Jews on some such charge.

[l] Bleeding crosses often bore witness of such crimes. There is one which converted many Jews; in Bolbon. Chronicon, Leibnitz, S. B. iii. 306. In the year 1422 a woollen manufacturer at Sobernheim, in the diocese of Mentz, was supernaturally directed to a cross near the mill, which he found mutilated, thrown down and covered with mud. As he reverently replaced it he heard a voice, "The four Evils are Jews, whores, bad priests, and pagans." Contin. Engelhus., Leibnitz, ii. 86.

[m] For SS. Simon of Trent and William of Norwich, see Alban Butler, Lives of Saints, both, March 24. The Bollandists for the same day give the juridical acts. It is remarkable to see the dawn of candour and charity freeing themselves on writers like Alban Butler. He will not venture to question legends sanctified by acts of canonization, but he ventures to add, "Nevertheless, it is a notorious slander of some authors who, from these singular and extraordinary instances, infer this to have been, at any time, the custom or maxim of this people."

[n] Chaucer, Prioress's Tale.

appealed to their humanity to tell her if they had seen her child. The Jews gave a hard, coarse denial, when suddenly from a deep foul pit was heard the child's voice, which

> "Alma Redemptoris 'gan to sing,
> So loud, that all the place 'gan to ring."

The scene of this is laid in Asia. There is a beautiful old Scotch ballad (imperfect) of the Jew's daughter of Merry-land (Milan).* As in Chaucer, the mother wanders into the Jews' quarter, seeking her missing child:—

> "My bonny Sir Hew, my pretty Sir Hew,
> I pray thee to me speak."
> "O lady, rin to the deep draw-well,
> Gin ye your sonne would seek."
> Lady Helen ran to the deep draw-well,
> And knelt upon her knee;
> "My bonny Sir Hew, so ye be here,
> I pray thee speak to me."
>
> "The lead is wondrous heavy, mither,
> The well is wondrous deep;
> A keen penknife sticks in my heart,
> A word I dounae speak.
> Gae hame, gae hame, my mither dear,
> Fetch me my winding-sheet;
> And at the back of Merry-land toune,
> It's there we twa shall meet."

But the Brussels legend surpasses all in the minuteness of its particulars, in its audacious incredibility, and in its vitality. It is commemorated, to their infinite shame, in the enlightened city of Brussels to the present day, by a solemn procession of the clergy and the exposition

---

* There is a French ballad among those published by M. Michel.

of the Host.[p] My account is taken from a book regularly reprinted and sold, and which all faithful members of the Church are directed to receive as undoubted truth, because "charity believeth all things"!!—A Jew, named Jonathan of Enghien, desired to possess himself of the consecrated Host in order to treat it with the sacrilegious insult by which that impious race delight in showing their hatred to Christianity. He applied to one John of Louvain, whose poverty could not resist the bribe of sixty golden coins, called moutons d'or. John mounted by night into the Chapel of St. Catherine, stole the pix with its sacred contents, and conveyed it to Jonathan. The Jew, triumphant in his iniquity, assembled his friends, when they blasphemed the Host in the most impious manner, but abstained from piercing it with their knives till the approaching Good Friday. In the mean time, on account of the murder of their son, Jonathan's wife persuaded him to migrate to Brussels. There the Host was borne into the synagogue, treated with the grossest insult, then pierced with knives. The blood poured forth profusely, but the obdurate Jews, unmoved by the miracle, dispersed tranquilly to their homes. Having done this, they resolved to send their treasure to Cologne. They made choice of a woman, unfortunately for them, secretly converted to the Catholic faith, as the bearer. Her poverty but not her will consented; but during the night, seized with remorse of conscience, she determined to denounce the crime to the clergy. The consequences may be anticipated: all the Jews were arrested, put to the torture,

---

[p] Compare Depping, p. 276, who says that when the festival was celebrated, in the year 1820, eighteen pictures were painted for the Church of S. Gudule, representing all the atrocities of the scene, even the execution of the three elders.

convicted, condemned to be torn by red-hot pincers, and then burned alive. The picture of their sufferings as they writhed on the stake is exhibited with horrid coolness, or rather satisfaction, in the book of the legend. And this triumph of the faith, supported, it is said, by many miracles, is to the present day commemorated in one of the first Christian cities of Europe.

BOOK XXV.

JEWS IN ENGLAND.

First Settlement — William Rufus — Henry II. — Coronation of Richard I. — Massacre at York — King John — Spoliations of the Jews — Henry III. — Jewish Parliament — Edward I. — Statute of Judaism — Final Expulsion from the Realm.

In the dark ages England was not advanced beyond the other nations of Europe in the civil or religious wisdom of toleration. While the sovereign authority—that of the Pope in Italy, of the Emperor in Germany, and of the Kings in Spain—frequently held in check the fierce animosities of the nobles, the clergy, and the populace against their Israelitish subjects, with rare exceptions the Kings of England, like those of France, joined in the inhuman and impolitic confederacy against them. There were Jews in England under the Saxons. The ecclesiastical constitutions of Egbright, Archbishop of York, A.C. 740, prohibit Christians from appearing at Jewish feasts. They are named in a charter to the monks of Croyland, A.C. 833, and named in the strange character of Benefactors, granters of land to the monastery.* They are said to have purchased from William

---

* "Omnes terras et tenementa, possessiones, et eorum peculia, quæ regns Merciorum et eorum proceres, vel alii fideles Christiani vel *Judæi*, monachis dederunt." Ingulph. Hist. p. 8. There are doubts, however, of the authenticity of these charters.

the Conqueror the right of settlement in the country. His son, William Rufus, shocked the devout feelings of his people by his open intercourse with the enemies of Christ. He appointed a public debate in London between the two parties, and profanely swore, by "the face of St. Luke," that if the Rabbins defeated the Bishops, he would turn Jew himself. The Jews boasted that they obtained the victory, while the trembling people, in a thunderstorm and an earthquake, recognised the wrath of God against the irreligious king. But William was unmoved; he received at Rouen the complaint of certain Jews, that their children had been seduced to the profession of Christianity.[b] Their petition was supported by a liberal offer of money. Many, either from conviction or confiding in the king's protection, abjured their new faith. One Stephen offered sixty marks for his son's restoration to Judaism, but the son had the courage to resist the imperious monarch. "Get thee hence quickly," said the king, "and obey, or, by the face of St. Luke, I will cause thine eyes to be plucked out of thine head." The young man temperately adhered to his determination. The king yielded, on which the Jew demanded back his money.[c] The king unwillingly restored half. Rufus gave still deeper offence by farming to Jews the vacant bishoprics. During this reign Jews were established in Oxford and in London. In the former city they had three halls, hostelries or lodging-houses, for the accommodation of youth:—Lombard

---

[b] Gul. Malmsb. sub ann. 1083. William usually swore "by the Cross of Lucca."

[c] This rests on the circumstantial but somewhat suspicious authority of Hollingshead. Indeed, considering the hatred of the monkish chroniclers, our only vouchers, for William Rufus and for the Jews, the historian, though relating these stories, as characteristic of the times and so far historical, may allow some reasonable doubt of their perfect veracity.

Hall, Moses Hall, and Jacob Hall. They taught Hebrew to Christian as well as Jewish students. They were not, however, permitted a burial-ground; their only cemetery was in St. Giles, Cripplegate, in London.[d] As history is silent about them for a short period, we may conclude that they were growing in opulence, and consequently in public detestation. In the 10th of Stephen the same dark tales began to be bruited abroad which were so readily credited on the Continent; they are said to have crucified a youth at Norwich. William of Norwich became a saint of wide repute. His wonder-working powers for some centuries brought pilgrims in multitudes, no doubt much to the benefit of that ancient and flourishing city.[e] "This crime," their historian shrewdly observes, "they are never said to have practised but at such times as the king was manifestly in want of money." The same atrocity was imputed to them at Gloucester, and at St. Edmondsbury (1160). At the latter place likewise the churchmen derived further advantage besides aggravating the general hatred against the Jews; the body of the youth was interred with great solemnity, and his tomb wrought frequent miracles.[f] Nor did the king (Henry the Second) overlook this favourable opportunity for filling his coffers: twelve years before he had extorted a large sum from the Jews

---

[d] They afterwards obtained a piece of burial-ground, the site on which the beautiful tower and part of Magdalene College stand.

[e] "In his reign [Stephen's] the Jews of Norwich bought a Christian child before Easter, and tortured him after the same manner as our Lord was tortured, and on Long Friday hanged him on a rood in memory of our Lord, and afterwards buried him. And they thought it would be concealed, but our Lord showed that he was a holy martyr, and the monks took him and buried him with high honour in the Minster; and through our Lord he worketh wonderful and manifold miracles, and is called S. William." Saxon Chronicle, sub ann. 1137.

[f] Gervas, sub ann. 1160.

—5000 marks—and banished many, probably those who refused to accede to his terms.[g] Other anecdotes illustrate their increasing wealth and unpopularity. They are charged with having lent money to some of the adventurers for Ireland, who undertook that enterprise contrary to the king's order; and with receiving in pledge some of the sacred treasures of the church of St. Edmondsbury:[h] it is to be hoped that this transaction had no connexion with the horrible charge of the crucified boy.[i] Their riches, which they were not so prudent as to conceal, kept alive the rankling jealousy. Their mansions were as stately as palaces.[k] The most

---

[g] Gervas, Ibid.

[h] These facts are well authenticated. The records of both transactions are quoted by Tovey from the Rolls. For the second, "Sancto Judæus de Sancto Edmundo reddidit compotum de v. marcis, ut sit quietus quod recepit in vadio vasa deputata obsequio altaris." We remember the severe and reiterated laws prohibiting, and necessarily prohibiting, the pledging the vessels and furniture of the Church in all countries.

[i] "Others," says the author of Anglia Judaica, "were grown so presumptuous as to scoff at and ridicule the highest dignitaries of the Church." For we read that a certain Jew, having the honour about this time to travel towards Shrewsbury in company with Richard Peche, archdeacon of Malpas in Cheshire, and a reverend dean, whose name was Deville; amongst other discourse, which they condescended to entertain him with, the archdeacon told him that his jurisdiction was so large as to reach from a place called Ill Street, all along till they came to Malpas, and took in a wide circumference of country. To which the Infidel, being more witty than wise, immediately replied, "Say you so, Sir? God grant me then a good deliverance! For it seems I am riding in a country where Sin is the archdeacon, and the Devil himself the dean—where the entrance into the archdeaconry is in Ill Street, and the going from It Bad Steps;" alluding to the French words "l'èché" and "Malpas." Our author is grievously offended at these liberties being taken with such reverend personages; but charitably concludes that so facetious a Jew would hardly have been concerned in such tragical crimes as they were charged with. The story rather indicates that the clergy and the Jews sometimes met on terms of amity; and it is curious as showing the mixture of French and English which seems to have prevailed in the language of the time.

[k] "Domus eorum quæ quasi palatia erectæ fuerunt." Ann. Waverl.

remarkable evidence of their wealth is, that at a parliament held at Northampton, to raise a tax for an expedition to the Holy Land, the whole Christian population was assessed at 70,000*l.*—the Jews alone at 60,000*l.*[1] The abandonment of the expedition, and the death of the king, prevented the levying of this enormous burthen. But Henry's death, instead of relieving them from oppression, was the accidental cause of a worse calamity—it gave an occasion for all the passions, which had long been brooding within the hearts of the people, to break forth into fierce and undisguised hostility. The whole nation crowded to the coronation of the brave Richard the First. Among the rest the Jews were eager to offer their allegiance, and to admire the splendour of the spectacle. They came in such apparel as suited the occasion, and were prepared with costly offerings to the new sovereign. But the jealous courtiers, and the whole people, demanded the exclusion of such dangerous guests from the royal presence, who were likely to blast all the prosperity of the reign by their ill-omened appearance. It was dreaded that these notorious and wicked sorcerers would bewitch the king. Peremptory orders were issued that none should be admitted.[m] A few strangers incautiously ventured, supposing themselves unknown, into the Abbey; they were detected, maltreated, and dragged forth, half dead, from the church. The news spread like wild-fire; the populace rose at once, broke open the houses of the Jews, whom they suspected, and found to conceal, under a modest exterior, incalculable wealth: they pillaged and set fire on all sides. The king sent the chief justiciary, Sir Richard Glanville, to arrest the tumult. Proclamation was made that the Jews were under

---

[1] Authorities in Anglia Judaica. | [m] Matt. Paris, sub ann. 1189.

the king's protection; they had supplied him largely with contributions for his Crusade.⁰ Avarice and hatred were too strong for authority, and during the whole night the work of plunder and havoc went on. "Blessed be God," is the pious ejaculation of the monkish historian, "who delivered up the wicked to death!"ᵒ The king, when the people, satiated with their booty, had retired, ordered a strict investigation. Many were apprehended—three were hanged; but such seems to have been the state of the public feeling, that the government either would not, or dared not, revenge the wrongs inflicted on the Jews: of the three, two suffered for robbing a Christian, on pretence of his being a Jew; one for setting fire to the house of a Jew, which burned down the next belonging to a Christian. One Benedict, to save his life, had submitted to baptism. He appealed to the king to release him from his compulsory engagement. The king referred this new case to the Archbishop of Canterbury, who was present. The Archbishop, Baldwin, who was more used to handle the battle-axe than to turn over tomes of casuistry, answered, though bluntly, perhaps with more plain sense than his more learned brethren might have done, "Why, if he is not willing to become a servant of God, he must even continue a servant of the devil."ᵖ The intelligence of the vengeance wrought by the citizens of London on the enemies of the Lord, probably likewise of the rich spoil they had obtained, spread rapidly throughout the country. All England was then swarming with fanatic friars preaching the Crusade, and fierce soldiers, of all classes, who had taken up the cross.ᵠ The example of London sounded

* Anglia Judaica, p. 29.
ᵒ "Per omnia benedictus Dominus qui tradidit impios." Ann. Waverl.
ᵖ Matt. Paris, sub ann. 1189.
ᵠ Brompton, sub ann. 1189.

like a tocsin, and directed their yet untried zeal and valour against the wealth and the infidelity of the Jews. At Norwich, at Edmondsbury, at Stamford, the Jews were plundered, maltreated, slain. At Lincoln they took timely warning, and, with the connivance of the governor, secured themselves and their more valuable effects in the castle. At York more disastrous scenes took place. Benedict, the relapsed convert, was a native of that city, but died in London of the ill-usage he had received. His friend Jacimus (Joachim) returned to York with the sad intelligence; but scarcely had he arrived when he found the city in a state of the most alarming excitement. The house of Benedict, a spacious building, was attacked; his wife and children, with many others who had fled there as to a place of strength, were murdered; the house was burned to the ground. Joachim, with the wealthiest of the Jews, took refuge in the castle with their most valuable effects; those who were not sufficiently expeditious were put to the sword—neither age nor sex was respected;[r] a few only escaped by submitting to baptism.

The Jews within the citadel, whether on good grounds or not, suspected that secret negotiations were going on between the governor of the castle and the populace, for their surrender; the governor, it was subtly spread abroad among them, was to be repaid for his treachery by a large share of the plunder. The desperate men felt that they had but one alternative; they seized the opportunity of the governor's absence in the town, closed the gates against him, and boldly manned the citadel. The sheriff of the county happened to be in the town

---

[r] The most complete account of all these transactions, at the accession of Richard I., is in Hemingford, sub ann. 1189.

with an armed force. At the persuasion of the indignant
governor, and of the populace, he gave the signal for
attack; but, alarmed at the frantic fury with which the
rabble swarmed to the assault, he endeavoured to revoke
his fatal order, but in vain. A more influential body,
the clergy, openly urged on the besiegers. A Canon
Regular, of the Premonstratensian order, stood in the
midst of the ferocious multitude, in his surplice, shouting
aloud, "Destroy the enemies of Christ; destroy the
enemies of Christ!" Every morning this fierce churchman took the Sacrament, and then proceeded to his
post, where he perished at length, crushed by a great
stone from the battlements. The besieged, after a
manful resistance, found their fate unavoidable. A
council was summoned. Their Rabbi, a foreigner, a
man educated in one of their schools of learning, and
universally respected for his profound knowledge of the
Law, rose up. "Men of Israel," he said, "the God of
our Fathers, to whom none can say, 'What doest thou?'
calls upon us to die for our Law. Death is inevitable;
but we may yet choose whether we will die speedily and
nobly, or ignominiously, after horrible torments and the
most barbarous usage: my advice is, that we voluntarily
render up our souls to our Creator, and fall by our
own hands. The deed is both reasonable, and according
to the Law, and is sanctioned by the example of our
most illustrious ancestors." The old man sat down in
tears. The assembly was divided; some declared that
he had spoken wisely; others that it was a hard saying.
The Rabbi rose again, and said, "Let those who approve
not of my proposal, depart in peace." Some few obeyed,
and left the place—the greater number remained unmoved upon their seats. They then arose, collected
their most precious effects, burned all that was com-

bustible, and buried the rest. They set fire to the castle in many places, cut the throats of their wives and children, and then their own. The Rabbi and Joachim alone survived. The place of honour was reserved for the Rabbi; he first slew Joachim, then pierced himself to the heart. The next morning the populace rushed to the assault with their accustomed fury. They beheld flames bursting from every part of the castle; and a few miserable wretches, with supplications and wild cries, running to and fro on the battlements, who related the fate of their companions; they entreated mercy, they offered to submit to baptism. No sooner were the terms accepted, and the gates opened, than the fanatic multitude poured in, and put every living being to the sword. Not content with this triumph, they rushed to the cathedral, demanded all the bonds and obligations, which had been laid up there in the archives, and cast them all into an enormous bonfire. The king might perhaps have forgiven their former crime, the massacre of his unoffending subjects, but this was an inexpiable offence—treason against his exchequer—as all these debts would have fallen to the Crown. Geoffrey Rydal, Bishop of Ely, the Chancellor, was sent to York, to investigate the affair, but the ringleaders of the riot fled for a time to Scotland,* the chief citizens entered into recognisances, nor does it appear that any persons paid the penalty of the law for this atrocious massacre, by which 500 or 1500 men—the numbers vary—were put to death.†

* During the reign of William the Lion (1165-1214; the accession of Richard was 1189), churchmen in Scotland were interdicted from pledging their beneficers for money borrowed from Jews. Innes, Sketches from Scottish History, ii. p. 36.

† There is a record of one person, whose land was seized to the king on account of his concern in this massacre: "Ricardus Malebisse r. c. de xi. marcis pro repetendâ terrâ suâ usque ad adventum regis quæ saisita fuit in manu Regis propter occisionem Judæorum

On his return from captivity, Richard directed his attention to the affairs of the Jews; the justices on their circuits were ordered to inquire who were the murderers, and what became of the property which had been seized: all who were in possession of these effects, and had not compounded by a fine, were to be brought to justice. The whole community was placed under certain statutes. The Jews were formally recognised as belonging to the Crown.[a] Their property was to be registered, on pain of forfeiture. No bonds and obligations were to be valid unless made in the presence of two lawyers, Jews, two lawyers, Christians, with two public notaries, and enrolled; a fee to the Crown was due on the enrolment of every bond. Two justices of the Jews,[v] were appointed, who attended at the Exchequer to superintend this important branch of the royal revenue. There was a special court in the Exchequer for the affairs of the Jews;[w] there was likewise an officer named the Jews' Escheator. All these contracts were to be made by indenture, one part to be held by the Jew, the second deposited in a common chest, of which

---

Eborac. Et ut Walterus de Carton et Ricardus de Kuheneiß armigeri ejus habeant pacem Regis usque ad adventum ejus." Magn. Rot. 4. R. I.; Anglia Judaica, p. 28. Perhaps the statement in the text above is too strong; there may have been others.

[a] This had long been the case, upon the feudal principle, in other countries. It was recognised in England by a law (a law, however, of which the authenticity has been doubted), that the Jews, and all that belongs to them, are the property of the king (Anglia Judaica): "Judæi et omnia sua regis sunt." Spelman admits the law, Prynne doubts it. In after-times this right was fully recognised. The Jews were taxable at the king's will. See authorities below.

[v] There seem to have been two kinds of justices, two Jewish justices, one named, no doubt, as representing the community (the record quoted in Anglia Judaica, pp. 31, 32), and the Christian justiciaries who represented the Crown. I think that more probable than the view in Anglia Judaica. List of Justices in Madox, p. 159, &c.

[w] Madox, Hist. of. Exchequer, pp. 150-178.

there were three keys, one to be kept by the Jewish, one by the Christian attorney, the third by the two public notaries. The chest was to be sealed with three seals; but in every step of all these processes the Crown contrived to wring out some emolument.[x]

John, previous to his accession, had probably many dealings with the Jews; he knew their value, as a source of revenue, and commenced his reign with heaping favours upon them, by which more were daily tempted to settle in the kingdom. It might almost seem that this weak and unprincipled, but crafty prince, had formed a deliberate scheme of allowing them to accumulate ample treasures, in order that hereafter he might reap a richer harvest of plunder, and render himself independent of his unruly subjects. Their high-priest received a patent for his office from the king. He was styled in the deed, "our Beloved and our Friend" (*dilectus et familiaris noster*).[y] The next year a charter was issued, restoring the Jews, in England and Normandy, to all the privileges enjoyed under Henry the First. They might settle where they pleased; they might hold lands and fees, and take mortgages. They might move about with perfect

---

[x] See in Anglia Judaica several forms of contract and release. In short (concludes Tovey of all these contracts) the king's will was the measure of everything; and upon paying generously for it, they might have a dispensation for anything. If the Jew's debtor would give the king a sum of money, he would order that the record should bear no interest; and unless the Jew would give him something too, he would perhaps compound the matter with the debtor, and make the Jew lose even his principal. But in no case was a Jew allowed to sue for his debt without paying poundage to the king. pp. 42, 43. Compare Madox throughout.

[y] He is called in the records Sacerdos and Presbyter; and it is amusing to see, where such questions run high, theology forcing itself into antiquarianism, and grave writers, like Selden and Prynne, debating whether he was priest or lay-elder. See the form of three or four such appointments, A. J., pp. 58, 60, and Madox, p. 177.

freedom with their chattels which, being the king's, could not be molested.[a] They were to be tried only in the king's court, or before the governors of his royal castles. Their oath was valid as evidence—a Christian and a Jewish witness were of equal weight. In disputes with Christians, Jews were to be tried by their own peers. They might freely buy and sell, excepting the sacred vessels and furniture of the Church. All the subjects of the realm were called upon to protect the Jews and their chattels, as the chattels of the king. Four thousand marks were paid for this charter.[a] By another statute, their own suits were to be determined by their own Law.

The favour of John was not likely to conciliate that of his subjects. All classes looked on the Jews with darker jealousy. The perpetual defamatory tales were repeated of their crucifying children; and the citizens of London, probably envious of their opulence, treated them with many indignities. The king wrote a strong rebuke to the Mayor and to the Barons of London, in which he complained that the Jews, who lived in peace in all other parts of England, were maltreated, in violation of the peace of the king and of the realm, in London alone;[b] he commended the Jews to their protection, stating that he attributed the recent outrages only to the fools—not to the discreet citizens[c]—of the

---

[a] "Et ubicunque Judei fuerint, liceat eis ire ubicunque voluerint, cum omnibus catallis eorum, sicut res nostra propria, et nulli liceat eos retinere, neque hoc eis prohibere."

[a] The Charter in Anglia Judaica, p. 63: "Et omnia illa quæ modo rationabiliter tenent in terris et feodis et vadiis et ablatis suis; et quod habeant omnes libertates et consuetudines suas, sicut eas habuerunt tempore prædicti Regis H. avi, patris nostri melius et quietius et honorabilius." Compare Madox, p. 173.

[b] The letter in Anglia Judaica, p. 67.

[c] "Per fatuos villæ, et non per discretos."

metropolis; he declared that he would require their blood at the hands of the civic magistrates.

On a sudden, in the next year (1210), impatient, as it were, that any part of his subjects should suppose him capable of a long effort of justice, or yielding with his accustomed weakness to the immediate pressure of his necessities, or perhaps rejoicing in thus having prepared himself subjects for spoliation, in whose behalf neither the imperious Pope nor his refractory Barons would interfere, John passed to the extreme of cruelty against the miserable Jews.[d] Every Israelite, without distinction of age or sex, was imprisoned, their wealth confiscated to the Exchequer, and the most cruel torments extorted from the reluctant the confession of their secret treasures. The story of the Jew of Bristol is well known—who was to lose a tooth a day till he betrayed his hoards. Ten thousand marks of silver were demanded of this wealthy merchant; he obstinately lost seven teeth, and saved the rest by paying the ransom demanded. The king gained 60,000 marks by this atrocious proceeding. A second time, demands equally extravagant were made, and these unhappy wretches, who paid so dearly for the privilege of being the vassals of the Crown, were still further plundered by the Barons, as belonging to the king. Their treasures in London were seized, and their houses demolished to repair the walls, by these stern assertors of the liberties of the land. Yet the regulations relating to the Jews in the Great Charter, though not perhaps quite equitable, were by no means wanting in moderation.[e] If a man died in debt to a Jew, the debt bore no interest, till the heir came

---
[d] Matt. Paris, sub ann. 1210. of Southampton, in Anglia Judaica,
[e] See the order for taxing the Jews p. 72.

of age. The wife was to receive her dower, and the children their maintenance; the debt was to be discharged out of the residue.[f]

The first act of the Guardians of the Realm under Henry the Third was to release the Jews who were in prison,[g] and to appoint twenty-four burgesses of every town where they resided, to protect their persons and property,[h] especially against the Crusaders. Among the towns in which they were settled in considerable numbers were Gloucester, Worcester, Hereford, York, Lincoln, Stamford, Bristol, Northampton, Southampton, Winchester, Oxford, Warwick, Norwich.[i] They were exempted from spiritual jurisdiction, and amenable only to the king and his judges; but they were commanded to wear a distinctive mark on their dress, two stripes of white cloth or parchment. This fatal distinction may have been intended in mercy to protect them as the king's property; it would, however, more surely designate them for popular insult, or more than insult; it was in fact the re-enactment or re-enforcement of the Canon of the Lateran Council. Power was also given to the Rabbins to excommunicate refractory Jews. The High Priest was presented to the king, and his authority so ratified.[j] But the avowed protection of the Crown could not shield them from the jealousy of the merchants whose traffic they injured, the hatred of the people, and the bigotry

---

[f] These clauses were not in the Charter as renewed by Henry III., A. J., p. 73.

[g] In the year 1232, Henry III. makes over the custody of the Jewry and all the Jews in Ireland to Peter de Rivaux. Royal Letters of Henry III., Appendix, p. 519.

[h] Many of these writs are now extant in the Tower, in a Roll marked "De Judæis deliberandis." Ang. Jud., p. 76.

[i] See writ to Gloucester, A. J., p. 77.

[j] One high-priest (he is called a bishop) was deprived, but, on his payment of three marks of gold, restored to his office. Rot., p. 29.

of the clergy. The Warden of the Cinque Ports imprisoned several Jews on their landing in England. The Government interfered, but enacted that all Jews should report themselves and be enrolled by the justices of the Jews immediately on their landing, and not quit the kingdom again without a passport.

But the Church was their more implacable enemy; among many enactments, similar to those which had been passed in other kingdoms, was one against Jews keeping Christian slaves,[k] one prohibiting the building any new synagogues, and another for the payment of all tithes or dues to the Church and the Bishop of Norwich.[l] Stephen Langton, Archbishop of Canterbury, and Hugh of Wells, Bishop of Lincoln, prohibited all Christians, on fear of ecclesiastical censure, from selling to them the necessaries of life.[l] The Crown again interfered in a royal precept addressed to the Mayor of Canterbury, the Sheriff of Lincoln, the Mayor and Provost of Oxford, and the Bailiff of Norwich, and commanded all good subjects to defy the spiritual interdict.[m] But these days of peace did not continue long. The Jews offered too great temptation to an impoverished king, in perpetual contest with his subjects. Their offences were said to call for punishment; they dared to sue even the clergy on their bonds;[n] probably

---

[k] The slaves were to be compelled to keep this law by ecclesiastical censure; the Jews, by canonical punishment, or by some arbitrary fine to be imposed and exacted by the diocesan.

[l] At the Synod of Oxford (held by Stephen Langton in 1222), a deacon, who had, from love of a Jewish woman, apostatised to Judaism, was hanged. A. J., p. 81; Matt. Paris, sub ann., with Watts' note and quotation from Lyndewood. Tovey says that the deacon was originally a Jew, but M. Paris does not bear him out. This Synod also enforced the wearing the badge.

[m] A. J., p. 82.

[n] The Prior of Dunstable permitted certain Jews to live in that town, on condition of offering two silver spoons yearly. The Jews were not duly grateful for this privilege. A Jew sued the Prior for 700 pounds (marks?)

in England as in other countries, their sordid spirit, ever watchful to make reprisals on society, might give countenance to many scarcely perhaps exaggerated stories of their usurious extortions. A crime was now laid to their charge, much more probable than the tales of their crucifying children, their tampering with and clipping the coin of the realm;[o] of this crime we shall soon hear more. On the occasion of the wars in France, a sudden demand was made (A.C. 1230) of a third of their moveables to be paid into the Exchequer. It was followed in two years by another, of 18,000 marks; in 1236, by a third, of 10,000 marks.[p] Yet the royal confidence in the inexhaustible resources of the Jews, and the popular prejudice that they could only be supplied by nefarious, if not by magical or supernatural means, were confirmed not only by the discharge of these enormous demands, but by other indications of opulence, which could not be drained even by such unprecedented exactions.[q] The daughter of Hamon, a Jew of Hereford, paid to the king 5000 marks as a relief. A baron's heir paid for his barony only 100 marks—a knight's fee 100 shillings. Aaron of York compounded for a payment of 100 marks a year to be free from taxes. Aaron solemnly declared

on a document said to have been proved a forgery. One of the proofs was that it contained bad grammar. The Jews paid a mark to the king for arrest of judgement; afterwards 100 pounds lest their Law should be disgraced by the Jew being hanged. Hearne, Preface to Chron. of Dunstable.

[o] A. J., p. 89.

[p] About this period a house was opened in London for the reception of Jewish converts; it was in Chancery Lane. Its site is now occupied by the Rolls Court. The extraordinary law which prevailed in France, that the Jewish convert to Christianity forfeited all his property (why should the lord lose his property in his Jew because the Jew would save his soul?) obtained in England also. Henry III. granted back his chattels in Kent to one Augustine, a convert from Judaism. See the Precept to the Sheriff of Kent, A. J., p. 87.

[q] A. J., p. 91.

to Matthew Paris, that the king had exacted from him in seven years 30,000 marks of silver—besides 200 of gold, paid to the queen.'

Yet a few years after, the nation beheld the curious spectacle of a Jewish Parliament regularly summoned. Writs were issued to the sheriffs, with most extraordinary menaces of punishment in case of disobedience,* to return six of the richest Jews from the more considerable towns, two from those where they were fewer in number.' This parliament met, and, like other parliaments, was graciously informed by the sovereign that he must have money—20,000 marks was the sum demanded. His Majesty's faithful Jews could boast no parliamentary privileges, nor were they permitted to demand freedom of debate. They were sent home to collect the money as speedily as possible; it was to be assessed and levied among themselves, and, as this enormous charge was not immediately forthcoming, the collectors were seized, with their wives and children, their goods and chattels, and imprisoned.

Jewish history has a melancholy sameness—perpetual

' Matt. Paris, sub ann. 1250.

* See, in A. J., Writ to the Sheriff of Northampton: "Sciturus quod nisi illuc ad terminum præfatum veneriut, ita manum nostram tam erga corpus quam catalla tua aggravabimus, quod ta perpetuo sentics non mediocriter pregravare." This threat must have been intended to alarm not only the sheriff, but rather the Jews; though, as their chattels were already the king's, they were liable to arbitrary seizure. "Prynne," observes the author of Anglia Judaica, "has given us above a hundred names of persons returned to this parliament, but as they make but indifferent musick, I shall not repeat them." See warrants in A. J., pp. 112, 113. Also in Royal Letters of the time of Henry III., p. 392, Precept to the Sheriff of Kent to send up the six most substantial Jews from Canterbury and from Rochester.

' Southampton and Newcastle had petitioned that no Jews might be permitted to reside within their walls. This privilege was extended to other towns—Derby, Rot. p. 32; Rumsey, p. 38. The exemptions to Southampton and Newcastle, A. J., pp. 102, 105. Madox, pp. 176, 177.

exactions, the means of enforcing them differing only in their degrees of cruelty. The Parliament of the Realm began to consider that these extraordinary succours ought at least to relieve the rest of the nation. They began to inquire into the king's resources from this quarter, and the king consented that one of the two justices of the Jews should be appointed by Parliament. But the Barons thought more of easing themselves than of protecting the oppressed. The next year a new demand of 8000 marks was made, under pain of being transported, some at least of the most wealthy, to Ireland;[u] and, lest they should withdraw their families into places of concealment, they were forbidden, under the penalty of outlawry and confiscation, to remove wife or child from their usual place of residence, for their wives and children were now liable to taxation as well as themselves. During the next three years 60,000 marks more were levied.[x] How then was it possible for any traffic, however lucrative, to endure such perpetual exactions? The reason must be found in the enormous interest of money, which seems to have been considered by no means immoderate at fifty per cent.; certain Oxford scholars thought themselves relieved by being constrained to pay only twopence weekly on a debt of twenty shillings.[y] In fact, the rivalry of more successful usurers seems to have afflicted the Jews more deeply than the exorbitant demands of the king. These were the Caorsini, Italian bankers, though named from the town of Cahors, employed by

---

[u] "Aliquos de ditioribus Judæis, at corpora eorum mittant ad Regem usque ad Gannock." Anglia Judaica, p. 118.

[x] Document, A. J., p. 119. They were obliged to contribute, at least in kind, to the building and decoration of Westminster Abbey, p. 138.

[y] A. J., p. 122.

the Pope to collect his revenue. It was the practice of these persons, under the sanction of their principal, to lend money for three months without interest, but afterwards to receive five per cent. monthly, till the debt was discharged: the former device was to exempt them from the charge of usury.* The king, at one time, attempted to expel this new swarm of locusts; but they asserted their authority from the Pope, and the monarch trembled. Nor were their own body always faithful to the Jews. A certain Abraham, who lived at Berkhampstead and Wallingford, with a beautiful wife who bore the heathen name of Flora, was accused of treating an image of the Virgin with most indecent contumely; he was sentenced to perpetual imprisonment, but released on the intervention of Richard Earl of Cornwall, on payment of 700 marks. He was a man, it would seem, of infamous character, for his brethren accused him of coining, and offered 1000 marks rather than that he should be released from prison. Richard refused the tempting bribe, because Abraham was "his Jew." Abraham revenged himself by laying information of plots and conspiracies entered into by the whole people, and the more probable charge of concealment of their wealth from the rapacious hands of the king. This led to a strict and severe investigation of their property. At this investigation was present a wicked and merciless Jew, who rebuked the Christians for their tenderness to his brethren, and reproached the king's officers as gentle and effeminate. He gnashed his teeth, and, as each Jew appeared, declared that he could afford to pay twice as much as was exacted. Though he lied, he

---

* See the bond in Matt. Paris to certain Milanese merchants.

was useful in betraying their secret hoards to the king.[a]

The distresses of the king increased, and, as his Parliament resolutely refused to maintain his extravagant expenditure, nothing remained but to drain still further the veins of the Jews. The office was delegated to Richard Earl of Cornwall, his brother, whom, from his wealth, the king might consider possessed of some secret for accumulating riches from hidden sources. The Rabbi Elias was deputed to wait on the prince, expressing the unanimous determination of all the Jews to quit the country, rather than submit to further burthens: "Their trade was ruined by the Caorsini, the Pope's merchants (the Jew dared not call them usurers), who heaped up masses of gold by their money-lending; they could scarcely live on the miserable gains they now obtained; if their eyes were torn out, and their bodies flayed, they could not give more." The old man fainted at the close of his speech, and was with difficulty revived.[b] Their departure from the country was a vain boast, for whither should they go? The edicts of the King of France had closed that country against them, and the inhospitable world scarcely afforded a place of refuge. Earl Richard treated them with leniency, and accepted a small sum. But the next year the king renewed his demands—his declaration affected no disguise: "It is dreadful to imagine the debts to which I am bound. By the face of God, they amount to 200,000 marks; if I should say 300,000, I should not go beyond the truth. Money I must have, from any place, from any person, or by any

---

[a] This characteristic scene is related by Matt. Paris, sub ann. 1250.
[b] Matt. Paris, sub ann. 1254.

means."[c] The king's acts display as little dignity as his proclamation. He actually sold or mortgaged to his brother Richard all the Jews in the realm for 5000 marks, giving him full power over their property and persons: our records still preserve the terms of this extraordinary bargain and sale.[d] Popular opinion, which in the worst times is some restraint upon the arbitrary oppressions of kings, in this case would rather applaud the utmost barbarity of the monarch, than commiserate the wretchedness of the victims; for a new tale of the crucifixion of a Christian child, called Hugh of Lincoln, was now spreading horror throughout the country. The fact was confirmed by a solemn trial, and the conviction and execution of the criminals. It was proved, according to the mode of proof in those days, that the child had been stolen, fattened on bread and milk for ten days, and crucified with all the cruelties and insults of Christ's Passion, in the presence of all the Jews in England, summoned to Lincoln for this especial purpose; a Jew of Lincoln sat in judgement as Pilate. But the earth could not endure to be an accomplice in the crime; it cast up the buried remains, and the affrighted criminals were obliged to throw the body into a well, where it was found by the mother.[e] Great part of this story refutes itself, but I have already admitted the possibility, that among the ignorant and fanatic Jews there might be some who, exasperated by the constant repetition of this charge, might brood over it so long as at length to be tempted to its perpetration.

---

[c] Matt. Paris, sub ann. 1255.
[d] "Noveritis nos mutuo accepisse a dilecto fratre et fideli nostro R. Comite Cornubiæ quinque millia Marcorum Sterlingorum, securum et integrorum, ad quorum solutionem assignavimus et tradidimus et omnes Judæos nostros Angliæ." A. J., p. 131; from Madox, p. 135.

[e] The Annals of Waverley are full on the death and canonization of Hugh of Lincoln.

I must not suppress the fearful vengeance wreaked on the supposed perpetrators of this all-execrated crime. The Jew into whose house the child, it was said, had gone to play, tempted by the promise of life and security from mutilation, made full confession, and threw the guilt upon his brethren. The king, indignant at this unauthorised covenant of mercy, ordered him to execution. The Jew, in his despair or frenzy, entered into a still more minute and terrible denunciation of all the Jews of the realm, as consenting to the act. He was dragged, tied to a horse's tail, to the gallows; his body and his soul delivered to the dæmons of the air. Ninety-one Jews of Lincoln were sent to London as accomplices, and thrown into dungeons. If, says the monkish historian, some Christians felt pity for their sufferings, their rivals, the Caorsini, beheld them with dry eyes. The king's inquest declared all the Jews of the realm guilty of the crime. The mother made her appeal to the king. Eighteen of the richest and most eminent of the Lincoln Jews were hung on a new gallows; twenty more were imprisoned in the Tower awaiting the same fate. But if the Jews of Lincoln were thus terribly chastised, the Church of Lincoln was enriched and made famous for centuries. The victim was canonized; pilgrims crowded from all parts of the kingdom, even from foreign lands, to pay their devotions at the shrine, to witness and to receive benefit from the miracles which were wrought by the martyr of eight years old. How deeply this legend sank into the popular mind may be conceived from Chaucer's Prioress's Tale alluded to above.

The rest of the reign of Henry the Third passed away with the same unmitigated oppressions of the Jews; which the Jews, no doubt, in some degree revenged by their extortions from the people. The contest between the royal and ecclesiastical jurisdiction over the Jews was arranged by certain constitutions, set forth by the king in council. By these laws no Jew could reside in the kingdom, but as king's serf. Service was to be performed in the synagogue in a low tone, so as not to offend the ears of Christians. The Jews were forbidden to have Christian nurses for their children. The other clauses were similar to those enacted in other countries: that the Jew should pay all dues to the parson; no Jew should eat or buy meat during Lent; all disputes on religion were forbidden; sexual intercourse between Jews and Christians interdicted; no Jew might settle in any town where Jews were not accustomed to reside, without special licence from the king.[f]

The Barons' wars drew on, fatal to the Israelites as compelling the king, by the hopeless state of his finances, to new extortions, and tempting the Barons to plunder and even murder them, as wickedly and unconstitutionally attached to the king. How they passed back from Richard of Cornwall into the king's jurisdiction as property appears not. It is not likely that the king redeemed the mortgage; but in 1261 they were again alienated to Prince Edward. The king's object was apparently by this and other gifts to withdraw the prince from his alliance with the Barons. The justiciaries of the Jews are now in abeyance. The Chancellor of the Exchequer was to seal all writs of Judaism, and account to the attorneys of the prince for the amount. But this was not the worst of their sufferings or the bitterest disgrace; the prince, in his turn,

---

[f] The law in Anglia Judaica, and Madox, p. 168, who dates it about the 37th year of Henry III., A.C. 1252.

mortgaged them to certain of their dire enemies, the Caorsini, and the king ratified the assignment by his royal authority.[e]

But for this compulsory aid, wrung from them by violence, the Jews were treated by the Barons as allies and accomplices of the king. When London, at least her turbulent mayor and the populace, declared for the Barons; when the grand justiciary, Hugh le Despenser, led the City bands to destroy the palaces of the King of the Romans at Westminster and Isleworth, threw the Justices of the King's Bench and the Barons of the Exchequer into prison, and seized the property of the foreign merchants, five hundred of the Jews,[h] men, women, and children, were apprehended, and set apart, but not for security. Despenser chose some of the richest in order to extort a ransom for his own people; the rest were plundered, stripped, murdered by the merciless rabble. Old men, and babes plucked from their mothers' breasts, were pitilessly slaughtered. It was on Good Friday that one of the fiercest of the Barons, Fitz John, put to death Cok ben Abraham, reputed to have been the wealthiest man in the kingdom, seized his property, but, fearful of the jealousy of the other Barons, surrendered one half of the plunder to Leicester, in order to secure his own portion.[i] The Jews of other cities fared no better, were pillaged, and then abandoned to

---

[e] Documents in A. J., pp. 157, 158.
[h] In his Charter to the City, King Henry exempts his Jews, who were to remain the exclusive property of himself and his successors: "De Judæis autem nostris nos et civitatem nostram tangentibus, providebimus, nos et heredes nostri, prout melius nobis videbitur expedire." The Barons no doubt seized them as the property of the king. Liber Albus, p. 255.

[i] Lingard, of our historians, has related this with the greatest spirit and felicity from Wikes and M. Westminster. Wikes is full; Westminster more pitilessly brief: "Ao in ipsâ Passione Dominicâ apud Londinium de quâdam proditione Baronibus simul ac civibus infenendâ, omnes fere Judæi

the mob by the Earl of Gloucester; many at Worcester were plundered and forced to submit to baptism by the Earl of Derby. At an earlier period the Earl of Leicester (Simon de Montfort) had expelled them from the town of Leicester; they sought refuge in the domains of the Countess of Winchester. Robert Grostête, the wisest and best churchman of the day, then Archdeacon of Leicester, hardly permitted the Countess to harbour this accursed race; their lives might be spared, but all further indulgence, especially acceptance of their ill-gotten wealth, would make her an accomplice in the wickedness of their usuries.[k]

After the battle of Lewes, the king, with the advice of his Barons (he was now a prisoner in their camp), issued a proclamation to the Lord Mayor and Sheriffs of London, in favour of the Jews. Some had found refuge, during the tumult and massacre, in the Tower of London; they were permitted to return with their

---

trucidati sunt, thesauro incomparabili assumpto in Judaismo." p. 286 (sub ann. 1264).

[k] Read the remarkable letter of Robert Grostête, then Archdeacon of Leicester, afterwards the famous Bishop of Lincoln, to the Countess on this subject, as showing the feelings of the most enlightened churchman in those times towards the Jews. His mercy, if it was mercy, would spare their lives. "As murderers of the Lord, as still blaspheming Christ and mocking His Passion, they were to be in captivity to the princes of the earth. As they have the brand of Cain, and are condemned to wander over the face of the earth, so were they to have the privilege of Cain, that no one was to kill them. But those who favoured or harboured them were to take care that they did not oppress Christian subjects by usury. It was for this reason that Simon de Montfort had expelled them from Leicester. Whoever protected them might share in the guilt of their usuries." There are some sentences evidently pointed at the king, for his dealings with them and his connivance (by extorting, it is presumed, a share in their ungodly gains) in their nefarious practices: "Principes quoque qui de usuris, quas Judæi a Christianis extorserint, aliquid acceperint, de rapinâ vivunt et sanguinem eorum quos tueri deberent, sine misericordia bibunt et induunt." Epist. Rob. Grostête, p. 30, Rolls Publication.

families to their homes. All ill-usage or further molestation was prohibited under pain of death. Orders of the same kind were issued to Lincoln; twenty-five citizens were named by the king and the Barons[l] their special protectors; so also to Northampton. The king (Prince Edward was now at war with the Barons, who had the king in their power) revoked the grant of the Jews to his son; with that the grant to the Caorsini, which had not expired, was cancelled. The justiciaries appointed by the prince to levy the tallage upon them were declared to have lost their authority; the Jews passed back to the property of the king. The king showed his power by annulling many debts and the interest due upon them to some of his faithful followers, avowedly in order to secure their attachment.[m] It was now clearly for the king's interest that such profitable subjects should find, we may not say justice, but something like restitution, which might enable them again to become profitable. The king in the parliament, which commenced its sittings immediately after the battle of Lewes, and continued till after the battle of Evesham, restored the Jews to the same state in which they were before the battle of Lewes. As to the Jews in London,[n] the constable of the Tower was to see not only that those who had taken refuge in the Tower, but those who had fled to other places, were to return to their houses, which were to be restored, except such as had been granted away by the king; and even all their property which could be recovered from the king's enemies. Excepting that some of the Barons' troops,

---

[l] Trivet, A. J., p. 166.
[m] "Ut nobis devotiores et obsequium nostrum promptiores efficiantur." See the Instrument, A. J., p. 167.
[n] Writ to the Mayor and Sheriffs, A. J., p. 161; Parliamentary Writ, p. 164.

flying from the battle of Evesham, under the younger Simon de Montfort, broke open and plundered the synagogue at Lincoln, where they found much wealth, and some excesses committed at Cambridge, the Jews had time to breathe. The king, enriched by the forfeited estates of the Barons, spared the Jews. We only find a tallage of 1000 pounds, with promise of exemption for three years, unless the king or his son should undertake a Crusade.°

Their wrongs had, no doubt, sunk deep into the hearts of the Jews. It has been observed that oppression, which drives even wise men mad, may instigate fanatics to the wildest acts of frenzy; an incident at Oxford will illustrate this. Throughout these times the Jews still flourished, if they may be said to have flourished, at Oxford. In 1244 certain clerks of the University broke into the houses of the Jews and carried away enormous wealth. The magistrates seized and imprisoned some of the offenders. Grostête, as bishop of the diocese (Oxford was then in the diocese of Lincoln), commanded their release, because there was no proof of felony against them.^p We hear nothing of restitution. The scholars might indeed hate the Jews, whose interest on loans was *limited*, by Bishop Grostête, to twopence weekly in the pound—between 40 and 50 per cent. Probably the poor scholars' security was not over good. Later, the studies in the University are said to have been interrupted, the scholars being unable to redeem their books, pledged to the Jews.^q

---

° Warrant, A. J., p. 167.

^p "Rons eorum innumerabilia asportaverunt." Wikes, sub ann. 1244. ". . . quia nullus apparuit qui eos directe convincere posset de crimine felonie." Ibid.

^q Compare Luard, Preface to Grostête Epistolæ, p. lxix.; for the latter fact, A. J., p. 209.

Four-and-twenty years after the outbreak of the scholars, years of bitterness and spoliation and suffering, while the chancellor and the whole body of the University were in solemn procession to the reliques of St. Frideswide, they were horror-struck by beholding a Jew rush forth, seize the cross which was borne before them, dash it to the ground, and trample upon it with the most furious contempt. The offender seems to have made his escape in the tumult, but his people suffered for his crime. Prince Edward was then at Oxford; and, by the royal decree, the Jews were imprisoned, and forced, notwithstanding much artful delay on their part, to erect a beautiful cross of white marble, with an image of the Virgin and Child, gilt all over, in the area of Merton College;[r] and to present to the proctors another cross of silver, to be borne in all future processions of the University.[s] The Jews endeavoured to elude this penalty by making over their effects to other persons. The king empowered the sheriff to levy the fine on all their property.[t]

The last solemn act of Henry of Winchester was a statute of great importance. Complaints had arisen that the Jews, by purchase, or probably foreclosure of mortgage, might become possessed of all the rights of lords of manors, escheat wardships, even of presentation to churches. They might hold entire baronies with all their appurtenances. The whole was swept away by one remorseless clause. The

---

[r] Walter de Merton purchased of a Jew the ground on which the front of his College now stands, Nov. 12, 1272.

[s] Wood's Hist. and Antiq. of Oxford, ad ann. 1268.

[t] See king's warrant, &c., A. J., p. 176.

Act[w] disqualified the Jews altogether from holding lands, or even tenements, except the houses of which they were actually possessed, particularly in the City of London, where they might only pull down and rebuild on the old foundations. All lands or manors were actually taken away; those which they held by mortgage were to be restored to the Christian owners, without any interest on such bonds. Henry almost died in the act of extortion; he had ordered the arrears of all charges to be peremptorily paid, under pain of imprisonment. Such was the distress caused by this inexorable mandate, that even the rival bankers, the Caorsini, and the Friars themselves, were moved to commiseration, though some complained that the wild outcries raised in the synagogue on this doleful occasion disturbed the devotion of the Christians in the neighbouring churches.[x]

The death of Henry released the Jews from this Egyptian bondage; but they changed their master, not their fortune. The first act of Edward's reign, after his return from the Holy Land, regulated the affairs of the Jews exactly in the same spirit: a new tallage was demanded, which was to extend to the women and children; the penalty of non-payment, even of arrears, was exile, not imprisonment. The defaulter was to proceed immediately to Dover, with his wife and children, leaving his house and property to the use of the king. The execution of this edict was committed, not to the ordinary civil authorities, but to an Irish bishop (elect) and to two friars.[y] This edict was fol-

---

[w] See the Act, which the author of Anglia Judaica discovered in the Bodleian, p. 198.

[x] Anglia Judaica, p. 106.
[y] See Commission, p. 196.

lowed up by the celebrated Act of Parliament concerning Judaism,[a] the object of which seems to have been the same with the policy of Louis IX. of France, to force the Jews to abandon usury, and betake themselves to traffic, manufactures, or the cultivation of land. It positively prohibited all usury, and cancelled all debts on payment of the principal. No Jew might distress beyond the moiety of a Christian's land and goods; they were to wear their badge, a badge now of yellow, not white, and pay an Easter offering of threepence, men and women, to the king. They were permitted to practise merchandize, or labour with their hands, and—some of them, it seems, were still addicted to husbandry—to hire farms for cultivation for fifteen years. On these terms they were assured of the royal protection. But manual labour and traffic were not sources sufficiently expeditious for the enterprising avarice of the Jews. Many of them, thus reduced, took again to a more unlawful and dangerous occupation, clipping and adulterating the coin. In one day (Nov. 17th, 1279) all the Jews in the kingdom were arrested. In London alone, 280 were executed, after a full trial; many more in other parts of the kingdom. A vast quantity of clipped coin was found, and confiscated to the king's use.[b] The king granted their estates and forfeitures with lavish hand. But law, though merciless, and probably not over-scrupulous in the investigation of crime, did not satisfy the popular passions, which had

---

[a] See the Act translated from the Norman French. It is remarkable that the king admits, notwithstanding, that they (the Jews) are and have been very profitable to him and his ancestors.

[b] Ann. Waverl., sub ann. 1278: "Inventa est maxima summa retonsionis [clipped coin] apud eos quae totaliter derenit ad fiscum Regis, ad magnum damnum totius regni et gravamen."

been let loose by these wide and general accusations. The populace took the law into their own hands. Everywhere there was full licence for plunder, and worse than plunder. The king was obliged to interpose. A writ[b] was issued, addressed to the justiciaries who had presided at the trials for the adulteration of the coin, Peter of Pentecester, Walter of Heylynn, John of Cobham, appointed justiciaries for the occasion. It recited that many Jews had been indicted and legally condemned to death, and to the forfeiture of their goods and chattels; but that certain Christians, solely on account of religious differences, were raising up false and frivolous charges against men who had not been legally arraigned, in order to extort money from them by fear. No Jew against whom a legal indictment had not been issued before the 1st of May was to be molested or subject to accusation. Those only arrested on grave suspicion before that time were to be put upon their trial. Jewish tradition attributes the final expulsion of the Jews to these charges, which the king, it avers, did not believe, yet was compelled to yield to popular clamour.[c]

But not all the statutes, nor public executions, nor the active preaching of the Dominican Friars, who undertook to convert them if they were constrained to hear their sermons (the king's bailiffs, on the petition of the Friars,[d] were ordered to induce the Jews to

---

[b] See the Writ, in A. J., p. 208.

[c] Schevet Judah: "Hac arte everterе Judæus aggressi Christiani fingunt et dictitant, adulterasse monetam." Though these charges were disproved, the king would not acknowledge his belief of their innocence, p. 140.

[d] The petition of the Friars was, "Quod omnes Judæos, ubicunque locorum in Ballivis vestris conversantes, efficaciter moneatis et inducatis, quod in locis ubi vobis de consilio Fratrum ipsorum magis expedire videbitur ad audiendum verbum Dei conveniant; et illud ab iisdem Fratribus, absque tumultu, contentione vel blasphemia, audiant diligenter et benigne." A. J., p. 219. The king was graciously

become quiet, meek, and uncontentious hearers), could either alter the Jewish character, still patient of all evil so that they could extort wealth; or suppress the still-increasing clamour of public detestation, which demanded that the land should cast forth from its indignant bosom this irreclaimable race of rapacious infidels. Still worse, if we may trust a Papal Bull, the presence and intercourse of the Jews were dangerous to the religion of England. In the year 1286, the Pope (Honorius IV.) addressed a Bull to the Archbishop of Canterbury and his suffragans, rebuking them for the remissness of the clergy in not watching more closely the proceedings of the Jews. The Archbishop, indeed, had not been altogether so neglectful in the duty of persecution. The number and the splendour of the synagogues in London had moved the indignation, perhaps the jealousy, of Primate Peckham. He issued his monition to the Bishop of London to inhibit the building any more of these offensively sumptuous edifices, and to compel the Jews to destroy those built within a prescribed time. The zeal of the Bishop of

---

pleased to accede to the wishes of the Dominicans, and to issue instructions accordingly, to be valid so long as he should think fit. The king did more; he generously waived his claim for seven years to more than a moiety of the goods of the converts; the other half was given to maintain the poor in the Hospital for Converts, already founded on ground now occupied by the Rolls Court. (The king had before granted deodands on the Jews to the Friars Preachers.) There are in Anglia Judaica several appointments of wardens, and other documents relating to this house and chapel. It is still more curious that allowances were made to converts from Judaism, after the grant of the house to the Master of the Rolls, out of the revenue of the house. One in the time of Richard II. to a female, said to have been the daughter of a bishop (Episcopi) of the Jews; she had one penny a day. Another as late as James II.; the convert had 1½d. a day (A. J., p. 226). Among the strange anomalies of the time was an action for defamation against certain persons (it was a litigation about the dower of a Jew's wife), for asserting that the Jewess had been baptized. A. J., p. 231.

London (Robert de Gravesend) outran that of the Archbishop; he ordered them all to be levelled to the ground. The Archbishop, prevailed on by the urgent supplications of the Jews, graciously informed the bishop that he might conscientiously allow one synagogue, if that synagogue did not wound the eyes of pious Christians by its magnificence.* But the Bull of Honorius IV. was something more than a stern condemnation of the usurious and extortionate practices of the Jews; it was a complaint of their progress, not merely in inducing Jewish converts to Christianity to apostatize back to Judaism, but of their not unsuccessful endeavours to tempt Christians to Judaism. "These Jews lure them to their synagogues on the Sabbath [are we to suppose that there was something splendid and attractive in the Synagogue worship of the day?]; and in their friendly intercourse at common banquets, the souls of Christians, softened by wine, and good eating, and social enjoyment, are endangered."† The Talmud of the Jews, which they still persist in studying, is especially denounced as full of abomination, falsehood, and infidelity.

The king at length listened to the public voice, and the irrevocable edict of total expulsion from the realm was issued. Their whole property was seized at once, and just money enough left to discharge their expenses to foreign

---

* A. J., pp. 302-304.

† "Præfati quoque Judæi non solum mentes fidelium ad eorum sectam pestiferam allicere moliuntur, verum etiam illos qui salubri ducti consilio infidelitatis abjurantes errorem ad lucem catholicæ fidei convolarunt donis multimodis ad apostatandum inducere non verentur." They invite Christians on the Sabbath to their synagogues, "quamobrem plerique Christicolæ pariter Judaizant." They buy Christian servants of both sexes.... "Christiani et Judæi in domibus propriis sæpe conveniunt, et dum simul commessationibus et potationibus vacant, erroris malitia præparatur." Apud Raynaldum, sub ann. 1286.

lands, perhaps equally inhospitable.* The 10th October
was the fatal day. The king benignantly allowed them
till All Saints' Day; after which all who delayed were
to be hanged without mercy. The king, in the execution of this barbarous proceeding, put on the appearance both of religion and moderation. Safe-conducts
were to be granted to the seashore from all parts of the
kingdom. The Wardens of the Cinque Ports were to
provide shipping and receive the exiles with civility and
kindness. The king expressed his intention of converting great part of his gains to pious uses, but the Church
looked in vain for the fulfilment of his vows. He issued
orders that the Jews should be treated with kindness
and courtesy on their journey to the seashore. But
where the prince by his laws thus gave countenance to
the worst passions of human nature, it was not likely
that they would be suppressed by his proclamations.
The Jews were pursued from the kingdom with every
mark of popular triumph in their sufferings; one man,
indeed, the master of a vessel at Queenborough, was
punished for leaving a considerable number on the shore
at the mouth of the river, when, as they prayed to him
to rescue them from their perilous situation, he answered, that they had better call on Moses, who had
made them pass safe through the Red Sea; and sailing
away with their remaining property, left them to their
fate.[b] The number of exiles is variously estimated at

---

* The Act for the expulsion of the Jews has not come down to us; we know not, therefore, the reasons alleged for the measure. Of the fact there can be no doubt (see Report on the Dignity of a Peer, p. 180), and there are many documents relating to the event, as writs to the authorities in Gloucester and York, to grant them safe-conduct to the parts where they were to embark.

[b] Coke's Institutes, p. 508. Matt. Westminster, sub ann. 1290.

15,060 and 16,511; all their property, debts, obligations, mortgages, escheated to the king. Yet some, even in those days, presumed to doubt whether the nation gained by the act of expulsion, and even ventured to assert that the public burthens on the Christians only became heavier and more intolerable.[i] Catholics suffered in the place of the enemies of the Cross of Christ. The loss to the Crown was enormous.[k] The convents made themselves masters of the valuable libraries of the Jews, one at Stamford, another at Oxford, from which the celebrated Roger Bacon is said to have derived great information; and long after, the common people would dig in the places they had frequented, in hopes of finding buried treasures. Thus terminates the first period of the History of the Jews in England.

---

[i] "Sane quantum emolumenti regis fisco deperiit per relegationem Judæorum a regno, multo amplius eidem per deplorabilem quintæ decimæ totius regni quam extorsit a Catholicis exaggerationem: sic quoque pro inimicis Christi crucis immisericorditer puniuntur." Wikes adds, "Nec quatenus æstimari potest occasione tanti sceleris deperiit, præsertim cum non tantum nullagiis, sed et placitis, demariis, escheatis, et exeniis ærarium Domini Regis conservarunt multipliciter augmentare." Wikes, sub ann. 1290.

[k] "Great," writes the author of Anglia Judaica, "were the spoils they left behind them. Whole Rolls, full of patents relating to their estates, are still remaining in the Tower, which, together with their rents in fee and their mortgages, all escheated to the King." p. 244.

BOOK XXVI.

JEWS EXPELLED FROM SPAIN.

Superiority of the Jews of Spain — Early period — Alfonso VIII. — Ferdinand III. — Alfonso X., the Wise — Siete Partidas — Attempt at Conversion — Ferdinand IV. — Alfonso XI. — Pedro of Castile and Henry of Transtamare — Zeal of the Clergy — Pope Benedict XIII. — Conversions — Vincent Ferrer — New Christians — The Inquisition — Ferdinand and Isabella — Expulsion of the Jews from Spain — Sufferings in Italy — In Morocco — In Portugal — Their subsequent History in the two kingdoms.

FRANCE and England had thus finally, it might appear, purified their realms from the infection of Jewish infidelity. Two centuries after their expulsion from England, one after that from France—Spain, disdaining to be outdone in religious persecution, made up the long arrears of her dormant intolerance, and asserted again her evil pre-eminence in bigotry. The Jews of Spain were of a far nobler rank than those of England, of Germany, and even of France. In the latter countries they were a caste—in the former, as it were, an order in the state. Prosperous and wealthy, they had not been, generally, reduced to the sordid occupations and debasing means of extorting riches, to which, with some exceptions, they had sunk in other countries. They were likewise the most enlightened class in the kingdom; they were possessors and cultivators of the soil; they were still, not seldom, ministers of finance; their fame as physicians was generally acknowledged, and no doubt deserved—for they had in their own tongue, or in Arabic, the best books of the ancient writers on medicine, and, by their intercourse with the East, no doubt obtained many valuable drugs unknown in the West.

Jewish tradition, which took the form of legend, looked back to Spain as the scene of a golden age. "For more than six hundred years beautiful and flourishing Spain might be looked on as the happy land, the earthly Paradise. There party madness had not inflamed the inhabitants against each other, and disturbed the sweet domestic peace. Everyone might worship God in his own manner, without on that account being despised and hated. Even Israel, that oppressed and persecuted people, found in happy Spain a haven of freedom. Everyone sat under his shady fig-tree or cluster-laden vine, singing hymns of thanksgiving to the mighty God of Israel, who again had mercy on His people, and gave them rest so long unknown. There were great men who sprang from the stock of Israel, men of learning, men of wisdom, poets, artists, whose names even to our own days are held in honour."* It might have been difficult for the author of these glowing sentences to make out his six centuries of peace. The Moorish persecution, which drove Maimonides from his native land, and other persecutions, related in my former pages, break in on this bright and serene retrospect. Whatever they were in other lands, in Spain they were more than a people within a people—they were a state within a state. The heads of the community, whether as princes or Rabbins, exercised not only religious, but civil authority also; they formed a full judicial tribunal

---

* I cannot call to mind from what Jewish writer I transcribed this, but can vouch for its accuracy.

in criminal as well as ecclesiastical affairs; adjudged not only in cases of property, but of life; passed sentences beyond that of excommunication, sentences of capital punishment. Many of the hostile statutes of the Kings, and of the Cortes, aim at depriving them of this judicial power; they are to cease to have judges. Even as late as 1391 they put to death, as unsound, Don Joseph Piehon.[b] It was only at that time, under John I., that they were deprived of this right.

We have seen the commencement of the Iron Age in Spain;[c] we must ascend again the stream of history to trace the gradually and irregularly darkening doom of the race in the Spanish peninsula.

Mariana would give the authority of history to the passion of the renowned Alfonso VIII. (A.C. 1158-1213) for the beautiful Jewess of Toledo, Rachel. To the judgement of God, for the sin of the king and his adultery, was attributed the loss of the great battle of Alarcos (A.C. 1195). The nobles released the king from the bonds of his unholy love by murdering the unhappy Jewess. The subject has been a favourite with Spanish dramatists.[d] In the great crusade of the Christian kings, of Castile, of Arragon, and of Navarre, which won the crowning victory of Navas de Tolosa (A.C. 1212), the wild cry, which had rung through the cities of France and on the Rhine against the Jews, was raised in Toledo. The king and the nobles interposed,[e] but it is said not before 12,000 miserable Jews had been maltreated or fallen by the sword. The triumph of the Christians threatened to

---

[b] Amador de los Rios, p. 188.
[c] See p. 203.
[d] Lope de Vega, Miradesperonus, Diamante, and La Huerta. I have read Diamante's play, which is very spirited. Huerta's is a more regular tragedy. See Mariana, xi. c. 18.
[e] Mariana, xi. c. 23.

be as fatal to the Jews as their arming for battle against the unbelievers; but the conquering monarch had power to restrain their ferocity.

Better times came with better kings. The silence of history as to the state of the Jews during the reign of Ferdinand the Saint, from 1217 to 1252, shows at least that he had a nobler title to sanctity than as a persecutor. Scarcely more is known than that at his remonstrance on the impracticability of branding the Jews with a peculiar dress, and so arraying the two races in irreconcileable hostility and exposing one to daily and habitual contempt, the mild Honorius III. suspended the execution of the stern law of his predecessor, Innocent III., unless under further instructions from the Papal See.[f]

Alfonso the Wise of Castile commenced his long reign in A.C. 1252. Already, before his father's death, in the settlement of the affairs of the city of Seville, the Prince showed manifest signs of favour to the proscribed race. He conceded to them certain lands; in Seville he gave them three mosques for synagogues. Their Jewry was enclosed by a wall which reached from the Alcazar to the Carmona Gate. He bestowed other heritable possessions on opulent Jews. He encouraged the residence of learned and distinguished Jews in the city. The Jews, in gratitude, presented to him a key of exquisite workmanship for the cathedral of Seville,

---

[f] "Quare nobis fuit, tam ex dicti regis [Ferdinand III.] quam ex tua parte humiliter supplicatum, ut executione constitutionis super hoc edictæ tibi supersedere de nostra provisione liceret, cum absque gravi scandalo procedere non valeat in eadem: volentes igitur tranquillitati dicti regis et regni paternâ solicitudine providere, præsentium tibi auctoritate mandamus, quatenus executionem constitutionis supradictæ suspendas, quamdiu expedire cognoveris, nisi forsan super exquundam eamdem apostolicum mandatum speciale receperis." Honor. III. ad Archiepiscopum Toletanum, April, 1219.

with the inscription, "God will open; the king will enter in." The same words in Hebrew characters ran round the ring of the key.[a] Soon after his accession Alfonso founded professorships at Seville, at Toledo, and other places, for the cultivation of the Hebrew language and literature. Perhaps the grant, under a sealed letter, to the metropolitan church of Seville, to impose the same capitation tax on the Jews which prevailed in other dioceses of Spain, may have been in some degree a protective measure. It is but natural, and no unfair imputation, to suppose that the zeal of the clergy would be somewhat mitigated by this tribute. Such useful tributaries would be less hateful, for money is a great peacemaker. But when the wise and just Alfonso was called on to draw up the great Statute Laws of the realm (the Siete Partidas),[b] he was constrained to make concessions to the sterner spirit of the times. In this code there is a severe enactment against the public preaching of Judaism and the endeavour to make proselytes (this ordinance, like all of the same class, betrays some dread of the strength of Judaism). There is an inhibition (perhaps a merciful one) for all Jews to keep within their houses on Friday, on pain of being exposed to insult and injury from the excited Christians. They are excluded from all public offices. The Christians are interdicted from living in familiarity with Jews. Jews are forbidden to have Christian servants; and finally they are condemned to wear some mark on their dress distinguishing them from other

---

[a] There is another version of this story, which would suppose that the Jews were not quite so grateful. The words in Hebrew, it is said, were— "The king of all the earth [meaning their Messiah] shall enter in." Amador de los Rios, p. 49, with note.

[b] Siete Partidas, vii. 24.

vassals of the realm. This last and severest clause was perhaps inevitable. The austere old Pope, Gregory IX., had retracted the concession of the mild Honorius III. (A.C. 1234). He had exacted from all the kings of Spain the strict enforcement of the canon of the Lateran Council concerning the distinctive dress of the Jews (A.C. 1235). The same Pope had issued two Bulls, one to the King of Castile, one to the whole of Spain, commanding, in the spirit of St. Louis, the interdiction of the Talmud to the Jews. But the execution of this ordinance, in Spain, was impossible. On the other hand, there were enactments in this code of a more liberal character. The Jews were permitted to rebuild their synagogues; severe penalties were attached to the Christian who should profane them. The Jews were exempt from arrest (save in cases of robbery or murder) on the Sabbath, lest the quiet of their religious observances should be disturbed. And there was a provision, that Jews who became Christians were to be held in honour: they were not to be reproached, neither themselves nor their families, with their Jewish blood. They were to be masters of their own possessions, to share with their brethren, and to inherit according to Jewish law, as if still Jews. They might hold all offices and honours open to other Christians.

This privilege was no doubt connected with a noble and generous movement for their conversion to the faith of the Gospel by fair argument, to which it was supposed that their high state of cultivation, their liberal learning, and the milder spirit of legislation, and of general usage, might open their minds with far greater success than hatred, contempt, and persecution. At the head of this movement stood Raimond de Pennaforte, confessor to King James of Arragon. The Dominicans, the fathers of the Inquisition, had not yet hardened themselves into the fatal belief that the fire and the stake were the lawful and the best instruments of conversion to the faith of Jesus. James of Arragon went so far as to permit a religious tournament to take place in his palace at Barcelona. A monk named Paul appeared on the Christian side; on that of the Jews, the famous Moses, the son of Nachman. Each combatant claimed the victory. The brother Paul received permission from the king to preach in all the synagogues of the Jews, and to receive the expenses of the journey out of the tribute paid to the Church by the Jews. Ben Nachman claimed the triumph, and received a valuable present in money from the king. But the dispute, like all such disputes, had little effect; no one was the better, not a convert was made.[1] The king ordered a

---

[1] It is, I presume, to Alfonso the Wise that is to be referred the curious conference, in the Schevet Judah, with Thomas the Philosopher. Though a Christian (see p. 42), Thomas was yet profoundly versed in Jewish erudition. A bishop had preached to the king, that the Jews never celebrated their Passover but with the blood of a Christian. "Though," says the king, "there are manifest signs of folly rather than of wisdom in that bishop, yet the populace fully believe a man of his position. What am I to do?" The king then enters into a strange view of Roman and Jewish history, not giving a high notion of his historical knowledge. The philosopher expresses his wonder that the king and a people so wise as the Spaniards could listen to such old wives' tables. He insists on the prohibition in the Law against murder, and against the tasting of the blood even of animals. The later part of the philosopher's defence is more curious: "All these calumnies against the Jews are from envy. When the Jews came into the kingdom, poor, and with tattered garments, no one heard of the charges of killing children and drinking Christian blood; now that the Jew appears like a king [regnare videtur], and if he has 200 florins buys for himself a robe of silk, for his sons gold brocade, such as princes whose annual revenues are 1000 crowns cannot afford, the Christians take counsel to expel the Jews from the realm. When the Christian was rich, the Jew poor, all was well; now that, through usury, the Jew is rich, the Christian poor, the Jews, by their superior cleverness, have scraped to-

censure upon Jewish books; all passages against Christianity were to be struck out. This Paul is the same monk who obtained great influence over Louis IX., and advised him to pass that persecuting law. But Alfonso the Wise rendered more important homage to the Jewish civilization of Spain. Of the Arabian science and the Arabian philosophy, which in older times had allured the more enlightened and inquiring minds of Europe, such as Gerbert (Pope Sylvester II.), to their schools in Spain, almost all which remained was with the Jews. In framing his famous Astronomical Tables, the king called in the aid of Jews, and it is probable that to them they owe their scientific value.

During all this time the perpetual and complicated money transactions between the Jews and the Christians

---

gether so much wealth that they possess one half of the lands and property in the kingdom." The king goes on to assign another cause for the hatred of the Jews—their unsocial disposition: "Nothing unites the hearts of those who differ so much as familiar and friendly intercourse; but if the lip of a Christian has touched a cup, the Jew pours out the wine as unclean." Thomas excuses this as a narrow Talmudic prejudice. He then gives advice to the king, of which the Jews assuredly would not approve; "Send out a herald and make proclamation that all the lands and possessions now occupied by the Jews be returned to their owners; from henceforth let no Jew wear silk, but every one wear the red fillet which distinguishes the Jew." The whole people applauded, as they might be expected to do, this wise proposal of the philosopher; and he was then enabled to pursue an investigation by which it appeared that the body of a dead Christian, found in the house of a Jew, had been placed there by a wicked conspiracy of some zealous Christians. Here, if the reader be tempted to open the Schevet Judah, let him pause, unless he would lose himself in a labyrinth of Talmudic nonsense. There is another singular conference of Alfonso the Wise with a Jewish deputation, on account of a charge of murdering a Christian at Osoma. The king avails himself of the knowledge which he has obtained from the philosopher Thomas. At the close of this inquiry, John de la Vera, who had brought a false (pp. 78-92) accusation against the Jews, is condemned to be buried alive, but, on his petition, only hanged.

throughout the Peninsula as elsewhere, if they did not require, were compelled to submit to legal regulation. Usury was prohibited by law, and the Jews were held to be violating their own law in demanding it. But necessity knows no law; and the supposition that the rich would lend their money without profit or advantage was an absurdity open to the coarsest common sense. The creditor, Lombard, Caorsin, or Jew, would lend on the highest interest he could extort, and in proportion to the precariousness of the security. The debtor, under the necessity of borrowing, would use every subterfuge and implore legal protection against the payment of his debts. In Spain the Jews probably held a monopoly in the money market; it was as yet too barren a province for the enterprising Italians; and the wealth was chiefly in the hands of the Jews.[j] The laws, and the kings and nobles, the authors of the laws, had the difficult task of adjusting the demands of concession to one class of their impoverished subjects with the least possible injustice to the other class, their useful, if despised subjects. Some laws of Alfonso VII, in the Fuero Viejo, of Castile had seemed to favour the Jews on this point. The Jewish as well as the Christian creditor might seize the moveables of a debtor, either for the debt, or the interest upon it, and sell them. He might even seize their lands, under certain restrictions, but not sell them. There were provisions, not unjust, for the proof of debts. In Arragon, King James limited interest to 20 per cent.;[k] but in the kingdom of Navarre it was otherwise. Not only was usury altogether forbidden, but a Bull was obtained from

---

[j] "Comperies tertiam agrorum et possessionum partem quæ in universa Hispania sunt, per immanes usuras jam evasisse Judæis." Schevet Judah, p. 33.

[k] Jost, vi. 296.

Pope Alexander IV. (A.C. 1254-1261), which empowered the kings to seize all estates obtained by the Jews through what were called usurious practices, and restore them to the owners—in default of owners, to give them to the Crown. In Navarre, too, the law of St. Louis prevailed, by which the Jew could recover only the capital, not the interest of his debt.

But of the wealth of the Jews there is extant a remarkable evidence, a detailed account of the capitation dues paid to the prelates and to the nobles of Castile, or to hidalgoes, who had obtained grants out of these funds, on the field of battle, or from the bounty of kings or prelates, or in commutation for other grants, in the archbishopric of Toledo, the bishoprics of Cuenca, Palencia, Burgos, Calahorra, Osma, Plasencia, Siguenza, Segovia, Avila, the kingdom of Murcia, the kingdom of Leon, the frontiers of Andalusia. The total sum was from two millions and a half to towards three millions of maravedis (the maravedi was reckoned at ten deniers); the number of Jews who paid the tax is stated at 850,961. But, as in the Aljama, this tax, which had been granted at the instigation of Alfonso before his accession to the throne, was paid only by males above seventeen years old, the Jewish population must have amounted to three millions; and as the commerce and industry, perhaps even in large part the profitable cultivation of the soil, was in the hands of the Jews, their flourishing state, under the administration of the Wise Alfonso, may be fairly estimated;—a state to be sadly changed under his fierce and barbarous successors. To the Jews in the kingdoms of Castile and Leon must be added those of Arragon and Navarre.[1]

---

[1] Unfortunately, in the account of this curious document, though the translation of Amador de los Rios detailed numbers are given, Magnabal's

In the frontier provinces, in Navarre and Catalonia, and the adjacent districts, the Jews suffered by the insurrection of the shepherds, which spread through those parts. They were accused in those districts, as in the South of France, of causing the dreadful plague of leprosy, which ensued, and of poisoning the fountains.[m] Still, on the whole they were protected by the wiser kings of Arragon and Castile from the growing jealousy of the nobles, and the implacable animosity of the clergy.

From the reign of Alfonso the Wise in Castile, under Sancho I.; and Ferdinand IV. to that of Alfonso XI.; during the wars of the Kings of Arragon with France

---

is deficient, and there seems to me an inexplicable contradiction between the text and the notes. It is a copy of an ordinance of the metropolitan church of Toledo, preserved in the city of Huete; the date is 1290, six years after the death of Alfonso the Wise. Neither the text nor the notes state how much each Jew paid per head, but no doubt it was three maravedis (thirty pence). In the text the sum total is given at 2,801,345; in the note at 2,564,855. Nor are we distinctly told, but left to infer, from the grant of the Aljama to the metropolitan church at Seville, that it was paid only by persons above seventeen years old (p. 48). But there is this further grave difficulty: Jost had before (vi. 380) printed this document. But the numbers in Jost differ in particular parts most materially; i.e., for Toledo and those that paid there, Jost has 18,505; Amador de los Rios 216,500. The total of the Archbishopric of Toledo in Jost is 558,216; in De Rios 1,082,902. The total in Jost is 2,100,000. They differ more formidably in the more important result, the number of the Jews (neither determines whether the tax was paid on the whole population or only by adults). Jost reckons only 80,000 taxable Jews (achtzig tausend); De Rios, as we see, above 800,000 ("nombre d'âmes qui payait," note). Jost calculates the Jews in Christian Spain at half a million. Considering that the Christian population of Spain, especially of Castile, must have been by no means great, the smaller number would appear more probable. In Ersch und Grüber there is a third transcript of this account, differing again in the numbers. Cassel thinks Jost incorrect.

[m] The Jewish historian (Schevet Judah) relates with pride that the wealthy Jews of Tudela, and even those of France and Germany, contributed largely to allay the sufferings of their brethren.

for the possession of the crown of Sicily, and throughout the contest for the Castilian throne, and the long strife of the king against the nobles, although the financial embarrassments were perpetual, and more than once the kings resorted to the ultimate remedy of tampering with the coin, yet the great desperate mode of alleviating taxation, the unfailing resource of France and England, the plunder of the Jews, does not seem to have occurred to the sovereign or to the nobles. The Jews of the great cities, Toledo, Seville, Burgos, still paid to the churches or chapters of those cities in their Aljamas, the three maravedis, or thirty pence, for each adult. The sum had long been fixed by the Christians, and the Jews might overlook, if they would, the ignominious significance of that special sum fixed in memorial of the betrayal of Christ.[b] The king, however, does not seem to have assumed or exercised the right of taxing them at his will, as his men, his feudal serfs. The great Queen Regent, Maria de Molina, on her resumption of the royal power, issued a singular edict against the Jews, partly a re-enactment from the Siete Partidas, that the Jews were not to assume Christian names under pain of being dealt with as heretics; that Christians were not to consort with Jews or Moors, or to allow Jews or Moors to educate their children.[c]

During the reign of Ferdinand IV., a Jew exercised great authority over the finances. Under Alfonso XI., Joseph, the famous Jew of Ecija, collected the royal rents, and appears to have been the financial minister.

---

[b] See in Amador de los Rios (p. 60, note) the remarkable proclamation of Ferdinand IV., enforcing these payments from the Aljama of the Jews in Segovia and other towns in that diocese.

[c] Flores, Reinas Catholicas, quoted by Amador de los Rios.

By his great power (he resided in the palace), he excited the jealousy of the nobles, who accused him, and the Christian Count Osorio, of having bewitched the king by magical beverages.[p] The nobles were at first content with the sacrifice of the Christian favourite, and condescended to despise the Jew; yet at a later period the Jew was accused of malversation, stripped of his office, and it was enacted that no Jew hereafter should administer the royal finances.[q] But, notwithstanding this prohibition, the king's physician, Samuel Abenhuer, obtained the privilege of coining money, on paying a fixed rent to the Crown.[r] He was also empowered to buy up the current coin at a lower price. The consequence of the Jew's financial operations is said to have been a general rise in provisions; from that rise came distress, from distress insurrection. The king by timely measures alone averted proscription and a general outbreak of popular fury against the whole race.[s]

---

[p] Chronique du Roi Alphonso XI., quoted in Amador de los Rios, p. 61. The nobles, according to Mariana, complained, "que el nuevo Conde, Alvaro Osorio, y un Judio llamado Juzeph, governavan todo el Regno, y lo trastornavan a su voluntad. Que tenian rendido el Rey como si los fuera esclavo, y como si le ovieron dado bevedizos." xv. 20.

[q] Amador de los Rios, p. 63.

[r] Amador de los Rios, with authorities. Is this Samuel the Samuel son of Wakeri, in the Schevet Judah?

[s] The Schevet Judah has a strange but particular history of the influence and fall of Joseph. Martin Gonzales, an officer under Joseph d'Ecija, became jealous of his master's wealth. He offered to the king an enormous sum (octo talenta) if he would sell to him ten Jews with all their families. The king agreed, and gave his seal as a pledge. Gonzales chose Joseph, and the King's physician Samuel, the son of Wakeri. The Jews were seized. Joseph died under the hands of the men sent to arrest him. The king gave him a splendid funeral in Cordova. In the house of Samuel, seized with his sons and two brothers, was discovered a vast mass of gold, silver, and other riches. He was cruelly tortured to make further disclosures, and died under the torments. Gonzales was rewarded with great honours, became Bishop of Alcantara, and persevered in his hatred of the

With the son of Alfonso, Pedro the Cruel, the Jews rose to more than their former power and influence. In defiance of the prohibitory law, a Jew, Samuel Levi, became the king's treasurer. Under his wise, it might be oppressive, administration, the royal rents were raised to an enormous amount. At a later period in the reign, Samuel Levi became too wealthy to be the trusted friend and minister, too temptingly wealthy not to be the victim of his unscrupulous master. He was arrested, accused of many malversations, thrown into prison, tortured with such horrible cruelty that he died on the rack. The king confiscated all his wealth, which amounted to 400,000 ducats; besides furniture, jewels, cloth of gold and silk,¹ and Moorish slaves. Still, during the power of Samuel Levi, as after his fall, the Jews were proud of the fatal favour of the detested king; to them alone Pedro was not the Cruel, if cruel, only so in his kindness. In his prosperity Samuel Levi had built a synagogue in Toledo in the Moorish style, which surpassed all their other temples in magnificence.ⁿ In the Hebrew inscription on the walls are commemorated the

---

Jews. In a war against the Saracens, Gonzales advised the king to confiscate all the wealth of the Jews. The bishop himself took arms, and inflicted a signal defeat on the Moors. But God heard the prayers of His people. The heart of the king was moved against Gonzales. Some of the nobles, even a bishop, took part with the Jews. Gonzales shut himself up in a strong fortress. It was stormed, Gonzales put to death, his body burned. His wealth was confiscated and restored to the Jews. pp. 98, 108.

¹ Mariana writes, "Con que juntò las grandes riquezas, y alcansò la mucha privança y favor que al presente se acarrearon su perdicion." The historian adds, "essa maravillosa que un Jodio juntasse tantas riquezas, y que no pudo ser sin grave daño del Reyno." xvii. 4.

La Fuente gives the confiscated treasures of Samuel Levi, 166,000 doblas d' oro, 4000 marcos de plata, 125 chests of cloth of gold and silk, 80 moros y moras. t. vii. p. 241.

ⁿ Can this be one of those alluded to in a former paragraph?

happy days and happy years of King Pedro. On the other hand the Jews were accumulating heavy arrears of public detestation, to be repaid in full measure after the fall and death of Pedro. In a poem written by the chronicler Lopez de Ayala, the chancellor of King Henry of Transtamare, prisoner in England after the battle of Najara, the exactions and oppressions of the Jews are described in the darkest terms.[x] "They are the blood-suckers of the afflicted people; they present their packed accounts, and propitiate the king by presents and precious jewels; they heap up his rents to an enormous height, as high as the walls; they exact fifty per cent., or eighty, or a hundred. Through them the land is desolate; where lived a thousand men, there are but three hundred; impositions fall upon them like hail; rich and poor fly together. Truly these Jews are skilful in inventing new taxes, new demands. Tears and groans touch not their hard hearts; their ears are deaf to petitions for delay." If this ardent partisan of Henry of Transtamaro be somewhat suspicious authority against the Jews, he is an unimpeachable witness to the popular detestation of them, and to the jealousy of their power and influence.

Henry of Transtamare and his partisans were not slow in appealing to the passion of popular hatred. In the first tumults in Castile, when he attempted to seize Toledo, the first act of his followers was to plunder and put to the sword the opulent Jews of

---

[x] I transcribe these stanzas from Amador de los Rios:—

"Alli vienen Judios que estan aparejados
Para beber la sangre de los pueblos cuitados;
Presentan sus escriptos, que tienen concertados,
Et prometen sus dones, et joyas muy preciadas.

Alli fazen Judios el su repartimiento
Sobre el pueblo que moere por mal defendimiento;
Et ellas lo maltrapian entre el medio ciento,
Que han de haber probados cual ochenta, cual ciento."—P. 64.

that city. The slaughtered were as many as 1000 or 1200, old and young, men, women, and children.[y] But the largest Jewry resisted their attack. King Pedro took terrible vengeance on the insurgents of Toledo; no doubt he would be represented by his enemies as not merely asserting his royal authority, but as avenging his beloved Israelites. In the war of Arragon and Castile, when Henry of Transtamare took the city of Najara, many Jews were killed, with the avowed design of grieving King Pedro.[z] But when Henry of Transtamare asserted his right to the crown, Pedro's favour to the Jews was urged in a bolder and more formidable way; Pedro himself became infected with their guilt and infidelity. Not only, was it everywhere hinted, did he consort with the Jews, and admit them to his councils—they ruled in his palace, and in his court; he was himself addicted to Judaism.[a] Worse than this, he was born a Jew. A rumour was industriously propagated in Spain, and spread into France, that he was a supposititious child. His mother, the queen of Alfonso XI., had borne a daughter—a Jewish boy had been substituted. At a later period, when the Black Prince took up arms to restore Pedro to his kingdom of Castile, Henry of Transtamare

---

[y] " Entrada fatal para los Judios de aquella ciudad, puesto que desfogando en ellos su saña las companias de Don Enrique mataron hasta mil docientos, entre hombres y mugeres, grandes y menos, y eso que no pudieron penetrar en la Juderia mayor, aunque la carcaron y atacaron." La Fuente, vii. p. 201.

[z] " Dieron la muerte a muchos Judios por hacer pesar al Rey, que los favoreció mucho por amor de Samuel Levi su tesorero major." Mariana, xvii. 4. This was before the fall of Levi, which I have anticipated.

[a] " Nihilominus dictus Rex Petrus per Judaeos, qui in maximâ abundantiâ erant in Hispaniâ, seipsum et domum suam regebat." Continuat. Nangis. " Legi Judaicae addictus," Ibid.

addressed Bertrand du Guesclin—"Will he set up that Jew, who calls himself King of Spain, on my throne!"[b] Nor was this all. Maria Padilla, the beautiful mistress for whom Pedro had deserted the bridal bed of Blanche of Bourbon, was called a Jewess.[c] This no doubt, as accounting for the bewitchment by other sorcery than that of beauty, more inflamed that indignation which roused the chivalry of France, even of England, to avenge the wrongs, and the murder (for it is impossible to clear Pedro of this crime) of the unfortunate Queen.[d] Bertrand du Guesclin's expedition was a crusade, not only because Pedro had been solemnly excommunicated by the Pope, but "because he was worse than a Saracen, and consorted with Jews." Saracens and Jews were said to be his chief partisans. If credit be due to a French historian, the Jews appeared in arms, and in a formidable body on the justly unpopular side of Pedro the Cruel. This, if true, can only have been at the final battle, after the restoration of Pedro by the Black Prince, and the second invasion of Henry of Transtamare, aided by Bertrand du Guesclin, near Monteil in Andalusia. There they were slain in vast numbers. Some escaped, and found their way to Paris and other cities in France, where they had recourse to the common usurious practices of their nation.[e] There, too,

---

[b] Froissart, L. cciv.
[c] Continuator Nangis.
[d] See the account of the murder in La Fuente, vii. 243. M. Merimée's quixotic defence of King Pedro certainly fails in this part.
[e] "Et potissime infinitos Judæos qui in potentia armorum regem Petrum adjuvabant, trucidando potenter in magnâ potentiâ. Qui interfecti, trucidati, et effugiati de illis partibus turpiter perierunt. De quibus sunt multi hodie in Parisiis et alibi in diversis civitatibus commorantes, per usuras Christianos nostros multas subtiliter defraudantes." Continuat. Nangis. This account of Jews in France, so long after their expulsion, is remarkable.

it must have been, if at all, that the order, attributed to Bertrand du Guesclin, must have been issued—"Kill all like sheep and oxen, unless they accept baptism." The Moors certainly, as well as the Jews, formed a powerful part of Pedro's army. Before the last death-struggle in the castle of Monteil, when Pedro fell by the hand of Henry of Transtamare, aided, it is said, by Du Guesclin, Froissart[f] repeats the uncourtly colloquy of the rival kings. "Where," said Henry of Transtamare, "is the son of a whore, the Jew, who calls himself King of Castile?" Don Pedro, who was a very brave and cruel man, advanced, and said—"Thou art the son of a whore. I am the son of the good King Alfonso."[g]

It is hardly probable that, in other parts of Spain, the Jews thus bound up with the odious cause of Pedro the Cruel would escape persecution. But, however Henry, in the battle or after the battle, might give the rein to his fierce French allies or his Spanish partisans in order to gain his throne, he was too wise (mercy was not in his character) to follow these destructive acts to extermination or expulsion, when the throne was won. On his triumphant progress through Castile to Andalusia, the Jews of Burgos and Toledo had paid

---

[f] Froissart, I. cclv.

[g] Amador de los Rios, as translated by Magnabal (p. 70, &c.), is not very accurate in his account of these transactions. The surrender of Seville, whether in the first or second invasion, must have been long after the massacres of Toledo, to which he seems to refer in the next sentence. He adds, "Et les champs de batailles étaient jonchés d'une multitude des Juifs, qui suivaient, fidèles, les étendards du monarque légitime." p. 72. Now it is remarkable that in these two revolutions there were but two great battles. Pedro, on the first invasion, fled the country without resistance. The battle of Najara, won by the Black Prince, replaced him on his throne. On the second invasion, Pedro retreated rapidly to Seville. Henry took peaceable possession of the Castiles; nor was there bloodshed before the closing victory of Montell.

him tribute, compulsory perhaps, but still valuable tribute.[h] It is said that two Jews (their names are given, Turquand and Daniel) betrayed Seville to Du Guesclin, and admitted his bands through the Jewry, which had been committed to their charge.[i] But, whatever their motive,[k] Henry of Transtamare, during the latter part of his reign, protected the Jews from popular excesses. They were again at peace, and with the Jews peace was prosperity.[l] A strange event, soon after the accession of John I., justly aroused the king's aversion to the Jews. Joseph Pichon, a Jew of great wealth and influence, held the office of collector of the royal rents, and of treasurer to the Crown. It seems that in these offices the Jews, notwithstanding all prohibitory laws, were indispensable. It is unknown from what cause, but many of the leading Jews became jealous of Joseph Pichon, and conspired against his life. They took an extraordinary and unaccountable course to compass their end; they obtained a warrant for his death, signed in ignorance by the king, and a second order to the royal headsman, suborned or deceived by them, to execute the sentence. The king was highly indignant at this abuse of his authority. Those guilty of

---

[h] "La Judería de Toledo le servió en cuento de maravedis, come la de Burgos." La Fuente, p. 271.

[i] Amador de los Rios, p. 270.

[k] Basnage has a remarkable story, utterly irreconcileable with the course of events and the character of the time. The Jews of Burgos refused to surrender. Henry was seized with so much admiration of their fidelity to King Pedro, that from that time he was favourably disposed towards the Jews. Ls. 18.§ 10. Basnage's whole account of these events is brief and worthless.

[l] This is admitted by Amador de los Rios, who perhaps exaggerates the vengeance; it was political vengeance, wreaked by the nobles and people on the Jews as partisans of Pedro. He quotes, however, from the archives of Toledo a fine imposed on the Jews of Toledo of 20,000 gold doubloons, and exacted by all kinds of torture.

the crime suffered death; and the Jews were deprived of the privilege of holding a tribunal for the judgement of their own causes, of which the Crown had not hitherto ventured to deprive them, lest they should suffer in the collection of their rents by offending or limiting the power of these useful subjects.* An interpretation of this strange story suggests itself, that Joseph Pichon was inclined towards, or suspected of an inclination to, Christianity; hence the hatred of the Jews. He was condemned to death in their courts, as unsound in the faith. Those courts were secret, as far as any knowledge of them by the Christians. They applied for the king's warrant to punish a convicted unbeliever, concealing or disguising the name. The warrant was granted without examination, and by their bribes and interest they urged on its immediate execution. When it was discovered, the wrath of the king, and of the Christians, would of course be intense.

After this time, the Cortes seized every opportunity of invading the privileges and increasing the burthens of the Jews; for the nobles, as in other countries, bore impatiently the mortgages with which their estates were encumbered, and were eager to revenge on their creditors the shame and inconvenience of their embarrassments. The Cortes of Burgos raised the protection money of the Jews—that of Valladolid attempted to renew an Act forbidding them to practise as physicians, surgeons, or apothecaries, as well as to hold high offices about the Court—they also made bitter complaints of

---

* Mariana, xvii. 3 : " Y se le quitó a esta nacion la potestad que tenia, y el tribunal para juzgar los negocios y pleytos de los suyos, desorden con que avian hasta allí dissimulado los Reyes por la necesidad y apretura de las rentas Reales, y ser los Judios gente que tan bien saben los caminos de allegar dinero."

their usurious practices. But the clergy beheld with still deeper sentiments of animosity so large a part of the population disdaining their dominion, and, if not refusing tribute to the Church (the Aljama payment was still regularly made), perhaps holding profitable bonds on the estates of the cathedrals and convents. Religious zeal was still further animated by pride, avarice, and jealousy. The clergy began to preach against them with fatal if not unceasing energy; the growing power and activity of the friars, especially the Preaching Friars, was even more fatal to their peace. The Jews themselves assert that they were popular with the king, the nobles, and the enlightened of the land; the populace hated and persecuted them as raising the prices of the necessaries of life. The monks were their deadly and irreconcileable enemies; with their fiery sermons, they were like tribunes of the people; constantly stirring up the rabble, of themselves savage enough, to more savage hostility.[a]

There was at Seville a fierce popular preacher, Ferdinand Martinez, Archdeacon of Ecija. During the reign of John I., his inflammatory harangues against the obstinacy and the usury and the wealth of the

---

[a] Schevet Judah: "Judæi enim in Hispania Regibus, proceribus, sapientibus atque prudentibus viris semper chari acceptique fuere; neque aliunde mata fuerunt odii et exiliorum semina nisi ex incondita plebe, quæ semper obstrepere solebat Judæis in regnum advenientibus rerum necessariarum pretia in immensum crevisse annotantemque indementissimè flagellatam esse.

"Altera vero malorum nostrorum tempestas orieliatur ex monachis qui, ut sanctimoniam suam populo probarent, acerrimi scilicet Christianæ religionis promotores quotidie a-perus et quasi tribunicias contra Judæos ad populum orationes habebant quibus hoc unum agebant ut plebis per se satis ferocis animus magis exasperarent. Quod vero ad cæteros Christianos attinebat, illi Judæos æstimabant et ut cives indigenas impensè amabant, ut admodum senes Hispani qui olim pueri istis rebus oculati testes interfuere, testari solebant." p. 309.

Jews, had excited the populace to some excesses. The Archbishop and the Chapter of Seville, to their honour, endeavoured to allay the tumult, and by their authority to silence the dangerous fanatic. A petition from the Chapter was presented to the King; the reply of the feeble king was, that holy and excellent as was the zeal of the Archdeacon, he ought to take care that he did not disturb the peace of the city. This mild rebuke was almost an encouragement. On the sudden death of the king, and the accession of the boy Henry III., the Archdeacon, who, if not silent, had been more moderate, broke out again, and with his hot sermons maddened the slumbering passions of the multitude. They began by insulting, plundering, pursuing to their quarters the unfortunate Jews. The city was in a wild uproar. The chief alguazil of the city, Alves Perez de Guzman, and his colleagues, the other alguazils, it is said, with the authority and in the personal presence of the Count of Niebla,* one of the Council of Regency (who can hardly have been in Seville), interposed to keep the peace. Two of the ringleaders in the riot were apprehended. The mob turned on the civil authorities, and, as usual, rescued the prisoners. On the triumph of the mob at the release of their accomplices, there was a momentary lull. But in a short time the tumult broke out with tenfold fury. The Jewries were attacked, forced; and a general pillage, violation, and massacre took place of men and women,

---

* In the former editions I was guilty of some errors by following Jost, in general a trustworthy guide. He made Martinez Archbishop of Niebla. This could not be, and I substituted *Bishop*. He was, however, according to Spanish authorities, Archdeacon of Ecija. The Count of Niebla was one of the six nobles and prelates who formed the Council of Regency. I have now chiefly followed Amador de los Rios, 76, 82.

old and young. Fire and sword raged unresisted through these quarters of the city. The streets of noble Seville ran with blood, and the wild voice of the Archdeacon in the pulpit rose over all, and kept up the madness. Four thousand Jews perished in the massacre.

The Cortes of the kingdom were assembled at Madrid. The Jews, who still farmed the royal revenues (they were yet indispensable in that capacity), appealed to the three Estates of the realm, and made strong representations concerning these sanguinary proceedings at Seville. The Cortes, superior to the popular passions, acknowledged the righteousness of their cause. Judges, called priors, were sent to Seville, armed with authority to do full justice, to allay the tumults, and punish the criminals; but the judges were either unable or unwilling to act with severity. Even the fierce Archdeacon was suffered to go unpunished. The Christians remained in possession of their plunder; they had seized two of the most splendid synagogues, and converted them into churches, Santa Croce and Santa Maria Bianca. The Jews, perhaps on account of their reduced numbers, reduced by the merciless massacre, were confined to one Aljama, that of St. Bartholomew. Instead of expiating their guilt, the plunderers had obtained a triumph.

The terrible example of their impunity, the fame of the blood which they had shed without rebuke, the wealth which they had acquired without restitution, spread throughout the kingdom. Hardly more than a year had passed, when in one day (Aug. 8) the populace rose in Cordova, in Valencia, in Toledo, in Burgos. Each of these cities, says a Spanish author, was another Troy. All the horrors of a town taken by storm were suffered by the Jewries: plunder, rape, massacre, conflagration.[p] In all these cities many Jews submitted to baptism (the only refuge from death), and from renegade Jews became unbelieving Christians. Redress, justice, punishment of the offenders, when the offenders were almost the whole population of these great towns, appeared impossible. To destroy a whole city on account of the destruction of the Jews' quarters would have been to heap disaster on disaster.

Nor were these enormities confined to the kingdom of Castile; the contagious thirst for plunder, and for blood, raged simultaneously in Arragon, even as far as the island of Majorca. The capital city of Barcelona was crowded with strangers to celebrate the Feast of St. Dominic (May 6, 1392); the day after, as if the worship of that stern saint had hardened their hearts, the silent streets were roused with a wild cry of extermination against the Jews. The city was thronged, besides its own rabble, with sailors and galley slaves; they broke into the Jewry, and perpetrated the most dreadful cruelties. The houses were sacked, the streets heaped with dead bodies. Some of the desperate Jews demanded baptism; that Christian rite was hastily administered in the midst of pillage, violation, and murder. Late in the day appeared the city militia, seized some of the more violent insurgents, and placed a guard over the Aljama; but, as in Seville, the interference of the civil authority only maddened to a greater height the irresistible populace. The next day the tumult was more wild and general. The Jews, abandoning all their wealth, fled to the Castello Nuevo. The castle

---

[p] See, for the persecutions of the Jews during the youth of Henry III. and King John, the Schevet Judah, 312, 313. But Solomon ben Virga leaps about strangely in his chronology.

was stormed; all who would not submit to baptism were put to the sword. Three hundred bodies lay in their agony. Amid the shrieks of their more faithful dying brethren, many abjured their faith, the only pride and consolation of their brethren in death; and embraced that of Christ, thus preached to them by the Mohammedan argument of the sword. Which were the least Christian, those who enforced, or those who embraced the faith?

It should be added, that the king of Arragon, John I., called the Amador de Gentileza, dared to punish these wickednesses perpetrated in Barcelona. Twenty-six of the ringleaders were beheaded; many were imprisoned, and only released on the supplication of the queen, and through the mercy of the sovereign. On the other hand, it is said that the severity of the king was chiefly provoked by the burning of many books and registers belonging to the Crown, by which the royal finances suffered serious loss.

The Jews of Navarre suffered no less than those of Arragon. In Pampeluna, and the other cities of that kingdom, their houses were burned; they were pillaged, massacred, compelled to baptism.*

Spain had throughout her borders destroyed these secret enemies, which, according to the notions of the day, preyed upon the wealth of the country, and heaped up in their secret hoards the riches which they extorted from the revenues of the king, the luxuries or warlike expenditure of the nobles, and the more grinding necessities of the indigent. To her astonishment and utter perplexity, Spain found herself poorer than before. "The Christians, who thus mercilessly indulged their madness against the Jews, did not

---

* MS. authorities quoted in Amador de los Rios, p. 83.

see that in destroying their industry, in depriving them of all means of employing it with profit, they threw upon themselves all the charges hitherto shared by the Jews, and that they smothered in blood every germ of prosperity and well-being. What became, in fact, of all the trade and commerce of Toledo and Seville? What became of those rich marts in which the Jews accumulated the products of the East and the West, the silks of Persia and Damascus, the skins of Tafilete, and the Arabian jewellery? They burned the shops in the Aljamas at Valencia, Toledo, Burgos, Cordova, Seville, Barcelona; and the rents of the kings and of the churches at once fell off. King Henry III. founded a magnificent mortuary chapel for himself and his family, and endowed it with part of the rents paid by the Jews of that city; but no rents could be exacted. During the wars with the Saracens, the coffers of the Jews had been a ready resource to the kings—they were now empty. The utter ruin of the only industry and commerce in the kingdom by an idle populace, and a king and nobles who disdained all occupation but war, was not only a grievous offence against humanity, against the Gospel, and against the laws of Spain, but it was profoundly impolitic, a prelude to that problem so fatally solved nearly a century later by the Kings of Spain. The whole crime is not to be charged on the Archdeacon of Ecija—the indolence and indifference of John I. must share the guilt and folly with the mad zeal of Martinez and the clergy."[*]

The clergy were emboldened and inspirited, by the success of these unchristian measures of conversion, to

---

[*] Of this passage some part is translated, part compressed, from Amador de los Rios, pp. 83, 84.

press their more legitimate means of influence, missions for the preaching of the Gospel. They would multiply the 200,000 who had by fiercer inducements submitted to baptism to save their lives. Among the most prominent and successful of these missionaries was Vincent Ferrer, afterwards a Saint; a man of the most earnest piety and, it was thought, of irresistible eloquence. Ferrer traversed the country, followed by a train of bare-headed penitents bewailing their sins and scourging themselves as they went till the earth was red with their blood. Ferrer's miracles and his preaching are said to have changed 35,000 Jews (there were Saracens too without number) into devout Christians. But it is difficult even in him to discriminate between the more gentle and more barbarous means of conversion. Vincent Ferrer witnessed, no doubt stood aloof from, the horrible cruelties of the persecution in Valencia. It is related in his Life (or Legend) that the Jews, before the insurrection in July, 1391, were assembled for worship in a noble synagogue, afterwards the Monastery of St. Christopher. A voice was heard three times, "Ye Jews, depart from my house." The Jews took no heed. On the ninth of the month, when they were again in prayer, the holy martyr spoke once more, rebuked their obstinacy, and threatened them with condign punishment. The perverse and blind race were not moved by this celestial monition. In the middle of the day a procession of boys, with crucifixes and white banners, appeared at the gates of the Jewry, crying out to the Jews to be converted to the faith of Christ and be baptized. The Jews, dreading the popular fury, closed their gates, some of the boys and some men remaining within; the men raised a cry that the Jews were murdering the boys; the rabble rose, burst the gates, slew 300, and sacked the whole quarter. At the sight of this carnage, the eyes of many Jews were opened (so, with no word of pity, writes the author of the Legend);⁕ they fled to the Cardinal Archbishop of Valencia, Don Jayme of Arragon, and, relating the marvel about St. Christopher (!), demanded baptism.¹ Search was made in the synagogue; an image of St. Christopher, two palms high (still an object of devout worship), was found. The saint took possession of the dwelling, and the dedication of the church was performed with many miracles.

To the wonderful and copious fruits of this day (so the legendist proceeds) contributed much the great zeal and fervent preaching of S. Vicente, who happened to be in Valencia. S. Vicente did not confine his labours to the city; in the towns on the seashore and in the kingdom more than 13,000 Jews submitted to baptism. Besides these, the biographer gives to the saint 20,000 in Castile, converted in thirteen months,ᵘ 30,000 in Arragon, without reckoning those in other parts of the kingdom.ˣ Much of this, of course, especially the numbers, is pure legend. But it is not less remarkable that of the humanity of the saint (as if beyond his comprehension) the admiring author of his Life is silent. It is stated, on other and more trustworthy authority,ʸ that S. V. Ferrer arrested by his single

---

⁕ Portentosa Vida de el Apostol de la Europa, S. Vicente Ferrer, por Francesco Vidal (Barcelona, 1777), pp. 46 and 66.

¹ "Entonces venianse ellos mismos a baptizar."

ᵃ "E despues, de baptizados se iban algunos a Portugal, b otros reynos h ser Judios." Bernaldez, Historia de los Reyes Catholicos; MS. quoted by De Castro, p. 5.

ˣ Amador de los Rios, p. 89, note, with authorities.

ʸ Rabbi Joseph perpetuates the hatred of V. Ferrer among the unconverted Jews: "In these days, in the days of Eugenius the Pope, in the days of Felix (the Antipope), the de-

commanding voice the massacre at Valencia. To this act we would attribute, even more than to his eloquence, the crowds who received baptism from his hands. Nor must it be disguised that Spanish authorities describe his mission as an utter failure, till aided by the more persuasive massacres committed by the populace.*

An attempt was made to bring the great question between Christianity and Judaism to a more solemn and decisive issue. The whole nation was to be publicly, and in the highest persons and by fair argument, convicted of its impious obstinacy. The antipope, Peter de Luna (Benedict XIII.), maintained

---

structions increased in Sphard, and Israel became very low. For there arose the priest, Friar Vincent, from the city of Valencia, of the sect of Baal Dominic, against the Jews, and he was unto them a Satan, and stirred up against them all the inhabitants of the country, and they arose to swallow them up alive, and slew many with the edge of the sword, and many they burned with fire, and many they turned away by the power of the sword from the Lord, the God of Israel. And they burned the books of the Law of our God, and trampled upon them as upon the mire in the streets; and the mothers they dashed in pieces upon the children in the day of the Lord's wrath. .... And some of them killed their sons and their daughters that they might not be defiled; for some of them changed their glory for one that does not profit from that day and afterwards. Those who were constrained to be baptized became numerous in the land of Sphard, and they put upon them a mark of distinction unto this day. ... Also upon the Jews that were in Savoy [compare Schevet Judah, p. 103] did this grievous oppressor turn his line of desolation. And I have seen in the book Mischath Marechu how they hid themselves in the castles of Savoy in those evil days. And this Belial was in their sight a saint; and the Pope Calixtus wrote his memory among the saints, and appointed feast days unto his name on the fifth of the month of April, May God recompense him according to his deeds!" L p. 265. Of the success of V. Ferrer there can be no doubt, but how much is to be attributed to his Christian preaching? how much to his un-Christian auxiliaries?

* "No pudo Fra Vicente convertir sino muy poco dellos. E las gentes con dispecho metieron en Castilla a espada, y mataron multos." Bernaldez, cited by De Castro, Religious Intolerance in Spain.

the last retreat of his authority in his native country of Arragon. The Pope had in his court a converted Jew of great Talmudic learning and ability, Joseph Halorqui, who had assumed the name of Hieronymo de Santa Fé. In the pride of his erudition, and with the zeal of a proselyte, Hieronymo suggested to the Pope a public disputation on the truth of the two religions. The disputation was held in the presence of the Pope at Tortosa. The Jewish record transports it to Rome (as if they had no notion of a Pope elsewhere), and encircles Benedict with the utmost pomp, his college of seventy cardinals and listening princes, far different from the lowly state of the exiled antipope. Fourteen of the most illustrious Rabbins appeared on behalf of the Jews. Sixteen questions were proposed, chiefly turning on the all-important one, whether the Messiah was come or not, and on the value and authority of the Talmud.[a] The abominations of this book Hieronymo denounced, and stood ready to prove and to expose. The Jews acknowledge that the Pope treated them with courtesy. Hieronymo de Santa Fé is said, by the Christian record, to have heaped confusion on the discomfited Rabbins.[b] All but two humbly submitted to

---

[a] The Christian account may be best read in Amador de los Rios; the Jewish in the Schevet Judah, as translated by Gentius, p. 225 et seqq. Amador de los Rios gives the sixteen questions from a MS. in the Escurial.

[b] Out of this disputation before Pope Benedict arose the work which for some time maintained its rank as the great armoury of offensive and defensive weapons employed by the clergy in their controversy with the Jews, the Pugio Fidei of Raymond Martin. From the vast range of Rabbinical learning, it has been concluded that the author of this book must have been a converted Jew. It seems, however, that he was a monk expressly educated to maintain the Christian cause against the profoundly learned Rabbins. The Rabbinical Hebrew seems as familiar to Raymond Martin as his native tongue or the Latin of the schools. Basnage has criticised the Pugio Fidei with justice. He gives due praise to the prodigious erudition of the author.

his arguments. The Jewish account breaks off abruptly, and modestly asserts that their champions departed "not without glory." Pope Benedict proclaimed and aided the triumph of his advocate by the summary argument of authority. He issued a Bull, commanding the Talmud, the bulwark of his antagonists, to be burnt. The reading of the execrable book was prohibited; the Deans and Chapters were to collect all these impious treatises for one vast holocaust. A singular clause in this Bull prohibited Jews from making crosses, chalices, sacred vessels, and from

---

The badness of his arguments (to which in those days no doubt Christian and Jew was equally blind) he exposes with severity, and not without truth: the very narrow base on which he builds the most lofty theories, the assertions and concessions which be ascribes to his adversaries (the Rabbins universally believe the Trinity), the wild ignorance of history, that of the old as well as the later world, the boldness of anachronism. One of the proofs of Christ's miracles is their acknowledgment by Constantine (seemingly a personal witness), who on that account made his famous Donation, submitted the empire and the whole world to the Pope, and set the example of kissing his foot.

I will venture to add one curious argument not noticed by Basnage. The Jew objects that the Messiah was not to be put to death, but rather slay the wicked by the breath of his life. "I answer: our Lord Jesus Christ, in his sufferings, Death, Burial, Resurrection, Ascension, if any one will attend closely, exactly resembles sometimes the sun, sometimes a rose. As the rose comforts the heads of some, so it pains (rheumatism) the heads of others; as much as its odour delights men, so much the more it afflicts the beetle. The beetle, so soon as it scents the rose, lies to all appearance dead. So our Lord Jesus, in his sufferings and death, is an odour of salvation to the Christian, to the Jew a scandal and the odour of death. As His death moves the Christian to love, so it moves the Jew to hatred and rancour." In the same way he plays with the similitude of Christ to the sun, who suffers sometimes the death of an eclipse. "But he dies one way to the wise, another to the foolish; as he appears loveable to those who have sound eyes, so he is hateful to those who have bad eyes; as he enlightens men, so he blinds bats and owls." There is much more in this strain. Yet, on the whole, the Pugio Fidei is a remarkable book, and has been the repertory from which even later controversialists have largely drawn.

vending books which contained the name of Jesus or that of the Blessed Virgin. The Jews seem to have had no objection to work in the way of trade on things which to them must have been absolutely idolatrous. The other clauses of this stern Bull aim at the complete isolation of the Jew, a relegation to a kind of social banishment, as infecting the Christian by any intercourse or communion. He was not to be physician, surgeon, shopkeeper, druggist, intendant, nor marriage broker,* nor to hold any public office which would mingle him up with Christians. He might not buy of or sell to Christians certain viands, nor be present at any banquet, nor bathe in any common bath. He was not to act as steward or agent of Christians, nor teach any science, art, or trade in a Christian school.

The civil laws had become as severe as the ecclesiastical; the Regent Queen Catherine had promulgated a famous ordinance secluding the Jews and the Moors in their separate quarters in every city; each Ghetto or Jewry was to be surrounded by a high wall, with only one gate of entrance. It rigidly prescribed their dress, a long mantle, reaching to the feet, without fringe, feather, or border of gold. It limited the cost of the cloth they wore to a low price. The Jewess who indulged in forbidden finery might be stripped of the whole, to her shift. The Jews might not change their place of residence; the magistrates might arrest any wanderers, and send them back to their homes. It is hardly conceivable that other clauses in this edict were intended to be carried into effect. They were neither to shave nor cut their hair. By the 20th clause they were

---

* " Provedor in casamentero."

neither to practise the veterinary art, nor to be carpenters, tailors, dressers of cloth, shoemakers, stocking weavers, peltcrers, nor butchers — these, it is presumed, not to Christians, lest clothes or meat from the hands of the unbaptized should infect the bodies and souls of the faithful. No Christian woman might on any account, lawful or unlawful, enter the Jewish quarter. The woman of character, if married, was fined 100 maravedis; if unmarried, she forfeited the dress which she wore. The loose woman was to be scourged, and turned out of the city, town, or hamlet.[d]

The Council of Zamora enforced with augmented rigour the Bull of Benedict XIII.[e] It annulled all the privileges of the Jews; they were only to be tolerated at all because they were human beings. There was a special clause, that during Wednesday in the Holy Week (the day of darkness) they were to keep within their houses. On Good Friday they were to close their doors and windows, lest they should seem to enjoy and mock the sorrow of good Christians.

During the long and disastrous reign of John II., it might seem that the Jews were quietly, with their wonderful vitality, rising again to wealth and importance. The Pragmatic, as it was called, issued (6th April, 1413) by John II. from Arévalo, assumed that feudal sovereignty, or rather right of possession over the Jews of Spain, which had been the general prerogative of the Crown in other kingdoms of Europe. The Jews were taken under the royal protection, as

---

[d] See this ordinance in substance in Amador de los Rios, p. 87.

[e] There is some confusion in the dates in Amador de los Rios. He speaks, p. 104, of the Bull of 1415 (?); of the Council of Zamora, 1413 (p. 107); of the Bull as published some years before.

his property, as belonging to his Chamber.^f A Bull of Pope Eugenius IV. had seemed to depart altogether from the milder Papal policy, and to aim at the total extirpation of the Jews. The king firmly, yet respectfully, asserts the prerogative of the Crown; he is bound to maintain the interests of the Church, his own, and those of his realm. The Jews are to be treated with humanity, according to the rights and the laws of Castile.^g

This state of affairs lasted through considerable part of the fifteenth century. The clergy, often seconded by the nobles, watched every opportunity of increasing the number of their willing, more often enforced, converts. The populace were ever ready to obey the tocsin of their spiritual leaders, and to indulge, under their holy sanction, their desire of plunder or revenge.

The old stories of the sacrilege of the Jews, of their murders especially of innocent children, whom they crucified in mockery, the stealing and insult of the consecrated Host, sprang up in Spain as elsewhere. Early in the century the Rabbins of one of the synagogues in Segovia were accused of some sacrilege. The Bishop, Don Juan de Tovdesllas, ordered them to be drawn on hurdles, hanged and quartered. The synagogue was confiscated, and turned into a church dedicated to the Corpus Christi. The Jews, it is said, in revenge, bribed the maître d'hôtel of the Bishop to poison him. The criminals suffered the same fate as the authors of the sacrilege.^h Nearly forty years after, a charge was brought against the Jews, probably less worthy of credit according to its atrocity. It was

---

^f "Cosa suya y de su Camera." ^g Amador de los Rios, p. 113.
^h Amador de los Rios, p. 115.

during the reign of Henry III., the Feeble. At the commencement of this reign (A.C. 1400) the nobles, who were in arms against the king, insisted, among the terms of their submission, that the king should dismiss from his service, and even from the kingdom, all Jews and Moors who defiled the religion and corrupted the morals of the people.¹ These were sinister times for an accusation against Jews. It was averred, that in the town of Sepulveda, on Good Friday (the Jews, shut up in the dark by the Christian law, are always said to have chosen that day for their deeds of darkness), they, by the advice of their Rabbi, Solomon Picho, carried off a child into a retired place, insulted it, and crucified it. The Bishop, Don Juan Arias d'Avila, caused sixteen of the most *culpable* to be arrested; some were burned, some hanged.ᵏ The populace only wanted countenance and authority to glut their growing hatred. Insurrections, massacres, took place in many cities of Andalusia, Cordova, Jaen, and of Castile, especially in Segovia.

The Popes at this period varied in their admonitions to the Kings of Spain. Eugenius IV. had issued his violent Bull denouncing the Jews of Castile and Leon, and prohibiting all intercourse between Jew and Christian. The Christian was not to receive medicine from a Jew. The wise and humane Nicolas V. prohibited compulsory baptisms, and all insults and injuries to Jews.¹

The union of Castile and Arragon, in the persons of Ferdinand and Isabella, was the crisis of their fate

---

¹ Amador de los Rios, p. 120.
ᵏ Ibid., p. 121.
¹ "Quo etiam tempore dixit Hispania, ne Judæus qui inter Ipsos dege-bant ad baptismata sacra suscipienda vi adigerent, neve afficerent injuriis." Raynald, sub ann. 1487.

to the unconverted, to a great extent to the converted, Jews. Another curious document, the assessment of all the Aljamas of the kingdom of Castile at the death of Henry III. (A.C. 1470), illustrates the numbers, the wealth, and the condition of the Jews at that period. Though the edicts of kings, the statutes of the Cortes, the Bull of Pope Benedict had prohibited the Jews from acting as collectors of the revenue or of the royal rents, as physicians, especially as judges, "even in Jewish affairs, yet at the head of this repartition appears the name of the Rabbi Aben Nunez, Physician to the King our Lord, and his Chief Judge, distributor of the services, and half-services, which the Jews in the Aljamas are bound to pay to the royal exchequer." The total assessment was 451,000 maravedis; each head of a family paid 45 maravedis, the maravedi being now, it is said, worth only six deniers. The Jews, then, on this calculation may be reckoned at towards 12,000 families, about 60,000 souls.[m] This was no doubt a great falling-off from the prosperous days of Judaism; and also a singular and melancholy testimony that in the most flourishing cities the decrease was the greatest. We need hardly suppose them driven out of these cities by the superior commercial activity of the Christians. Andalusia, including the great capital cities Seville and Cordova, paid only 59,500; the great archbishopric of Toledo, 64,300; while Palencia paid 54,500; Placentia 57,300. Such seems to have been the number of declared Jews who passed under the dominion of Ferdinand and Isabella.[n]

---

[m] Amador de los Rios, p. 131.

	Maravedis.
The Aljama of the Bishopric of Burgos	30,800
The Aljama of Calahorra	30,100
" Palencia	84,500
" Osma	19,600

Under these sovereigns Spain became one great monarchy. But were these (allowing, as it seems to me we must, for the incompleteness of these returns for all the Hebrews of both the kingdoms) all the Jews which became subjects of Ferdinand and Isabella? It is utterly and absolutely inconsistent with the lowest estimate of the numbers a few years afterwards expelled from the kingdom. But, even multiplied by at least three, they were not all. Notwithstanding their apparent and recorded triumphs in the conversion of the Jews, the clergy had long mistrusted their own success. Not only in the conformists themselves did there appear a secret inclination to their former religious usages, and but a cold and constrained obedience to the laws of the Church, but from generation to generation the hereditary evil lurked in their veins. The New Christians, as they were called, formed a kind of distinct and intermediate class of believers. Many of them no doubt had aspired to and had filled the highest offices in the State, and even in the Church. Some had become eminent in Christian knowledge, and in all the accomplishments of the age—statesmen, soldiers, poets, monks, friars, bishops. We have seen the distinction of Hieronymo de Santa Fé. Paul de Santa Maria had become Bishop of Burgos; Gonzalo Garcia was entrusted by Pope Benedict with the execution of the Bull of Valencia. Alphonso and Peter of Carthagena, John Alphonso of Baena, Friar Alphonso d'Espina, John the

---

	Maravedis.		Maravedis.
The Aljama of Siguenza	15,500	Bishopric of Placencia	57,300
„ Segovia	10,750	„ Andalusia	50,500
„ Avila	59,950		451,000
„ Salamanca and Ciudad Rodrigo	12,700		
„ Zamora	9,500	Amador de los Rios supposes the odd 1000 to have been the expense of collection.	
„ Leon and Astorga	37,100		
The Archbishopric of Toledo	64,500		

Old, and others, were illustrious names in their day. Some, no doubt from the noble desire of imparting to others the hopes and consolations of the religion in which they had found peace and knowledge and happiness—some, it may be feared, from the baser desire of inducing others to share the apostasy—had been most active in the conversion of their brethren. There were two (Paul of Burgos was of these) who, not content with enlightening, had become the most bitter and cruel persecutors of their more stedfast brethren. Many had intermarried, doubtless for their wealth, into the noblest families, families which boasted the richest and purest Gothic blood. It was the bitterest reproach in later days to prove this indelible contamination,° though there was scarcely a noble house in the land unimpeachably clear from this stain. But the mass of them, it was believed by the jealous clergy, and no doubt for this belief they had strong grounds, were still, at heart and in secret, Jews. They attended the services, they followed the processions, they listened to the teaching of the Church, but it was too evident that their hearts were far away, joining in the simpler service of the synagogue of their fathers, and in their secret chambers the usages of the Law were observed with the fond stealth of old attachment. To discover how widely Jewish practices still prevailed, nothing was necessary but to ascend a hill on their Sabbath, and look down on the town or village below; scarce half the chimneys would be seen to smoke; all that did not, were evidently

---

° The Mala Sangra, as it was afterwards termed, could not be purged away by centuries of transmission. See in Prescott the note concerning the Tizon de España, a rare volume, most carefully suppressed, which traced up most of the famous families to Jewish or Moorish ancestry. Prescott's Ferdinand and Isabella, i. pp. 355, 356.

those of the people who still feared to profane the holy day by lighting a fire.

The clergy summoned to their assistance that stern and irresistible ally, the Inquisition. This dread tribunal had already signalized its zeal by the extermination of the Albigenses, and the desolation of the beautiful province of Languedoc. Alphonso di Oyeda, prior of the Dominicans in Seville, urged the monarchs to bless their kingdom by the erection of a similar office, that the whole realm might be reduced to the unity of the faith. The religion of Ferdinand was his policy; Isabella's policy was religion.[p] Isabella was endowed with every virtue except that of humanity to those of another creed. And even the want of that (no doubt deemed by her subjects, perhaps by herself, to be her crowning excellence) was mitigated by her natural womanly benignity. Ferdinand, therefore, hesitated from worldly wisdom; Isabella from gentleness of heart. But the fatal Bull was obtained from the Pope, Sixtus the Fourth, empowering the monarchs to nominate certain of the clergy, above forty years of age, to make strict inquisition into all persons suspected of heretical pravity.[q] In this evil hour a work was published by some

---

[p] Compare Prescott (Ferdinand and Isabella). In this brief sketch, which remains as originally written, I find pride and pleasure in having anticipated the more elaborate statements of my dear friend as to the reluctant struggles of Isabella.

[q] Mariana hails the establishment of the Inquisition in these words:— "Mejor suerte y mas venturosa para España fue el establecimiento que per esto tiempo si hizo en Castilla, de un nuevo y santo tribunal de juezes severos y graves, a proposito de Inquerir y castignr la heretica pravidad y apostasia, diverso de los obispos, a cuyo cargo y autoridad Incumbia antiquamente este officio." xxiv. 17. I have no belief in the political rather than religious objects for which, according to some later writers, the Inquisition was founded, and introduced into Spain. In this case the politic Ferdinand would not have felt any reluctance for its establishment. Amador de los Rios, p. 174, adopts this theory

misguided Jew, reflecting on the government of Ferdinand and Isabella, probably on the Christian religion. It was answered by Ferdinand of Talavera, the queen's confessor, who thus acquired new influence, unfavourable to the Jews, over the vacillating mind of the queen. In September, 1480, two Dominicans, Michael Morillo and John de St. Martin, were named Inquisitors. Even the Cortes beheld with reluctance—the very populace with terror—the establishment of this dreadful tribunal; and, as it were to enlist still worse passions in the cause, a third of the property of all condemned heretics was confiscated to the use of the Holy Office; another third was assigned for the expenses of the trial—the last third went to the Crown. The tribunal established its head-quarters at Seville, and assumed at once a lofty tone; denouncing vengeance against all, even the highest nobles—the Duke of Medina Sidonia, the Marquis of Cadiz,[r] Count d'Arcos, into whose domains many of the New Christians had fled—if they should presume to shelter offenders from their justice. The dreadful work began. Victims crowded the prisons. The convent was not sufficiently spacious for their business, and the Inquisitors moved to the Castel de Triana, near Seville. Secret denunciations were encouraged—not to denounce was a crime worthy of death. The Inquisitors published an edict of grace, inviting all who sincerely repented of

---

on the subject. See the remarkable disclosures in the very recent Introduction to the Calendar of State Papers from Simancas, of the time of Henry II. (Rolls Publications, 1862), by G. A. Bergenroth—I regret to say, far less favourable to Queen Isabella—pp. 41 et seqq.

[r] I had fallen into an error, following Llorente, my chief authority in much of this, making two persons out of one. Rodrigo Ponce de Leon had both these titles. Note in Prescott.

their apostasy to manifest their repentance; in which case they might escape the confiscation of their property, and receive absolution. If they allowed the time of grace to elapse, they incurred the severest penalties of the law. Many came in and surrendered, but a dreadful oath was extorted from them to inform against their more criminal brethren. In one year 280 were burned in Seville alone; 79 were condemned to perpetual imprisonment in their loathsome cells; 17,000 suffered lighter punishments. A spot of ground was set apart near this beautiful city, not for the innocent amusement of the people, nor even for their more barbarous, yet manly, bull-fights, but as the Quemadero, the Place of Burning. It contained four statues, called the Four Prophets, to which the unhappy victims were bound. The diagnostics of this fatal disease of New Christianity were specified with nice minuteness. There were twenty-seven symptoms of the disorder. Among these (we have not space to recite the whole), were the expectation of the Messiah—the hope of justification by the Law of Moses—reverence for the Sabbath shown by wearing better clothes, or not lighting a fire—by observing any usage of their forefathers relating to meats—honouring the national fasts or festivals—rejoicing on the Feast of Esther, or bewailing the fall of Jerusalem on the 9th of August—singing psalms in Hebrew without the *Gloria Patri*—using any of the rites, not merely of circumcision, but those which accompanied it—those of marriage or of burial—even of interring the dead in the burying place of their forefathers.* Mariana himself,

---

* Prescott adds: "If he sate at table with Jews, or ate the meat of animals slaughtered by their hands, or drank a certain beverage held in much estimation by them; if he washed a corpse in warm water, or, finally, if he

the Spanish historian, while he justifies the measure by its success, ventures to express the general terror and amazement of the whole people that children were thus visited for the offences of their forefathers—that, contrary to the practice of all tribunals, the criminal was not informed of the name of his accuser, nor confronted with the witnesses—that death should be the punishment awarded for such offences—and that informers should be encouraged to lurk in every city or village, and listen to every careless conversation:—" a state of things, as some thought, not less grievous than slavery, or even than death." In some places they were not content with burning the living; their insatiable vengeance warred on the dead. Sepulchres were broken open, and the bodies of suspected Jews, which had wickedly intruded themselves into consecrated ground, but had long slumbered in peace, and their souls gone to their

---

gave Hebrew names to his children,—a most whimsical provision, since by a law of Henry II. he was prohibited, under severe penalties, from giving them Christian names. He must have found it difficult to extricate himself from the horns of this dilemma." This is not quite accurate; the prohibition of Henry II. was to the unconverted Jew. The converts, of course, were expected to give Christian names to their children. The perplexity must have been, that so many Christian names being of Jewish origin, a Christian may very innocently have given an odious Hebrew name to his child, a name, for instance, of one of the Apostles. I think therefore that my friend has here confused the persecutions of the New Christians and those of the Jews.

I do not believe that the early Inquisition took cognisance of Jews; no inquisition was necessary into their tenets, nor were they, strictly speaking, heretics. They were hardly under ecclesiastical jurisdiction. It was the secret Judaism which lurked in the heart of professed Christians which was to be searched out with such cruel acuteness, and punished with such remorseless barbarity. 17,000 or 18,000 may appear a large number of New Christians; but more than a generation had passed since the great conversions: it was acknowledged to be an hereditary evil. Seville was, in fact, the great seat of these suspected New Christians. "Daño que en Sevilla, mas que en otra parte prevalecio." Mariana, xxiv. 17.

account, were torn up and exposed to shame and insult. Miserable malice, which had all the guilt of cruel vindictiveness, yet was baffled by its senseless victims!

The ministers of confiscation and execution spread through Spain; many of the New Christians fled to France, to Portugal, and to Africa. Some, condemned for contumacy, ventured to fly to Rome, and to appeal to the Pope against their judges. The Pope himself trembled at his own act. He wrote to the sovereigns, complaining that the Inquisitors exceeded their powers. It was but a momentary burst of justice and mercy. Under the pretext of securing their impartiality, the number of Inquisitors was increased; the whole body was placed under certain regulations; and at length the Holy Office was declared permanent, and the too-celebrated Thomas de Torquemada placed at its head. Its powers were extended to Arragon; but the high-spirited nobles of that kingdom did not submit to its laws without a resolute contest— for many of those who held the highest offices were descended from the New Christians. The Cortes appealed to the King and to the Pope, particularly against the article which confiscated the property of the criminals—contrary, as they asserted, to the laws of Arragon. While their appeal was pending, the Inquisitors proceeded to condemn several New Christians. The pride of the nation took fire; an extensive conspiracy was organized; and the Inquisitor Arbues was assassinated in the cathedral of Saragossa.[1] But the effects of

---

[1] Compare the account of the murder of Arbues in Prescott, v. ii. p. 84. The whole scene, be justly observes, will readily remind the English reader of the assassination of Thomas à Becket.

this daring act were fatal, instead of advantageous, to the New Christians. The horror of the crime was universal. The old Christians shrunk from their share in the conspiracy, and left their confederates to bear all the odium and the penalty of the atrocious deed. The Inquisitors proceeded to exact a frightful retribution. Two hundred victims perished. Many of the noblest families were degraded by beholding some one of their members bearing the *san-benito*, as confessed and pardoned heretics. Though their chief victims were selected from those who were suspected of secret Judaism, yet the slightest taint of Judaism in the blood (and among the Arragonese nobility—the nobility of all Spain—this was by no means rare) was sufficient to excite suspicion, and, if possible, the vengeance of the Inquisitors.

The unconverted Jews, however they might commiserate these sufferings, still, no doubt, in their hours of sterner zeal, acknowledged the justice of the visitation which the God of their fathers had permitted against those who had thus stooped to dissemble the faith of their ancestors. Their pusillanimous dereliction of the God of Abraham had met with severe, though just retribution, while those who, with more stedfast hearts, had defied their adversary to the utmost, now enjoyed the reward of their holy resolution in their comparative security. But their turn came. In 1492 appeared the fatal edict commanding all unbaptized Jews to quit the realm in four months; for Ferdinand and Isabella, having now subdued the kingdom of Granada, had determined that the air of Spain should no longer be breathed by anyone who did not profess the Catholic faith. For this edict, which must make desolate the fairest provinces of the kingdom of its most industrious and thriving population, no act of recent conspiracy, no disloyal demeanour, no reluctance to contribute to the public burthens, was alleged. The whole race was condemned on charges, some a century old, all frivolous or wickedly false—crucifixions of children at different periods, insults to the Host, and the frequent poisoning of their patients by Jewish physicians. One of these charges was that they perverted back to Judaism their brethren who had embraced Christianity.[u] The story of the crucifixion of a child at Guardia had found ready belief (Juan de Passamento had been added to the saints and martyrs of the Church); it was working with unresisted effect on the popular belief.[x] The edict raked up every worn-out tradition of these atrocities, a crucifixion at Saragossa in 1250, in Segovia in 1406, one near Zamora, one at Sepulveda, an infernal conspiracy at Toledo to blow up a procession of the Host. The edict was issued only eighty-nine days after the conquest of Granada. The Jews made an ineffectual effort to avert their fate. Abarbanel, a man of the greatest learning, the boast of the present race of Jews, and of unblemished reputation, threw himself at the feet of the king and queen, and offered in the name of his nation an immense sum, 30,000 ducats, to recruit the finances of the kingdom, exhausted by the wars of Granada.[y]

---

[u] Llorente, c. 8.

[x] Amador de los Rios, p. 158. The author, though sharing in modern enlightenment, has still some old Spanish prejudices. He would throw the guilt of this act rather on the people than on the sovereigns; to the latter it was a matter of necessity. I have no doubt that the whole nation must share in the condemnation; and the whole nation bore the inevitable penalty.

[y] Solomon ben Virga (in the Schevet Judah) inserts Abarbanel's description of the causes and of the horrid scenes which accompanied the expulsion: "The king, more fierce than Esau (ipso Esavo ferocior), thought that he could not show his gratitude to God for the conquest of Granada so fully as by compelling the Jews to baptism, or expelling them from the kingdom." Abarbanel's offer rests on

The queen, sad to say, made a bitter speech against the suppliant. The Inquisitors were alarmed. Against all feelings of humanity and justice the royal hearts were steeled, but the appeal to their interests might be more effectual. Thomas de Torquemada advanced into the royal presence, bearing a crucifix. "Behold," he said, "him whom Judas sold for thirty pieces of silver. Sell ye him now for a higher price, and render an account of your bargain before God."[a]

The sovereigns trembled before the stern Dominican, and the Jews had no alternative but baptism or exile. For three centuries their fathers had dwelt in this delightful country, which they had fertilized with their industry, enriched with their commerce, adorned with their learning. Yet there were few examples of weakness or apostasy: the whole race—variously calculated at 160,000, 300,000, 650,000, or 800,000[b]—in a lofty spirit of self-devotion (we envy not that mind which cannot appreciate its real greatness) determined to abandon all rather than desert the religion of their fathers. They left the homes of their youth, the scenes of their early associations, the sacred graves of their ancestors, the more recent tombs of

---

his own authority. The queen supported Ferdinand in his stern determination. "Adstitit quoque a dextris Regina, Judæis inimicissima, quæ Regem acri oratione identidem hortabatur, quod feliciter cœpisset, fortiter exequeretur." p. 321.

[a] Amador de los Rios questions this story as improbable, p. 181. Mr. Prescott, like myself, received it as perfectly consistent with the character of the actors and of the times.

[b] As to the numbers, I am disposed, with Mr. Prescott, to take the lower, but not quite the lowest, as

more nearly approximating to probability. The whole population of the kingdom of Castile at that time was 6,750,000. Yet Abarbanel states the number of exiles at 800,000 (not a very large proportion of that population), and Abarbanel was one of the exiles. "Uno die trecenta peditum millia sine armis ex omnibus regni locis confluxere, juvenes, senes, infantes atque mulieres ituri omnes quocunque viam fata monstrarent, in horum numero ipse quoque fui." Schevet Judah, p. 322.

their own friends and relatives. They left the synagogues in which they had so long worshipped their God; the schools where those wise men had taught, who had thrown a lustre which shone, even through the darkness of the age, upon the Hebrew name.[b] They were allowed four months to prepare for this everlasting exile. The unbaptized Jew found in the kingdom after that period was condemned to death. The persecutor could not even trust the hostile feelings of his bigoted subjects to execute his purpose; a statute was thought necessary, prohibiting any Christian from harbouring a Jew after that period. Many were sold for slaves;[c] Christendom swarmed with them. The wealthier were permitted to carry away their moveables, excepting gold and silver, for which they were to accept letters of change or any merchandize not prohibited. Their property they might sell; but the market was soon glutted, and the cold-hearted purchasers waited till the last instant, to wring from their distress the hardest terms. A contemporary author states that he saw Jews give a house for an ass, and a vineyard for a small quantity of cloth or linen.[d] Yet many of them concealed their gold and jewels in their clothes and saddles; some swallowed them, in hopes thus at least to elude the scrutiny of the officers. The Jews consider this calamity almost as dreadful as the taking and ruin

---

[b] I had again anticipated my friend: "This extraordinary act of self-devotion by a whole people for conscience' sake may be thought by a contemporary of the nineteenth century to merit other epithets than those of perfidy, incredulity, and stiffnecked obstinacy, with which the worthy curate of Los Palacios in the charitable feeling of the time has seen fit to dogmatise it." Prescott, ii. p. 228.

[c] "Multi, ut vilia mancipiorum capita, per Christianorum terras, pretio venditi." Abarbanel, in Ben Virga ut supra."

[d] Bernaldes, as quoted by Llorente, and also by Mr. Prescott.

of Jerusalem. For whither to fly? and where to find a more hospitable shore? Incidents, which make the blood run cold, are related of the miseries which they suffered. Some of those from Arragon found their way into Navarre; others to the seashore, where they set sail for Italy, or the coast of Morocco; others crossed the frontier into Portugal. "Many of the former were cast away, or sunk," says a Jewish writer, "like lead, into the ocean." On board the ship, which was conveying a great number to Africa, the plague broke out. The captain ascribed the infection to his circumcised passengers, and set them all on shore, on a desert coast, without provisions. They dispersed: one, a father, saw his beautiful wife perish before his eyes—fainted himself with exhaustion—and, waking, beheld his two children dead by his side.* A few made their way to a settlement of the Jews. Some reached the coast of Genoa, but they bore famine with them; they lay perishing on the shore,—the clergy approached with the crucifix in one hand and provisions in the other,—nature was too strong for faith—they yielded, and were baptized. A Genoese, an eye-witness, describes their landing and their sufferings. He commences with these expressive words: "At first sight their treatment might seem praiseworthy, as doing honour to our God; perhaps there was some little cruelty in it, since we considered them not as beasts, but as men created by God." It was wretched to witness their sufferings; they

---

* Abarbanel, p. 323.

† "Res hæc primo aspectu laudabilis visa est, quia decus nostræ religionis respiceret, sed aliquantulum in se crudelitatis continere, si eos non belluas sed homines a Deo creatos consideravimus." Mr. Prescott, who translated the whole passage (ii. p. 232), omitted this characteristic sentence. Seneraga de Reb. Gen. apud Muratori, xxiv. 521, 522.

were wasted away with hunger, especially sucklings and infants; mothers half alive carried their children famishing with hunger in their arms, and died holding them. Many expired from cold, others with squalor and thirst. The tossing about on the sea and the unaccustomed miseries of the voyage had destroyed an incredible multitude. I speak not of the cruelty and rapacity with which they were treated by the captains of the ships. Some were thrown into the sea by the cupidity of the sailors; some lived to sell their children to pay for their passage. Many came into the city, but were not permitted to stay long—by the ancient laws of Genoa not above three days. They were allowed, however, to refit their vessels, and to recruit themselves some days from their fatigues: except that they could move, and that with difficulty, you would have thought them dead. They were crowded on the Mole with the sea on all sides; so many died that the air was infected; ulcers broke out, and the plague which visited Genoa the next year was ascribed to that infection." The acts of the clergy and the compulsory baptism rest on Jewish tradition.[a] Into Rome the fugitives were admitted, but they were received with the utmost inhospitality by their own brethren, fearful that the increased numbers would bring evil upon the community: even the profligate heart of Alexander the Sixth was moved with indignation.—" This is something new," he exclaimed; "I had always heard that a Jew had ever compassion on a Jew." The Pope commanded the resident Jews to evacuate the country; they bought the revocation of the edict at a considerable price.[b] Those who reached Fez were not permitted to enter the town; the king,

---

[a] Schevet Judah.   [b] Abarbanel, ut supra.

though by no means unfriendly, dreaded the famine they might cause among his own subjects. They were encamped on the sand, suffering all the miseries of hunger; living on the roots they dug up, or the grass of the field, "happy," says one Jewish authority, "if the grass had been plentiful:"[1] yet, even in this state, they religiously avoided the violation of the Sabbath by plucking the grass with their hands; they grovelled on their knees, and cropt it with their teeth. Worse than all, they were exposed to the most wanton barbarities of the savage people. An Arab violated a maiden before her parent's face—returned and stabbed her to the heart, lest he should have begotten a child infected with the Jewish faith. Another woman, unable to bear the sight of her pining child in his agony, struck him dead to the earth with a large stone. Many sold their children for bread. The king of the country afterwards declared all such children free. A pirate of Sallee allured a number of youths—one hundred and fifty—on board his ship, with the promise of provisions —and, amid the shrieks of the parents on the shore, set sail, and sold his booty in some distant port. The captain had intended to murder them all; a merchant on board the ship remonstrated; "how can I otherwise avenge the blood of Christ, whom the Jews slew?" argued the avaricious captain, intent on his plunder; "Christ himself," was the reply, "allowed his blood to be shed to redeem mankind."[k] It was not thought wrong to cast them out on the wild shore. Another party were landed by a barbarous captain of a ship, entirely naked and utterly desolate on the African coast: the

---

[1] Abarbanel, ut supra, in Schevet Judah, p. 324.
[k] Abarbanel, ut supra, 328, 331.

first, who ascended a hill to survey the country, were devoured by wild beasts, which came howling down upon the rest of the miserable crew. They plunged into the sea, and stood shivering in the water till the wild beasts retreated; they then crept back to the beach. For five days they remained in this miserable plight, and were rescued by the humane activity of the captain of another vessel, who sent his boat to their relief.

But these were the acts of savage barbarians or lawless pirates. In Portugal they trusted to the faith of kings. They offered to Joam II. a large sum, for permission to enter his kingdom. The more intolerant of his advisers urged him to refuse all terms; but the poverty of the king triumphed over his bigotry. They were admitted at the price of eight crusadoes a head— children at the breast alone excepted from the tax. The frontier was lined with toll-gatherers, and they were permitted to enter only at particular places. They were merely to pass through the country, and embark for Africa; with the exception of artificers in brass and iron, who were to enter at half-price, and, if they chose, might remain. They brought the plague with them, and many lay perishing by the wayside. Eight months elapsed, and many still lingered in the country—either too poor to obtain a passage, or terrified by the tales of horrid cruelty inflicted on their brethren by the Moors. All these were made slaves—the youth were baptized by force, and drafted off to colonize the unwholesome island of St. Thomas. The new king, Emmanuel, commenced his reign with a hopeful act of mercy: he enfranchised the slaves—he seemed inclined to protect the resident Jews within his realm. But he wedded the daughter of Ferdinand and Isabella, and brought home a dowry of cruelty and intolerance. The son-in-law must follow the example of his parents: he deserved to win their favour by surpassing them even in their own barbarity. He named a day for all Jews to quit the kingdom, and appointed certain ports for their embarkation. Before that time he issued another secret order to seize all children under fourteen years of age, to tear them from the arms, the bosoms of their parents, and disperse them through the kingdom, to be baptized and brought up as Christians. The secret transpired, and, lest they should conceal their children, it was instantly put in execution.—Great God of Mercy, this was in the name of Christianity! Frantic mothers threw their children into the wells and rivers,—they destroyed them with their own hands. One mother threw herself at the feet of the king as he was riding to church. She had already lost six children; she implored that her youngest might be spared to her. The courtiers repelled her with scorn and ill-usage. The king told them to let her go, "the poor bitch deprived of her whelps!" But, though stifled in the heart of the monarch, the voice of Nature still spoke in that of the people, however bigoted. They assisted the Jews to conceal their children. By a new act of perfidy, Emmanuel suddenly revoked the order for their embarkation at two of the ports which he had named. Many were thrown back upon Lisbon, and the delay made them liable to the law. The more stedfast in their faith were shipped off as slaves, but the spirits of many were broken: on condition that they might receive back their children, and that government would not scrutinize their conduct too closely for twenty years, they submitted to baptism. Yet most of these were reserved, if possible, for a more dreadful fate. About ten years after, some of them were detected celebrating the Passover, or by one account eating bitter herbs before the Passover For this offence some were imprisoned. The heavier charges inflamed the popular resentment against them. In this state of the public mind, it happened that a monk was displaying a crucifix to the eyes of the wondering people, through a narrow aperture in which a light streamed—the light, he declared, of the manifest Deity. While the devout multitude were listening in blind devotion, one man alone was seen to smile; he had, in fact, discovered a lamp behind the mysterious crucifix. In a rash moment he dropped the incautious expression, that if God would manifest himself by water (the year had been unusually dry and sultry), rather than by fire, it would be for the public advantage. The scandalized multitude recognized in the infidel speaker a New Christian. They rushed upon him, dragged him by the hair into the marketplace, and there murdered him. His brother stood wailing over the body; he instantly shared his fate. From every quarter the Dominicans rushed forth with crucifixes in their hands, crying out, "Revenge, revenge! Down with the heretics; root them out; exterminate them!" A Jewish authority asserts that they offered to every one who should murder a Jew, that his sufferings in purgatory should be limited to a hundred days. The houses of the converts were assailed: men, women, and children involved in a promiscuous massacre—even those who fled into the churches, embraced the sacred relics, or clung to the crucifixes, were dragged forth and burned. The king was absent: on his return he put on great indignation. The ringleaders of the riot were punished; and the New Christians, who escaped, became for the future more cautious.

My History may well close this melancholy scene with the description of it in somewhat later Jewish tradition, instinct as that description is with touches of biblical pathos: "In that year the exiles from Jerusalem were driven away from Sphard by command of the wicked ones, Ferdinand, King of Sphard, and his wife Isabella, and were thence dispersed into the four wings of the earth. And they went in ships, whither the wind allowed them to go—unto Africa and Asia, and the land of Yavan and Turkey; and they dwell therein unto this day. And there came upon them many sorrows and afflictions, and the souls of the people became weary on the way. For some of them the Turks killed, to take out the gold which they had swallowed to hide it; and some of them hunger and the plague consumed; and some of them were cast naked by the captain upon the isles of the sea; and some of them were sold for menservants and maidservants in Genoa and its villages; and some of them were drowned in the sea. See, O Lord, whom hast thou afflicted so much that a man should consume his fruit! For there were among them who were cast into the isles of the sea upon Provence, a Jew and his old father fainting from hunger, begging bread; and there was no one to break unto him in a strange country. And the man went and sold his little son for bread, to restore the soul of the old man. And it came to pass, when he returned unto his father, that he found him fallen down dead, and he rent his clothes. And he returned unto the baker to take his son, and the baker would not give him back. And he cried out with a sore and bitter cry for his son, and there was none to deliver. All this befell us in the year RABBIM (for the sons of the desolate are רבים many) . . . . Yet have we not forgotten thee, neither have we dealt falsely in thy covenant. And now, O God, be not far off; hasten to help us, O Lord! For thy sake we are killed all the day; we are counted as sheep for the slaughter. Make haste to help us, O God of our salvation! Plead our cause and deliver us.

"And also unto them that had changed their glory for an unprofitable one, in the days of the priest Fra Vincenzio Sadi. This Isabella was a Satan in those days. And she set searchers and spies over them, to see if they walked in the law of their Messiah or not. And they burned by hundreds of them for no cause; and all that they had they plundered daily. And then they began to flee, and to go unto Turkey, to serve God as at this day." R. Joshua fiercely adds, "And the Lord was zealous for his people, and gave unto those kings the recompence of the works of their hands. For their daughter died in Portugal while she was labouring with child; and her eldest son died in Prague, and there was no male child left to inherit her dominion. And the Queen Isabella became weary of her life, and half of her flesh was consumed by the evil and lasting plague that is called cancer, and she died.

"In Portugal also the destructions increased; and the enemies decreed by the power of the sword that none should walk according to the Law of Moses the servant of the Lord. And the Jews took their sons and their daughters, and sent them unto the isles of the sea wherein no one dwelled. And many hallowed the Holy One of Israel; but many fell down and worshipped the Image, and changed their glory for an unprofitable one."

R. Joshua proceeds to say that there arose upon the fugitives a priest as a Satan. The inhabitants killed them, and had no compassion upon man or woman. The king was absent from Lisbon. On his return, he ordered the priest to be burned, his accomplices to be put to death.

"And many Jews went out from Portugal at that time, and went unto the East country to serve the Lord our God as at the first; and they have dwelled there unto this day. And many were left halting between two opinions; they feared the Lord, yet swore by the image of the uncircumcised, and went daily unto their churches. And they have increased, and become mighty in riches until this day. From that day and afterwards there was not a man left in all the kingdoms of Sphard who was called by the name of Israel."[1]

How deep a wound was inflicted on the national prosperity by this act of "the most Christian sovereign" cannot easily be calculated; but it may be reckoned among the most effective causes of the decline of Spanish greatness. It was not only the wealth, which notwithstanding the most vigilant perquisition they carried away, though that for those times no doubt was enormous. A Jew, probably an African refugee, after the taking of Malaga, ransomed 450 of his brethren at a cost of 27,000 doubloons. We have seen the vast sum offered to the king by Abarbanel to buy off the edict of expulsion. There are many records of the secret luxury and magnificence of the Spanish Jews in the darkest times. What was a much more severe loss, they carried away all the industry and the commerce of the land. The loss of the gold and silver (alone considered wealth in those days) which disappeared with them, would have been replaced before

---

[1] R. Joseph, I. 322, 326. R. Joseph's own ancestors fled from Navarre to Avignon; some of his relations fled to Turkey. His father, when he was five years old, migrated to the neighbourhood of Genoa; exiled from Genoa, he lived at Novi (p. 415).

long by the influx of the precious metals from America. But the loss of industry was irreparable in a country where pride and indolence proscribed all such pursuits as base and sordid; and where the richest body, the Church, contributed nothing, either directly, or by the improvement of the land, to the support of the State. With the Moors and with the Jews vanished all the rich cultivation of the soil, and all internal and external commerce.[m] "You call this," the Sultan Bajazet is reported to have said of Ferdinand, "a politic king, who impoverishes his own kingdom to enrich mine!"[a]

Nevertheless, it is certain that in the Peninsula Judaism still lurked in the depth of many hearts, inac-

---

[m] Amador de los Rios, p. 166.

[a] There is a correspondence between the Jews of Spain and the Jews of Constantinople, such palpable forgeries as to be in themselves of no value, but curious as showing the Spanish notion of the motives and character of the Jews. The Jews' letter runs thus: "Honourable Jews, health and grace be with you! Know ye that the King of Spain, by a public proclamation, wishes to make us Christians, and to rob us of all our property. He takes away our lives, destroys our synagogues, and inflicts upon us other vexations, which trouble us, and make us uncertain what to do. By the Law of Moses we pray and entreat you to summon an assembly, and to send us, as speedily as possible, the result of your deliberations." The Jews of Constantinople replied: "Beloved brethren in Moses, we have received your letter, in which you describe the torments and miseries which you suffer, in which we fully participate. This is the advice of the great Satraps and of the Rabbins. For what you say concerning the King of Spain wishing to make you Christians, do so, since you cannot do otherwise. As to the order to plunder you of your goods, make your sons merchants, and plunder them of theirs. For what you say of taking away your lives, make your sons apothecaries and physicians, and take away theirs. They destroy, you say, your synagogues: make your sons clergymen, that they may profane their religion and their churches. If they afflict you with other vexations, strive to get State employments for your children, in order to revenge yourselves upon them. Do not depart from these instructions, and you will see, by experience, that, from down-trodden as you are, you will soon be held in consideration. Usaaf, Prince of the Jews of Constantinople." Amador de los Rios, from MSS. in the Library of Madrid. The Spaniard will not absolutely give up the authenticity of these letters.

cessible even to the searching scrutiny of the Inquisition. Secret Jews are said to have obtained the highest offices of the State, and even of the Church, to have worn the cowl of the monk, and even to have sat on the tribunal of the Inquisition. The celebrated Jewish physician Orobio stated that he had personal knowledge of many of his brethren who thus eluded the keen eye of the bloodhounds of the Holy Office. Cloisters, of monks and nuns, were full of Jews; there were canons, bishops, Inquisitors, not only of Jewish descent, but in heart Jews.[o] They were rich, many of them, and money could easily obtain certificates of pure Christianity. This profound and widespread hypocrisy may seem to some almost to justify the Inquisition; but it shows also how it was baffled in spite of all its zealous cruelty. Mr. Borrow relates a strange story of secret Jews in the Church of Spain in our own days; some of the most learned performing, with seeming solemnity and earnestness, the ceremonial of the Church, but in spirit still faithful to the Law of Moses.[p]

---

[o] "Quid dicam de Hispaniâ et Portugalliâ? Ubi ex Judæis apostatis fere omnes et principes et nobiles et populares originem ducunt, quod In eis regionibus adeo notum est, ut nemo dubitaverit; quamvis pro insignis nobilitatis et dignitatibus præsertim ecclesiasticis obtinendis Judaismum abjurare oportet, et informationes exhibere quod ab Israeli oriundi non sunt: quod falsis testibus adhibitis, ut in regiâ, curo etiam favente facile consequuntur. Adeo omnia monachorum claustra atque monialium Judæorum plena, Canonici, Inquisitores, Episcopi plurimi ex Judæis procedunt. Non pauci in corde Judaismut, et propter ea bona temporalia Christianismum simulant; ex quibus aliqui resipiscunt, et, ut possunt, effugiunt." Limborch, in his answer, says: "Monachorum quorumcunque cænobia in Hispaniâ istiusmodi sceleratis hominibus esse repleta." Limborch, Amica Collatio (Gouda, 1687), pp. 102, 209, 276.

"And many were left halting between two opinions; they feared the Lord, yet swore by the Image of the uncircumcised, and went daily into their churches, and they have increased and become mighty unto this day." Rabbi Joseph, p. 327.

[p] Mr. Borrow, Bible in Spain, p. 233 (see also the story on p. 300), gives

If these proofs were insufficient, the lurid light of Autos da Fé still betrayed the fact that Jews, undisguised Jews, lingered on the forbidden soil of Spain. At the burning of a young Jewish woman, Philip III. had the weakness to shudder. The Inquisitor declared that the king must atone for this crime by his blood. He was bled; the pale guilty blood burned by the executioner.[q]

At all events, if Jews did not, as they certainly did, still defile the soil of Spain, their contaminating blood lingered in the veins of the greatest and noblest—the dukes with the most magnificent titles and hereditary dignities. That blood, both in Spain and Portugal, was as ineffaceable as negro blood in the United States of America—the pure red of princes, even of kings, was tainted. The shrewd Venetian Ambassador, in the reign of Philip the Second and his successor, observing how deeply the priesthood, as well as the laity,[r] were polluted with Jewish blood, doubted whether

---

this extraordinary conversation between himself and a Jew who passed for a Christian. "Have you reason," says Mr. Borrow, "to suppose that many of you are to be found among the priesthood?" Abarbanel: "Not to suppose, but to know it. There are many such as I amongst the priesthood, and not amongst the inferior priesthood either. Some of the most learned and famed of those of Spain have been of us, or of our blood at least; and many of them at this day think as I do. They perform all the Catholic ceremonies, and then sit down upon the floor and curse." Abarbanel mentions an archbishop who, having acknowledged his inclinations at heart to Judaism, died in the odour of sanctity.

[q] Grégoire, Régénération des Juifs, quoted by M. Bédarride, note, p. 553.

[r] "E chi sa la poca conscienza, che la maggior parte cosi dei preti, cosi dei laici tiensi nelle cose essenziale, e che molti di loro frescamente descendono da Mori e da Ebrei, dubità grandemente, che il cuore e l'animo non corrisponda alle apparenze. Alle Gerbe, innanzi che si perdesse il forte, molte passarono a i Turchi, lasciando i compagni e la fede. Alcuni nella Goletta, poco fa trattarono di darla agli infideli: e in Murcia, come scrissi, si scoperse una grandissima copia d' Ebrei." Relazione di Paolo Tiepolo, 1563 (in the reign of Philip II.), vol. v. p. 18. See also Relazione di Soranzo, 1565, p. 82.

their Christianity was more pure than their descent. And as late as towards the close of the last century, it is told of Pombal, that the King of Portugal, Joseph I., proposed to issue an edict that all who were descended from Jews should wear a yellow cap. Pombal appeared in the Council with three yellow caps. The king demanded the meaning of this strange accoutrement: "One is for your Majesty, one for the Grand Inquisitor, one for myself."

Spain—even in her lowest decrepitude—indulged in what might seem the luxury of persecution. The Marquis de Villars, Ambassador of France from 1678 to 1682, describes as an eye-witness a scene almost incredible in its cruel and cowardly details. On the last day of June the theatre was erected in the public Place of Madrid for a general gaol delivery of all the Inquisition Courts in Spain, which had not taken place for forty-eight years. The trials lasted from nine in the morning to nine at night. The King was present—that king, the poor idiot, Charles II. Above the King sat the Grand Inquisitor.[*] The most noble grandees of Spain —men with the most glorious names and titles—acted as familiars of the Inquisition, and led the miserable victims upon the stage of the theatre. Eighteen Jews, men and women—two relapsed and one Mohammedan— were condemned to the flames. Fifty other Jews and

---

[*] I cannot refrain from citing from Llorente a passage relating to the great persecutor: "In the year 1498 died Thomas de Torquemada, who had presided over the Inquisition, and governed all its proceedings for sixteen years. In that time it is reckoned that under this Christian judge 8800 victims had perished at the stake; 6500 had been burned in effigy. Those who had suffered other penalties, infamy, perpetual imprisonment, confiscation, amounted to 90,000. And with this mass of human bloodshed and human misery upon his soul, Thomas de Torquemada was prepared to undergo, according to his own creed, the judgement of Jesus Christ.'

Jewesses were condemned to bear the *san-benito*, and to imprisonment for different terms. The king sat there the whole day, staring with his stupid eyes on the scene as if it had been a play, and saw the ignorant monks savagely beating the wretched victims to compel them to kneel at the altar. The following night those condemned to the flames were executed without the city. The monks, not content with harassing them by arguments, according to Villars' words, little likely to shake their faith in their religion, burned them with torches in order to force them to confess Christianity. Some persons, it may be hoped in mercy, despatched them with their swords. The howling people heaped stones upon them. The Jews bore their sufferings with admirable constancy, "worthy," says Villars, "of a better cause. Some plunged into the fire. These executions," continues Villars, "by no means diminished the number of Jews in Spain; while these wretched Jews were burned for their faith, other Jews held high offices, especially in finance, and lived in credit and respect."[1]

I close this dreary Book with this touching incident. To a late period the Jews scattered over the world retained the precious recollection of their glorious and pleasant days in Spain, and their fond hopes of return to that delicious climate. It was recorded in their prayers. Long afterwards they sought, for their Feast of Tabernacles, branches of the orange-trees under whose fragrant shade they had reposed in Spain and Portugal. Even in the seventeenth century German Jews travelled to Spain to obtain branches of these hallowed trees for their synagogues.[2]

---

[1] From the Mémoires de Villars, printed by Mr. Stirling for the Philobiblian Society, pp. 187, 191.

[2] Buxtorf, Synagoga Judaica, c. xxi. Depping, p. 434.

BOOK XXVII.

JEWS OF ITALY.

Early Period — The Popes — The family of Peter Leonis — Martin V.

On the Jews of Italy my History has maintained almost total and significant silence. During the darker ages, if they attained not in Italy the same dangerous and distinctive opulence, neither were they exposed to the same cruel and sweeping calamities. The feudal system, so far as it was established in Italy (most fully in the Norman kingdom of Naples[a]), degraded them, as in France, England, and Germany, into the property of the lords. They were assigned over by one feudal sovereign to another, granted as gifts, made objects of bargain, sale, and merciless exaction.[b] But the feudal system died out earlier and with more rapid dissolution in Italy than in the rest of Europe. The free cities assumed their independence, and in these the Jews seem generally to have lived in happy obscurity. The cities and

---

[a] On the Norman conquest of Sicily, deeds of purchase and sale, or contracts, were equally valid in Arabic, Greek, or Hebrew, "in linguâ Arabicâ, Græcâ, et Hebraicâ, per manus notariorum Saracenorum, Græcorum, et Hebræorum, etsi solemnitatibus careant Christianorum." Const. Panormit. apud Gregorio, Considerazioni sopra la Storia di Sicilia, t. 1, Prove, i. 11.

Latins, Greeks, Jews, Saracens, were to be judged each by his own law. Diplom. 1168, Ibid. iv. 21, Prove.

King Roger of Sicily brought Jewish silk-weavers to Sicily from the Morea. Ann. Cavenses; Muratori, vii. 924.

[b] See examples from Muratori, Ant. Med. Æv. cited above, p. 160.

the petty sovereigns were too perpetually occupied with wars within themselves, and wars with their neighbours, to take up any systematic policy concerning these scattered strangers; and the Jews cared little, so they were left in peace, for Guelph or Ghibelline, Pope or Emperor.[c] Neither was religious zeal in the peninsula so easily inflamed, so frantic or so bloodthirsty, as beyond the Alps. Italy, if cold to the glorious enthusiasm, was exempt from the blind fanaticism of the earlier Crusades. The cry of "Hep! Hep!" was not raised, or, if raised, but feebly and rarely, in the Italian cities; their streets did not run with Jewish blood.

But the great cause of the comparative quiet and security of the Italian Jews was that they were not the sole, and therefore not the few, envied and odious possessors of wealth. They did not engross the commerce. In Naples and Sicily, Frederick the Second, though he published the terrible edicts of the Canon-law, as enacted by Innocent III., yet, with that premature political wisdom with which he fostered trade and industry in all their branches, skilfully turned the political incapacity of the Jews to their advantage and to the advantage of the State. He deliberately, it might seem, made over to them the whole trade in money. Usury, which he could not, in the teeth of the Papal edicts and the popular feeling, declare to be lawful to the Christian, was not forbidden by the Divine law to the Jew: aliens from the Christian

---

[c] Cassel rather asserts that they were mostly Ghibellines. They appear, in the wars of the Angevins and Arragonese for Sicily and Naples, to have been against the Pope and the French.

Cassel quotes a letter of Pope Martin III. "A li perfidi Judei dilla Isula di Sicilia Martinu Papa terzu manda quilli saluti, siccomu a corrompitari di paci, e di Christiani ucidatori e spargituri de lu sangue di nostri figli." p. 143. The article has much more on Jews in Sicily. Compare also Amari, Vespro Siciliano.

Church, they could not be bound by its laws, and under the royal licence might carry on this baleful, as it was thought, but, as he knew, necessary traffic.[4] But in Italy generally the money transactions were not entirely in their hands; they were not alone enriched by and hated for the practice of usury. From an early period the Lombards, the Florentines, the Caorsini, were their rivals in that business. so necessary, yet so detested, and which, beyond the Alps, marked out the Israelites, and them alone, as the victims of hate and rapacity. The Christians are the objects of Dante's withering scorn for their exaction and avarice. Even beyond the Alps the Italians became the rivals of the Jews and competitors for gain and its inevitable consequences. The direct taxes levied by the Popes on Latin Christendom, annates, first fruits, Peter's pence, assessments on rich conventual foundations, the votive offerings of pious kings and nobles to the Holy See, the contributions for the Crusades, of which the Popes constituted themselves the treasurers; the vast expense of all ecclesiastical suits, and of those offices of the Roman Court which had long been proverbial for their cost; in short, all the sources of the remorseless rapacity, venality, and extortion with which Rome was taunted for centuries,—all these world-embracing

---

[4] "A nexu tamen præsentis Constitutionis nostræ Judæos tantum excipimus, in quibus non potest argui fœnus illicitum divinâ lege prohibitum, quod constat non esse sub legibus a beatissimis patribus institutis, quos etiam auctoritate nostrâ licentia improbum fænum volumus exercere." Const. Reg. Siculæ, apud Cancianl, i.

307. (What did they pay for the licence?) See also, in Gregorio III., Prove, p. xxxvi., Frederick's Regest concerning Jewish gardeners in Palermo. They were very skilful in the cultivation of fruit-trees; they were no doubt much employed by the enlightened Emperor in translations from the Arabic. See back, p. 200.

financial operations required agents, and by degrees bankers, in foreign countries for their collection and transmission. Italians, even churchmen, even cardinals, soon became adepts, active, sagacious adepts, in all these pecuniary transactions. We more often hear these Papal tax-gatherers taunted with Jewish avarice and usuriousness than with Jewish descent or creed. It is true that on the expulsion of the Jews from France by Philip Augustus many of the richest Jews took refuge in Northern Italy. There they are said—but the fact is by no means certain—to have invented letters of change and credit, which their extensive correspondence and honourable fidelity to each other rendered a safe means for these incipient dealings with the money market of Europe. But even if the Jews had, it may be in a ruder way, forestalled this simple invention, the Lombards and Italians were not slow in availing themselves of, and securing an ample share, if not almost the whole, of these profits. Philip the Fair found his Italian bankers not less tempting objects of plunder (some of them he had himself employed to levy his grinding taxation) than the Jews. At all events, the Jews, if we may so speak, were held not to be the only or the worst Jews in Italy. If they enjoyed not the monopoly of moneymaking, they escaped the monopoly of detestation, and that which followed detestation, persecution, pillage, sometimes massacre.

If the Popes, faithful to the milder tradition of Gregory the Great, were on the whole more humane and Christian, it must be acknowledged that they had not the same temptations as the poorer and more embarrassed sovereigns of Europe. The Jews of Paris or of Languedoc, of London or of York, of the cities on the Rhine, offered a rich prey to the rapacity of the kings or the great feudal nobles. These potentates felt, too, occasionally, or affected, commiseration for their people, heavily burthened with debts, these debts iniquitously and irreligiously, as it was universally believed, aggravated by usury. In Rome the Jews were, some few of them probably of a higher, others of a much lower class. The higher were obliged to content themselves with more moderate gains, and therefore more moderate wealth, moderate at least as contrasted with that of the higher clergy, the officials of the Papal Curia, and the religious foundations. The lower probably kept up the hereditary and traditionary offices of pedlers and dealers in small wares, which they held during the old Empire. Contempt and poverty would secure them against violent persecution. History and legislation, even the legislation of the Church, are totally or almost totally silent about the Italian, and especially the Roman, Jews during the ninth and tenth centuries. In those wild times of the law of the strongest, even Jews would not venture, or would be unable to become perilously wealthy. In the eleventh century occurs one persecution. Some poor Jews were executed on account of an earthquake.* In the latter half of that century one family alone, but that a renegade family, the Peter Leonis,† having submitted to baptism, rose, during the

---

* Ademar, Hist. lii. 52.

† "Cujus avus, cum inæstimabilem pecuniam multiplici corrogasset usurâ, susceptam circumcisionem baptismatis undâ damnavit . . . . Factus dignitate Romanus, nam genus et formam regiæ pecuniæ donat, alterois matrimoniis omnes sibi nobiles civitatis asciviL." According to Arnulf, the Antipope had a Jewish countenance, "qui et Judaicam facie repræsentat imaginem, et perfidiam voto refert." Arnulf, Monum. Germ. viL p. 711. But the hatred of the Jews appears even more strongly. After accusing the Antipope of bestial incest, he adds as an aggravation—"Jam ore Judæus quidem sed Judæo deterior." Arnulf speaks of the numerous progeny and infinite wealth of the Peter Leonis. Compare

strife between the Popes and the Emperors, to great power, gave consuls, patricians to the city of Rome, and if not a Pope, an Antipope, who was crowned and for a time maintained his authority in the Vatican. It is from the invectives of the enemies of Anacletus II. that we obtain our fullest knowledge of the rise of this remarkable family. Its founder, according to these writers, a Jew, in the days of Pope Gregory VII., had scraped up enormous wealth by nefarious usury. This wealth made him a useful, in the days of his exigency no doubt a welcome, partisan of the Pope. Had the commanding mind of Hildebrand anything to do with Peter's conversion? At all events he became a Christian, and was admitted to the rank and dignity of a Roman. The haughtiest and noblest families of Rome did not disdain to ally themselves to the Jew by intermarriages with his sons and daughters. Peter Leonis, the second of the race, had a strong tower palace near the Temple of Marcellus, not far from which is now the Ghetto, even then no doubt occupied by his Jewish kindred. If an inscription which was once in the Church of S. Alesio marks the grave of that Peter Leonis, he had attained the rank of consul. The son of the same Peter Leonis became cardinal, became Antipope under the title of Anacletus II. St. Bernard, the ardent partisan, the maker almost of Innocent II., does not scruple to taunt Anacletus with

---

Compare Chron. Mauriu. Duschesne, iv. 570.

If the epitaph quoted by Baronius, ann. 1111, refers to Leo, the founder of the family, the Jew himself had a noble mother:—

"Ille jacet in tumulo Leo, vir per cuncta fidelis

Sedis apostolicae tempore quo viguit,
Romae natus, opum dives, probus et satis alius,
Sanguine materno nobilitatus erat.
Prudens et sapiens, et caelo pene sub omni
Agnitus et celebris, semper in urbe manens,
Virgo ter sena fuerat cum sole dierum
Quando suum vitae finierat spatium."

the indelible reproach of his Jewish descent. He is indignant that the offspring of a Jew should occupy the chair of St. Peter.[a] The Archbishop of Ravenna brands the schism of Anacletus as the heresy of Jewish unbelief.[b]

It is in their homage to the successful rival of their renegade descendant that the Jews in other parts of Europe, those especially of Rome, in a more marked manner on the accession of Alexander II., emerge into notice. To Innocent no doubt they would be eager to show their allegiance, as disclaiming all sympathy with him who was mocked by his enemies as a Jewish pontiff, and would be more odious to them as sprung from an apostate. On the entrance of Alexander II. into Rome they appear as a guild or corporation. (This may seem to imply an ancient and recognized establishment.) They have their place in the solemn processions, with their standard, among judges, clergy, and other guilds. They carry, as it appears according to custom, the Book of the Law, the Old Testament, as their badge. The grateful Pope not only accepts their homage as faithful subjects; he issues an edict, prohibiting all interference with their synagogues, all insult to their religious rites. In the twelfth century Benjamin of Tudela found the Jewish congregation at Rome (they amounted only to two hundred) held in respect, and exempt from tribute. As in other countries, the Pope's (Alexander III.'s[c])

---

[a] "Ut constat Judaicam sobolem sedem Petri in Christo occupasse injuriâ." Epist. 134.

[b] "Judaicæ perfidiæ hæresis." Apud Mansi, xxi. 434.

[c] Asher's edition, p. 38 et seqq. Alexander III. was Pope from 1159 to 1181, but during a great part of his pontificate was not at Rome. Zunz dates Benjamin's visit between 1159 and 1167. Benjamin's strange stories of the sights of Rome are very curious. He mentions St. Peter's on the site of the large palace of Julius Cæsar. "The

stoward and minister of his private property was a Jew, R. Jechiel, a handsome, prudent, and wise man. Benjamin found Jews in other cities: 300 in Capua, 500 in Naples, 600 in Salerno (the principal medical university in Christendom), 20 principal men in Amalfi, 200 in Benevento, 200 in Melfi, 40 in Ascoli, 200 in Trani, none in Bari, 300 in Taranto, 500 in Otranto.[a]

The Acts of Innocent III. and of the Lateran Council were addressed rather to the Jews of the Catholic world than to those of Rome, the prohibition to hold offices of dignity and trust (they were to forfeit all the emolument of such charges to the poor); the fatal statute commanding them to wear a distinctive mark on their dress. The protective law of Honorius III., looked to the Jews of

---

extent of ground covered by ruined and inhabited parts of Rome amounts to four and twenty miles. You there find eighty halls of the eighty eminent kings who are called Imperator, from King Tarquin to King Pepin, the father of Charles who first conquered Spain and wrested it from the Mohammedans. In the outskirts of Rome is the palace of Titus, who was rejected by three hundred senators in consequence of his having wasted three years in the conquest of Jerushalaim, which task, according to their rule, ought to have been accomplished in two years !" He mentions also the hall of the palace of King Vespasianus, a very large and strong building (qy. the Coliseum?), as the marvellous Hall of King Galba; also S. Giovanni in Porta Latina, in which place of worship are two copper pillars, constructed by King Schlomo (o. b. m.), whose name, Schlomo ben David, is engraved upon each. The Jews in Rome told him that every year, about the time of the 9th of Ab, these pillars sweat so much that the water runs down from them. There is a cave, too, in which Titus hid the vessels of the Temple, and another containing the sepulchres of those holy men, the ten martyrs of the kingdom.

[a] R. Jacob ben Jehudah, who travelled in Provence 140 years later (Minchath Kenaoth, Letter 53, p. 115), reports that no Jews were to be found in his time from Provence to Rome; and even the small number found at Genoa, Pisa, and Lucca by our author, had disappeared. The latter city was also visited by Aben Ezra. In the eastern and central parts, however, of Northern Italy, Jewish congregations were to be met with at Venice, Ancona, Rieti, Pesaro, Bologna, Fano, Forli, Ferrara, Fermo, Febriano, Ascoli, Perugia. R. Mashe Zins (1400) mentions the Jewish traders at Lucca. Zunz, note on Benjamin of Tudela, p. 16.

Spain. Gregory IX., though in general he maintained the more tolerant policy, yet enforced some restrictions. He prohibited the Jews from having Christian slaves, and forbade Christians to enter into religious disputations with the Jews.

During the pontificate of Alexander IV.[1] there was a fierce persecution of the Jews in the kingdom of Naples. Jewish tradition affirms that among the Jews of Trani, Bari, and Naples, there were men of science, orators, and poets, superior to all in the world except in France. Was this the result of the enlightened rule of the Emperor Frederick II. (we have seen his patronage of learned Jews) and that of King Manfred? The tradition gives the cause of the popular outburst against the Jews. In Trani a monk, worsted in a quarrel with a Jew, revenged himself by hiding a crucifix in a dung-heap near the Jew's house. He pretended to have received in a dream a revelation of this profane insult to Christianity. The people were in a fury; the magistrate, suspecting the monk, but unable to arrest the rage of the populace, advised the Jews to turn Christians. Some yielded; some fled to Naples. There they fared worse: the story had spread; the rabble was up. Some abandoned their faith; others concealed themselves, and when the storm was over fled to distant countries. Alexander IV. interfered, but without much effect, in favour of the Jews. The king afterwards detected the fraud of the monk, but was afraid to put him to death—he was banished to one of the islands.[m]

We have heard the solemn voice of Innocent IV. raised in favour of the Jews. The ambitious Nicolas III.[o]

---

[1] 1245-1261.
[m] Schevet Judah, p. 141.
[o] On the character of Nicolas III. comp. Latin Christianity, iv. 452, &c.

scrupled not to arrest the fierce zeal of the Franciscans, on whom he otherwise leaned as the most useful allies of the Papal power. The Franciscans demanded the forcible conversion of the Jews. The just edict of Nicolas III. appeals to the Christian example of the Popes, his predecessors, protects the Jews in their rights, in their property, and in their religion; their festivals were to be respected, their cemeteries undisturbed; they were to be subject to no insult or molestation.

The Jews, however, during the ensuing pontificates made, it would seem, extraordinary reprisals for these actual or threatened forcible conversions. Clement IV. published a Bull,* complaining that there were Christians who embraced Judaism. Possibly these were the enforced converts, who fell back in more quiet times to their old faith; but the Bull broadly acknowledges Christian converts of both sexes to Judaism.[p] The Pope commanded the Inquisition to search out and punish the apostates, and the Jews who had abetted such apostasy. Nicolas IV. renewed this Bull in 1288.

During more than a century the Jews of Italy almost disappear; that century was mostly occupied by the eventful pontificate of Boniface VIII.,[q] the Babylonian Captivity of the Popes at Avignon, and the great schism During the absence of the Popes from Rome their edicts and acts had more to do with the Jews of Provence and Languedoc than with those of Rome.

---

* Bullarium sub ann. 1278. There is a copy of this Bull, on parchment, which once belonged to the Jews, in the Trésor des Chartes at Paris. Depping, p. 465.

[p] "Judæos autem qui Christianos utriusque sexus ad eorum ritum execrabilem induxerint, aut invenerites de cetero inducentes, pœnâ debitâ puniatis; contradictores per censuram ecclesiasticam appellatione postpositâ compescendo; invocato ad hoc, si opus fuerit, auxilio brachii secularis." Apud Raynald. sub ann. 1288.

[q] Sub ann. 1299.

At the close of the schism, in the Council of Constance, on the election of Martin V.,[r] the Jews of Constance appeared in the procession, as those of Rome were wont to do, with burning torches, and chanting Hebrew psalms, to do homage to the new Pontiff. They offered to him the Book of the Law. The Pope received it, and returned it with these words, " Ye have a Law, but ye understand it not: old things are gone by; all things are new."[s]

Martin V. issued a Bull from Mantua, which commenced with words of unusual liberality. " Since the Jews are made in the image of God, since a remnant of them shall be saved, since, further, their trading is profitable to Christians, and, lastly, since they solicit our countenance and our compassion, thus will we, in the same sense as Calixtus, Eugenius, Alexander, Clement, Cœlestine, Innocent, Honorius, Gregory, Urban, Nicolas, and other former Popes of blessed memory." He proceeds to protect their synagogues, their rites, their privileges, usages, and constitutions, as far as they do not violate public morals, or insult the Catholic faith. No Christian shall compel a Jew, even of the most tender age, to baptism; no one shall disturb them in their festivals; they must pay on their part respect to the Christian worship of God. Pope Martin repealed all the hostile statutes of the Spanish Antipope, Peter of Luna: it was a temptation to annul the acts of an Antipope. Martin V.

---

[r] On the character of Martin V., Latin Christianity, vi. 73.

[s] There is another version of this story. The Pope refused to accept the book; the Emperor took it and said: " Your laws are just and good; none of us rejects them; but ye observe them not as ye ought." The Pope added: " May God remove the veil from your eyes, that ye may behold the everlasting light." He blessed them in the name of the Father, Son, and Holy Ghost. L'Enfant, Conc. de Constance, ii. 167.

also restrained the zeal of the monks, who endeavoured to compel the Jews to baptism, by prohibiting the traffic of Christians with them. He annulled the order of the General of the Dominicans to compel them to hear sermons; he gave full licence for trade with Jews. These were wise measures; how far counselled by the poverty or parsimony of Pope Martin—how far his imputed avarice, which, at the close of his life, left him master of a great treasure, prompted them—neither the traditions of the grateful Jews nor the taunts of Martin's enemies, as far as I have observed, furnish any evidence.

We have seen the violent Bull of Eugenius IV.; the wise and humane edict of Nicolas V. relating to the Jews of Spain ; the reception of the wretched fugitives from Spain, at Genoa, and at Rome. I shall hereafter show the conduct of the later Popes to the children of Israel.[1]

---

[1] See the preceding Book.

BOOK XXVIII.

Jews in Turkey — In Italy — In Germany before the Reformation — Invention of Printing — Reformation — Luther — Holland — Negotiation with Cromwell — False Messiahs — Sabbathai Sevi — Frank, &c. — Spinoza.

PROSCRIBED in so many kingdoms of Europe, exiled from Spain, the Jews again found shelter under the protection of the Crescent. In the North of Africa, the communities which had long existed were considerably increased. Jews of each sect, Karaïtes as well as Talmudists, are found in every part of that region. In many countries they derive, as might naturally be supposed, a tinge from the manners of the people with whom they dwell; and, among these hordes of fierce pirates and savage Moors, their character and habits are impregnated with the ferocity of the land. In Egypt their race has never been exterminated; they once suffered a persecution under Hakim (A.C. 1020), which might remind them of the terrors of former days, but they seem afterwards to have dwelt in peace: Maimonides was the physician of Saladin. But the Ottoman Empire, particularly its European dominions, was the great final retreat of those who fled from Spain. 50,000 are estimated to have been admitted into that country, where the haughty Turk condescended to look down on them with far less contempt than on the trampled Greeks. The Greeks were Yeshir, slaves, they held their lives on sufferance; the Jews, Monsaphir, or visiters. They settled in Constantinople and in the commercial towns of the Levant, particularly Salonichi.[a] Here the Rabbinical dominion was re-established in all its authority; schools were opened; the Semicha, or ordination, was re-enacted; and R. Berab entertained some hopes of re-establishing the Patriarchate of Tiberias. The Osmanlis beheld with stately indifference this busy people, on one hand organizing their dispersed communities, strengthening their spiritual government, and labouring in the pursuit of that vain knowledge which, being beyond the circle of the Koran, is abomination and folly to the true believer, even establishing that mysterious engine, the printing-press; on the other, appropriating to themselves, with diligent industry and successful enterprize, the whole trade of the Levant.

Their success in this important branch of commerce reacted upon the wealth and prosperity of their correspondents, their brethren in Italy. At a somewhat later period the famous Savonarola founded a Monte della Pietà in Florence with the avowed purpose of rescuing the poor from the exactions of the Israelites, whom he denounced with his own peculiar vehemence. The good Friar might well undertake this work of charity, if the Jews obtained thirty-two and a half per cent. on their loans, with compound interest.[b] But the

---

[a] Rabbi Joseph describes a terrible fire at Salonichi, which broke out in the house of a Jew grocer, Abraham Catalan, and destroyed eight thousand houses, and two hundred lives were lost: "Woe unto the eyes which have seen eighteen of our prayer-houses, and our glory, and the books of our Law, and the believers of our Law, become a burning and a fuel of fire." The misery which followed this fire caused a great plague, "until those who buried became weary, and the mourners and bewailers ceased. And the Jews retained no strength at that time, and Israel became very low." The grocer whose house took fire was imprisoned by the Turks, and died in prison. R. Joseph, ii. 403.

[b] Villari (Vita di Savonarola, i. 278)

Friar was not content without an edict, hunting the Jews out of the land.[c]

As early as 1400 the jealous republic of Venice had permitted a bank to be opened in their city by two Jews. In almost every town in Italy they pursued their steady course of traffic. They were established in Verona, Genoa, Pisa, Parma, Mantua,[d] Pavia, Padua, Sienna, Bassano, Faenza, Florence, Cremona, Aquila, Ancona, Leghorn,[e] besides their head-quarters at Rome.[f] Their chief trade, however, was money-lending; in which, at least with the lower classes, they seem to have held a successful contest against their old rivals, the Lombard bankers.[g] An amiable enthusiast,

---

says that this enormous amount of interest is stated in the decree which founded the Monte della Pietà. The precariousness of the security should be taken into account.

[c] " La pestifera voragine e pessimo veneno della usura, già sopportata in Firenze 60 anni, da quella pessima e di Dio inimica setta Ebraica." The Jews were allowed a year to depart. Ibid. p. 279.

[d] Henry II. of France permitted the Jew merchants of Mantua to come into the cities of the kingdom. " And they went into the king's gate, and bowed themselves before him to the ground; and he accepted their persons and made a release to them according to the hand of our God, upon him: and they went from him in peace, for he was a faithful man." R. Joseph, ii. 454. Probably from this time, if not before, the Jews crept unobserved into France. R. Joshua also relates that the Regent Duchess of Mantua took away the Jews' burial ground in that city, for which God visited her with the death of the Duke, her eldest son (467).

[e] At a somewhat later period (under the Medici) it became a proverb in Leghorn, that a man might as well strike the Grand Duke as a Jew.

[f] Many Jews were slaughtered at Rome in the great siege by the Constable Bourbon (R. Joshua, p. 72). On the coronation of Charles V. at Rome, the Jews had been threatened with pillage. "And had it not been for the mercies of the Lord, which never fail, the Jews would have been soon given up to pillage on that day. For the men of the Emperor gaped with their mouths, hissed, and gnashed with their teeth against them, but the Lord delivered them" (p. 114). There are many curious details as to the Jews in all the cities of Italy in Emek and Grüber, pp. 155, 163.

[g] In Rabbi Joshua's History (for, like Tacitus, he affected to write Annals and Histories) there are a few incidents relating to the Jews of Italy. He himself

Bernardino di Feltre, moved to see the whole people groaning under their extortions, endeavoured to preach a crusade, not against their religion, but against their usury. His language towards the Jews was full of wisdom and humanity;[b] but the effect was, in many places, to raise the populace against them. Nor indeed did the preacher altogether abstain from language which could not but inflame the popular mind: "The Canon-law prohibits all intercourse with Jews, specially their employment as physicians; the presence of Christians at feasts is expressly interdicted. Yet did the Jew Leo celebrate the wedding of his son with a feast which lasted eight days, and how many crowded to his banquets, to his balls! In the present day everybody who is suf-

---

resided usually near Genoa, or at Rome. One is perplexing enough: "The Jews also Lautrec grievously oppressed when he was at Milan, and commanded them to put green helmets on their heads as high as those of the *Muscovites* [?], in order to deride the people of the living God. Howbeit the Eternal suffered him not, but thrust him out that day from the territory of Milan" (p. 22). The Jews had been expelled by the Fregosi, no doubt from commercial jealousy, from Genoa. "But in those days the Jews returned to dwell at Genoa, for the Adorni were men of kindness towards the Jews, and they brought my brother-in-law, the Rabbi Joseph, the son of David, thither, contrary to the laws of that perverted city, and he abode there many days, and was physician unto them." This was during the plague. R. Joseph was ill of this plague for forty days, but recovered (p. 39).

There is a curious passage in the

Continuation of the Chronicle of the Abbas Uspergensis, which says that, at the storming of Rome by the Constable Bourbon, the Jews, who were numerous in the city, not only bought their own security, but made vast sums by purchasing the plunder at the cheapest prices: "Judæi, quorum magnus numerus illic, ne sint omnia sancta Romæ, persolutis pretiis sese redemerunt, ex prædâ omnis generis vili empta, ingens lucrum facientes" (p. 357). The Jews assert that they suffered in the general plunder and massacre. Both accounts are probably true. Compare Ersch und Grüber, p. 152, note.

[b] "Si de Hebræis loquendum est, dicam, qnod in aliis civitatibus dico: neminem, quantum cuique sua anima cara est, posse nocere Hebræis, in personâ sive in facultatibus, sive in quacunque aliâ re: nam etiam Judæis justitia, Christiana pietas, et dilectio exhibenda est cum et illi naturæ humanæ sint." Acta SS. p. 010.

fering from illness openly calls in a Jewish doctor."[1] This was in Piacenza; the infuriated rabble wreaked their rapacity or their vengeance; gibbets were loaded with Jews; some were torn in pieces, their bodies cast to the dogs or wild animals. Bernardino di Feltre sought better means for rescuing his beloved poor from the hands of the usurious Ismelites. He attempted to enforce the doctrines of his sermons by active measures of benevolence, the establishment everywhere of banks on a more moderate rate of interest for the accommodation of the poor, called Mounts of Piety—Monti della Pietà. He met with great success in many towns; in Mantua, Monselice, Montefiore, Rimini, and Brescia: in Padua he forced the Jews to close their banks, from whence they had drawn an enormous profit. But the people were either so deeply implicated with their usurious masters, so much the slaves of habit, or so much repressed by the honest shame of poverty, as to prefer secret though more disadvantageous dealings with the Jews, to the publicity required in these new banks. The scheme languished, and in many places speedily expired.

The conduct of the Popes, as of old, varied, as bigotry, policy, or humanity predominated in the character of the Pontiff. In 1442, Eugenius the Fourth had deprived the Jews of one of their most valuable privileges, and endeavoured to interrupt their amicable relations with the Christians; they were prohibited from eating and drinking together: Jews were excluded from almost every profession, were forced to wear their badge, to pay tithes; and Christians were forbidden to bequeath legacies to Jews. The succeeding Popes had been more wise

[1] Acta SS. Sept. 30; Annal. Placentini, apud Muratori, xx. 945. Much of this, with the citations, is from Cassel, Ersch and Grüber, pp. 150, &c.

or more humane. In Naples, the celebrated Abarbanel became the confidential adviser of Ferdinand the Bastard, and of Alphonso the Second; the Jews experienced a reverse, and were expelled from that city by Charles the Fifth. Some of the Popes, wiser than the Most Catholic Kings, began to discover that by casting forth the Jews Christendom cast forth Jewish wealth from her kingdoms. They began to perceive and to be jealous of the Turks, whose stately indifference had permitted the Jews to settle and to trade in their dominions, and had thus secured a much larger share of the money market of Europe.[j] They were unwilling to lose such profitable subjects. Leo X. in an edict rebuked the popular preachers who inveighed against the tables of the Jewish money-changers. Paul III. openly espoused the cause of the Jews expelled from Portugal, and the New Christians against whom the Inquisition continued to work with all its stern and implacable vigilance. The Pope forbade in his own dominions all such cruel investigations. He granted an amnesty for all former offences.[k] His aim was to encourage the prosperity of his rising port, Ancona. In this city the Pope permitted Turks, Jews, heretics, to trade with perfect freedom without any inquiry into their creed. They paid the same taxes as Christians; they were not compelled to wear their ignominious badge. It was especially permitted that Jews

---

[j] "Ne ad eas nationes quæ Christum Salvatorem nostrum as conferant." Cassel, p. 152. "Et quia tanta multitudo istorum est apud Turchas et in partibus Africæ et sicut Judæi vivunt, et quod pejus est: contra aliquos fuit a Papa consistorio temporibus meis propositum et fuit determinatum quod viverent sicut Judæi." Ibid., from a letter of Coutinho, Bishop of Algarve.

[k] "Impetravano del l'apa una perdonanza generale di tutti li crimini che havesno commessi contra la santa e cattolica fede fino al di che si publicasse la bulla della Inquisitione nel regno di Portugalla." MS. authority quoted by Cassel.

and New Christians from Portugal and Algarve should fully enjoy this privilege. Ancona rapidly grew in opulence, and in commerce, the parent of opulence. There were two Jewish communities, an Italian and a Levantine synagogue. Julius III. not merely confirmed the wise edict of his predecessor. On the establishment of the Inquisition at Rome on account of the perilous progress of the Reformed opinions, he specially exempted the Jews of Ancona from this jurisdiction. The Cardinals and other delegates of the Papal power were instructed to pay the utmost respect to the religious observances of the Jews. They were forbidden, under pain of the Papal displeasure, to inquire into the religious observances or religion of the Jews, or into their former confession of Christianity, to dispute with them, to drag them into their courts, to burthen or molest them in any way.

Nevertheless, under Julius III. the Jews were endangered by a rash proselyte. A Franciscan Friar, Corneglio of Montalcino, embraced Judaism, circumcised himself, and "set his face as a flint" to preach against Christianity in the streets of Rome. He was seized and burned. Julius issued a mandate, considering the circumstances, of no great severity. The Talmud, to which the guilt of the conversion of the friar was attributed, was ordered everywhere to be burned: at Rome, at Bologna, and at Venice. Throughout Italy the Jews, dreading some more awful vengeance, sat in terror—they fasted and put on sackcloth—but the merciful Pope was contented with punishing their books; no violence was committed on the Jews.[1]

---

[1] Rabbi Joseph, ii. 523 : "And he was long-suffering with them, because he delighteth in mercy."

But the reawakening zeal of the Popes, startled from its serene and mild slumbers by Protestantism, soon returned to its ancient bigotry and ignorance; ignorance the parent and offspring of bigotry. They hastened to discard their wiser policy, to reject the first dawnings of political economy, which in calmer times had forced themselves into their councils.

The stern and haughty Pope, Paul the Fourth, renewed the hostile edicts; he prohibited the Jews from holding real property;[m] that which they held was to be sold, and within six months: therefore property estimated at 500,000 crowns was sold for a fifth of that sum. The Pope endeavoured to embarrass their traffic, by regulations which prohibited them from disposing of their pledges under eighteen months; deprived them of the trade in corn and in every other necessary of life, but left them the privilege of dealing in old clothes.[n] Paul IV. first shut them up in their Ghetto, a confined quarter of the city, out of which they were prohibited from appearing after sunset; he reduced them to one synagogue—the rest were to be destroyed.[o] They were to wear a distinctive dress; they were not to work on the Christian Sabbath, to keep their accounts in Italian or Latin, not to have any conversation with Christians, not to practise among them as physicians. Pius the Fourth relaxed the severity of his predecessor. He enlarged the Ghetto, and removed the restrictions on their commerce; he permitted them to hold real property up

---

[m] Bullarium, ann. 1555.

[n] "Nullam mercaturam frumenti vel horrei aut allarum rerum usui humano necessariarum." Art. 10.

[o] According to Bartolocci (ill.), there were nineteen synagogues in Campania, eight in Umbria, thirty-six in the March, thirteen in Romagnola, eleven at Bologna, two at Benevento, six at Avignon, nine at Rome, thirteen in other parts of the Roman States. They paid 1380 scudi annually to the Hospital of the Catechumens at Rome.

to a certain value, 1500 ducats; to have direct conversation with Christians; to wear a black instead of a yellow hat; the owners of the houses in the Ghetto were prohibited from exacting exorbitant rents; the Jew became almost a citizen and a man. Pius the Fifth expelled them from every city in the Papal territory, except Rome and Ancona; he endured them in those cities with the avowed design of preserving their commerce with the East; in other respects he returned to the harsh policy of Paul IV. Gregory the Thirteenth pursued the same course; a Bull was published, and suspended at the gate of the Jews' quarter, prohibiting the reading of the Talmud, blasphemies against Christ, or ridicule against the ceremonies of the Church. All Jews, above twelve years old, were bound to appear at the regular sermons delivered for their conversion; where it seems, notwithstanding the authority of the Pope and the eloquence of the Cardinals, that their behaviour was not very edifying. At length the bold and statesmanlike Sixtus the Fifth annulled at once all the persecuting or vexatious regulations of his predecessors, opened the gates of every city in the ecclesiastical dominions to these enterprising traders, secured and enlarged their privileges, proclaimed toleration of their religion, subjected them to the ordinary tribunals, and enforced a general and equal taxation.*

The great events of this period—the invention and rapid progress of printing, and the Reformation—could not but have some effect on the condition of the Jews. This people were by no means slow to avail themselves of the advantages offered to learning, by the general use of printing. From their presses at Venice, in Turkey,

---

* Sixtus V. limited the interest on loans to 18 per cent.

and in other quarters, splendid specimens of typography were sent forth,[q] and the respect of the learned world was insensibly increased by the facilities thus afforded for the knowledge of the Scriptures in the original language, and the bold opening of all the mysteries of Rabbinical wisdom to those who had sufficient inquisitiveness and industry to enter on that wide and unknown field of study. A strong effort was made by struggling bigotry to suppress all these works, which a pusillanimous faith knew to be hostile, and therefore considered dangerous to the Christian religion. Pfefferkorn, a convert from Judaism, earnestly persuaded the Emperor Maximilian to order the entire destruction of all books printed by the Jews. The celebrated Capnio, or Reuchlin (such are the names by which he is best known), interfered; he abandoned certain books, which contained offensive blasphemies against the Redeemer (the Nizzachon and the Toldoth Jesu) to the zeal of his antagonist: but pleaded, and not without success, the cause of the sounder and more useful parts of Jewish learning.

The Reformation affected the people of Israel rather in its remote than in its immediate consequences. It found the Jews spread in great numbers in Germany and Poland. They were still liable to the arbitrary caprice of the petty sovereigns or free cities of the Empire. But great changes had already come over the Jews in Germany. The days were long gone by when,

---

[q] R. Joseph speaks of Rabbi Tobias Phoall as one of the first who used the press for Hebrew works: "His mind also did not rest until he had propagated the good doctrine which is the perfect Law among Israel; and he instituted the printing-office at Sabionetta, his dwelling-place, which was under the government of the Lord Vespasian Gonzaga Colonna (exalted be his glory!), from whence the Law goeth out unto all Israel." II. 475.

according to the fine expression, the Imperial Eagle brooded over the Jews to protect and to prey upon them; when, according to the Sachsen Spiegel,^r the Emperor Titus, or his father, Vespasian, had made over all, or a third of the Jews for ever to his successors the Roman Emperors; when the haughty Hohenstauffen, Frederick I., could grant as a favour to the Duke of Austria all the Jews and usurers in his domain without any molestation or interference from the Imperial Courts;^s when in a more merciful spirit, in the proclamations of the Truce of God, with the clergy, women, nuns, husbandmen, merchants, travellers, fishermen, Jews came under the general protection.^t By Frederick II., whose stern Imperial despotism contrasted with his wise policy as King of Sicily,^u the Jews had been first declared serfs of the Imperial Chamber. Later emperors, Rodolph of Hapsburg, Louis of Bavaria, Charles IV., Wenceslaus, Sigismund, had asserted the same broad and indefeasible supremacy, or rather proprietorship in all the Jews of the Empire.^x Certain taxes had been levied upon the Jews, with more or less regularity, according to the poverty or the power of the Emperor, as protection-money (they were at all times, not alone during the Truce of God, under the peace of the Emperor). The amount of this, usually paid on St. Martin's Day, was somewhat arbitrary; there was also the headpenny, paid on the coronation of the Emperor; and, it seems, a golden penny specially belonging to the Imperial Treasury which he could not alienate.^y But the

^r Sachsen Spiegel, quoted by Cassel.
^s See the Grant, in Pertz, Leges, II. p. 101.
^t See the proclamations of the Treuga Dei, ibid. p. 207.
^u See back, p. 336.

^x Compare Cassel, in Ersch und Grüber, p. 85 et seqq.
^y The account of these various taxes and offerings in Cassel is not quite so clear as might be desired.

power of the Emperor had long been on the wane.
Half of the Jew-tax had been ceded, or wrung from
him by the Electors and sovereign princes, who still,
however, acknowledged the right of the Emperor to do
as he would with the Jews, to kill them or burn them,
of course to tax them according to his good pleasure.
The Golden Bull reserved the Imperial rights, but, to a
certain extent, made over their protection, and in consequence the power of oppressing them, to the sovereign
princes.[a]

The Jews were still, at least in theory, under Imperial
protection, if not as serfs, as a kind of vassals. But
the power of the Emperor had sunk still more. In the
great strife between the princes of Germany and the
free cities towards the close of the fourteenth century,
both parties at one time came to a kind of truce, and
magnanimously agreed to suspend their hostilities in
order to persecute and plunder the Jews. At Nuremberg (in the year 1389) it was resolved, by common
consent, that neither princes nor cities should pay their
debts or interest to the Jews; that all contracts and
pledges should be demanded back. The only commerce
between Christian and Jew should be of sale and purchase. The Emperor, or rather King of the Romans,
the feeble Wenceslaus, only stipulated for his share, a
large share, of the spoil. The king's chief councillors,
Duke Frederick of Bavaria, the Bishops of Bamberg,
Wurtzburg, Augsburg, the Margrave of Nuremberg, the
Counts of Oeting and Wertheim, bought the sovereign's
assent to their robbery, by a percentage on their gains.
The cities paid 40,000 florins, the Bishop of Wurtzburg
and the Duke of Bavaria, each 15,000. The king rati-

---

[a] See the declaration of Albert Achill (A.C. 1462), Cassel, p. 86.

fied the compact, commanded the Jews (he their protector) to surrender their pledges, and proclaimed that whatever prince, count, knight, or squire would not aid the Throne against the Jews should be placed under the ban of the Empire.[a] Yet in his own dominions, in Prague, Wenceslaus was afterwards accused of favouring the Jews.[b] Rupert, the Palsgrave, the Antiking of the Romans, followed a wiser and more humane policy. On his coronation day he took the Jews of Oppenheim and Nuremberg under his special protection, and induced persecuting Nuremberg to do the same. What they were to pay to the city appears not; but every Jew and Jewess of full age was to pay yearly a gulden to the royal treasury.[c] They were the property of the king, but they made payments to the cities as well as to the king. On these terms also the Jews of Cologne, Mayence, Frankfort, Worms, Spiers, Landau, Schelstadt, Ratisbon, Colmar, Haguenau, Muhlhausen, Kaisersberg, and Eherhausen obtained letters of enfranchisement. In Frankfort they had a special right of appeal from the Imperial tribunal to that of the city.

I have no space to enlarge on the local oppressions and persecutions, which may be detected at every period during this intermediate century in almost every province and city in Germany, sometimes told with frightful but significant brevity:[d] their frequent ejection, and worse than ejection, by the Landgrave of Thuringia; popular commotions in Nuremberg, Frankfort, Worms, almost everywhere; massacres in Gotha and Erfurt; their expulsion from the Mark of Brandenburg. Ex-

---

[a] See the authorities for this in a recently published book, Hoefler, Ruprecht von der Pfalz, pp. 74-77, with citations.
[b] Ibid., pp. 86, 88, 91.
[c] Ibid., p. 377. Rupert had raised money on the Jew Tax, perhaps for his inroad into Bohemia. See also p. 356.
[d] "Judæi occisi," "combusti," perpetually occurs in the chronicles.

cluded from one city or state, they found refuge in another till the storm blew over. It is clear, however, that wherever they had an opportunity, though usually more addicted to money-lending and the sale of gold trinkets and jewellery, they opened larger branches of traffic. In Poland they seem early to have entered into the great corn trade of that kingdom.

On the history of the Jews in Prague alone I would willingly have dwelt; that community which boasts itself the oldest, at times has been the most prosperous, but which has suffered the most frightful disasters—that community, with all its hoary traditions, and its wild, crowded, weed-and-hemlock-overgrown cemetery, the graves and the epitaphs of which might seem to reach up to the remotest antiquity, and in which a Jewish "Old Mortality" might spell out records of times when Bohemia was still heathen. Rabbi Joseph boldly declares that the Jews "had dwelled in Prague from the day that they were led captive." Strange traditions tell of their removal, prophesied by the heathen Queen Libussa, of their solemn reception a century after by Duke Hostiwit. Jewish learning has lately illustrated their history, and turned passages into romance out of a history more wonderful and romantic than romance. The Sippurim of Dr. Wolff Pascheles has well been called the Acts of the Jewish Martyrs.* In the Hussite wars, and later, in the days of Luther, the Jews of Prague were suspected by the Reformers of fidelity to the Catholic Emperors; they were strangely accused of aiding the Turks, the common enemies of the Emperor and the Reformers. But the tradition of their

---

* Compare Sipporim, by Wolff Pascheles, Prague, 1838-1856; and an able notice of this curious book which contains two or three very powerful and characteristic tales, in Fraser's Magazine, Dec. 1862.

sympathy with the Imperialists is preserved by Rabbi Joseph. "Then Bohemia rebelled against her king and her God, because of the wrath of the Lutherans: and in these days they drove out the Jews from the provinces of Bohemia and of Prague the capital; and they removed from thence in waggons, and went into Poland and abode there. And many died on the road, and many were slain by the edge of the sword."[1] They returned, at least some of them, under Emperor Ferdinand, " who spake kindly to them," and invited them back. It is believed that they showed their gratitude by their fidelity, and by useful service during the Thirty Years' War.

During the Reformation period, about A.C. 1542, terrible conflagrations broke out in many cities of Germany which were laid to the account of the Jews. "In that year," writes Rabbi Joseph, "there were burned in Germany many cities both large and small, and their smoke went up toward heaven; and it was not known who had kindled the fire, and they wrongfully accused the Jews and the shepherds [peasants?], saying, 'Ye have done this wicked thing;' and they chastised them and afflicted their souls, so that the Jews confessed what never came into their hearts; and they burned them with fire." As if to prove their guiltlessness, " God took away their reproach" (writes the Rabbi); "Linz was burned after they went out—it was a great city, the perfection of beauty, the joy of the whole earth; and only twenty houses were left in the midst thereof; and it was a lasting heap for many days."

The tone in which Luther spoke of the Jews varied, as on many other points not immediately connected with his main object, according to the period of his life.

---

[1] Rabbi Joseph, ii. p. 337.

and the light in which he viewed the race. As sordid usurers he detested them, and at first he seems to have approved of violent means of conversion; but at other times he spoke of them with humane consideration rather than anger, and reprobated all means of attempting their conversion, except those of gentleness and Christian love.*

---

* Dr. Scheidler, in his article Juden Emancipation, in Ersch und Grüber, p. 271, reverses this view. According to the dates of his citations, Luther began by being more mild and just, and ended in being more fiercely cruel and fanatical against the Jews. In his Exposition of the Twenty-second Psalm (A.C. 1519) are these words on the conversion of the Jews:—

"Daher ist das Wüten einiger Christen (wenn die andern noch Christen können genannt werden) verdammlich, welche meinen sie than Gott daran einen Dienst, wenn sie die Juden auf das gehässigste verfolgen, alles Böse über sie denken, und bei ihren beweinen - würdigsten Unglück ihrer noch mit dem äussersten Hochmuth und Verachtung spotten; denn sie vielmehr sollten, nach dem Exempel dieses Psalms (Ps. xiv. 10, und Paulus Röm. ix. 1, 2), von Herzen über sie traurig seyn, sie bedauern, und ohne Unterlass für sie beten. Dergleichen Gottloser Christen theilen sowohl zum Christlichen Namen als Volke durch diese ihre Tyrannie nicht geringern Abbruch, und sind an der Gottlosigkeit der Juden schuldig; sintemal sie dieselben durch dieses Exempel der Grausamkeit gleichsam mit Gewalt vom Christenthum zurück treiben, da sie vielmehr sollten mit aller Freundlichkeit, Geduld, Gebeth, Sorgfalt, har-

beiziehen. Und diese ihre Wuth vertheidigen noch einige sehr abgeschmackte Theologi, und reden ihnen das Wort; indem sie aus grossem Hochmuth daher plaudern, die Juden wären der Christen Knechte und dem Kaiser unterworfen. Ich litte euch darum, sagt mir, wer wird zu unser Religion übertreten, wenn er auch der allersanftmüthigste und geduldigste Mensch wäre, wenn er siehet, dass er so grausam und feindselig, und nicht allein nicht Christlich, sondern mehr als viehisch von uns tractirt wird. . . . Die meisten Passions Prediger thun nichts anders als dass sie der Juden Muthwillen, so sie an Christo verübet sehr schwer und gross machen, und die Herzen der Gläubigen wieder sie erbittern; so dass das Evangelium einzig und allein damit umgehet, dass es uns in diesem Stücke die Liebe Gottes und Christo einzig und allein auf höchste anpreise."

Is it possible that later in life Luther (alas, for the power of polemic strife to harden the heart!) should do more than declare the conversion of the Jews impossible? "Doubt not, beloved in Christ, that after the Devil you have no more bitter, venomous, violent enemy, than the real Jew, the Jew in earnest in his belief." Luther inveighs against their usury with all the fierceness of the darkest of the dark ages. Is it credible that he should give

THE REFORMATION.

It was partly by affording new and more dangerous enemies to the power of the Church that the Reformation ameliorated the condition of the Jews; they were forgotten or overlooked in the momentous conflict: but to a much greater extent, by the wise maxims of toleration, which, though not the immediate, were not less the legitimate fruits of this great revolution in the European world.[b] The bitterness of religious hatred

---

this counsel to those who asked the question, what was to be done by Christians with that accursed and reprobate people?—" I. Burn their synagogues and schools; what will not burn, bury with earth, that neither stone nor rubbish remain. II. In like manner break into and destroy their houses. III. Take away all their prayer-books and Talmuds, in which are nothing but godlessness, lies, cursing, and swearing. IV. Forbid their Rabbis to teach, on pain of life and limb. V. Forbid them to travel: 'as they are neither lords nor officials [Amtsleuter], nor traders, they should stay at home'| VI. Interdict all usury: 'we are not their subjects, but they ours.' VII. In the hands of all young Jews and Jewesses should be placed flails, axes, mattocks, spades, distaffs, spinning-wheels, and let them get their livelihood in the sweat of their brow, as should all the children of Adam."

There are above 400 pages, mostly of bitter vituperation (Luther's Werke, p. 2471), but with vigorous argument against the Jews, curious but most painful to read (2290-2632). Walch's Edition, t. xx. p. 2478.

[b] Rabbi Joshua's account of the Reformation is so curious as to be worthy

of insertion: "And it came to pass, when the Pope Julius [the Second] began to build the great high place which is in Rome [St. Peter's], that he sent the Franciscan Friars into all the districts of the uncircumcised. And he gave them power to loose and to bind, and *to deliver souls from perdition*. And they departed and cried with a loud voice, 'Take off the earrings of your wives and daughters [the words in Exodus, xxxii. 2] and bring them for the building of the high place; and it shall come to pass when ye shall come, that ye shall save the souls of your generation from perdition.' And it came to pass, after the death of Julius, that the Pope Leo sent again, and they went, as before, into the cities of Ashkenaz [Germany], and they were lifted up. And it came to pass whenever the Germans would speak, saying, 'How could ye any this thing? and how can the pope do it?' they answered them proudly, saying, 'Ye shall be cursed if ye do not believe, for there is no faith in you; and ye shall be an abhorrence to all flesh.' And there was one Martin [Luther], a monk, a skillful and wise man, and he also said unto them, 'Why are ye not ashamed when ye let your voice be heard on high speaking such dreams?' And the priests could not

was gradually assuaged; active animosity settled down into quiet aversion; the popular feeling became contempt of the sordid meanness of the Jewish character, justified no doubt by the filthy habits, the base frauds, and the miserable chicanery of many of the lower orders who alone came in contact with the mass of the people, rather than revengeful antipathy towards the descendants of those who crucified the Redeemer, and who, by their obstinate unbelief, inherited the guilt of their forefathers.

During the Thirty Years' War the Jews, it has been said, assisted with great valour in the defence of Prague, and obtained the protection and favour of the grateful Emperor. Before this, the Reformation had been the remote cause of another important benefit—the opening the free cities of Holland, where a great number of Portuguese Jews settled, and vied in regularity, enterprise, and wealth with the commercial citizens of that flourishing republic.¹ The Jews of Amsterdam and other cities bore a high rank for intelligence and punctuality in business.

From Holland they long looked for some favourable

give an answer; and they behaved with madness after their manner, and they anathematized him in the year 1518, and the wrath of Martin was much kindled. And Martin opened his mouth and preached with a loud voice against the pope, and against the dreams and the abominations of the popes, but still he delighted in THAT MAN [Jesus], and many gathered themselves unto him. And he made them statutes and ordinances, and spake revolt against the wise men of the Church; and he would explain from his own heart their law *and the words of Paul*; and they went not after the precepts of the popes; and their laws are two different laws until this day." l. p. 430.

¹ In 1590, three Portuguese Jews were hospitably received in Holland. Many soon followed. The first synagogue was founded in 1598. The States publicly avowed their determination to open a place of refuge for those who were expelled by the tyrannical governments of Europe. About twenty years after, German Jews settled in Holland, but their first community was not formed in Amsterdam till 1630. Ersch and Grüber, p. 120.

opportunity which might open the exchange, the marts, and the havens of England to their adventurous traffic. But the stern law of Edward I. was still in force, and though, no doubt, often eluded, the religious feeling of the country, as well as the interests of the trading part of the community, would have risen in arms at a proposition for its repeal.[j] Yet it can hardly be doubted that Jews must have walked the streets of London, and, though proscribed by the law, must, by tacit, perhaps unconscious, connivance, have taken some share in the expanding commerce of England during the reign of the Tudors.[k] If it were not a creation of Shakespeare, it would be difficult to believe his Shylock a pure creation, or to suppose that the poet drew entirely from his own mind the Jewish character and feelings, the mutual heart-deep hatred of Jew and Christian.[l] It was

[j] I know not on what authority Amador de los Rios asserts that England was among the first countries which received the Spanish Jews on their expulsion from Spain by Ferdinand and Isabella. He names London, York, and Dover, as three cities where they settled, p. 419. He says (p. 440) that they built synagogues in London as well as in most of the Hanseatic towns, and drove a flourishing trade.

[k] "I pass over a period in our own history, in which it is supposed there were no Jews in England—the reigns of Elizabeth, James, and Charles I. My researches might show that they were not then unknown in this country. Had there been no Jews in England, would that luminary of the law, Sir Edward Coke, have needed to inveigh against the Jews as 'Infidels and Turks'?—delivering them all alike to the Devil; stigmatised and infamous persons, 'perpetui inimici,' says Littleton, 'and not admissible as witnesses.'" Disraeli, Genius of Judaism, 240.

[l] This is more remarkable if, as Charles Lamb has done, with his fine originality of criticism and felicitous language, we contrast Shylock with Marlowe's Jew of Malta: "Marlowe's Jew does not approach so near to Shakespeare as his Edward II. does to Richard II. Shylock, in the midst of his savage purpose, is a man; his motives, feelings, resentments, have something human in them: 'If you wrong us, shall we not revenge?' Barabbas is a mere monster brought in with a large painted nose to please the rabble. He kills in sport, poisons whole nunneries, invents infernal machines. This is just such an exhibition as a century or

not, however, till the Protectorate of Cromwell that the Jews made an open attempt to obtain a legal re-establishment in the realm. The strength of ancient prejudice, co-operating with the aversion of a large part of the nation towards the Government, gave rise to the most absurd rumours of their secret proposals to the Protector. It was bruited abroad, and widely believed, that they had offered £500,000 on condition of obtaining St. Paul's Church for their synagogue, and the Bodleian Library to begin business with. Harry Martin and Hugh Peters were designated as the profane or fanatic advisers of this strange bargain.™ Another equally ridiculous story was propagated of certain Asiatic Jews, who sent a deputation to inquire whether Cromwell was not the Messiah, and went to Huntingdon with the ostensible design of buying the Hebrew books belonging to the University of Cambridge, but with the real object of searching the Protector's pedigree to find whether he could claim Jewish descent. The plain fact was this—a physician of great learning and estimation among the Jews, Manasseh ben Israel,"

---

two earlier might have been played before the Londoners by the Royal command, when a general pillage and massacre of the Hebrews had been previously resolved on in the Cabinet." Lamb's Specimens, p. 31.

It is very curious that the Jews have the same story, only with everything reversed. Shylock, the Jew, is the liberal, unsuspecting merchant. Antonio, the Christian, insists on the forfeited pound of flesh. But the noble Portia is even more cruelly used; she is employed in that worst and basest calling to which women can be self-degraded, the procuress who is to in-

veigle the gentle Jessica. The whimsical part is, that the Jews place the story at Rome, in the time of Pope Sixtus V. (Elizabeth's contemporary); the Pope plays a great part in it. Shakspeare's authorities for his version ascend high in the Middle Ages. It is almost more whimsical that the story, in its Jewish form, found its way into Gregorio Leti's Life of Sixtus V. See Sippurim, No. lv. p. 202, &c.

" This rumour is mentioned in Manasseh ben Israel's Defence of the Jews, p. 7.

" See Manasseh Ben Israel, Sein Leben und Werken, von Dr. M. Kay-

presented a petition to the Protector for the readmission of his countrymen into the realm. The address was drawn with eloquence and skill—it commenced by recognising the hand of God in the appointment of Cromwell to the Protectorate, it dexterously insinuated the instability of all Governments unfavourable to the Jews, and it asserted the general joy with which the ambassadors of the Republic had been received in their synagogues in Holland and elsewhere.* Manasseh ben Israel issued a second address to the Commonwealth of England. He complimented the general humanity of the nation, stated his sole object to be the establishment of a synagogue in the kingdom; he adroitly endeavoured to interest the religious enthusiasm of England on his side, by declaring his conviction that the restoration of Israel, and of course the Last Day, was at hand. He did not neglect the temporal advantages of the worldly, the profits to be derived from their traffic; and concluded with expressing his sincere attachment to a Commonwealth abounding in so many men of piety and learning. Whether moved by one or all these reasons, Cromwell summoned an assembly of two lawyers, seven citizens of London, and fourteen divines, to debate the question, first, whether it was lawful to admit the Jews; secondly, if lawful, on what terms it was expedient to admit them. The lawyers decided at once on the legality; the citizens were divided; but the contest among the divines was so long and so inconclusive, that Oliver, having so spoken that one present asserted, "I have never heard a man speak so well," at length grew weary, and the question was ad-

---

wrting (Berlin, 1861)—a careful, and seemingly accurate, account of the life of this remarkable man.

* See the Vindiciæ Judaicæ, in the Phœnix, vol. ii. pp. 391 et seqq.

journed to a more favourable opportunity.[p] It is a curious fact of the times, that so far were some of the Republican writers from hostility to the Jews, that Harrington, in his 'Oceana,' gravely proposes disburthening the kingdom of the weight of Irish affairs, by selling the island to the Jews. The necessities of Charles II. and his courtiers quietly accomplished that change on which Cromwell had not dared openly to venture.[q] The convenient Jews stole insensibly into the kingdom, where they have ever since maintained their footing,

---

[p] When the Jews desired leave to have a synagogue in London, they offered him, when Protector, 60,000l. Cromwell appointed a day for giving them an answer. He then sent for some of the most powerful among the clergy and some of the chief merchants of the City to be present at their meeting. It was in the long gallery at Whitehall. Sir Paul Rycaut, who was then a young man, pressed in among the crowd, and said he never heard a man speak so well in his life as Cromwell did on this occasion. When they were all met, he ordered the Jews to speak for themselves. After that he turned to the clergy, who inveighed much against the Jews as a cruel and accursed people. Cromwell, in his answer to the clergy, called them 'Men of God,' and desired to be informed by them whether it was not their opinion that the Jews were to be called, in the fulness of time, into the Church. He then desired to know whether it was not every Christian man's duty to forward that good end all he could. Then he flourished a good deal on religion prevailing in this nation, the only place in the world where religion was taught in its full purity. 'Was it not,' he said, 'then, our duty in particular to encourage them to settle where they could be taught the truth, and not to exclude them from the light, and leave them among false teachers, Papists and idolaters?' This silenced the clergy. He then turned to the merchants, who spoke of their falseness and meanness, and that they would get their trade from them. 'And can ye really be afraid,' said he, 'that this mean and despised people should be able to prevail in trade and credit over the merchants of England, the noblest and most esteemed merchants of the whole world?' Thus he went on till he had silenced them too, and so was at liberty to grant what he desired to the Jews." Spence's Anecdotes, p. 215.

Burnet gives rather a different view of Cromwell's policy. He wished to avail himself of their rapid and accurate intelligence on foreign affairs. Burnet's Own Time, i. 1[?]2, Oxford Edition.

[q] "Under Charles II. Lord Keeper North found no difficulty in swearing a Jew on his Pentateuch." Disraeli, p. 241.

and no doubt contributed their fair proportion to the national wealth.

I have not thought it expedient to interrupt the course of my History with the account of every adventurer who, from time to time, assumed the name of the Messiah. It is probable that the constant appearance of these successive impostors tended, nevertheless, to keep alive the ardent belief of the nation in this great and consolatory article of their creed. The disappointment in each particular case might break the spirit and confound the faith of the immediate followers of the pretender, but it kept the whole nation incessantly on the watch. The Messiah was ever present to the thoughts and to the visions of the Jews: their prosperity seemed the harbinger of his coming; their darkest calamities gathered around them only to display, with the force of stronger contrast, the mercy of their God and the glory of their Redeemer. In vain the Rabbinical interdict repressed the dangerous curiosity which, still baffled, would still penetrate the secrets of futurity. "Cursed is he who calculates the time of the Messiah's coming," was constantly repeated in the synagogue, but as constantly disregarded. That chord in the national feeling was never struck but it seemed to vibrate through the whole community. A long list of false Messiahs might be produced—in France, in Fez, in Persia,' in Moravia; but their career was so short, and their adventures so inseparably moulded up with fictions, that I have passed them by.' Some few, however,

---

' Benjamin of Tudela relates at length the insurrection and death of David Elroy, a Persian. Asher's Edition, pp. 122, 127.

' See the curious treatise of John b

Lent, De Pseudo-Messiis, in Ugolini, Thesaurus. Moses Cretensis, A.C. 434 (see p. 32). Dunaan in Nigra, a city of Arabia Felix, A.C. 520. Some Jews hailed Julian, some Mohammed, as the

I will endeavour to rescue from oblivion. During the reign of Charles V, a man named David appeared in the Court of the King of Portugal; he announced that he had come from India, sent by his brother, the King of the Jews, to propose an alliance in order to recover the Holy Land from the Sultan Solyman. Many of the forced Christians believed in him. He passed through Spain, where he made many proselytes; into France, to Avignon, into Italy. He inscribed banners with the holy name of God. In many cities, Bologna, Ferrara, Mantua, many believed that he was commissioned to lead them back to the Holy Land. He had even an interview with the Pope. But some of his more sagacious brethren detected the imposture; and he fell for a time into contempt. The false David was followed by a false Solomon. There was a Portuguese New Christian, who apostatised openly to Judaism, and set up as the prophet of the movement, Solomon Molcho. It does not indeed appear that either David or Solomon Molcho assumed the title of Messiah. The Jews relate that Solomon was utterly ignorant while he was a Christian; immediately at his circumcision the Lord gave him wisdom; he became rapidly endowed with profound knowledge; he became master of the Cabala; he possessed inspiring eloquence. He preached Judaism before kings; even the Pope, Clement VII., admitted him to an audience, and gave him a privilege to dwell wherever he would. Solomon Molcho seems to have been permitted to pour out his apocalyptic rhapsodies

---

Messiah (see Baronius, A.C. 1009; Math. Paris.); a Syrian, A.C. 721; one in France, 1137; in Persia, 1138; in Spain, 1157; in Fez, 1167 (vide Maimonides, Epist. ad Judæos in Mantissa agentes); another beyond the Euphrates, who went to bed a leper and rose a man of great beauty; in Morocco, David Almusser, a great Cabalist, 1174.

(pages of them may be read) without restraint. Bishops, the Bishop of Ancona—princes, the Duke of Urbino—from credulity, curiosity, or compassion, protected him against his enemies. Two of his prophecies, inundations of the Tiber in Rome, earthquakes in Lisbon, could hardly fail of accomplishment. But he came to a woful end. He attempted to convert the Emperor at Ratisbon. Charles was hard-hearted; the Prophet and the Prince, David and Solomon, were thrown into prison. After the peace with Solyman the Turk, they were conveyed to Mantua. Solomon was condemned to be burned as an apostate Christian. He was offered his life and a maintenance if he would recant his recantation and again become a Christian. He answered, "like a saint and an angel of God," with stedfast refusal. He was cast into the fire; "and the Lord" (so closes the Jewish relation) "smelled the sweet savour, and took to Him the spotless soul."[1] Yet there were Jews who believed that the fire had no power over him, and that he departed—God only knew whither.

But there was one who appeared in more enlightened days, in the middle of the seventeenth century, who demands a more extended notice. This man formed a considerable sect, which—notwithstanding that the conduct of its founder might, one would suppose, have disabused the most blind and fanatic enthusiasm—long existed, and still continues to exist.

In the year 1655, a certain Samuel Brett published a Narrative of a great Meeting of Jewish Rabbins in the

---

[1] R. Joseph seems in great perplexity about him: "And would to God I could write in a book with certainty and security, whether the words were true or not!" Whether he was impostor, fanatic, or madman, may be reasonably doubted. His visions favour the last conclusion. Rabbi Joseph, 149, 192.

Plain of Ageda, about thirty miles from Buda, in Hungary, to discuss their long-baffled hopes of the Messiah, and to consider the prophetic passages applied by Christian writers to their Redeemer. The author declared himself an eye-witness of the pomp of this extraordinary general assembly, where 300 Rabbins pitched their tents, and gravely debated, for seven days, this solemn question. But the authority of Samuel Brett is far from unexceptionable. The Jews, particularly Manasseh ben Israel, disclaim the whole transaction as a groundless fiction. Many circumstances of the Narrative—the setting Pharisees and Sadducees in array against each other, and the manifest design of the whole to throw odium on the Church of Rome—concur in inducing me entirely to reject the story.[a]

But a few years after the date of this real or fictitious event, in 1666, the whole Jewish world, coextensive almost with the globe itself, was raised to the highest degree of excitement by the intelligence of the appearance and the rapid progress of a pretender who had suddenly risen up in Smyrna, and assumed the name and the authority of the Messiah. Sabbathai Sevi was the younger son of Mordechai Sevi, who first followed the mean trade of a poulterer at Smyrna, and afterwards became broker to some English merchants. He was born A.C. 1625. Sabbathai was sent to school, where he made such rapid progress in the Cabala, that in his eighteenth year he was appointed a Hakim or Rabbi; he even then had many followers among the youth, and indeed among the elders of the place, with whom he practised rigid fasts, and bathed perpetually in the sea.

---

[a] Brett's Narrative is printed in the Phœnix, a collection of scarce tracts. Some of Brett's errors may have arisen from ignorance rather than from mendacity.

At twenty years old he married a woman of great beauty and rank among his people, but declined all conjugal connexion with her. The father cited him for this neglect of his duty: he was forced to give a bill of divorce. A second time he married; and a second time, on the same plea, the marriage was dissolved. Sabbathai announced that "the voice from heaven" assured him that neither of these women was the meet and appointed partner of his life. His partizans asserted that he was actuated by a holy desire of triumphing over human passion: his enemies gave a different turn to the affair. Still his fame increased. He sometimes fasted from Sabbath to Sabbath, and bathed till his life was endangered; yet his beauty, which was exquisite, seemed daily to increase. His whole body was said to breathe a delicious odour, which the physician of the family, suspecting to be perfume, declared, on examination, to be a natural exhalation from the skin. He now began to preach and to announce himself openly as the Son of David, and had the boldness to utter, in proof of his divine mission, the Ineffable Name, Jehovah. The offended Rabbins, horror-struck at this double crime, declared him worthy of death, and denounced him before the Turkish tribunal. Sabbathai took refuge in Salonichi. There the Rabbins again rose against him. He fled to Egypt; thence to Jerusalem. As he passed by Gaza, he made an important proselyte, named Nathan Benjamin, who, admitted trembling to his presence, declared, by the great Almighty and dreadful God, that he had seen the Lord in his cherub-borne chariot, as Ezekiel of old, with the ten Sephiroth murmuring around him like the waves of the sea: a voice came forth—"Your Redeemer is come; his name is Sabbathai Sevi; *he shall go forth as a mighty one, in-*

flamed with wrath as a warrior; he shall cry, he shall roar, he shall prevail against his enemies." In Jerusalem Sabbathai preached, and proclaimed himself the Messiah, with such success, that the Rabbins trembled before him; and the Elias of the new sect, Nathan of Gaza, had the audacity to issue an address to the brethren of Israel, in which he declared that before long the Messiah would reveal himself, and seize the crown from the head of the Sultan, who would follow him like a slave. After residing thirteen years in Jerusalem, Sabbathai made a second expedition to Egypt, where he married again, by the account of his enemies, a woman of light character—by that of his partizans, a maiden designated as his bride by the most surprising miracles. She was the daughter of a Polish Jew, made captive by some marauding Muscovites. At eighteen years of age she was suddenly seized from her bed by the ghost of her dead father, set down in a burying-place of the Jews, where she was found, told her story, and declared that she was the appointed bride of the Messiah. She was sent to her brother in Amsterdam; thence to Egypt. After passing three years more in Jerusalem, Sabbathai went openly into the synagogue, and proclaimed himself the Messiah. A violent commotion took place; the Rabbins launched their interdict against him: he fled to his native place, Smyrna. There the ban pursued him; but the people received him with rapture. Ono Anakia, a Jew of high rank, denounced him on the Exchange as an impostor. The unbeliever returned to his home, fell from his chair, and died: this singular accident was at once recognized as from the hand of God. The Rabbins feared to pursue their interdict;

---

* Isaiah xlii. 13.

Sabbathai assumed a royal pomp; a banner was borne before him with the words "The right hand of the Lord is uplifted." He divided among his partizans the kingdoms of the earth; he named his two brothers Kings of Judah and Israel; he himself took the title of King of the Kings of the Earth. One man, of high rank, nearly lost his life for opposing the prevailing delusion. The Head of the Rabbins was degraded; the Vice-President openly espoused the party.

The fame of Sabbathai spread throughout the world. In Poland, in Germany, in Hamburg, and Amsterdam, the course of business was interrupted on the Exchange, by the gravest Jews breaking off to discuss this wonderful event. From Amsterdam inquiries were sent to their commercial agents in the Levant; they received the brief and emphatic answer, "'Tis he, and no other." In the mean time rich presents were poured in to the Court of Sabbathai, and embassies were sent from the different communities of the Jews—some of these were detained three or four weeks before they could obtain an audience. His picture was surmounted by a crown of gold; the Twenty-first Psalm was sung before him, and a public prayer offered in the synagogue, in which he was acknowledged as the Messiah. In all parts, as if to accomplish the memorable words of Joel, prophets and prophetesses appeared—men and women, youths and maidens, in Samaria, Adrianople, Salonichi, Constantinople, and in other places, fell to the earth, or went raving about in prophetic raptures, exclaiming, it was said, in Hebrew, of which before they knew not a word, "Sabbathai Sevi is the true Messiah of the race of David: to him the crown and the kingdom are given." Even the daughters of his bitterest opponent, R. Pechina, were seized, as Sabbathai had predicted, with the same frenzy, and burst out in rapturous acknowledgment of the Messiah in the Hebrew language, which they had never learned. One wealthy Israelite, of Constantinople, more cautious than the rest, apprehending that this frenzy would bring some dreadful persecution against the Jews, went to the Grand Vizier, and requested a certificate that he had never been a believer in the Messiah. This reached the ears of the partizans of Sabbathai; they accused their crafty opponent of treasonable designs against the Turks, brought forward false witnesses, and the over-cautious unbeliever was sentenced to the galleys. Among the Persian Jews the excitement was so great that the husbandmen refused to labour in the fields. The governor, a man, it would seem, of unusual mildness, remonstrated with them for thus abandoning their work, instead of endeavouring to pay their tribute. "Sir," they answered with one voice, "we shall pay no more tribute—our Deliverer is come." The governor bound them in an obligation, to which they readily acceded, to pay 200 tomans if the Messiah did not appear within three months. But Sabbathai had now advanced too far to recede: his partizans were clamorous for his passing over to Constantinople, to confront the Grand Seignior. He arrived, escorted by a vast number of his friends, and was received with the loudest acclamations by the Jews of Constantinople. The Sultan was absent—he demanded an audience of the Grand Vizier. The Vizier delayed till he had received instructions from his master. The Sultan sent orders that Sabbathai should be seized and kept in safe custody. The Grand Vizier despatched an Aga and some Janissaries to the dwelling of Sabbathai, but the superstitious Aga was so overawed by the appearance of Sabbathai, "bright," he said, "as an angel," that he returned trembling and confounded to his master. Another Aga was sent, and returned in the same manner. Sabbathai, however, surrendered himself of his own accord; he was committed to the Castle of Sestos, as a sort of honourable prison, where his partizans had free access to him. From thence he issued a manifesto, suspending the fast religiously kept on the 9th of August, on account of the destruction of Jerusalem, and ordered the day to be celebrated, with the utmost festivity, as the birthday of the Messiah Sabbathai Sevi. In Sestos he admitted a deputation from Poland into his presence, whom he astonished with his profound knowledge and ready application of the Cabala. But there was in Constantinople one stubborn unbeliever, named Nehemiah, who for three days resisted all the arguments of the Messiah, and at the end, openly proclaimed him an impostor. The partizans of Sabbathai rose in the utmost fury; and, when Sabbathai threatened his opponent with death, rushed forward to put his mandate in execution. The Rabbi burst out of the chamber, and fled, pursued by the adherents of Sabbathai; escape was hopeless, when he suddenly seized a turban from the head of a Turk, placed it on his own, and cried aloud, "I am a Mussulman." The Turks instantly took him under their protection, and he was sent to Adrianople to the Sultan, who summoned Sabbathai to his presence. Sabbathai stood before the Grand Seignior; he was ignorant of Turkish, and a Jewish renegade was appointed as interpreter. But the man before whom the awe-struck Agas had trembled, now before the majesty of the Sultan, in his turn, totally lost his presence of mind; when the Sultan demanded whether he was the Messiah, he stood in trembling silence, and made no answer. He had some reason for his apprehensions, for the Sultan made him the following truly Turkish proposal:—"That he, the Sultan, should shoot three poisoned arrows at the Messiah: if he proved invulnerable, the Turk would himself own his title. If he refused to submit to this ordeal, he had his choice, to be put to death, or to embrace Mohammedanism." The interpreter urged him to accept the latter alternative—Sabbathai did not hesitate long; he seized a turban from a page, and uttered the irrevocable words, "I am a Mussulman." The Grand Seignior, instead of dismissing him with contempt, ordered him a pelisse of honour, named him Aga Mohammed Effendi, and gave him the title of Capidgi Basha. Consternation at this strange intelligence spread among the followers of Sabbathai; prophets and prophetesses were silent, but Sabbathai was daunted only by the death-denouncing countenance of the Sultan. He issued an address to his brethren in Israel:—"I, Mohammed Capidgi Basha, make it known unto you that God hath changed me from an Israelite to an Ismaelite. He spake, and it was done: he ordered, and it was fulfilled. Given in the ninth day of my renewal according to His holy will." He most ingeniously extracted prophetic intimations of his change both from tradition and Scripture. In the book called Pirke Elieser it was written, "that the Messiah must remain some time among the unbelievers." From the Scripture the example of Moses was alleged, who, "dwelt among the Ethiopians;" and the text of Isaiah, "he was numbered among the transgressors." For some time he maintained his double character with great success, honoured by the Moslemites as a true believer, by the Jews as their Messiah. Many of the latter followed his example, and embraced Islamism. St. Croix had frequently heard him preach in the synagogue, and with so much success, that scarcely a day passed but Jews seized the turbans from the heads of the Turks, and declared themselves Mussulmen. His Polish wife died; he again married the daughter of a learned man, who was excommunicated, on account of the unlawful connexion, by the Rabbins. She also embraced Islamism. At length the Rabbins, dreading the total extinction of Judaism, succeeded in gaining the ear of the Sultan. The Messiah was seized, and confined in a castle near Belgrade, where he died of a colic in the year 1676, in the fifty-first year of his age.⁷

It might have been expected that his sect, if it survived his apostasy, at least would have expired with his death; but there is no calculating the obstinacy of human credulity: his followers gave out that he was transported to heaven, like Enoch and Elijah; and, notwithstanding the constant and active opposition of the Jewish priesthood, the sect spread in all quarters. His forerunner, Nathan of Gaza, had abandoned his cause on his embracing Islamism, and prophesied against him in Italy and Corfu. But it is the most extraordinary fact of all, that Nehemiah, his most vehement opponent, recanted his enforced Islamism, and after all embraced Sabbathaism. A prophet of Smyrna proclaimed that the Messiah would reappear in 111½ years. But the doctrine of Michael Cardoso, which spread rapidly from Fez to Tripoli, and even to Egypt, was the most extravagant—the Son of David, he said, would not appear till all Israel were either holy or wicked: as the latter was far the easier process, he recommended all true Israelites to accelerate the coming of the Mes-

---

⁷ I have gathered from various Jewish and Christian accounts of Sabbathai Sevi. See Jost, t. viii. There is a Life of Sabbathai in the Sippurim, ii. 55.

siah, by apostatizing to Mohammedanism—numbers, with pious zeal, complied with this advice. Sabbathaism still exists as a sect of Judaism; though, probably, among most of its believers, rather supported by that corporate spirit which holds the followers of a political or religious faction together, than by any distinct and definite articles of belief.

But in the middle of the last century, an extraordinary adventurer, named Frank, organized a sect out of the wrecks of the Sabbathaic party. Before the appearance of Frank, an earlier sect, that of the Hassidin,[a] the New Saints, the Pietists, had spread from Podolia, its birthplace, into Wallachia, Moldavia, Hungary, Gallicia. Its founder was named Israel Baal-Schem, the Lord of the Home, or Israel the Wonder-Worker. The sect had its special worship, its books of faith, its doctors, called Tsadikin (the Just). It claimed the Zohar as its organ, but the Zohar with its mysticism alone, and that mysticism reduced to its simplest form. Its sole worship was prayer, prayer sublimed to silent contemplation, ravishment, ecstasy. The whole thought was centred on God, but on God alone. It is strange how limited, after all, are the forms of religious extravagance: whatever the faith, Indian, Heathen, Jewish, Christian, Mohammedan, this detachment from earth, this concentration on the Invisible, is the aim and the boast. But Nature will have her course; the exhausted mind loses its command over the body. The

---

[a] Compare on these Hassidin, Jost, and a long note at the end of Franck, La Kabbale, which contains extracts from the Autobiography of Solomon Maimon—a curious and rare book. Solomon Maimon joined the sect for a short time, obtained full insight into their tenets and practices, and, after a strange ramble through all conceivable creeds, settled down as a follower of Kant.

Hassidin not only threw aside all the cumbrous ceremonial of the Talmudists; they threw aside likewise the restraints of morality, even of decency. With the founders and leaders of this vast sect, there was the wild mixture of enthusiasm and imposture, with which this mysticism has sometimes commenced, into which it has almost always degenerated. Israel the Wonder-Worker assumed unbounded spiritual power; he could absolve from all sins; he maintained his power by working miracles; his prayer could cure all diseases. He was endowed with all knowledge, with the gift of prophecy. A witness, at one time a convert to this creed, discovered before long that this extraordinary knowledge was derived from a vast army of spies, great acuteness in reading the countenances of men, and skill in inducing them to reveal the secrets of their thoughts. The sect, spread through a large part of the Judaism of Eastern Europe, resisted alike its proscription by the Talmudic Rabbins, and the attempt of the Government to enslave and to convert the race; it is said still to exist, for these religious lunacies are immortal, unless absorbed by some kindred fanaticism. Frank and his followers, a very few years later, assumed the name of Zoharites. The founder astonished the whole of Germany, by living in a style of Oriental magnificence, encircled by a retinue of obsequious adherents. No one knew, or knows to this day, the source of the enormous wealth with which the state of the man was maintained during his life, and his sumptuous funeral conducted after his death. The early life of Jacob Frank did not forebode this splendour. He was born in Poland; in his youth he had been a distiller of brandy, and wandered into the Crimea, thence into Turkey, where he acquired great fame as a Cabalist. He returned to Podolia in his thirty-eighth year, and gathered together the wrecks of the followers of Sabbathai Sevi. He was persecuted by the Talmudists, revenged himself by throwing himself under the protection of the Bishop of Kaminiek, publicly burned the Talmud, announced himself a believer in the Zohar, and promulgated a new creed.

Yet for a time he attempted to maintain his lofty intermediate eclecticism. But those were not the days, nor was Poland the country, in which men could safely halt between two opinions. The Bishop, his protector, died. The Rabbins, his deadly enemies, denounced him at Warsaw to the Government and to the Papal Nuncio, as an apostate Jew, and a heretic Christian. His creed was certainly neither pure Judaism nor orthodox Christianity. The Zoharites began to see the fires of persecution already prepared for them, and themselves at the stake. They set forth for Turkey. As the first pilgrims entered Moldavia, the stern Kadi was as intolerant of men neither Jews, nor Christians, nor Mussulmen, as the Christians. They were left to be plundered by the populace. Those who remained behind openly embraced the Catholic faith, yet retained their secret Judaism. Many were detected, and sent forth, with their beards half-shaved, to the scorn and insult of the people. Some were condemned to hard labour. Yet many succeeded in concealing their doubtful opinions, intermarried, founded families, and attained rank and honour in Warsaw. Frank himself was imprisoned in the fortress of Czentschow. When this fortress was taken by the Russians he was set free. He travelled as ostensibly a Catholic Christian, but levying vast sums of money from his countrymen through Poland, Bohemia, Moravia. The new creed leant towards Christianity rather than Islamism. It rejected the Talmud, but insisted on a hidden sense in the Scriptures. It admitted the Trinity and the Incarnation of the Deity, but preserved an artful ambiguity as to the person in whom the Deity was incarnate, whether Jesus Christ or Sabbathai Sevi. As, however, the great head of this sect, Jacob Frank, afterwards openly embraced Christianity, and attended mass, he scarcely belongs to Jewish History. Suffice it to say that this adventurer lived in Vienna, in Brunn, and in Offenbach, with a retinue of several hundred beautiful Jewish youth of both sexes; carts containing treasure were reported to be perpetually brought in to him, chiefly from Poland—he went out daily in great state to perform his devotions in the open field—he rode in a chariot drawn by noble horses; ten or twelve Hulans in red and green uniform, glittering with gold, rode by his side, with pikes in their hands, and crests on their caps, eagles, or stags, or the sun and moon. Water was always carefully poured over the place where he had paid his devotions. He proceeded in the same pomp to church, where his behaviour was peculiar, but grave and solemn. His followers believed him immortal, but in 1791 he died; his burial was as splendid as his mode of living—800 persons followed him to the grave. But with his body the secret of his wealth was interred; his family sank into a state of want, and almost beggary. In vain they appealed to the credulity, to the charity of their brethren; they fell into insignificance, and were obliged to submit to the ordinary labours of mortal life.[*]

But while these men, half enthusiasts, perhaps more than half impostors, agitated the Jewish mind in the

---

[*] Peter Beer, in his Geschichte der Juden, is the great authority for the life and opinions of Jacob Frank. See also Jost, viii. 231. See, too, a note at the end of Franck, La Kabbale.

more rude and barbarous parts of Europe, and formed sects hateful alike to Jew, Christian, and Islamite—sects which soon either died out or dwindled away into insignificance and oblivion,—the despised race of Israel produced a man in every respect the direct opposite to these crazy or designing fanatics or impostors. He formed no creed, organised no sect, had during his lifetime no single avowed follower, yet long after his death he has risen to extraordinary fame and influence.

Towards the latter half of the seventeenth century lived, in an obscure village in the neighbourhood of the Hague, a Jew by birth, the influence of whose writings for good or for evil has been extensive, beyond that of most men, on the thoughts and opinions of modern Europe. The Politico-theological Treatise of Benedict (Baruch) Spinoza is the undoubted parent of what is called the Rationalist system, and from his arid and coldly logical Pantheism has grown up the more exuberant and imaginative Pantheism of modern Germany. It may be truly said that to Judaism mankind owes the doctrine of the Unity, the distinct and active Personality and Providence of God; from a Jew came forth the conception most antagonistic to the conception of the Godhead revealed through Moses, and accepted, as its primary truth, by Christianity. Such modes of thought as Spinoza's, however concealed, not from timidity, but because they were the inward, almost unconscious, workings of his own mind, would naturally lead to indifference for, and what would seem contemptuous neglect of, the rigid and minute ceremonies of his people and for the authority of his people's acknowledged teachers: and this neglect would vaguely and indistinctly transpire, and from its vagueness and indistinctness appear the more odious and repulsive to the popular feeling. Spinoza was denounced and expelled from the community as a dangerous apostate.[b] The excommunication fell light upon his calm, solitary, self-concentered, and self-sufficing mind. Though Spinoza always treats Christianity with respect, and throughout his famous Treatise cites the Evangelic writers as of equal authority with those of the Old Testament, he can certainly at no period of his life have been called a Christian. The fundamental axioms of his philosophy are utterly irreconcileable, not only with the peculiar and vital doctrines of Christianity, but even with the moral system of Socinus and his school. Spinoza ceased to be a Jew in language as well as in thought and in conviction. Though deeply read in the works of his Jewish forefathers, he wrote in the learned Latin of the day; for he wrote, if in his time for himself and a few congenial readers, for mankind, not for his own people.

This remarkable man had all the virtue, the abstemiousness, the self-denial, the frugality, and, as far as we know, the purity of the most rigid ascetic. He was entirely above the proverbial reproach of his race, avarice. He had no wants beyond the simplest sustenance. He engaged in no trade, followed no calling; mathematical and scientific instruments (which it seems that he constructed, perhaps for sale), and books, were his only expense. He was as superior to ambition. An enlightened German prince offered to found and endow a professorship for him, on one not illiberal condition,

---

[b] "The form of excommunication, dated 1656, may be read (it is the old, terrible form, with all its awful curses) in the Supplement to Spinoza's works (p. 290). No one might communicate with him orally or by writing, no one show him any favour, no one be under the same roof with him, or within four ells' distance, no one read any writing executed or written by him."

that he should not assail the established religion. Spinoza gratefully declined the dazzling offer. The instruction of youth would interfere with his entire and exclusive devotion to his philosophical studies; though he professed great respect for religion, he would not trammel the freedom of his speculations by any restriction.

This was the admirable part of his character; his intrepid assertion of the absolute freedom of human thought, his perfect independence, and consecration of his whole life to the laborious and conscientious investigation of truth, and this with no zealous ardour for proselytism, no fanatic hatred of religion, such as broke out later in Europe. He was content to dwell almost alone (though he would willingly admit the intercourse of congenial minds), in the hermitage of his own thoughts, and we must remember that though his kindred, the Jews, could proceed no further than a harmless excommunication (his life was once attempted), half a century had hardly elapsed, since religious, mingled with political fury, had reddened the streets of the Hague with the blood of the De Witts, and Grotius had suffered a long and ignominious imprisonment.

If ever any man was pure intellect, it was Spinoza. He had neither passions nor affections, of imagination not a gleam; to him, imagination was the source of all fallacy and delusion. He had no domestic ties—none, as far as we know, of the appetencies of our nature. He had friendships, but friendships which grew out of mental sympathies alone, a common interest in mathematical and scientific researches, inquiries into moral and metaphysical truth. Such was his relation, shown by his correspondence, with very acute and distinguished men, Oldenburg, Blyenberg, Leibnitz.

But it may be fairly said that the strength of Spinoza

was his weakness. His virtue isolated him, not only from the common vices and follies of mankind, but from all real knowledge of human nature, from that great part of the vast domain of philosophy, the mental constitution of the human race. With his unrivalled power of abstraction, of reducing everything to metaphysical entities, almost all truths to mathematical truths, his delight was in everything to approach as nearly as possible to the forms of geometry—to make, as it were, an algebra of metaphysical science.[c] Of the religious instincts, of the universal, if not inborn, notion of God as a Providential Agent; of the religious wants, hopes, and fears, he had no comprehension, for he had no experience. The philosophy of Spinoza, his metaphysical system, in its close logical coherence, lies beyond the scope, and could not find room in the space of this work.[d] I would consider him as a born Jew, yet, if I may so say, the prot-antagonistic adversary of Judaism, more especially of Rabbinical Judaism; and as an obscure Jew, in process of time, taking in his toils, and claiming as his followers, some of the leading intellects of modern Europe.

Spinoza began, like other philosophers of his race, with an aversion for, almost an absolute hostility towards, the anthropomorphism of the Hebrew Scriptures. From this, Philo had taken refuge in Allegory, Maimonides in what bordered on Rationalism; it had been held by most thoughtful men, at least among

---

[c] He uses this strange illustration, singularly characteristic of his mathematical metaphysics: "Hæc non miror, quia credo quod Triangulus, si loquendi facultatem haberet, eodem modo diceret, Deum eminenter triangulum esse, et Circulus divinam naturam eminente ratione circularem esse, et hac ratione quilibet suas attributa Deo adscriberet, similemque se Deo redderet reliquumque et deforme videretur." Epist. xlvii. p. 658.

[d] I would refer, for the only just, candid, and distinct view of the whole, to the Introduction to the French translation of his works by M. Emile Saisset.

Christians, to be an anthropomorphism only of language. But Spinoza carried this principle, as it were, into the Moral Being, at least into our conceptions of the Moral Being of God. Those conceptions of the active love, goodness, righteousness of God, were not merely inadequate, and far below their transcendent and inconceivable excellence, but were utterly without meaning. It was as unphilosophical, as entirely a figure of speech, to speak of the justice, mercy, patience, forbearance, loving-kindness of God, as of his right hand, his footstool, or his countenance; not merely was God without corporeity, but his moral nature was without kindred, affinity, or resemblance to the same qualities in man. These attributes were reflected back by man from his nature upon God, whom he, as it were, created in his own image. Thus, in his remorseless logic, Spinoza cut off all religious motives and incentives to virtue, rooted up the foundations of morality in our conceptions of God, and in the relations of God and man. And this did a man, himself of unimpeachable virtue, who, if his icy words ever kindle to any warmth, it is in commendation of purity, of kindness, of humanity, of universal charity; who even, in one of his letters, makes the distinct admission that the wisdom of God is the groundwork of truth and falsehood, good and evil; that that wisdom was pre-eminently manifested in Jesus Christ and his Apostles; and that in the practice of such virtues consists true and enduring beatitude. In this contradiction the old Jew, or the unformed Christian, might seem to linger indelibly, if almost unconsciously, in the mind of Spinoza.* In his latest work, his Posthumous

---

* "Denique ut de tertio etiam capite | salutem non esse omnino necessaria, mentem meam clarius aperiam, dico ad | Christum secundum carnem noscere

Ethics, he adheres to his reverence for virtue, will not altogether yield up the immortality of the soul, and admits a certain retribution after life; "virtuous souls, as partaking of the Divine wisdom, will endure for ever;" to the vicious he seems to assign something like a natural extinction. But how he reconciled this with his great system, appears to baffle the sagacity of those who judge him most fairly and most charitably. Throughout the Theologico-political Treatise, he writes as a Theist; his leading political object is anti-Judaism, to show that all nations are, and ever were, equally with the Jews, under the providential care of God. The name of Atheist he indignantly rejects ᶠ (and, indeed, however their consequences may seem the same to a

---

[he utterly denied the Incarnation], sed de æterno illo filio Dei, hoc est Dei æternâ sapientiâ, quæ sese in omnibus rebus et maximè in mente humanâ et omnium maximè in Christo Jesu manifestavit, longe aliter sentiendum. Nam nemo absque hac ad statum beatitudinis potest pervenire, utpote quæ sola docet quod verum et falsum, bonum et malum sit. Et quia, uti dixi, hæc sapientia per Jesum Christum, maximè manifestata fuit, ideo ipsius discipuli eandem, quatenus ab ipso ipsis fuit revelata, prædicaverunt, semque spiritu illo Christi supra reliquos gloriari posse ostenderunt." Epist. xxi. ad Oldenburg, Opera, I. p. 510.

These Epistles are the most curious, perhaps most trustworthy, depositories of Spinoza's opinions. They were published in his lifetime. They answer the objections raised by his friends, men of great acuteness, to the views maintained in the Tractatus Theologico-Politicus. They are the vain struggles of the strong man to break the bands in which he has inextricably involved himself.

The Resurrection of Christ he explained away in a spiritual sense. See the remarkable passage in the Letter xxiii. p. 414, to Oldenburg. Oldenburg, in his reply, strongly presses him with the usual arguments. He rejoins, " Christi passionem, mortem, et sepulturam tecum literaliter accipio; ejus autem resurrectionem allegoricè." p. 419.

ᶠ " Primo ait parum interesse scire cujus gentis ego sum, nec quod ritæ institutum sequor. Quod sanè si novisset, non tam facile sibi persuasisset, me Atheismum docere. Solent enim Athei summos et divitias ultra modum quærere, quæ ego semper certò contempsi; quod omnes qui me norunt, sciunt." Epist. xlix. p. 629. Compare also the newly discovered Treatise De Deo et Homine. Supplem. ad B. de Spinoza Opera, Amsterdam 1862.

theologian, the words Atheist and Pantheist are in absolute opposition). He repudiates, too, Materialism; he does not identify God with gross and brute matter.ᵃ But God, according to Spinoza, being the whole universe, the one primal Substance, all emanating from Him as attributes of his Being, or existing but as modes or affections of his Being; God, being the immanent, not the passing,ᵇ Cause of all things, was immutable—everywhere and in all respects alike immutable.

I cannot soar to the speculative, but rather dwell on the practical part of his system, as contrasted with that of his original faith, and with that of Christianity—the rejection of that active Theism, which is the first axiom of both these religions—indeed, it may be said, of all religion. This immutability of God, and the consequent immutability of all that God was, or that was God, bound up all things in an inevitable necessity. Of course all supernaturalism was discarded; miracles were believed only from the ignorance of man or his superstition; it is difficult to find room even for the remotest influence of Providential government. The free will of man was but an illusion of his pride; indeed any free will of God seemed equally inconceivable.ⁱ The individual man

---

ᵃ "Attamen quod quidam putant, Tractatum Theologico-Politicum eo niti quod Deus et Natura, per quam massam quandam, sive materiem corpoream, intelligunt unum et idem sunt, totâ errant viâ." p. 509.

ᵇ "Transeuntem." Neither of our words *transient* or *transitory* quite expresses the thought of Spinoza.

ⁱ Read in Mons. E. Saismet's Introduction to the French Translation the excellent chapter " Du Libre Arbitre," p. 148 et seqq.: " D'où vient donc que la masse entière du genre humain proclame le libre arbitre ? C'est que la masse entière du genre humain vit sous l'empire de l'imagination et des sens, dans un profond oubli de la raison. Le vulgaire s'est-il pas convaincu que l'âme meut le corps à son gré? Or, peut-on concevoir qu'une pensée donne du mouvement à une étendue? ... Et tout ce que je puis dire à ceux qui croient qu'ils peuvent parler, se taire, en un mot, agir, en vertu d'une libre décision de l'âme, c'est qu'ils rêvent les yeux ouverts."

could not be other than he was. For it is difficult to understand how any man, predestined, as it might seem, by the irresistible impulse of his nature, could be anything but what he became. Nero could be only Nero; the matricide was the consequence of his unalterable nature. Paul could be but Paul; he had no merit, as he could not choose but be an apostle and a martyr.

During his own time (till the posthumous publication of his Ethics, his system cannot be said to have been complete), and in the following period, Spinoza was more denounced, dreaded, and hated, than read. The world contented itself with the contemptuous sarcasm, that his system was only the philosophic dream of an obscure Jew. Though he wrote in Latin—the language of European learning—and had long been disclaimed by, and had disclaimed his race, I doubt not that with the natural apprehension and aversion to his tenets mingled much of the disdain and detestation which still in the general mind adhered to his descent. The most sceptical of sceptics, Bayle (as is the wont of sceptics, who seem glad to throw over some one more obnoxious to the religious prepossessions of the age than themselves), in an elaborate Life of Spinoza, acute, desultory, but copious and amusing, denounced him as a bold and declared Atheist. His virtuous life Bayle acknowledges, on the testimony of the peasants among whom Spinoza lived, and refrains from taunts upon his Jewish origin. From this Article of Bayle was probably derived most of the knowledge of Spinoza which prevailed till towards the close of the last century. His name was the by-word for Atheism and impiety. By degrees, however, Spinoza could not but find a place in histories of philosophy; and historians were not content to rest on the authority or on the citations of Bayle. His works were translated into German; and with the rise of what is called "the German school of criticism," as also with that of German philosophy, his name and his influence became more and more manifest and avowed. Lessing spoke of him with respect, almost with reverence. Goethe (whose abstract speculations found vent chiefly in his poetry, and that poetry, even in its most abstruse views, and its wildest dreams, though fathoming the depths of human thought, singularly distinct and luminous) declared, it is said, that the three master-spirits which had formed his mind were Shakespeare, Linnæus (in Goethe must be remembered the discoverer of the metamorphoses of plants), and Spinoza. He who knows the influence of Goethe upon the mind and thought of Germany, and through Germany on that of Europe, will hardly think that the name of Spinoza ought not to find room in the History of the Jewish race. It is still more extraordinary that the religious mystic Novalis found, or fancied that he found, in Spinozism a philosophical system which supplied the wants and harmonised with the aspirations of his pious mind.[1] In France there has been a curious controversy. No Frenchman must be acknowledged as the teacher of so unpopular a writer as Spinoza. The memory of Descartes must be relieved from this imputation, and M. Cousin, with his wonted patriotism, has undertaken this desperate task—desperate, for Spinoza himself declares that he was a follower of Descartes—that he began with the study of the works, deduced much of his reasoning from the axioms, of Descartes, and avowedly adopted his method. But France, in the

---

[1] On Novalis compare M. de Saisset's Introduction.

translation of his works and in the Introduction of M.
Emile Saisset, has, with a distinct and eminently judicious disclaimer of Spinozism, done justice, not more
than justice, to the character and to the writings of the
remarkable Jew. In Germany most of the philosophers,
Schleiermacher, Fichte, Schelling, Hegel (Fichte especially), paid him the homage, either of transplanting
his system into their own, or of transmuting it into
another form.

BOOK XXIX.

MODERN JUDAISM.

Change in the relative State of the Jews to the rest of Mankind — Jews in Poland — In Germany — Frederick the Great — Naturalization Bill in England — Toleration Edict of Joseph II. — Jews of France — Petition to Louis XVI. — Revolution — Bonaparte — More recent Acts for the Amelioration of the Civil State of the Jews — General Estimate of the Number of Jews in Africa, Asia, Europe, America — Conclusion.

I HAVE followed the sect of Sabbathai and his disciples to the close of the eighteenth century; I have placed in strong but appropriate contrast the singular phenomena of the life and philosophy of Spinoza. I must now retrace my steps, and terminate this History by a rapid sketch of the more important events which influenced the condition of the Jews in the different countries of the world, during that period, down to our own days. The lapse of centuries, and the slow improvement in almost the whole state of society, had made a material alteration in the relative position of the Jews towards the rest of mankind. They were still, many of them, wealthy; but their wealth no longer bore so invidious and dangerous a proportion to that of the community at large as to tempt unprincipled kings, or a burthened people, to fill their exchequer, or revenge themselves for a long arrear of usurious exaction, by the spoliation of this unprotected race. A milder spirit of Christian forbearance with some, of religious indifference with others, allayed the fierce spirit of animosity, which now, instead of bursting forth at every opportunity, was slowly and with difficulty excited and forced to a violent explosion. Still, in the midst of society, the Jews dwelt apart, excluded by ancient laws from most of the civil offices, by general prejudice and by their own tacit consent from the common intercourse of life; they were endured because mankind had become habituated to their presence, rather than tolerated on liberal principles, still less courted by any overtures for mutual amity. The Jew was contented with this cessation of hostilities: he had obtained a truce; he sought not for a treaty of alliance. Where commercial restrictions were removed, he either did not feel, or disdained, civil disqualifications. So long as he retained, unmolested, the independent government of his own little world, he left to the Gentiles to administer the politics of the kingdoms of the earth. If he might be permitted to live as a peaceful merchant, he aspired not to become statesman, magistrate, or soldier. So that the equal law protected him in the acquisition and possession of personal property, he had no great desire to invest his wealth in land, or to exchange the unsettled and enterprising habits of trade for the more slow returns and laborious profits of agriculture. He demanded no more than to be secured from the active enmity of mankind; his pride set him above their contempt. Like the haughty Roman, banished from the world, the Israelite threw back the sentence of banishment, and still retreated to the lofty conviction that his race was not excluded, as an unworthy, but kept apart, as a sacred people; humiliated indeed, but still hallowed, and reserved for the sure though tardy fulfilment of the Divine promises. The lofty feeling of having endured and triumphed over centuries of intolerable wrong, mingled among the Jews with the splendid recollections of the past and the hopes of the future, which were sedulously inculcated by their Rabbinical instructors; and thus their exclusion from the communities of the world, from the honours and privileges of social life, was felt, by those who were highminded enough to feel at all, rather as a distinction than a disgrace. This at once compelled and voluntary unsocialness was still the universal national characteristic of the Jews: yet in process of time they became in some degree assimilated to the nations among whom they lived; their relative state of civilization materially depended on the manners of the surrounding people, and there was nearly as great a difference between the depressed and ignorant Jew of Persia, the fierce fanatic of Barbary or Constantinople, and his opulent and enlightened brethren of Hamburg or Amsterdam, as between the Mussulman and Christian population of the different countries. The dominion of the Rabbins was universally recognized, except among the Karaïtes, whose orderly and simple congregations were frequent in the East, in the Crimea, in Poland, even in Africa. Rabbinism was still the stronghold and the source of the general stubborn fanaticism: yet even this stern priestcraft, which ruled with its ancient despotism in more barbarous Poland, either lost its weight, or was constrained to accommodate itself to the spirit of the age, in the West of Europe.

At the beginning of the eighteenth century, Poland, Galicia, and the adjacent provinces, had long been the head-quarters of the Jews.* Into these regions they had

---

* Cassel, in Ersch und Grüber, pp. 130-138, enters into many minute details on the settlement in Poland and Galicia, and Red Russia. In Kiew they

spread at an early period, silently and obscurely, from Hungary, Moravia, Bohemia. Some had taken refuge from the atrocities perpetrated by the early Crusaders as they passed through those realms; some from the persecutions by the Flagellants, and those which arose out of the Black Plague. It is usual to date their flourishing state and protection by the paternal government from the reign of Casimir the Great in the fourteenth century.[b] Casimir, however, only confirmed a law of Duke Boleslaw, the regent of the realm during the minority of his nephew.[c] This was the first enlightened edict which secured to the Jews with unusual precision their privileges, their rights, and their duties, as subjects. Boleslaw, and still more Casimir avowed the policy that by encouraging the Jews they encouraged the commerce of the kingdom. They had the premature wisdom to appreciate the value of trade and industry to the wealth and happiness of their country. To the influence of a beautiful Jewish mistress, Esther, was attributed, probably to a certain extent not without justice, this humane policy of Casimir the Great.[d] Esther was permitted to bring up her daughter by the king in her own

---

were in great numbers in the year 1113. A persecution followed the death of Swatopulk.

[b] Casimir reigned from 1337 to 1370.

[c] See Depping, p. 237, who translates the original charter of 1264, first published in Archiv für Geschichte, Vienna, 1826. In case of a mulct, they paid, as in the South of France, so much pepper instead of so much money. Boleslaw adopts the maxim of some of the Popes, that the modern Jews are not guilty of the blood of Christ.

[d] Casimir's law, however, is dated 1343; Esther was not his mistress till 1350. All his subjects were not so tender or so courteous to the Jews, "quorum fœtor olidus usque in hanc diem perseverat." Dlugloss, Hist. Polon. quoted by Cassel. Cassel will not subscribe to the passage in the Corpus Polon. Hist. ii. 602: "Hujus Hester operâ gens Judaica magnas prærogativas in Polonia a rege adepta est, cum novas tum quam ipsis Boleslaus . . . concesserat." p. 132.

faith; the sons had liberal appanages. Many circumstances concurred in advancing the comparative security, with the security, the numbers, wealth, and influence of the Jews in this part of Europe. In the Slavonian kingdoms the feudal system never prevailed to the same extent as in Germany and the West. Though under the royal protection, the Jews were not the liegemen, the vassals of the royal chamber, the property of the king. The Slavonian clergy never, even when the Papal power was recognized, attained the same authority; the nobility were in constant strife with the hierarchy; the Canon-law had far less power. In vain did the clergy make, as under the reign of Sigismund I.,* a desperate struggle to draw the rigid line of demarcation between the Jew and the Christian, to prohibit social and commercial intercourse, to demand their exclusion from offices of State and public service, even to enforce the peculiar and distinctive dress upon the Jew. The Jews living on the estates, and under the protection of the independent nobles who would brook no interference with their authority, defied the edicts of synods and even of kings. Not that the kings were adverse to them; the greatest and the best, as John Sobieski, looked on them with favour, and maintained them in their rights and in their industry. Nor indeed were the Slavonian Jews always secure against the calumnies, against the popular tumults, the plunders, and the massacres perpetrated so much more frequently, so much more cruelly, in Western Europe. Posen and Cracow, the chief seats of the most powerful Roman

---

* 1506-1526: "Indignum et Juri divino contrarium censentes, ejus generis homines aliquibus honoribus et officiis inter Christianos fungi debere." Apud Cassel, p. 133.

Catholic hierarchy, may claim distinctive infamy for these persecutions. The building of a synagogue in Posen was the signal for a rumour about an insult to the Host, an outbreak of the populace, and pillage and murder of the Jews. In Cracow, in 1407, a priest, Budeek, craftily spread a report of a murdered child. The authorities of the city would have protected the Jews; but the great bell tolled (it is said, through some mistake), the mob rose, the Jews' houses were fired, and a terrible conflagration wasted the city. The Crusaders against the Jews sometimes followed the fatal examples of the Crusaders to the Holy Land. In 1464 the Jews were plundered in Cracow, and thirty men killed. In 1500, the gates of the Jewish quarter, notwithstanding the king's protection, who had removed the Jews to a safer place, were forced by another band of Crusaders, and a great slaughter perpetrated. Even as late as 1737 in Posen, as in 1753 in Kiew, the child-murder fable rose anew against the Jews. An appeal was made to the Pope, Benedict XIV. His successor, Clement XIII., did not shrink from the investigation. By his orders the Nuncio wrote to Count Bruhl, commanding that nothing should be done on hearsay evidence—nothing without clear and substantial proof.[f] Wonderful as it may seem, such things have taken place in our own times, in the nineteenth century. It needed Russian Imperial Ukases to interpose. In the province of Witepck in 1805 a child was found drowned in the Dwina; the Jews were accused of the murder. In 1811, a child eight weeks old disappeared out of its cradle; the Jews were arraigned

---

[f] "C'est pour ça, que dans le cas des pareilles accusations l'on ne doit pas appuyer le jugement sur les dits fondements, mais aux preuves légales, qui peuvent regarder l'affaire et rendre certain le crime qu'on leur impute." Quoted by Cassel, p. 134.

as having stolen it for their evil purposes. The process lasted till 1827. An Imperial Ukase appeared in 1817 prohibiting such charges, yet they continued to be made and heard till 1835; the date of the great Imperial Edict concerning the Jews. Nevertheless, the Jews in Poland gradually grew up into a middle order between the nobles and the serfs; the only middle order, between the nobles, however gallant yet the haughtiest in Europe and most contemptuous of trade or industry, and the serfs perhaps the most degraded, wretched, and unimproved in their condition and in their minds. Almost every branch of traffic was in the hands of the Jews. They were the corn merchants, shopkeepers, innkeepers. In some towns they formed the greatest part of the population; in some villages almost the whole.[g] If heavily, it does not appear that they were exorbitantly taxed either by the nobles or the government.[h]

The Jews suffered with the rest of the inhabitants of that unhappy country, when Poland and its neighbouring provinces, already in the middle of the seventeenth century,[i] became the battle-ground, hereafter to be the

---

[g] Schlosser ascribes their settlement to the deliberate policy of Kasimir III. the Great:

"Kasimir nämlich wollte Gewerbe, Handel, Regsamkeit schaffen, nicht langsam entstehen sehen: er wollte Geld und Deutsche ins Lande ziehen; die damals gedrückten Juden folgten seinem Rufe am ersten, und er begünstigte ihre Einwanderung. Die zahlreich in Galizien einwandernden Juden bemächtigten sich bald aller Gewerbe und Geschäfte, welche einträglich gemacht werden können ohne mühsam zu seyn und körperliche Arbeit zu fordern, und drängten sich auf diese Weise als Bürgerstand in die Mitte eines Nations von Herrn und leibeigener Bauern. Diese Juden vermehrten sich, wie in Ægypten, und überliessen gern Ehre und Rang in Staat anderen, wenn ihnen nur das Geld bleibe." Schlosser, Weltgeschichte, iv. p. 162.

[h] Cassel, in Ersch und Gruber, p. 134.

[i] 1674 to 1697.

prey, of its ambitious neighbours. In an invasion by the Grand Duke of Muscovy, in 1655, of twelve thousand Jews in Wilna when that city was laid waste with fire and sword, eight thousand submitted to baptism; four thousand, more heroically obstinate, were burned alive.[1]

If Poland was hospitable, Russia Proper, from ancient times, was sternly inhospitable to the race of Israel. Paulus Jovius in his 'Embassies' relates that they are hated by the Russians. The mischievous race could not be permitted to dwell within their frontiers; the Jews are accused of having perfidiously furnished the Turks with iron artillery. There was a deeper and more enduring cause of this enmity. Towards the end of the fifteenth century (in 1490), in Novogorod, a Jew named Zacharias, with the aid of some of his brethren (it is added, through the mysterious and attractive Cabala, with the dark sentences of which he bewildered their minds), induced several Priests and many Boyars to renounce Christianity; to believe that Moses alone had a divine mission; that the whole Gospel was a fable; that the Christ was not yet come. One of the converts, a priest, Alexis, took the name of Abraham; his wife that of Sarah.[2] They became Jews in all but the rite of circumcision, which, to avoid detection, they had the prudence or the cunning to dispense with. The sect spread rapidly among Ecclesiastics and Boyars. It

---

[1] "Le Grand Duc de Moscovie est entré dans la Pologne d'un autre côté que le roi de Suède : Il a assiégé Vilna, qui est la capitale de la Lithuanie, qu'il a pris par force, où il a tout fait mettre à feu et à sang. De douze mille Juifs qui y ont été trouvés, il y en a eu huit mille qui ont composé et qui ont reçu le baptême, et quatre autres mille, avec la loi de Moïse gravée dans leur cœur, ont été brulés, n'ayant pas voulu se convertir." Lettres de Guy Patin. ii. 208, dated 21 Sept., 1655.

[2] Compare Cassel, p. 135.

was embraced among the rest by Zozimus, Archimandrite of the Monastery of St. Simon. They still performed the Christian ceremonies, and kept the fasts of the Church with the utmost rigour. The two leading heretics, Denis and Alexis, became arch-priests, one of the Cathedral of the Assumption, one of the Church of St. Michael the Archangel. The sovereign, Ivan III., listened, without suspicion of heresy, to the Cabalistic teaching of these men. The Princess Helena became a convert. Even more wonderful, the Archimandrite Zozimus was promoted to the Metropolitan throne of All the Russias. "The son of Satan sat on the throne of the Holy Saints who had Christianized the realm." At length the dire spiritual conspiracy was discovered by Gennadius, Archbishop of Novogorod. The Czar could not but summon a council of Bishops, Archimandrites, Abbots, and Priests. Before this council the depositions were laid, implicating a great number of ecclesiastics and laymen at Novogorod, Moscow, and other cities. Zozimus only and Kouritzin the Secretary of State were not involved in the charge. Zozimus was obliged to listen while the others were arraigned by the zealous Archbishop as guilty of cursing Jesus Christ and the Blessed Virgin, of spitting on the crucifix, of calling the sacred images idols, and biting them with their teeth while they seemed to kiss them with their lips; of casting them into foul places; of denying Paradise and the Resurrection of the Dead. Some were for putting the accused, even priests of the highest rank, to the torture, and condemning them to death. The mild Iwan interfered; the council by his direction was content with launching an anathema against the terrible heresy, and banishing its adherents. The zealous Archbishop, Gennadius, sent some of the most notorious to Novogorod (the council was held at Moscow). These were set on horses, with their faces to the tails, their garments turned inside out, and with horned caps, like the paintings of the Devil, and crowns of straw, with a writing thereon, "Behold the Host of Satan!" They were thus paraded through the streets; the rabble spat upon them, and jeered them, "Lo, the Enemies of Jesus Christ!" The mildness of this punishment among the rude Muscovites might put to shame the bloody hecatombs and flaming Autos-da-Fé of more civilized kingdoms. Zozimus, the Metropolitan, still wore the mask of consummate hypocrisy. In public he was a pious Christian; it is said that he practised the Christian virtues. In secret he mocked at the kingdom of God, at Christ, and the Resurrection; "at Him who never was and never will be." In the palace of the Metropolitan, in the palace of the Secretary of State, meetings were held, it was said, sumptuous banquets, in which the Cabala, with its profound questions, its subtle allegories, its astrology, were the common conversation. A general Pyrrhonism spread abroad; monks and laymen were heard in public discussing the mysteries of the Holy Trinity. Zozimus abused his power by degrading orthodox and advancing Judaizing priests. He affected the fullest Christian toleration: "Bear no malice to any one, not even to heretics: the pastors of the Church should always and only preach peace."

At length some discovery was made. It is not known how far these secret proceedings were divulged to the sovereign. But the wise Iwan would avoid the scandal of the degradation of a Metropolitan—a Metropolitan promoted by himself. Zozimus was quietly dismissed and sent back to his monastery. He was afterwards (we may perhaps mistrust the charges of his enemies), on account of drunkenness, removed from that of St. Simon to that of the Trinity. But Kouritzin, the Secretary of State, long enjoyed the favour of his master. This Crypto-Judaism lurked long in the bosom of the Russian Church; when it was entirely extinguished, if extinguished, remains unknown.*

Russia in the following centuries still adhered to her hostility to the Jews; but her ambition was too strong for her intolerance. As province after province was added to her vast empire, and as of almost all these provinces a large part of the population, at least the wealthiest and most industrious, were Jews, expulsion was impossible; Russia did not conquer to rule over a desert. Her policy became of necessity more wise and humane. The partition of Poland, or rather the two partitions, with the enormous share which fell into her iron grasp, gave her nearly half a million of Jewish subjects. Though, like other Poles, they were unwilling subjects (many Jews fought bravely in the army of Kosciusko), yet their numbers, their wealth, their importance, enforced only moderate oppression.

Of the millions of Jews upon the face of the earth, loosely and vaguely estimated at five, seven, or eight millions, two millions ⁿ are subjects of the Russian empire. I return to the subject.

Poland was the seat of the Rabbinical Papacy. The Talmud ruled supreme in the public mind; the

---

* All this is from Karamsin's Hist. of Russia (French translation), t. vi. pp. 242-250.
ⁿ Cassel, Ersch und Grüber, gives

for the year 1838: — In Russia, 1,507,993 souls; In Poland, 453,646, of which 36,390 are in Warsaw.

synagogues obeyed with implicit deference the mandates of their spiritual superiors, and the whole system of education was rigidly conducted, so as to perpetuate the authority of tradition. Lublin and Cracow were the great seats of Jewish learning. How far in more recent times these barriers have been broken down by the more free and liberal spirit of Western Judaism, it would be hard to determine. We have seen in the last Book some insurrections—insurrections which ended in almost general submission, and so added to the strength of the ruling authority.

In the West of Europe, during all this period, those great changes were slowly preparing, which, before the close of the century, were to disorganize the whole framework of society. The new opinions not merely altered the political condition of the Jews, as well as that of almost all orders of men, but they penetrated into the very sanctuary of Judaism, and threatened to shake the dominion of the Rabbins, as they had that of the Christian priesthood, to its base. It is singular, however, that the first of these daring innovators, who declared war alike against ancient prejudices and the most sacred principles, excluded the Jews from the wide pale of their philanthropy. The old bitter and contemptuous antipathy against the Jews lurks in the writings of many of the philosophic school, especially those of Gibbon and Voltaire. It was partly the leaven of hereditary aversion, partly, perhaps, the fastidiousness of Parisian taste, which dreaded all contamination from a filthy and sordid, as well as a superstitious race; but, most of all, it arose from the intimate relation of the Mosaic with the Christian religion. The Jews were hated as the religious ancestors of the Christians; and, in Paley's phrase, it became the accustomed mode of warfare "to wound Christianity through the sides of Judaism." Strange fate of the Jews, after having suffered centuries of persecution for their opposition to Christianity, now to be held up to public scorn and detestation for their alliance with it!*

The legislation of Frederick the Great almost, as it were, throws us back into the Middle Ages. In 1750 appeared an edict for the general regulation of the Jews in the Prussian dominions. It limited the number of Jews in the kingdom, divided them into those who held an ordinary or an extraordinary protection from the Crown. The ordinary protection descended to one child, the extraordinary was limited to the life of the bearer. Foreign Jews were prohibited from settling in Prussia; exceptions were obtained only at an exorbitant price. Widows who married foreign Jews must leave the kingdom. The protected Jews were liable to enormous and special burthens. They paid, besides the common taxes of the kingdom, for their patent of protection, for every election of an elder in their communities, and every marriage. By a strange enactment, in which the king and the merchant were somewhat unroyally combined, every Jew on the marriage of a son was obliged to purchase porcelain, to the amount of 300 rix-dollars, from the king's manufactory, for foreign exportation. Thus heavily burthened, the Jews were excluded from all civil functions, and from many of the most profitable branches of trade—from agriculture, from breweries and distilleries, from manu-

---

* Montesquieu, if he may be justly reckoned with this school, is a bright example of the opposite spirit. Read the striking letter, supposed to be addressed on the occasion of the burning of a young Jewess in an Auto-da-Fé at Lisbon, to the Inquisitors, showing that the persecution of the Christians in Japan was only an antitype of theirs. Esprit des Lois, x. 14.

factures, from innkeeping, from victualling, from physic and surgery.

Nor in more enlightened countries was the public mind prepared for any innovations in the relative condition of the Jews. In England, from the time of Charles II., they had lived in peace in their two communities of Portuguese and German origin. At first, indeed, the favour which was said to be shown to them by Cromwell was looked on with jealousy by the Royalists after the Restoration. A remonstrance was addressed to the King.[p] It dwelt on the mischiefs perpetrated by the Jews from the time of William the Conqueror to that of Edward I.; their privileges obtained by bribery, their usuries, and mal-practices; their expulsion from the realm at the petition and amid the general joy of the nation. They had returned, resumed their fraudulent practices, and in their prosperity presumed to offer to buy the Cathedral of St. Paul's for a synagogue. The remonstrants prayed for a commission to seize their property for the people's use, and to banish them for ever from the kingdom. They were in some danger in those loose days. Some of their wealthiest were threatened with the seizure of their whole property, as illegally trading, even as residents in the land, by some of the profligate courtiers (Mr. Rycaut and others), who, no doubt from their Christian zeal, declared both their estates and lives to be forfeit. The Earl of Berkshire betrayed the secret of that zeal; he pretended to have received a verbal order from the

---

[p] Mrs. Everett Greene, Calendar of State Papers, 1666, p. 566. There is a petition from two converted Jews to share in the charity of Henry III. settled on the Rolls House. The Master of the Rolls of that time had charged the estate with 20*l.* 0*s.* 4*d.* for the charity. p. 171.

King to prosecute them and seize their estates, *unless they made agreement with him.* To do the King (Charles II.) justice, he received their petition graciously, utterly denied the verbal order, and gave them permission to enjoy the same favour as before, so long as they should live peaceably and in obedience to the laws.[q]

The Jews had obtained relief under James II. from an alien-duty, which restricted their traffic; the indulgence was revoked under William III. The Lord Treasurer Godolphin was tempted with an offer of the Jews to purchase the town of Brentford (was it the situation or the dirt of Brentford which attracted the Jews?) at the price of £500,000,—it might be a million. Godolphin dreaded the fanaticism of the clergy and the jealousy of the merchants, and declined the offer.[r]

Under Queen Anne a regulation was made to facilitate conversions among the Jews; the Chancellor was empowered to enforce from the father of a convert to Christianity a fair and sufficient maintenance. The baptism of a rich and influential person of the sect, named Moses Marcus, excited a considerable sen-

---

[q] See the notice of the Petition of Emanuel Martinez Dormido (doubtless a Portuguese Jew) and others in behalf of the Jews trading in and about London, in Mrs. Everett Greene's Calendar of State Papers, Aug. 22, 1664, p. 672.

[r] "The Jews offered my Lord Godolphin to pay 500,000l. (and they would have made it a million), if the Government would allow them to purchase the town of Brentford, with leave of settling there entirely, with full privilege of trade, &c. The agent from the Jews said that the affair was already concerted with the chief of their brethren abroad, that it would bring the riches of their merchants hither, and of course an addition of more than twenty millions of money to circulate in the nation. Lord Molesworth was in the room with Lord Godolphin when this proposal was made, and, as soon as the agent was gone, pressed him to close with it. Lord Godolphin was not of his opinion. He foresaw that it would provoke two of the most powerful bodies in the nation, the clergy and the merchants. He gave other reasons, too, against it, and, in fine, it was dropped." Spence's Anecdotes, 215.

sation at the time. At the beginning of the eighteenth century, the cause of the Jews was brought forward under the unpopular auspices of Toland the Freethinker. In 1753 a more important measure was attempted. A Bill was introduced into Parliament for the naturalization of all Jews who had resided three years in the kingdom, without being absent more than three months at a time. It excluded them from civil offices, but in other respects bestowed all the privileges of British subjects. The Bill passed both Houses, and received the royal assent. But the old jealousies only slumbered—they were not extinguished. The nation, as if horror-struck at finding those whom it had been accustomed to consider as outlaws thus suddenly introduced into its bosom, burst into an irresistible clamour of indignation. The Mayor and citizens of London (for mercantile jealousy mingled with religious prejudices) took the lead in denouncing this inroad on the Constitution and insult on Christianity.[*] The bishops were everywhere insulted for not having opposed the Bill. The Bishop of Norwich on his Confirmation circuit was hooted in almost every town. At Ipswich the youths who were to be confirmed called out for circumcision. A paper was affixed on the door of one of the churches, that his Lordship would the next day, Saturday, their Sabbath, confirm the Jews, on Sunday the Christians.

The pulpits thundered: a respectable clergyman, Tucker, who had written a defence of the measure, was maltreated by the populace. The Ministry and the

---

[*] Among the arguments for the Naturalization Bill in England was the manifest extent to which the Jews had contributed to the wealth and prosperity of the great trading cities of Europe—Amsterdam, Leghorn, Venice,

Houses of Parliament found it necessary to repeal the obnoxious statute.[1]

The number of the Jews in England was then reckoned at 12,000.

In Italy, till the French Revolution, the Jews enjoyed their quiet freedom. In Rome they were confined to their Ghetto, and still constrained to listen to periodical sermons. In the maritime towns they continued to prosper. An attempt by the king himself to secure their re-establishment in the kingdom of Naples is remarkable for the politic boldness on the part of the king, and its failure through the unmitigated hostility of the clergy and the populace. On the separation of the kingdom of the Two Sicilies from the Spanish monarchy, the king, Charles, seemed determined to repudiate the Spanish policy. With a view probably to the restoration of the commerce of the realm, a royal edict was issued, inviting the Jews to settle for sixty years in the Two Sicilies. The edict, by the rights and privileges which it conferred, might seem studiously to reverse all the policy of the Middle Ages. They might trade in all parts by sea and land, exempt from tolls, and on the same footing as other corporations. They might practise every handicraft, hold lands, except such as had feudal jurisdiction. They might import the necessaries of life without custom dues; they might practise medicine even upon Christians, under Christian superintendence; they had their special judicature, and were exempt from all other civil magistracy; they might print books in all languages; they might have Turkish slaves and Christian domestics, men· of twenty-five

---

[1] Coxe's Lives of the Pelhams. In this work there is a good account of | the debate, with an abstract of the speech of Mr. Pelham (ii. 290).

years old, women of thirty-five; they might bear arms; they might have their special meat markets and granaries. The excommunicating power of the Rabbins was acknowledged; they might choose the heads of their communities in Naples, Messina, Palermo. Christians were strictly forbidden to insult or injure them, or to make proselytes of their children. The Jews crowded at the royal summons to Naples; perhaps not without ostentation of their newly-acquired privileges, and of their wealth. But they ought to have known better the public mind at Naples. The hatred, which was here universal, broke out into fury. The clergy thundered against them from the pulpits; the Pope, and the king's confessor, held almost a saint, denounced them in the sternest sermons. A Capucin Friar threatened the king himself: "for this impious deed he would die childless." There were brooding murmurs of a massacre. The Jews dared not open shops; they withdrew, except a few of the lowest. The premature scheme of toleration utterly failed.[a]

In Germany the public mind was surprised at the unusual phenomenon of a Jew suddenly starting forward in the career of letters, and assuming a high and acknowledged rank in the rapidly awakening literature of that country, as a metaphysical and philosophical writer. This was the celebrated Moses Mendelssohn, who, by genius and unwearied application, broke through the most formidable obstacles, poverty, dependence, and the spirit of his sect. The Jews were proud of his distinction, but trembled at his desertion of their ancient opinions; the Christians confidently looked forward to the accession of so enlightened a mind to the Church; the

---

[a] Muratori, Ann. d'Italia (sub ann. 1740); Mémoire Historique et Politique.

philosophers expected him to join in their fierce crusade against religion. Mendelssohn maintained his own calm and independent course. He remained outwardly a member of the synagogue, while he threw aside disdainfully the trammels of Rabbinism; to a letter of Lavater, urging him to embrace Christianity, he returned a firm and temperate vindication of his adherence to his former faith; his mild and amiable spirit had little in common with the unprincipled apostles of unbelief. It would be difficult to define the religious opinions of Mendelssohn, whose mind, in some respects singularly lucid, in others partook of the vague and dreamy mysticism of his German countrymen; but if he had any fixed view, it probably was to infuse into a kind of philosophic, or, as it would now be called, rationalizing, Judaism the spirit of pure Christian love. But whatever the opinions of Mendelssohn, whether Jew or Christian, or with an undefined and blended creed, his translations of the Pentateuch and of the Psalms into German forbid all doubt as to the sincerity of his belief; his success in letters exercised an important influence both on the minds of his own brethren, and on the estimation in which the Jews were held, at least in Germany. Many of the Jewish youth, emancipated by his example from the control of Rabbinism,[z] probably rushed headlong down the precipice of unbelief; while, on the other hand, a kindlier feeling gradually arose towards the brethren of a man whose writings delighted and instructed much of the rising youth of Germany.

---

[z] For the double effect of the progress of more liberal opinions, and the overthrow of the Rabbinical rule without any counterbalancing method of instruction, or books of authority, read a remarkable passage in Jost, ix. 107, 110.

Jost's account of his own youth, and the lamentable state of the Jewish schools, in his Autobiography (Sippurim, iii. p. 141), is instructive.

It is impossible to over-estimate the influence of Mendelssohn in Europeanizing, if I may so say, and civilizing his German brethren, in throwing down the barriers behind which the Jews were self-exiled, or exiled by the scorn and hatred of mankind, and introducing them imperceptibly within the pale of society. No one, except perhaps a hard orthodox Rabbi, could refuse to admire, to love Mendelssohn, and that admiration and that love spread unconsciously over his race.

In the year 1780, the imperial avant-courier of the Revolution, Joseph the Second, ascended the throne. Among the first measures of this restless and universal reformer, was a measure for the amelioration of the condition of the Jews. In Vienna, they had been barely tolerated since their expulsion by Leopold the First. This monarch had a Jewish mistress, named Esther, who was shot crossing the bridge from Leopoldstadt to the capital. The crime was, most improbably, charged on the Jews, and the afflicted monarch revenged her death by the expulsion of her brethren from the city. But this exile was not lasting. Under Maria Theresa, the Jews were permitted to reside in Vienna, and enjoyed some sort of protection. They might exercise certain trades,[y] as money-changers, jewellers, manufacturers; they had full freedom of worship in their synagogues, but might not leave their houses during the hours of Divine service on Sundays and holidays. In the other provinces of the Empire they had lived unmolested, unless perhaps by some vexatious local regulations, or by popular commotions in the different cities. Joseph published his edict of toleration A.C. 1782, by which he opened to the Jews the schools and the uni-

[y] Jost, ix. 66.

versities of the Empire, and gave them the privilege of taking degrees as doctors in philosophy, medicine, and civil law. It enforced upon them the wise preliminary measure of establishing primary schools for their youth. It threw open the whole circle of trade to their speculations, permitted them to establish manufactories of all sorts, excepting gunpowder, and to attend fairs in towns where they were not domiciliated. In all the cities of the Empire it made them liable to a toleration-tax, and certain other contributions; but it gave them equal rights, and subjected them to the same laws, with the Christians. Some years after, they were made liable to military conscription; but, according to the established Austrian code, not being nobles, they could not rise above the rank of non-commissioned officers.

The publication of Dohm, 1781, upon the rights of the Jews as citizens, with many valuable suggestions on the elevation of their position and character, and especially their education, excited public attention. It reserved certain powers to the Rabbinical priesthood, particularly that of excommunication. Mendelssohn raised his voice loudly and fiercely against this last vestige of spiritual domination.

Frederick William the Second repealed to a great extent the barbarous edicts of Frederick the Great. The Jews were permitted to redeem for a certain sum the compulsory purchase of porcelain at the royal manufactory.

The French Revolution was advancing, that terrible epoch in which all that was wise and sound, as well as all that was antiquated and iniquitous in the old institutions of Europe, was shattered to the earth—but from which All-merciful Providence has educed much, and will no doubt, as from the tornado, the earthquake, and the volcanic eruption, educe much further eventual good. The Revolution found Jews in France: after their final expulsion, a few Portuguese fugitives had been permitted to take up their abode in Bordeaux and Bayonne. These passed at first under the name of New Christians. Letters patent of Louis XIII. recognise their civil existence. By degrees they were emboldened to marry without the intervention of the clergy, and to elude baptism. The clergy were too busily employed in the persecution of the dangerous Protestants to waste their intolerance on a few contemptible Jews. But the Jews were gradually accumulating wealth; and wealth, taxable wealth, was profitable, not dangerous, to the State. New letters patent (in 1623) recognised them as Jews. They had already built a synagogue; the Parliament of Bordeaux did not hesitate to reject the royal edict. The Jews paid 110,000 francs for their privilege. It was understood that the registration was to be renewed at the commencement of each* reign. The Jews of Bayonne, which included those of St. Jean de Luz, Biarritz, and other towns, at first wore the same disguise, and by degrees obtained the same privilege, as did also the Jews of Marseilles; letters patent in their favour were registered in the Parliament of Aix (1688). There were a certain number in the old Papal dominions in Avignon. The conquest of the city of Metz, and afterwards of Alsace, included some considerable communities under the dominion of France. There, especially in the Comtat de Venaisin, they had been exposed to the zeal of the clergy, who decoyed, or even stole, their children in order to baptize them. Many of them, however, attained to wealth, and indulged in great luxury. Within houses modest, humble, even rude in their outward appearance, lurked Oriental splendour; costly furniture, silken hangings, sumptuous plate, and all the show and reality of wealth. The Jews of this latter province presented a remarkable petition, in 1780, to the king in council. It displayed the almost intolerable grievances[1] under which their communities had especially suffered from the time of their remote establishment. The Parliament of Metz had burned many Jews on the old charge of murdering an infant at Glatigny on Easter-day, A.C. 1670. On the annexation of Alsace, Louis XIV. extended, for his own advantage, the privileges of free commerce, enjoyed by those of Bordeaux, Bayonne, Marseilles, to the Jews of Metz. They paid a head-tax of forty francs a family, afterwards compounded for by 2000 francs annually. This revenue had been granted, as in days of old, as a gift to the Duke of Brancas. The Jews complained of the burthen of the seignorial rights. Besides the royal patent of protection, for which they paid, the lords of the soil exacted a capitation-tax for the right of residence within their domains, from which not even the aged or infirm, nor children, nor the Rabbins and officers of the synagogue, were exempt. These privileges were not hereditary; they expired with the person of the bearer, and for each child a special patent was to be purchased. They complained likewise of the restrictions on their commerce, and of the activity of the clergy, who seduced their children at a very tender age to submit to baptism. They proposed, with great justice, that no abjuration of Judaism should be permitted under twelve

---

[1] See on these grievances, and the acts of Louis XIV., Bédarride, pp. 377 et seqq., as also on the condition of the Jews of Lorraine.

years of age. In later days an appeal to the equity of Louis the Sixteenth was not in vain—the capitation-tax was abolished in 1784; and in 1788, a commission was appointed, with the wise and good Malesherbes[a] at its head, to devise means for remodelling on principles of justice all laws relating to the Jews. The celebrated Abbé Grégoire gained the prize for a dissertation, which was received with great applause, on the means of working the regeneration of the Jews. But the revolutionary tribunals were more rapid in their movements than the slow justice of the sovereign. In 1790, the Jews, who had watched their opportunity, sent in petitions from various quarters, claiming equal rights as citizens. The measure was not passed without considerable discussion; but Mirabeau and Rabaut St. Etienne declared themselves their advocates, and the Jews were recognised as free citizens of the great republic.[b]

A parallel has often been instituted between Cromwell and Bonaparte; it is a curious coincidence that both should have been engaged in designs for the advantage of the Jews. In the year 1806, while Bonaparte was distributing to his followers the kingdoms of Europe, and consolidating the superiority of France over the whole Continent, the world heard with amazement, almost bordering on ridicule, that he had summoned a grand Sanhedrin of the Jews to assemble at Paris. We are more inclined to look for motives of policy in the acts of Napoleon, than of vanity

---

[a] Malesherbes first abolished the toll which the Jews paid, like animals, at the gates of the cities, especially in Alsace and the neighbouring provinces. Depinart has given the tariff paid at Château-neuf-sur-Loire:—

For a Jew . . . . . 12 deniers
For a Jewess with child . 9 „
For an ordinary Jewess . 6 „
For a dead Jew . . . . 5 sous
For a dead Jewess . . . 30 deniers.
(Quoted by Bédarride, p. 555.)

[b] 27 Sept., 1791, and 30 Nov. Hist. Parlementaire, ii. 457.

or philanthropy; nor does it seem unlikely that in this singular transaction he contemplated remotely, if not immediately, both commercial and military objects. He might hope to turn to his own advantage, by a cheap sacrifice to the national vanity, the wide-extended and rapid correspondence of the Jews throughout the world, which notoriously outstripped his own couriers; and the secret ramifications of their trade, which not only commanded the supply of the precious metals, but much of the internal traffic of Europe, and probably made great inroads on his Continental system. At all events, in every quarter of Europe, the Jews would be invaluable auxiliaries of a commissariat; and as the reconstruction of the kingdom of Poland might at any time enter into his political system, their aid might not be unworthy of consideration. It must, however, be acknowledged, that the twelve questions submitted first to the deputation of the Jews, and confirmed by the Sanhedrin, seem to refer to the Jews strictly as subjects and citizens of the empire. They were, briefly, as follows: — I. Is polygamy allowed among the Jews? II. Is divorce recognised by the Jewish law? III. Can Jews intermarry with Christians? IV. Will the French people be esteemed by the Jews as strangers or as brethren? V. In what relation, according to the Jewish law, would the Jews stand towards the French? VI. Do Jews born in France consider it their native country? Are they bound to obey the laws and customs of the land? VII. Who elect the Rabbins? VIII. What are the legal powers of the Rabbins? IX. Are the election and authority of the Rabbins grounded on law or custom? X. Is there any kind of business in which the Jews may not be engaged? XI. Is usury to their brethren forbidden by the Law? XII. Is it permitted or forbidden to practise usury with strangers? The answers of the deputies were clear and precise.[c] They were introduced by some general maxims, skilfully adapted to the character or the ruling power, and to that of the French nation. They declared that their religion commanded them to acknowledge the supremacy of the law enacted by sovereigns in all civil and political affairs. If their religious code, or its interpretation, contained any civil or political regulations inconsistent with the Code of France, they would be overruled, as it was the primary duty to acknowledge and to obey the law of the sovereign. They further declared that France was their country, all Frenchmen their brothers. "This glorious title, so exalting to us in our own estimation, is the true guarantee for our stedfast endeavours to deserve it. Our relations to Christians are the same as to Jews; the only distinction is, that each should be permitted to worship the Supreme Being in his own way." As the special answers tend to elucidate the opinions of the more enlightened Jews, they are subjoined, with as much conciseness as possible, though I suspect that they are not universally recognised as the authoritative sentence of the nation.[d] I. Polygamy is forbidden,

---

[c] The President of the Sanhedrin's first deputation was Abraham Furtado, of Bordeaux; the imperial commissioners, MM. Molé, Portalis the younger, and Pasquier. The deputation met July 26, 1806. The Sanhedrin met Feb. 8, 1807.

[d] See the curious scene described by the elder Disraeli (Genius of Judaism) p. 74—the dispute between the freethinker and the orthodox Jew whether the Law should be called the Law of God or the Law of Moses. Mr. Disraeli's conclusion is somewhat magniloquent: "It is not surprising that the Parisian Sanhedrin was not only a mockery but a failure of the mocker. Even despotism shrinks into the weakness of infancy when Heaven itself seems to place an impassable barrier to its design; and it encounters minds inscrutable as the laws which govern

according to a decree of the Synod of Worms, in 1030. II. Divorce is allowed, but in this respect the Jews recognise the authority of the civil law of the land in which they live. III. Intermarriages with Christians are not forbidden, though difficulties arise from the different forms of marriage. IV. The Jews of France recognise in the fullest sense the French people as their brethren. V. The relation of the Jew to the Frenchman is the same as of Jew to Jew. The only distinction is in their religion. VI. The Jews acknowledged France as their country when oppressed,—how much more must they when admitted to civil rights! VII. The election of the Rabbins is neither defined nor uniform. It usually rests with the heads of each family in the community. VIII. The Rabbins have no judicial power; the Sanhedrin is the only legal tribunal. The Jews of France and Italy being subject to the equal laws of the land, whatever power they might otherwise exercise is annulled. IX. The election and powers of the Rabbins rest solely on usage. X. All business is permitted to the Jews. The Talmud enjoins that every Jew be taught some trade. XI., XII. The Mosaic institute forbids unlawful interest; but this was the law of an agricultural people. The Talmud allows legal interest to be taken from brethren and strangers; it forbids usury.

There was a preparatory assemblage of Jewish Deputies selected from the different provinces in proportion to the Jewish population in each: A. Furtado of Bordeaux was President of that assembly. In 1807 the

---

them." With due respect, I do not see the failure. Napoleon wished to conciliate the Jews (for their religious opi- alone be cared not a jot); the Jews obtained what they wanted, the right of citizenship.

Sanhedrin was formally assembled, according to a plan then proposed for the regular organization of the Jews throughout the empire. Every 2000 Jews were to form a synagogue and a consistory, of one head and two inferior Rabbins, with three householders of the town where the consistory was held. The consistory chose twenty-five Notables, above thirty years old, for their council. Bankrupts and usurers were excluded; the consistory was to watch over the conduct of the Rabbins; the central consistory of Paris was to be a Supreme Tribunal, with the power of appointing or deposing the Rabbins; the Rabbins were to publish the decrees of the Sanhedrin, to preach obedience to the laws, to urge their people to enter into the military service; to pray in the synagogues for the Imperial House! The Sanhedrin, assembled in this manner, generally ratified the scheme of the Deputies. The Imperial edict confirmed the whole system of organization, though the triumph of the Jews was in some degree damped by an ordinance, aimed chiefly at those of the Rhenish provinces. It interdicted the Jews from lending money to minors without consent of their guardians, to wives without consent of their husbands, to soldiers without consent of their officers. It annulled all bills for which "value received" could not be proved. All Jews engaged in commerce were obliged to take out a patent, all strangers to invest some property in land and agriculture. The general effect of these measures was shown in a return made in 1808. It reported that there were 80,000 Jews in the dominion of France, 1232 landed proprietors, not reckoning the owners of houses, 797 military, 2360 artizans, 250 manufacturers.

The extension of the French kingdoms and the erection of tributary kingdoms were highly beneficial to the Jews;

in Italy, in Holland, in the kingdom of Westphalia, the old barbarous restrictions fell away, and the Jew became a citizen with all the rights and duties of the order. The laws of France relating to the Jews have remained unaltered, excepting that the Law of the Restoration, which enacted that the teachers of Christianity alone should be salaried by the State, was modified at the accession of Louis Philippe. Since that period the Rabbins have received a stipend from the State. In Italy, excepting in the Tuscan dominions, they have become again subject to the ancient regulations. In Germany, some hostility is yet lurking in the popular feeling, not so much from religious animosity, as from commercial jealousy, in the great trading towns, Hamburg, Bremen, Lubeck, and particularly Frankfort, where they are still liable to an oppressive tax for the right of residence. Nor did the ancient nobility behold, without sentiments of natural indignation, their proud patrimonial estates falling, during the great political changes, into the hands of the more prosperous Israelites. Nevertheless, the condition of the Jews, both political and intellectual, has been rapidly improving. Before the fall of Napoleon, besides many of the smaller states, the Grand Duke of Baden in 1809, the King of Prussia in 1812, the Duke of Mecklenburg Schwerin in 1812, the King of Bavaria in 1813, issued ordinances, admitting the Jews to civil rights, exempting them from particular imposts, and opening to them all trades and professions. The Act for the federative constitution of Germany, passed at the Congress of Vienna in 1815, pledges the Diet to turn its attention to the amelioration of the civil state of the Jews throughout the empire. The King of Prussia had, before this, given security that he would nobly redeem his pledge; he had long paid great attention to the encouragement of education among the Jews; and in his rapidly improving dominions, the Israelites are said to be by no means the last in the career of advancement. Nor has his benevolence been wasted on an ungrateful race; they are reported to be attached, with patriotic zeal, to their native land; many Jews are stated to have fallen in the Prussian ranks at Waterloo. During the year 1828, while the States of Wirtemberg were discussing a Bill for the extension of civil rights to the Jews, the populace of Stuttgard surrounded the Hall of Assembly with fierce outcries, " Down with the Jews! Down with the friends of the Jews!" The States maintained their dignity, and, unmoved, proceeded to the ratification of the obnoxious edict.

Russia, it has been said, if we take the low estimate, which I am altogether disinclined to do, of four millions for the whole Jewish population in the world, contains half the descendants of Abraham. In the earlier period of her empire, dating that empire from Peter the Great, before her wider southern conquests and the Polish annexations, she still maintained her stern inhospitality. In Muscovy Proper, by law, no Jew could reside within the frontiers. Under Peter the Great a few stole in unobserved and unmolested. They were expelled by an Ukase of the Empress Elizabeth, A.C. 1795, for a crime unpardonable by a Russian autocrat. They had, by letters of change, secured the property of certain exiles to Siberia and foreign countries; and invested, out of Russia, the savings of foreigners employed in the Russian service. In later years, the policy of the Russian Government seems to have been to endeavour to overthrow the Rabbinical authority, and to relieve the crowded Polish provinces by transferring the Jews to less densely peopled parts of their dominions, where, it was hoped, they might be induced or compelled to become an agricultural race. An Ukase of the Emperor Alexander, in 1803-4, prohibited the practice of small trades to the Jews of Poland, and proposed to transport numbers of them to agricultural settlements. He transferred, likewise, the management of the revenue of the communities, from the Rabbins, who were accused of malversation, to the Elders. A decree of the Emperor Nicholas appears to be aimed partly at the Rabbins, who are to be immediately excluded by the police from any town they may enter, and at the petty traffickers, who are entirely prohibited in the Russian dominions; though the higher order of merchants, such as billbrokers and contractors, are admitted, on receiving an express permission from the government: artizans and handicraftsmen are encouraged, though they are subject to rigorous police regulations, and must be attached to some guild or fraternity. They cannot move without a passport. The important Ukase of 1835 is the charter, we must not say of their liberties, but limits the oppression to which the Jews were formerly liable, and gives them a defined state and position in the Russian Empire.

It only remains to give the best estimate I can obtain of the number of the Jews now dispersed throughout the four quarters of the world. Such statements must of necessity be extremely loose and imperfect. Even in Europe it would be difficult to approximate closely to the truth; how much more so in Africa and Asia, where our conclusions depend on no statistic returns, and where the habits of the people are probably less stationary!

It is usually calculated that there exist between four

and five millions [a] of this people, descended in a direct line from, and maintaining the same laws with, their forefathers, who, above 3000 years ago, retreated from Egypt under the guidance of their inspired lawgiver.[f]

In Africa we know little more of their numbers than that they are found along the whole coast, from Morocco to Egypt; they travel with the caravans into the interior; nor is there probably a region undiscovered by Christian enterprise which has not been visited by the Jewish trafficker. In Morocco they are said to be held in low estimation, and to be treated with great indignity by the Moors. That empire has about 540,000.[g]

In Egypt, 150 families alone inhabit that great city, Alexandria, which has so often flowed with torrents of Jewish blood, and where, in the splendid days of the Macedonian city, their still-recruited wealth excited the rapacious jealousy of the hostile populace or oppressive government.[h]

In Cairo, the number of Jews is stated at 2000, including, it appears, sixty Karaïte families.

The Felashas, or Jewish tribe named by Bruce, inhabit the borders of Abyssinia; and it is probable that in that

---

[a] Monsieur Rénan (Langues Semitiques, p. 43) sets down the Jews scattered over the whole world at four millions. Beldarride (himself a Jew) gives six or seven millions (Preface, p. v.). I am assured, on good authority, that there cannot be less than three millions in Europe. I should think this a low statement.

[f] I have made inquiries in many quarters, among some of our best-informed Jews, yet have been able to obtain very few satisfactory results. It does not appear that they themselves keep any regular statistics: the only certain statements are from the official population returns in some of the kingdoms of Europe.

[g] Ersch und Grüber, p. 234. Compare also this page on their occupation and condition.

[h] In the Weimar Statement, quoted in my first edition, the Jews of Africa stand as follows:—Morocco and Fez, 300,000; Tunis, 130,000; Algiers, 30,000; Gabes or Ilabesh, 20,000; Tripoli, 12,000; Egypt, 12,000. Total, 504,000.

singular kingdom many Jews either dwell or make their periodical visits.[1] In Asia the Jews are still found in considerable numbers on the verge of the continent; in China, they are now found in one city alone, and possess only one synagogue.[a] On the coast of Malabar, in Cochin, two distinct races, called black and white Jews, were visited by Dr. Buchanan.[m] The traditions of the latter averred that they had found their way to that region after the fall of Jerusalem; but the date they assigned for their migration singularly coincided with that of a persecution in Persia, about A.C. 508, from whence, most likely, they found their way to India. The origin of the black Jews is more obscure: it is not impossible that they may have been converts made by the more civilized

---

[1] The Felashas have been recently visited by a pious missionary, M. Stern. See his account, his simpler account, reprinted from the *Jewish Intelligencer* by the London Missionary Society (for in his later volume, 'Wanderings among the Felashas in Abyssinia,' he has been unfortunately seized with the ambition of fine writing). His earlier account contains some curious particulars, but is silent on many points on which we should most desire knowledge. According to M. Stern, the Felashas are miserably priest-ridden; and among the priests were a number of Jewish monks, less like to the Essenes and Therapeutæ of old, than to the Faquirs of India, and to the most fanatic Christian ascetics of the East. The fulfilment of the Levitical Law, of which they were proud, seemed to be their highest notion of religion. They boasted that they had Moses and David; but, if I understand right, their Scriptures were in the Ethiopic language and character. They had no Hebrew writings. Of their numbers M. Stern appears to have formed no estimate. On that subject, as on many others of interest, his expressions are vague and unsatisfactory. See Account of a Missionary Visit to the Felashas, London, 1861; Wanderings among the Felashas of Abyssinia, by the Rev. H. A. Stern, London, 1862.

[a] "Kai-fung, the capital of the latter province [Hoo-nan], and famous to Europeans by being the city in which the small and only tribe of Jews in China have their synagogue and carry out their religious observances." Brine, The Taeping Rebellion in China (London, 1862), p. 184.

[m] Buchanan's Researches. I was promised further information on this subject, but it never reached me.

whites, or, more probably, are descendants of black slaves. The Malabar Jews were about one thousand; they possessed a copy of the Old Testament. Many are found in other parts of the East Indies.

In Bokhara reside two thousand families of Jews; in Balkh, 150.

In Persia they have deeply partaken of the desolation which has fallen on the fair provinces of that land; their numbers were variously stated to Mr. Wolff at 2974 and 3590 families. Their chief communities are at Shiraz and Ispahan, Kashaan and Yazd. They are subject to the heaviest exactions, and to the capricious despotism of the governors. "I have travelled far," said a Jew to Mr. Wolff; "the Jews are everywhere princes, in comparison with those in the land of Persia. Heavy is our captivity, heavy is our burthen, heavy is our slavery; anxiously we wait for redemption."

In Mesopotamia and Assyria, the ancient seats of the Babylonian Jews are still occupied by 5270 families, exclusive of those in Bagdad and Bassora. The latter are described as a fine race, both in form and intellect; in the provinces they are broken in mind and body by the heavy exactions of the pashas, and by long ages of sluggish ignorance. At Bagdad the ancient title of Prince of the Captivity, so long, according to the accounts of the Jews, entirely suppressed, was borne by an ancient Jew named Isaac. He paid dear for his honour; he was suddenly summoned to Constantinople and imprisoned.

At Damascus there are seven synagogues and four colleges.

In Arabia, whether not entirely expelled by Mohammed or having returned to their ancient dwellings in later periods, the Beni-Khaibar still retain their Jewish descent and faith. In Yemen reside 2658 families, 18,000 souls.

In Palestine, of late years, the Israelites have greatly increased; it is said, but I am inclined to doubt the numbers, that 10,000 inhabit Safet and Jerusalem. They are partly Karaites; some very pathetic hymns of this interesting Israelitish race have been published in the Journals of Mr. Wolff, which must have a singularly affecting sound when heard from children of Israel, bewailing, upon the very ruins of Jerusalem, the fallen city, and the suffering people.[n]

In the Turkish dominions, not including the Barbary States, the Israelites are calculated at 800,000.[o] In Asia Minor they are numerous, in general unenlightened, rapacious, warred on, and at war with mankind.

---

[n] The accuracy of the following statement of the Jewish population of Palestine and Syria may be relied on :—Jerusalem, 5,700; Safed, 2,100; Tiberias. 1,514; Hebron, 400; Jaffa, 400; Saida, 150; St. Jean d'Acre, 120; Kharfa, 100; Schafamer, 60; Peykin, 50; Nablous, 40; Ramah, 5. Total, 10,689.

Damascus, 5,000; Beyrout, 180; Deir el Kamar, 100; Charbera, 100; Tripolis, 40. Total, 5,420. Syria and Palestine, 16,059.

From 'The Jews in the East,' by Dr. Frankl (translated by J. R. Beaton), vol. ii. p. 20.

Dr. Frankl, himself a Jew, and a very liberal one, was employed by a devout lady of Vienna to found an educational institution for the Jews of Jerusalem. He gives a most deplorable account of their state. They are divided into sects, and sects of sects, hating each other with unmitigated cordiality. The chief divisions are the Sephardim (the Spanish), the Ashkonasim, the Khasin (Germans and Poles). All the munificent charities founded by Mr. Cohen, Sir M. Montefiore, the Rothschilds, except one hospital, have sunk into decay and utter uselessness. The poor and indolent Jews, the dregs of the people, are drained from Europe, Asia, and indeed from all parts, to live in Judæa upon the alms of the most wealthy and most bountiful people in the world. This is a kind of Poor-law fund paid by the rich and flourishing houses of the race, with all the evil effects of a Poor-law, and none of its benefits. For these lavish donations are intercepted and swallowed up by the Rabbins and Priests, who live in idleness and luxury, while the poor starve in idleness and misery.

[o] This number I should think over rated.

In Constantinople they are described as the most fierce and fanatical race which inhabit the city: hated by and hating the Greeks with the unmitigated animosity of ages, they lend themselves to every atrocity for which the government may demand unrelenting executioners. They were employed in the barbarous murder and maltreatment of the body of the Patriarch; on the other hand, the old rumours of their crucifying Christian children are still revived: the body of a youth was found pierced with many wounds; the murder was, with one voice, charged upon the Jews. Their numbers are stated at 40,000.

At Adrianople reside eight hundred families, with thirteen synagogues.

In Salonichi, 30,000 possess thirty synagogues;[p] and in this city, the ancient Thessalonica, the most learned of the Eastern Rabbins are reported to teach in their schools, with great diligence, the old Talmudic learning.

In the Crimea the Karaites still possess their wild and picturesque mountain-fortress, so beautifully described by Dr. Clarke, with its cemetery reposing under its ancient and peaceful grove, and retain the simple manners of an industrious and blameless people, who are proverbial elsewhere, as in this settlement, for their honesty. Their numbers amount to about 1200.[q]

In the Russian Asiatic dominions, about Caucasus and in Georgia, their numbers are considerable. In Georgia some of them are serfs attached to the soil; some,

---

[p] Luzzato, according to Camel, reckons 80,000 in Adrianople and Salonichi. Ersch und Grüber, p. 200. The other towns which they inhabit are recorded in the same page.

[q] Among the most interesting passages in Dr. Wolff's Journal is the account of his intercourse with the Karaites in the Crimea. Read their two simple and striking hymns (iii. p. 148), inferior, however, to those of the Karaites in Jerusalem, i. 263.

among the wild tribes about Caucasus, are bold and marauding horsemen, like their Tartar compatriots.

But the ancient kingdom of Poland, with the adjacent provinces of Moravia, Moldavia, and Wallachia, is still the great seat of the modern Jewish population.[1] Three millions have been stated to exist in these regions; but no doubt this is a great exaggeration. In Poland they still to a great extent form the intermediate class between the haughty nobles and the miserable agricultural villains of that kingdom. The rapid increase of their population, beyond all possible maintenance by trade, embarrasses the government. They cannot ascend or descend; they may not become possessors, they are averse to becoming cultivators, of the soil; they swarm in all the towns. In some districts, as in Volhynia, they were described by Bishop James as a fine race, with the lively, expressive eye of the Jew, and forms, though not robust, active and well-proportioned. Of late years much attention, under the sanction of the government, has been paid to their education, and a great institution established for this purpose at Warsaw. The last accounts in Ersch und Grüber for the year 1838 gave for Poland 453,646 (36,390 in Warsaw); for the whole Russian dominions altogether, 1,507,995 souls.[2] A later statement, which I owe to the kindness of Mr. Alderman Salomons, gives for Russia 1,250,000; for Austria 1,049,871; Poland, 600,000.[3]

The number of Jews in the Austrian dominions is estimated, not including Poland, at 650,000; in Prussia 242,000; in the rest of Germany, by conjecture,

---

[1] See the account of the Polish Jews, Jost, ix. 167.
[2] Ersch und Grüber, p. 139.
[3] It would seem, as far as I can conjecture, that the Polish Jews are not comprehended in the Russian, but are in the Austrian, calculations.

108,000. The Emperor of Austria afforded to Europe, some years ago, the novel sight of a Jew created a Baron, and invested with a patent of nobility.

In Denmark and Sweden the Jews are in considerable numbers; those resident in Copenhagen were stated, in 1819, at 1491. They enjoy freedom of trade and the protection of the government. In Sweden King Charles John gave a free constitution to the Jews in the four cities which they chiefly inhabited—Stockholm, Gothenburg, Norköping, and Carlscrona—but the States would not accept it. The king, however, obliged to yield in some points, maintained his authority.* They are not permitted to enter into Norway. A law of Christian VIII. in Denmark was in like manner rejected by the States; but the Jews are protected by the government.

The kingdom of Belgium contains by the last census only 1843. In Holland the best authenticated returns state the numbers at no less than about 65,000.

In France the Israelites were reckoned in 1829 at about 40,000 or 50,000. By the last accounts, they are thought to be underrated at 100,000. Many Jews have attained to the highest political dignities: M. Crémieux was a member of the Provisional Government; M. Fould is now the finance minister, as in the older days of France and of Spain, to the Emperor Louis Napoleon.

In Spain, the iron edict of Ferdinand and Isabella still excludes the Israelite. At the extremity of the land, in Gibraltar, 3000 or 4000 are found under the equitable protection of Great Britain. Yet there are Jews, or reputed Jews, in the highest ranks and offices.

In Portugal they have been tolerated since the time

---

* Ersch und Grüber, p. 140.

of King John VI., who remunerated their services in introducing large cargoes of corn during a famine, by the recognition of their right to inhabit Lisbon.[r]

In Italy their numbers are considerable.[s] It is said that many took refuge in Tuscany from what was the sterner government of Sardinia; where, under the French dominion, among a Jewish population of 5543, there were 182 landed proprietors, 402 children attended the public schools: 7000 is given as their number in the Austrian territories in Italy.

In Great Britain the number of Jews was variously stated at from 12,000 to 25,000.[s] They may now fairly be reckoned at 30,000 in England; but this is uncertain, as no accurate register is kept. In 1829 I wrote thus, "They are entitled to every privilege of British subjects, except certain corporate offices and seats in Parliament, from which they are excluded by the Act which requires an oath to be taken on the faith of a Christian. They cannot vote for Members of Parliament, at least might be disqualified from so doing by the form of the Oath of Abjuration; and they are excluded from the higher branches of the learned pro-

---

[r] Europe:—In Russia and Poland, 658,809; Austria, 453,524; European Turkey, 321,000; States of the German Confederation, 138,000; Prussia, 134,000; Netherlands, 80,000; France, 60,000; Italy, 36,000; Great Britain, 12,000; Cracow, 7,900; Ionian Isles, 7,000; Denmark, 6,000; Switzerland, 1,970; Sweden, 450. Total number of Jews in Europe, 1,818,053; or a proportion of an 113th part of the population, calculated at 227 millions.—*Weimar Statement*. (I retain this note from the older edition.)

[s] I was informed, in 1829, on the authority of a very intelligent Italian, that the number of Jews in Italy is greatly underrated. Some suppose that they amount to near 100,000. In the Austrian dominions they are extremely numerous. In the district of Mantua alone, under the former kingdom of Italy, they were reckoned at 5,000. In Parma and Modena, 7,000. In Venice, Tuscany, and the Papal States, they abound.

[s] Since the first edition of this work, their number has been stated in Parliament at near 30,000.

fessions by the same cause, and probably by restrictions on education; from the lower chiefly by popular opinion and their own habits. In the City of London they are prevented by municipal regulations from taking out their freedom—a restriction which subjects them to great occasional embarrassment and vexation, as no one can legally follow a retail trade, without having previously gone through this ceremony."

Since that time (1829) all the high offices of the City of London have been filled by Jews. A Jew, Mr. Salomons, has been Lord Mayor: it may be said that few have maintained the office with greater dignity, liberality, or popularity. The act of the City of London in electing a Jew, Baron Rothschild, as one of its Members of Parliament, eventually broke down the one remaining barrier which insulated the Jews from the other subjects of the realm. Notwithstanding the opposition of several years, during which the House of Lords stedfastly adhered to the principle of exclusion, the Bill in their favour at length passed; and the oath, the great obstacle, was modified so as to admit conscientious Jews to the Legislature. There are now four Jewish Members of Parliament.

Perhaps the most remarkable fact in the history of modern Judaism is the extension of the Jews in the United States of America. Writing in 1829, I stated, on the best authority then attainable, their numbers at 6000. They are now reckoned at 75,000. In New York alone there are thirteen large synagogues. The few in the former dominions of Spain and Portugal are descendants of those who, under the assumed name of Christians, fled from the Inquisition. In Surinam, a prosperous community is settled under the protection of the Dutch;

they were originally established at Cayenne; there are some in Jamaica. There are now considerable numbers in our Australian colonies. A late account mentions Jews in the new colony of Vancouver's Island.

Such, according to the best authorities to which we have access, is the number and distribution of the children of Israel; they are still found in every quarter of the world, under every climate, in every region, under every form of government, wearing the indelible national stamp on their features, united by the close moral affinity of habits and feelings, and, at least the mass of the community, treasuring in their hearts the same reliance on their national privileges, the same trust in the promises of their God, the same conscientious attachment to the institutions of their fathers.

History, which is the record of the Past, has now discharged its office; it presumes not to raise the mysterious veil which the Almighty has spread over the Future. The destinies of this wonderful people, as of all mankind, are in the hands of the All-wise Ruler of the Universe: His decrees will be accomplished; his truth, his goodness, and his wisdom vindicated. This, however, we may venture to assert, that true religion will advance with the dissemination of knowledge. I cannot but think that the doom of the Talmud, with that of much of our mediæval legend, is pronounced. The more enlightened the Jew becomes, the less credible will it appear that the Universal Father intended an exclusive religion, confined to one family among the race of man, to be permanent; the more evident that the faith which embraces the whole human race within the sphere of its benevolence, is alone adapted to a more advanced and civilized age. On the other hand, Christianity, to work any change on the hereditary religious pride of the Jew, on his inflexible confidence in his inalienable privileges, must put off the hostile and repulsive aspect which it has too long worn; it must show itself as the faith of reason, of universal peace and good-will to man, and thus, unanswerably, prove its descent from the All-wise and All-merciful Father.[b]

---

[b] I find from Dr. Frankl's book that there is an opinion widely spread among the more enlightened Jews, that Christianity was the publication of true religion among the Gentiles, and therefore but an expanded Judaism. This notion probably confines true religion to the belief in the Divine Unity, and in the universal principles of morality. But of the peculiar doctrines of Christianity it takes no note. It may perhaps be admitted as groundwork for a treaty of amity and mutual respect, but not as a complete and lasting harmony of the two religions.

BOOK XXX.

Survey of Influence of the Jews on Philosophy, Poetry, History, &c.

THE History of the Jews will be fitly closed by a brief and rapid view of the services (the intellectual services, exclusive of those connected with the industry and commerce of the world) rendered to mankind by this remarkable race during the ages which they have passed through, alone, unmingled with the other families of mankind—services either direct and manifest, or through remoter influences more difficult to trace in their effects on the knowledge, civilization, and humanity of the world.

The religious obligations of mankind to the Jews it is impossible to appreciate in all their fulness. Up to a certain time they are the sole designated conservators of the great primary truths of religion, the Unity of the Godhead, and that Godhead an ever-present, overruling Providence, present not only as the One Power which originated and the One Force which sustains with conscious goodness and wisdom the whole universe, but also, in some mysterious way, as the Supreme Will, exercising its dominion over the (inexplicably but unquestionably) free will of man. The Jews are the religious parents, in a certain sense, both of Christianity and Mohammedanism. Mohammedanism, it has been justly said, is but a republication of Judaism, with all its stern Monotheism hardened into a rigid Predestinarianism, and with the Lawgiver and the Prophets centered, and as it were condensed, in Mohammed and his successors. To the Christian the Jews are the appointed conservators, not only of their sublime Monotheism, but guardians of the oracles of that One God, oracles predictive of a nobler, purer, more comprehensive faith, significant of the Christ to come; oracles which they have, fatally for themselves, interpreted in a more narrow and unspiritual sense. Their sacred Scriptures, therefore, in what we believe to be their true scope, became the common property of mankind, at least of Christianized mankind, subordinate to, or rather preparatory for, the Christian New Testament.

But the Hebrew sacred books, as interpreted by the Jews, withdrew with the Jews into their total isolation from the rest of mankind. The language itself kept them in almost complete seclusion. Before Jerome, very few of the Christian writers—still fewer after Jerome— had any knowledge of Hebrew. The Greek Version of the LXX. was in general the Old Testament of the early Christian Church. But around the Hebrew Books, as has appeared, had grown up a mass of tradition, according to the common view and according to the teaching of the Jewish schools coeval with, and of equal authority with the Law itself. The study of this tradition, and its adaptation to the sacred books, furnished full scope for the restless ingenuity, and occupation for the indefatigable activity, of the Jewish mind. An authorised interpretation fenced round the original Law. Even the Masora, the insertion of the vowel points and of the other grammatical signs, as well as the Targums or commentaries on the sacred writings, was part of this system of interpretation. By degrees arose the Mischna; upon the Mischna was accumulated the Gemara; the Jerusalem and the Babylonian Talmud comprehended the vast stores of Jewish erudition. And the Mischna and the Talmud were to the Jew what the Roman law was to the lawyers, the canons of Councils, the decrees of Popes, the whole authorised theology of the Church, to the clergy of Christendom.*

But to the world at large, to the Pagan and Christian world, or to the half-Pagan and half-Christian world of Alexandria, all this Rabbinical theology was utterly unknown and unapproachable. Neither Gentile nor Christian student found his way into the schools of Tiberias, Nahardea, Sura, or Pumbeditha. Even the Syrian Christians, speaking a cognate dialect, seem to have stood altogether aloof from the Jews and their seats of learning. The estrangement, of course, had been gradual. The Judaizing Christians of the earlier ages had kept up some communication between the synagogue and the rapidly Christianizing world, at least in usages and tone of thought. The ceremonial law was among them but slowly abrogated; and those who had been bred in obedience to the ceremonial law, would not renounce at once all allegiance, and break off all intercourse with the authorised interpreters of the Law. The Judaizing Christians split up, it appears, into countless sects, of which it is difficult, and has taxed the

---

* I omit all notice of the countless Jewish commentators on the Old Testament, valuable as many of them are.

Nothing can be more uninteresting—if I may judge by myself, so uninstructive—as a long, barren list of authors, and of their works. The bibliography, therefore, of Jewish literature I would leave to Wolff, Bartolocci, De Rossi; to the Spanish writers, De Castro and other expounders of Rabbinical learning. (For the writers on geography, see the elaborate Essay of Dr. Zunz in the Supplement to Asher's Benjamin of Tudela.)

ingenuity of the most profound Christian scholars of our day, to trace the shadowy differences. Some of the Gnostic sects blended Judaism with Christianity, and their Judaism betrays their lingering intimacy with the teaching of the Jewish schools. In some regions, in parts of Arabia and of Africa, the divorce between Judaism and Christianity was less complete. Jewish apocryphal books,[b] entirely lost in Asia, have been recovered in the dialect of Abyssinia. At a later period, Hebrew tradition (no doubt through the Arabian Jews) found its way, to a remarkable extent, into the Koran.[c]

In general, however, Rabbinical literature, excepting in the few indistinct glimpses obtained by Jerome, was for a long period a sealed volume to the Christian mind. And all this vast literature to the Jew himself was fatal to freedom and originality of thought, to science properly so called, to all invention, to all bold inquiry. It was theological, if with some of the deep devotion and some of the sublimity of theology, with its fetters riveted even more closely than any system belonging to a less insulated people, a people more in contact with the rest of mankind, more inevitably swept forward by the stream of progress, could ever be. Within its circle man might move with some freedom; without that circle he dared not venture a single step. He was the galley slave of the most rigid orthodoxy. No Church authority, no Articles of the narrowest sect have been more jealous, more imperious, more vigilant, than the perpetual dictatorship of the Rabbins. The sacerdotalism of the Middle Ages was not more tyrannous and intolerant than were the schools of Jewish learning. They had their anathemas, their excommunications, of course, more

---

[b] The Book of Enoch, the Ascensio Isaiæ.
[c] Geiger, Was hat Mohammed aus dem Judenthum genommen?

awful, more terrible, to the member of a small community than the ban of Pope or Council; at times they claimed, and even exercised, the right of capital punishment over the obstinate heretic. Within its sphere the Rabbinical lore is infinitely copious and various; its Scholasticism is as acute and subtle, as much delighting in its peculiar subtlety as that of Bradwardine or Duns Scotus; its casuistry is as ingenious, as wiredrawn, as perplexing, and as perilously tampering with morals, as that of Suarez or Del Soto. Not that there were any determinate creeds or articles of belief.[4] These were of a later period, such as the articles drawn up by Maimonides. But it was the awful and unlimited and admitted authority of the Rabbins which, notwithstanding certain differences which at times arrayed master against master, school against school, held the Jews of all countries in passive, and, if it may be said, eager, unstruggling submission. Of the purity of each man's faith, the Rabbins, the authoritative expounders of the Law, the guardians of the hallowed traditions, were the supreme, irrefragable judges.

Yet even under the most revered and time-hallowed tyranny, under the severest and most watchful sacerdotal despotism, the uncontrollable human mind will strive to make a way to its emancipation. In Judaism it was not by impugning (excepting in the case of the Karaïtes) or lowering this uncontested authority,

---

[4] Delitzsch may be right in his statement:—" Die Juden haben seit ihre Zerstreuung nie Synagogale von der Nation bestätigte und angenommene Bekenntnisschriften gehabt. . . . Die Talmude haben deshalb gar keine dogmatische Einheit; selbst die gesetzwissenschaftlichen Resultate sind individuell und provisorisch gültig, die Synagoge hat ihnen als durch eine Sanction des Ansehn anerkannter, allgemeingültigen Decretalen gegeben." Yet the Rabbinical system was sternly and severely orthodox, impatient of heretical teaching. Zur Geschichte der Jüdischen Poesie, Vorrede, p. 9.

that it strove for freedom. The philosophic Cabala aspired to be a more sublime and transcendental Rabbinism. It was a mystery not exclusive of, but above their more common mysteries; a secret more profound than their profoundest secrets. It claimed the same guarantee of antiquity, of revelation, of tradition; it was the true, occult, to few intelligible, sense of the sacred writings and of the sayings of the most renowned Wise Men; the inward interpretation of the genuine interpretation of the Law and the Prophets. Men went on; they advanced, they rose from the most full and perfect study of the Talmuds to the higher doctrines, to the more divine contemplations of the Cabala. And the Zohar was the Book of the Cabala which soared almost above the comprehension of the wisest.

The mysterious Cabala appears at length to have disclosed its secrets to the general reader. The Dissertation of M. Ad. Franck of Paris,* comprehensive, yet not too minute, profound, yet perfectly clear, has determined, on grounds to which (if I may do so without presumption) I subscribe in almost every respect, its age, its origin, its doctrines, and its influence. In its traditional, no doubt unwritten form, the Cabala, at least a Cabala, ascends to a very early date, the Captivity; in its proper and more mature form, it belongs to the first century, and reaches down to the end of the seventh century of our era. The 'Sepher Yetzira,' the Book of Creation,' which boasts itself to be derived from Moses, from Abraham, if not from Adam, or even aspires higher, belongs to the earlier period; the Zohar, the Light, to the later. The remote origin of the Cabala belongs to

---

* La Kabbale, ou la Philosophie religieuse des Hébreux, par Ad. Franck, Paris, 1843. Professeur à la Faculté des Lettres, &c., f Pp. 362, 369.

that period when the Jewish mind, during the Captivity, became so deeply impregnated with Oriental notions, those of the Persian or Zoroastrian religion. Some of the first principles of the Cabala, as well as many of the tenets, still more of the superstitions of the Talmud,[a] coincide so exactly with the Zendavesta (the Zendavesta not only as expounded by Anquetil du Perron and Klenker, but by the higher authority of Bournouf, in his Commentary on the Yaçna) as to leave no doubt of their kindred and affiliation. They found their first Western home in Palestine after the return from the Captivity. Some of their doctrines, or doctrines closely analogous, found their way to Alexandria, and may be traced in the Translation of the LXX. (as well as in the Book of Ecclesiasticus and the Targums of Onkelos) and in Philo. With Philo they were crossed, blended, and modified by the Greek philosophy, especially Platonism, which in a later period expanded into the mystic school of Porphyry, Proclus, and Plotinus. This Alexandrian system could not have been their source. The Cabala is essentially Jewish in thought, in language, in its utter aversion to, or rather ignorance of, Greek philosophers and Greek philosophy.

But while it is undoubtedly Zoroastrian in many of its primary conceptions, and still more in its wild imaginations, in what may be called its mythology, yet in its unalterable Monotheism, it is strictly and rigidly

---

[a] Franck shows that this secret doctrine, the history of the Creation, and the Mercaba (the Chariot), are mentioned in the Mischna and Gemara, and therefore are older. R. Akiba and Simon ben Jochai were their first compilers: "Les partisans enthousiastes de la Kabbale la font descendre du ciel, apportée par les anges, pour enseigner au premier homme, après sa désobéissance, les moyens de reconquérir sa noblesse et sa félicité premières." According to others, Moses received it from God on Mount Sinai, and entrusted it to the seventy elders. Franck, p. 51.

Mosaic. It repudiates altogether the Dualism, into which the Persian Monotheism seems, even with Zoroaster himself, to have degenerated. There is an absolute Unity in its Pantheism, for Pantheism it undoubtedly is, open and undisguised, as all mysticism either is by nature or has an irresistible tendency to become; as the Pantheism of India, Brahminical and Buddhist, as the Pantheism of Spinoza, even of Hegel. The base of the Cabalistic system is absolute Unity: a God who is at once the cause, the substance, and the form of all that is or all that can be. The Ensoph,[h] the One Infinite, the Mystery of Mysteries, Light of Lights,[i] remains above in its solitary, unapproachable majesty. Below this, but far below, is the common Emanation System of the East. First comes the Word, the Creator, and the Demiurgos, as it were the Godhead in action or development. The impersonated attributes of God, at once metaphysical and abstract conceptions, become real beings, the Sephiroth, the Æons of Gnosticism, of which Cabalism was to a great degree the parent. (Some of the most famous Gnostics were Jews; Simon Magus was Jew or Samaritan.) The ten Sephiroth are the manifestation of God, the triple Trinity, in concentric circles around the central Godhead. Then follows the primal and archetypical Man, the Man Above to be carefully distinguished from the Man Below; the conflict of Good and Evil, of Spirit and Matter, of Light and Darkness; the pre-existence of human souls, their imprisonment in matter, their reunion with God by faith and love.

---

[h] The Ensoph, p. 183.
[i] "Ainsi Dieu est à la fois, dans le sens le plus élevé, et la matière et la forme de l'univers. Il n'est pas seulement cette matière et cette forme; mais rien n'existe, ni ne peut exister, en dehors de lui; sa substance est au fond de tous les êtres, et tous portent l'empreinte, tous sont les symboles de son intelligence." p. 160.

There are beautiful images illustrative of this, and of the tender remonstrances of the souls of men against being submitted to this gross trial; the death, the release, of the just, is the kiss of love.[k] Among the Cabalists there is the universal sacred horror of anthropomorphism, from which sometimes, in their coarser moods, they take refuge in monstrous allegories. Infinity is represented by immensity, the Incomprehensible by heaping upon each other inconceivable masses of numbers, of times, and of distances (as in the Indian poets) by which at last the Immaterial is materialized. The Ancient of Ancients has a face of the length of 370 times 10,000 worlds. The light of the head illuminates 400,000 worlds. Every day issue from his brain 400,000 worlds, the inheritance of the just in the life to come.[l] Nothing indeed is absolutely bad, nothing eternally accursed ; the great fallen archangel himself will resume his former nature, the venomous beast lose his venom.[m] Yet it is remarkable, and especially Jewish, that there does not seem to have been that deep sense of the malignity of matter which prevailed in kindred systems. Marriage, the lawful union of the sexes, was not in itself an evil, a necessary but still fatal contamination, as it was held even by Philo, and by some of the early Christian Fathers, and by Monachism Oriental as well as Christian. Marriage was acquiesced in by the Cabala as in the natural order of things, with no aversion or proscription. The Cabalists, as has been said, anti-

---

[k] Pp. 178 (a remarkable passage) and 182.
[l] Franck, p. 171; see the whole strange passage.
[m] P. 217. The whole of this passage is very curious. There has been a succession of worlds. Before they were created, all things appeared in the sight of God. See, too, about the Demons as inferior to men :— "The souls of the just are above the angels." p. 223.

cipated or coincided with Origen in the final restoration of Satan, or rather Samael (the great Evil Spirit) himself.[a] On the whole, the notion of man in the Cabala is of singular elevation: not only the primal and celestial man, the Adam Caedmon, who as the image of God comprehends within himself the Sephiroth, the Divine attributes, but the man of the lower sphere. Man was the consummation and perfection of Creation, and therefore not formed till the sixth day. He is inferior to the angels; the Dæmons seem to be but other names for his passions, pride, avarice, cruelty. Thus, throughout, the Cabala differs from its parent the Zendavesta. The impersonated beings of the Zendavesta are metaphysical entities in the Cabala. Zoroastrianism is a mythology; the Cabala approaches to a philosophy. In the Cabala, too, are some singular premature gleams of scientific knowledge. The Cabala, as well as the Talmud, dares to assert the earth to be spherical and rotatory,[o] and the existence of antipodes; there is even an approach to the Copernican system. This, too, about the time when, according to the Christian Fathers Lactantius and Augustine, such opinions bordered close on damnable heresy. Of the human brain, its triple division, and peculiar integuments, and thirty-two nerves which ramify through the whole body, the Cabala had a clear and distinct apprehension.[p] And

---

[a] P. 217.

[o] "Dans le livre de Chammoune le Vieux, on apprend, par des explications étendues, que la terre tourne sur elle-même en forme de cercle; que les uns sont en haut, les autres en bas; que toutes les créatures changent d'aspect suivant l'air de chaque lieu, en gardant pourtant la même position; qu'il y a telle contrée de la terre qui est éclairée tandis que les autres sont dans les ténèbres; ceux-ci ont le jour, quand pour ceux-là il fait nuit; et il y a des pays où il fait constamment jour, ou au moins la nuit ne dure que quelques instants." p. 102; compare 187.

[p] "Dans l'intérieur du crâne, le cerveau se partage en trois parties, dont

this exalted view of man, even when immersed in the material world, supports the theory of Franck, that the Cabala belongs to the end of the seventh century, when the Jews were yet in some independence and prosperity; not to the thirteenth (as Tholuck and others have argued, confuted, as I think, by Franck), when they were in their lowest state of depression, trampled on by the rest of mankind.

Such was the high speculative Cabala; but, like the neo-Platonic philosophy, the Cabala degenerated into a theurgic system of magic and wonder-working. Not only was the Bible one vast allegory, in which the literal sense was cast scornfully aside, and a wild, arbitrary meaning attached to every history and every doctrine, but at the same time there was a superstitious reverence of the letter; the numbers of the letters, 10, 7, 12, 32, every single letter, the collocation of every letter, the transposition, the substitution, had a special, even a supernatural power. The traditional Fathers of the Cabala, R. Akiba and Simon ben Jochai, had wrought miracles with the letters of the Scripture;[q] and later there was no kind of vulgar conjuring trick that was not performed by the Adepts,[r] till Cabalism sank into contempt and suspicion. Though studied with fond perseverance and patient industry, as something above and beyond genuine Talmudical learning, yet

---

chacune occupe une place distincte. Il est en outre recouvert d'un voile très mince, puis d'un autre voile plus dur. Au moyen de trente-deux canaux, ces trois parties du cerveau se répandent dans tout le corps en se dirigeant par deux côtés: c'est ainsi qu'elles embrassent le corps sur tous les points et se répandent dans toutes ses parties."

It is suggested that the legal practice of dissecting animals to separate the clean from the unclean, must have led to some study of anatomy. p. 138.

[q] See on the worship of the letters, Franck, p. 69. The Cabalists had an alphabet of their own. p. 76.

[r] On the powers of letters, pp. 79, 145, 154.

the ordinary Talmudists looked on the Cabalists with not ungrounded jealousy, as tampering with forbidden things, as aspiring to knowledge of unrevealed mysteries, and practising unlawful arts. The Cabalistic pretensions to enchantments, amulets, charms, justified to the more sober, if not the proscription, the discouragement of these, in their essence lofty, in their practice vulgar and degrading studies.

But the influence of the Cabala was not confined to the Jewish mind; some of the strange, powerful intellects of the Middle Ages, when the borders of science and wonder-working were utterly confounded, were tempted at once by the abstruseness, the magnificent pretensions, and the mysticism of the Cabala, to penetrate into its secrets and appropriate its powers and virtues. From Raymond Lully to Van Helmont, the Adepts boasted, perhaps too boldly, their familiarity with the Jewish Cabala. How far they were really indebted to it, it is perhaps impossible to determine.

The Cabala is purely Jewish; it may be said to represent the Oriental or Asiatic part of the Jewish mind. But the European philosophy of the Jews assumed a more European cast. It is impossible, I apprehend, to separate and distinguish between the Jewish and Arabian influences which created what is usually called the Arabian philosophy of Spain. The earliest, by some thought the greatest, of this school, who passed under the name of Avicebron, turns out to be, under this disguised appellation, Salomon ben Ghebirol of Malaga, the famous Jewish hymnologist.* Of this philosophy, the Judæo-Arabic of Spain, the value and the originality are now called in question. Its immense

---

* This discovery is due to M. Munk. (See Ernest Rénan, Averroes, p. 100.)

mass rivals that of Christian scholasticism. Is it more than the opinions of the Greeks, passing through the Jewish and Arabian minds?—more than in a great part Aristotelism in other forms and in other language?—the Eternity of matter, on which the Eternity of thought or intelligence is eternally operating—the Eternal Thought, which swallows up and absorbs, and so is one with, all active intelligence, and of which, whether individual or that of collective humanity, human intelligence is a part or an efflux? This philosophy also would issue in a kind of Pantheism; or, if the Divine be co-ordinate with the same all-absorbing one Matter, in a Dualism.

But if the Jews were the primary authors, they were likewise the conservators, of the Arabian philosophy; through them these tenets were no doubt propagated into the Christian schools. Considerable parts of the works of the Arabian writers are to be read only in Hebrew translations.

The doctrines of Averroes and his followers, contained in their Commentaries on Aristotle, were translated by the Spanish Jews who took refuge, after the expulsion of the Jews from Spain, in Languedoc; the family of the Tibbon at Lunel, Solomon ben Job at Beziers, Calonymus ben Meir at Arles, Judah ben Meschullam at Marseilles. Besides these were Judah ben Solomon Cohen of Toledo, who flourished under the protection of the Emperor Frederick II.; and another Provençal Jew, settled at Naples, Jacob ben Abba Mari, who enjoyed the patronage of the same enlightened monarch.

"None," writes a distinguished Orientalist of our day, M. Ernest Rénan, "were in earnest about the Arabian philosophy but the Jews."[t] He acknowledges at the same time that the first impulse to that philosophy

---
[t] Ernest Rénan, Averroes, pp. 176, 186, et seqq.

came from the Oriental Jewish school of Sura, that of Saadi.

The time is perhaps approaching in which at least some award may be made of the share of the Jews in that philosophy to study which the Adelards,[a] the Gerberts, visited the schools of Toledo and Cordova, and from which, in the days of Frederick II., Jews certainly assisted in restoring the genuine Aristotle to the knowledge of the West. It may be impossible to discriminate between the converging and harmonising thought of Jew and Arabian, or their common debt to the Greek philosophy, which they joined in disguising and passing off on themselves as their own. Hebrew writings are not necessarily the produce of Hebrew thought, nor Arabic of Arabian. No one will ever perhaps thread completely the bewildering labyrinth; perhaps it may not at last be worth the labour.[x] But no one is more likely to succeed than M. Munk; and, as a descendant of the race of Israel, M. Munk, we may be assured, will render full justice to his ancestors.

The old Hebrew poetry, that of the Bible, by its transcendent excellence, dooms to obscurity all later Hebrew verse. With a religious people, and through their religion alone the Jews persevere in being a people, their poetry must be, and almost always has been, essentially religious. But every avenue to the heart and

---

[a] For Adelard see Sprenger's Preface to his Life of Mohammed.

[x] " Les Juifs remplissaient dans ces relations un rôle essentiel, et dont on n'a pas tenu assez de compte dans l'histoire de la civilisation. Leur activité commerciale, leur facilité à apprendre les langues en faisaient les intermédiaires naturels entre les Chrétiens et les Musulmans, . . . Le peuple seul les avait en antipathie. Quant aux hommes désireux de s'instruire, ils n'éprouvaient aucun scrupule à s'en faire en philosophie les disciples de maîtres appartenant à d'autres religions. La science était quelque chose de neutre et commun à tous." Rénan, p. 202. See also the following paragraph.

soul of the Jew is preoccupied by hymns, by odes, by Gnomic verse, which have cloven to the universal heart and soul of man to a depth, and with a tenacity, never surpassed or equalled. Every emotion, every thought, almost every occurrence in the somewhat narrow sphere of Jewish life, has already found its expression in words so inimitable, in music so harmonious, that all other words must seem pale and feeble. What can be the choral hymns of the Synagogue compared with those which resounded in the courts of the first, or even of the second, Temple? What lyric language can refuse to borrow its tone from, and therefore but faintly echo, the devotional Psalms of David, and of those who followed him? What Odes on all the awful events of human or national life can approach those of the Prophets? The sorrows of centuries can hardly wring from Jewish hearts any lamentations approaching to those of Jeremiah. According to the historian of later Jewish poetry, the three treasure-houses of Jewish song are, their History, their Law, and their Legends.⁷ But their older History is in itself such poetry that it can only be expanded into a comparatively flat and lifeless paraphrase. If by the Law be meant their Gnomic poetry, the Proverbs, and the firstfruits of their poetic wisdom, subsequent to the Sacred Books, the Book of Ecclesiasticus, will hardly be rivalled by the wisdom and ingenuity of the later Rabbinical school. Even the Legend, from which the Arabic writers, the Koran itself, have drawn so abundantly, in its most creative and imaginative form is found in the Targums.⁸ Their wild and fantastic apocalyptic writings

---

⁷ Delitzsch. Zur Geschichte der Jüdischen Poesie, von Franz Delitzsch. Leipsic, 1836. I believe that the continuation of this work, promised by the author, has not appeared.

⁸ "Die ganze Sagen-welt der spätern Moslemen, der Araber, Perser, und Turken, soweit sie zur die alttesta-

are full of poetry, extravagant, it is true, but still rich in invention, in bold and striking imagery, and with a luxuriant and lavish symbolism.[a]

Nevertheless, Hebrew poetry boasts a succession of writings as copious as that of most modern nations. The lineage of their poets, if occasionally interrupted, has gone on, singing the songs of Zion in strange lands, but in strains audible only to the Jewish ear. It is acknowledged, indeed, that the whole Mischna is hard and arid prose;[b] that what is poetical occasionally in the Talmuds is without poetic form or language; that the age of the Gaonim, nearly five hundred years, from A.C. 540 to 997, was barren, uncreative, without invention or fancy.[c] But then began, it is said, in Spain the golden age, from 940 to 1040.[d] It was succeeded by a silver age, 1090 to 1190. At a later period winter fell on the poetic Jewish mind.[e] Yet there is no form which the poetry of modern European nations has taken which Hebrew poetry has not attempted to domiciliate. It had its Troubadours, with their amorous con-

---

mentliche Geschichte berührt, findet sich ein Jahrtausend früher schon in den Jüdischen Targumen weit einfacher, reiner und würdiger abgeschildert; die Geschichte wird in ihnen zur reitzendsten, lehrreichendsten Poesie; diese Poesie ist aber nicht Einkleidung, Dichtung, Phantasma des Schreibers, sondern die alte und volksthämliche, venerable Sage, deren Redacteren die Targumisten sind: die Targumen sind Exegese, Geschichte, altsynagogales Bekenntnis, und bei dem allen poetisch in ihrem Inhalt, poetisch in ihre Form." Delitzsch, p. 27.

[a] René Hilgenfeld, Die Jüdische Apocalyptik, and many passages in Ewald's History, especially his account of the apocryphal Esdras.

[b] Delitzsch, p. 120. He says, indeed, " In den Talmuden ist uns eine grosse Vergangenheit des Jüdischen Volkslebens nicht in der Copie einer blossen Relation, modern wie in einer Mumie erhalten, ihr eignes Fleisch und Bein: der Dichter löss die künstlichen Specereien ab, deren Hülle sie so lange vor der Zerstörung sicherte, und stelle uns das Leben wieder lebendig dar." p. 121.

[c] Delitzsch, p. 29.
[d] Ibid., p. 35.
[e] Ibid., p. 42.

ceits. It had its epic poems, its Mosaides, its Zionides,[f] even its drama,[g] the form of poetry, notwithstanding the early attempt of the Judæo-Alexandrian Ezekiel to mould the wonders of their early history into a Greek tragedy, the most irreconcileable with their older models. A late poet in Italy has even ventured on a harlequinade for the joyous festival of the Purim.[h] The Jewish poets either borrowed rhyme from the Arabian poets, as is most probable, or, as some with national partisanship aver, imparted it to them.[i] They have their Dantes,[k] but it is not writing in triple rhymes, nor attempting to unfold the mysteries of the unseen world, which can make a Dante; they have their sonnets, but sonnets make not a Petrarch; they have even, they confess it with shame, their Aretin.[l] Their poetry is that of all countries in which they dwell, Spain, Italy,[m] Germany, Holland, Poland, even Russia.[n] But, after all, these are still foreign lands. There is something deeply pathetic in a sentence of the historian of Hebrew poetry—"The pure poetry of Nature cannot be the national poetry of the Jews, for down to this time the Jewish people has

---

[f] The Zionida. Delitzsch, p. 162.
[g] The earliest Jewish dramas were written in Holland in the seventeenth century. p. 77.
[h] The Harlequinade, by Rappoport, p. 119.
[i] "Selbst in der Mischna und Gemara findet sich nichts von Metrum und Reim, sondern diese sind erst den Arabern entlehnt und dann von den Dichtern in der Provence, Catalonien, Arragon und Castilien ausgebildet worden." Delitzsch, p. 5. Compare p. 132, and on rhyme, p. 137.
[k] The Hebrew Dante was Mose de Rieti (p. 54). Compare pp. 72, 73.

[l] Delitzsch, p. 523. This Hebrew Aretin was Imanuel Romi ben Salomo, of the March of Ancona, author of The Divan.
[m] On the different character of the older Italian and the Spanish Hebrew poetry, see Delitzsch, p. 43: "Die Spanische Poesie mahlt mit dem Pinsel Rafaels; die Italienische bildet mit dem Meisel Michel Angelos." It The world ought not to be deprived even of a faint copy of the works of such masters.
[n] Jewish Poets in Russian Poland, p. 83.

been a nationality without a native country, and neither the luxuriant nature of the Barbaresque lands, nor the vine-clad shores of the Rhine, can make up to them for Judæa. A naturalized Jew cannot be a national poet."* I presume not to judge of these hidden treasures, secluded in their own libraries, and veiled in their own peculiar language. But it is remarkable that even in translations, however it might be that translation could hardly transfuse poems, retaining much of an indelible Oriental cast, with full justice into European tongues, so far as I know, hardly any of these boasted treasures have been communicated to the general ear of Europe; and those which have been communicated have fallen dead on the ear. I have never read any piece of modern Hebrew poetry in any translation in which I have not felt that I had heard it before —its images, its thoughts, its passion, its very cadence, is that on which I have dwelt in the Bible.

I cannot but apprehend too that all this poetry labours under another fatal cause of inferiority. It is an immutable law that no great poet has ever been inspired but in his native tongue. Now, Hebrew, though no doubt fully comprehended, and fluently spoken, it may be, by the instructed or educated Jew, is after all a foreign or a dead language. It is not his vernacular; not the language of ordinary every-day life; not the language in which the man, if we may so say, speaks, thinks; not the language of his emotions, his passions. It is what the Latin was to the clergy, and to the few educated men of the Middle Ages; and as European poetry was only born with the young European languages, as Dante would never have been Dante had

---

* Delitzsch, p. 123.

he fulfilled his original fatal scheme of writing the Divine Comedy in Latin; as Petrarch, after labouring for years on the unread, unreadable Africa, fortunately condescended to the vulgar tongue in his Sonnets, so, however the Hebrew poets may learn to move with some ease in the fetters of their ancient language, they are still fetters. No one perhaps can derive more pleasure than myself (through education, familiarity with Greek and Latin through Eton and academic studies and practice) from writers of modern Latin verse, the Italians, some of the French Jesuits, the Poles, our own Milton, Cowley, Gray, R. Smith, still I feel, everyone feels, that the whole is admirably ingenious, but no more; the play of fancy, the feeling, the passion, all is artificial. They neither rouse, nor melt, nor transport us out of ourselves. So I suspect it is, I believe that it must be, with most of the later Hebrew poetry. It is the Synagogal poetry in which I conceive rests all its true strength and beauty. The legitimate son of such a parent could not so altogether forget its rich inheritance as to fall into absolute poverty. The heirlooms could not but retain some of their original splendour, though but reflected splendour.

The historian indeed admits that the Synagogal hymns (in which, as the devotional outpourings of souls in whom devotion must have been their one consolation, the very life-blood of their miserable being, and therefore all the emotional part at least of their poetry must have found vent) are but an echo of those in the Bible;[p] still that echo may be of deep solemnity—its

---

[p] This Delitzsch asserts broadly of the older Synagogal poetry, the Liturgic, which was "Reminiscenz und gleichsam das Echo der Bibel." The new school aspired to be neither the echo of the Bible nor of the Talmud; yet "Sie will aus der Bibel als der reinsten, idealsten Darstellung des lle-

dying wail of exquisite tenderness. A late writer, unrivalled, I believe, among his compatriots for the vast range of his knowledge—knowledge which he pours forth with such overflowing copiousness and minute particularity as to overload and weary the most patient reader—has taken upon him the office of doing justice to the Synagogal poetry of the Middle Ages.[q] Its continuous history, its various forms, its use in the public services, its measures, its rhythm, the construction of its verse, are followed out into the utmost detail; but what is more valuable, and more likely to obtain it a fair hearing, is that he has rendered some of its best passages into that flexible German, which Goethe and Rückert have shown can accommodate itself with such ease and harmony with Oriental thought, imagery, and melody. I will not attribute to Dr. Zunz the unrivalled skill and facility of these great poets,—Zunz indeed complains that of one passage no European language can render the thunderstrokes of the continuous rhymes, that the lightning of its beauty is quenched in the dull auxiliaries and pronouns. I venture, however, on a few lines:—

Him sings the voice of every living creature,
Echoes from above, from underneath his glory;
"One God," shouts forth the Earth, and "Holy One," the Heavens;
From the waters songs are sounding to the Mighty in the Highest:
Majesty from the abyss, hymns come chanting from the stars;
Speech is from the day, and music from the night;
His name the fire proclaims,
And melodies are floating o'er the forest,—
The beasts proclaim God's overpowering greatness.

---

braismus, sich bloss dem Sprachshatz aneignen, ihn aber dann selbstandig handhaben." But if all the power of the language is Biblical, it would be very difficult to rise much above imitation.

[q] Die Synagogalen Poesie des Mittelalters, von Dr. Zunz, Berlin, 1855.

The work of Zunz will try, but we think will reward, the patience of the curious reader. Still, in the long line of Jewish Hymnology, transferred into German verse or rhythm, there is a wearisome sameness, and a constant reminiscence of the Biblical language, spun out into enfeebling length, and prolonged with perpetual iteration. There are, however, fine thoughts, bold expressions, and the constant allusions to the sufferings of the people, and their lofty and undying trust in the faithfulness and promises of their God, are not without tenderness and sublimity. They may be but variations on the unapproachable music of Job and the Psalms, but these variations are full of sweetness and grandeur, almost of genius and originality.

The true poetry of the Jews was secluded in the isolation of their own language. But on their expulsion from Spain, the Sephardim bore with them to different countries, to Italy,[r] to France, to Holland, to Greece, and Constantinople, the noble language which was hereafter to be made illustrious by Cervantes and Calderon. So entirely were they Spaniards, that parts of their religious services were in Spanish.[s] Among the earliest typographical works was a Spanish translation of the Old Testament, issued by Abraham Usque at Ferrara,[t] and frequently reprinted, in a more correct form, in the Low Countries. They had Spanish poets, too, in many countries. In Spain, before the Expulsion, the Hebrew Spanish poets had been almost exclusively

---

[r] Qualir the Sardinian is the first great name in the Mediæval Synagogal poetry. Delitzsch, p. 51.
[s] Amador de los Rios, li. c. 5.
[t] On the Bible of Ferrara, Amador de los Rios, p. 432. Ten years before the publication of the Bible at Ferrara, Francesco Frellon published at Lyons a poem in Spanish, Retratos o tablas de las Historias del Testamento Viejo. See for extracts from this poem, ibid., pp. 437, 442.

converts.* They had had their Troubadour poets in Catalonia. The Rabbi Abner, Santo de Carrcon, the famous Paul, Bishop of Burgos, Hieronymo di Santa Fé, find their place in the history of Spanish poetry.[x] The Sephardim with singular fidelity adhered in foreign lands to that which had become the native tongue. This can hardly indeed be said of Moses Pinto Delgado. He had embraced the Gospel in Spain, but fell back to his old religion. He fled from the searching eye of the Inquisition and found refuge in France. There he published his Poem of Esther,[y] the Lamentations of Jeremiah, and the Poem of Ruth the Moabitess.[z] The Jews likewise printed books in Spanish at Constantinople and Salonichi, as well as at Venice and Amsterdam, of a much higher order than the poems of Delgado, such as the translation of the Psalms by David Abenatar Melo. This remarkable man had been baptized. Either from some suspicion of his sincerity, or, to crush out of him the betrayal of some of his kindred, he was committed to the prison of the Inquisition. There he lived for some years, and was released (no crime being proved against him) in 1611. He found refuge in Germany; at least the rare volume of his Psalms was printed at Frankfort in 1626. This translation, if I may judge from extracts, is one of the finest in any European language, and shows that the lingering Orientalism in the Spanish language is singularly adapted for the bold and lofty imagery of the Hebrew poetry. It is of strange interest, too, to find a Jew, a prisoner escaped from the Inquisition, uttering his own sorrows

---

* For the Judæo-Arabic Chronicle of the Cid, see Dellitzsch, p. 65.
[x] Amador de los Rios, ch. v.
[y] See, for the extracts from Esther, which have much sweetness and tenderness, Amador de los Rios, ch. iii.
[z] Extracts are given at length in Amador de los Rios, p. 469, &c.

and thanksgiving in the words of the Psalmist. These verses are inserted into the Thirtieth Psalm:—

" Nel Infierno metido
De la Inquisicion dura,
Entre fieros loones de alvedrio,
De allí me has redimido
Dando a mis males cura,
Solo porque me viste arrepentido.'

(Doomed in the depths to dwell
Of the Inquisition's Hell,
At those fierce lions' hard arbitrement,
Thou has redeemed me,
Healed all my misery,
For thou didst see how deeply I repent.)

Michael Silveyra was the author of one of those long and wearisome epic poems which encumber the literature of Spain, 'The Conquest of Jerusalem by the Maccabees,' a poem written in rivalry of Tasso, but in the inflated style of Gongora, which, nevertheless, found admirers in Spain. Michael Silveyra was a converted Jew, who adhered faithfully to his new religion, and escaped the jealousy of the Holy Office. Not so a man of more versatile genius, Enriquez de Paz, better known under the name of Antonio Enriquez Gomez.[a] Son of a Portuguese Jew, captain, and enrolled in the Order of St. Michael, accused, not without justice, of Judaism by the inexorable Inquisition, he fled from his country, A.C. 1636, wandered over many parts of Europe, and settled in the centre of Judaism, Amsterdam; he was burned in effigy at Seville in 1660. During all this time he was pouring

---

[a] See on Gomes, Amador de los Rios, c. vii. and viii., and Ticknor, iii. 67. According to the Spanish writer, his lyrics are not without grace and beauty, and there is something of the fine old chivalrous extravagance of the Spanish drama in some of the plays of the Jewish exile.

forth Spanish verse without ceasing; an epic poem on Samson, lyrics in profusion, a satirical poem called the 'Age of Pythagoras,' and many dramas. These dramas were acted at Madrid. By a strange anomaly, the people of Madrid were listening, not without applause, to the verses of a man under the proscription of the Holy Office, known no doubt to be an avowed Jew. Nor was Enriquez de Paz the last of the exiled race who in foreign countries perpetuated the language of their native land, and gave to Spanish poetry an European fame in regions into which, without their aid, it would hardly have penetrated.

I may sum up in one word—to be poets, in Europe and in our days, the Jews must cease to be Jews; whether retaining their creed or not, they must abandon their language. One, who I fear abandoned much more of his Judaism than his language, Heinrich Heine, may prove how deep a vein of true poetry can spring from such sources. The one German whose short lyrics can be read after Goethe's, may show what Jewish poets can become, if they will, I would that I could in his case say, Christianize (though I believe that Heine's last hours were far different from his earlier ones), at all events fully and entirely Europeanize themselves. Jews may be English, German, Spanish, Italian, French poets,—they will hardly be Hebrew poets.

History, of all departments of letters, might appear, at first sight, that for which, as the Jews possessed special advantages, so they might seem specially designated. Dwelling in the seclusion of their own communities, yet those communities spread over the face of the earth, and maintaining more or less intimate and frequent intercourse with all nations; many of them merchants, travellers, with every opportunity of observation; excepting when they were immediate objects of persecution, unimpassioned and above the ordinary interests of men; for centuries they surveyed the world, and yet were not of the world. They saw the mightiest revolutions among the Gentiles, which they could look on with impartial indifference; empires rising and falling, kingdoms established and passing away; migrations from east to west, from north to south; powers temporal and spiritual, in the ascendant, in their supremacy, and in their decline; revolutions as complete in human thought, in human laws, in human manners, as in their rule and in their polities. Like the Wandering Jew of the legend, the nation might be the calm witness of the revolutions of ages—the chronicler of all the untold vicissitudes. But of History, in its highest sense, Jewish literature is absolutely barren. The historical faculty seems to have been altogether wanting. As if, either in their pride or their misery, they had obstinately or desperately closed their eyes to all but the narrow concerns of their own race, they have left us no trustworthy record even of their own interworking into the frame of society, their influence, their commerce, their relations to the rest of mankind. Still more, of their degradation and their sufferings they have preserved but broken and fragmentary notices, hardly to be dignified with the name of History.[b] There are

---

[b] "A thousand years had been suffered to elapse without the appearance of a single historian; but when the Rabbins saw that the antiquity, that is the authenticity, of their traditions became doubtful, and was disputed by the anti-traditionists, they attempted to demonstrate their antiquity by a meagre catalogue of generations, always opening with the year of the Creation, by which they pretended they had preserved an unbroken line of tradition." Disraeli, Genius of Judaism, p. 9.

traditions of their Babylonian Principality, of the rise and fall of their schools in Palestine, and in the East; but of their influence in the great struggle between Mohammedanism and Christianity, when they stood between the decaying civilization of the East and the dawning civilization of the Arabian dynasties at Damascus and Bagdad, there is nothing which can even compare with a Monkish Chronicler, far less with the works of a Froissart, a Comines, a Villani.

Even in their early narratives, of their fall in the war of Titus, of the insurrection under Bar-cochab, history is so overgrown with legend, truth is so moulded up with fiction or with allegory, that we wonder less at their want, in later times, of grave and sober annals. Of their own historian Josephus they either knew little, or chose to know little.[c] His vernacular History, which he wrote, by his own account, in the language of his people, doubtless the Aramaic Hebrew of the day, seems soon to have perished. The Greek they could not, or would not, read. Of Justus, the rival and adversary of Josephus, they seem equally ignorant.[d]

But the place of Josephus was usurped by one of the most audacious of romancers, who wrote under the name of Joseph ben Gorion, and is known in later times as Josippon. It is inconceivable that this strange rhapsody should be accepted as genuine history, as it was even by some of the most learned of the Jews. No Mediæval Chronicle ever indulged in such bold latitude of ana-

---

[c] See Gagnier's Preface, pp. xxviii., xxix.:—

"Nam quod ad Josephum Græcum adtinet, illum non in magno habere solent pretio, imo ei nullam habent fidem, et tanquam in Historicum mendacem et adulatorem adversus illum acriter invehuntur; Suum vero Josephum quasi hominem veracem et pene divinum summis laudibus ad sidera evehunt, extollunt, et prædicant."

[d] Gagnier, p. xlii.

chronism. The author asserts himself to have been born during the Empire of Julius Cæsar, whom he had seen; by his own account he must have lived about two hundred years. From King Tsepho the Arabian, son of Eliphaz, the contemporary of Joseph in Egypt, general and son-in-law of Agnias King of Carthage, he leaps to Daniel, from Daniel to Alexander the Great; whose history is related after the mediæval poem or romance. Romulus and David are contemporaries and allies. Hannibal, on his way to Italy, subdues the Goths in Spain and all Germany. To complete all, he describes the election and coronation of a Roman Emperor (Vespasian?), which he himself witnesses. The Emperor was chosen by the seven electors; he scatters golden florins among the mob. He is received in Rome by the Patron, the Father of all the Prefects, evidently the Pope, who gives him the sceptre, the ring (made of the bone of a dead man), and the chalice on which is the golden apple, sets the crown on his head, and cries "Long live our Lord the Cæsar!" And all the people, Pope, electors, princes, shout "Amen!"

The history of the calamities of the Jewish nation by Solomon ben Virga,* a Spanish Jew, a physician, is trustworthy as to the events concerning which he may have received immediate traditions, and those which occurred in his own time. All above and beyond is clouded with fable. The whole is desultory and unequal; some passages, as the histories of many persecutions in different parts of Europe, are disappointingly brief and without particulars, while the disputation with

---

* This work was translated into Latin by Gentius (Amsterdam, 1690). In the dedication to the Consuls, Senate, and people of Hamburg, is related the Apologue of Abraham and the Fire-worshipper quoted by Franklin, who probably took it from Jeremy Taylor.

Thomas di Santa Fé runs out into disproportioned prolixity, though not without its interest. The close of this History is perhaps the most remarkable. It is a bold attempt by an apologue, which assumes the form of history, to place the Jews under the protection of the Pope. After their expulsion from Spain, ambassadors from the King of Spain appear before the Supreme Pontiff, urging him to exterminate them from his dominions. The wise and gentle Pope betrays great reluctance to comply with this request, and bears a kind of unwilling testimony to the piety and virtue of the Jews. He himself moves the somewhat perilous question of the image-worship of the Christians, as resembling that of the Egyptians, which the Jews were taught to abominate. The Pope's scruples relieved on that head, the enemies of the Jews revert to the old calumnies. A Jew is accused of having stolen a silver image, and melted it in scorn of the Christians. He is hanged for the offence. The Pope issues Bulls commanding that all the Jewish infants should be immediately baptized; that those of the adults alone who embraced Christianity should escape; the rest must perish by the sword. That very night the bishop, or cardinal, their most bitter persecutor, falls dead from his chair. The Pope, deeming this a sign from heaven in favour of the Jews, suspends the execution of his orders. On the following night the other bishop, or cardinal, gives a splendid banquet to all the magnates, the bishops, and ambassadors, who had come to Rome to demand the banishment of the Jews. That night Rome is shaken with an earthquake more terrible than was ever before known. But it does no harm to any of the private or sacred edifices of the city; only the palace where this banquet was held falls on the cruel guests, and crushes them all to death.

The Pope acknowledges that Heaven has thus declared the Jews guiltless of the sacrilege: "I am almost induced to believe that the crucifixion of Christ by the Jews is a calumny, falsely charged upon them from hatred of their race." The Bulls are rescinded, and from that time the Jews have been held in the utmost honour by that benignant Pope.

Unquestionably the most valuable historic work of the Jews which has been made accessible to the European reader is the Chronicle, often cited in these pages, of Rabbi Joseph ben Joshua ben Meir.¹ But this is the work of a late writer, subsequent to the Reformation, and therefore obtaining his knowledge chiefly from the remote and troubled stream of tradition. Its Biblical style, wisely retained by the translator, gives an attractive character to the Chronicle, and the author has thrown aside much of the fable and wild imagination which render almost worthless all other Rabbinical histories.²

As in poetry, so it would seem in history, a man must cease to be a Jew to take a place in the goodly cata-

---

¹ Translated for the Oriental Fund, by C. H. F. Bialloblotsky, Lond., 1835.

² The translator of this work has observed, in accordance with the views expressed above, "An extensive mercantile correspondence, and frequent wanderings and pilgrimages, afforded to the Jew many opportunities of acquiring information during centuries in which the greater part of the nations professing Christianity remained in comparative ignorance. Jews were, during the Middle Ages, admitted into the secrets of European and Asiatic Cabinets, and consulted on questions of political importance. The interests of their nation were then, much more than at present, interwoven with those of almost every people, both barbarous and civilized; and while self-interest quickened the perceptive faculties of the children of Israel to the observation of passing events, their natural bias was also so essentially different from that of the nations among whom they sojourned, that the misconceptions and misstatements of their historical writers could hardly ever coincide with those of any contemporary party, either political or religious."

logue of the annalists of the world. Had Neander remained a Jew, would he have aspired to the rank which he now so justly holds as the historian not of the events only, but of the intimate spirit of Christianity? I would gladly hail a Jewish Neander; but even Jost (and I am too deeply obliged to Jost not to do him ample justice) will hardly fill that place which no Christian, perhaps, has a right to occupy—not even Ewald in the earlier scenes of Jewish History, certainly not Basnage in the later, least of all one like myself, who began too early, and have been called off too much by other studies, fully to appropriate or worthily to execute this work of universal, of perpetual interest to mankind.[h]

---

[h] To one of the fine arts alone, the enchanting science of music, the Jews have made vast contributions; but even in music the son of Mendelssohn had passed over to Christianity before he achieved his immortal fame.

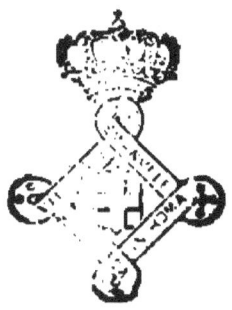

(457)

INDEX.

A

AARON, brother of Moses, L. 76; before Pharaoh, 77; his rod transformed into a serpent, 79; himself and his sons designated for the priesthood, 146; confirmed in the office by a miracle, 196; his death and burial on Mount Hor, 200.

ABARIS, city of, L. 60; shepherd kings expelled from, 107.

ABENATAR Melo, his Spanish translation of the Psalms, iii. 447; his escape from the Inquisition celebrated in, 448.

ABIMELECH, conspiracy of, L. 252; is made king, 253.

ABRAHAM, the "Father of the Faithful," L. 3; his eminent place in Oriental tradition, 4; he worships one God, 5; traditionary fictions respecting, 6; his migration westward, 7; in Egypt, 8; returns to Canaan, 9; rescues Lot, 11; divine promise to, 12; birth of his son Ishmael, 14; birth of his son Isaac, 19; trial of his faith, 20; offers up Isaac, 21; his death, 27; as to date of his sojourn in Egypt, 108; his conspicuous rank in Mohammedanism, iii. 91.

ABSALOM, his beauty, L. 298; his rebellion against David—takes possession of Jerusalem, 299; his death, 300.

ADONIBEZEK, king of Jerusalem, L. 222.

ADULTERY, Jewish law of, L. 171.

ÆLIA Capitolina, founded by Hadrian on the site of Jerusalem, ii. 417; Jews prohibited from entering—made a bishopric, 418.

AGOBARD, Archbishop of Lyons, iii. 138; his laws against the Jews, 139; his charges against them, 140; his mission to Paris, 141.

AGRIPPA, his friendship with Herod, ii. 75.

AGRIPPA, Herod, ii. 126; his early life, 127; in prison at Rome, 129; liberated by Caligula—made king of Palestine, 130; at Alexandria, 135; before Caligula, 148; his treaty with Claudius, 156; returns to Jerusalem, 157; his magnificence, 158; persecutes the Christians, 159; his death, 160; exultation at his death, 161.

AGRIPPA, the Second, ii. 166; his interests promoted by Claudius, 171; his residence in Jerusalem, 174; adorns the city of Berytus, 176; his speech after the massacre by Florus, 187; sends troops to Jerusalem, 191; endeavours to avert the war between Jews and Romans, 205; espouses the Roman party, 211; joins the army of Vespasian, 240; at the siege of Gamala, 281; his death, 394.

AHAB, destruction of the prophetic order by, i. 344; defeats Benhadad —covets Naboth's vineyard, 349; his death, 352.

AHASUERUS, L. 428.

AHAZ, king of Judah, L. 168; his idolatry, 173; his death, 174.

AHITOPHEL.

AHITOPHEL, i. 298; his advice to Absalom, 300.

AI, destruction of, i. 22.

AKIBA, Rabbi, ii. 426; his sayings, 427; he acknowledges the pretended Messiah, 428; his fate, 436.

ALBINUS, governor of Judæa, ii. 175.

ALEXANDER, the Great, before Jerusalem, i. 447.

ALEXANDER, son of Herod and Mariamne, his education at Rome, ii. 75; his return to Jerusalem, 78; accused by Herod before Augustus, 79; reconciled to his father, 80; imprisoned, 82; his trial and condemnation—his execution, 84.

ALEXANDER Jannæus, ii. 35; rebellion against, 17; death of, 19.

ALEXANDER Severus, ii. 474.

ALEXANDRA, reign of, ii. 19.

ALEXANDRA, the mother of Mariamne, ii. 62; corresponds with Cleopatra, 63; imprisoned by Herod, 65; her invectives against Mariamne, 69; her execution, 70.

ALEXANDRIA, foundation of, i. 445; Jews in, ii. 111; tumults in, 101.

ALEXANDRIAN Jews, i. 445—ii. 24; romantic history of their persecution, 26; persecuted by Flaccus Aquilius, 136; deputation of to Caligula, 141; its reception, 143.

AMBROSE, bishop of Milan, iii. 31; his letter to Theodosius, 71.

AMERICAN Jews, number of, iii. 431.

AMMIANUS Marcellinus, attempt to rebuild the Temple described by, iii. 20, and note.

AMOS, the prophet, i. 369.

AMRAM, father of Moses, i. 68.

ANAN, the Karaite, iii. 116.

ANANUS, the chief priest, ii. 216; takes the lead in defence of Jerusalem, 237; incites the people against Zealot robbers, 291; harangues the assembly, 295; murdered by the Idumæans, 301; his character, 302.

ARISTOBULUS.

ANILAI, exploits of, in Babylonia, ii. 151.

ANTIGONUS, the last of the Asmonean race, ii. 55; put to death at solicitation of Herod, 59.

ANTIOCH, surrender of, to Chosroes, iii. 82.

ANTIOCHUS, the Great, i. 452.

ANTIOCHUS Epiphanes, i. 454; succeeds to throne of Syria, 456; his character, 457; invades Egypt, 460; persecution of the Jews by, 461; his miserable death in Persia, ii. 8.

ANTIPATER, ii. 41; before Pompey, 44; assists Cæsar in Egypt, 51; is appointed procurator of Judæa, 52.

ANTIPATER, son of Herod the Great, ii. 79; declared heir to the throne, 80; his intrigues, 81; conspires to poison his father, 85; his trial, 86; and condemnation, 87; executed, 89.

ANTONIA, fortress of, taken by Jewish insurgents, ii. 192; described, 331; taken and razed by the Romans, 357.

ANTONINUS, accession of, ii. 442; his treatment of the Jews, 443.

AQUINAS, Thomas, his axiom about the Jews, iii. 162, note.

ARABIA, the Happy, Jews in, iii. 15.

ARCHELAUS, his accession to the throne of Judæa, ii. 93; his address to the people, 94; his journey to Rome, 96; will of Herod in his favour confirmed by imperial edict, 102; he assumes the dominion of Judæa, 103; is deposed and banished, 104.

ARIANS, faction of, joined by Alexandrian Jews, iii. 15; favourable to the Jews, 17.

ARISTOBULUS, the First, ii. 14.

ARISTOBULUS, the Second, ii. 40; attacked by Aretas, king of Arabia, 42; applies to Pompey for protection, 43; besieged in the Temple by Pompey, 46; carried prisoner to Rome, 48; escapes, but is again defeated and sent back, 49.

INDEX.

ARISTOBULUS.

ARISTOBULUS, son of Herod and Mariamne, his education at Rome, ii. 75; his return to Jerusalem, 78; accused by Herod before Augustus, 79; reconciled to his father, 80; his trial and condemnation—his execution, 84.

ARK, the, i. 145; capture of by Philistines, 263; restored, 264; removed to Jerusalem, 292.

ARTAXERXES orders Jerusalem to be rebuilt, i. 414.

ASCALON, battle of, ii. 218.

ASCHE, Rabbi, superintends compilation of Babylonian Talmud, iii. 4; his mode of teaching, 5.

ASINAI, exploits of, in Babylonia, ii. 151.

ASMONEANS, the, ii. L

ASSYRIAN Empire, power of the, i. 367.

ATHALIAH, her usurpation, i. 361; her death, 362.

ATHANASIANS, the, iii. 15.

AUGUSTUS, decree of, ii. 101.

AVERROES, the doctrines of, translated by Spanish Jews, iii. 438.

AVODA Sara, tract of, on foreign worship, in the Mischna, ii. 460, note.

AZARIAH, his prosperous reign, i. 365.

B

BABYLON, captivity of Jews in, i. 408; taking of, 415.

BABYLONIA, Jewish schools of, ii. 472; submit to Patriarch of the West, 471; their high reputation, 486.

BABYLONIAN Jews, their remarkable history, ii. 150; their historical importance, 152, note; massacre of, 155; their wealth, 486.

BALAAM, the prophet, i. 201; falls in the general massacre of Midianites, 206.

BALAK, King of Moab, i. 201.

BARBARIANS, irruption of the northern, iii. 4.

BRITTANY.

BAR-COCHAB, the pretended Messiah ii. 425; the Jews flock to his banner, 430; takes the ruins of Jerusalem, 431; killed at the storming of Bither, 435.

BARONS, wars of the, in England fatal to Jews, iii. 251; slaughter of Jews in London by faction of the, 252.

BATHSHEBA, i. 296.

BELISARIUS, Jews defend Naples against, iii. 76; checks the advance of the Persians, 79.

BELSHAZZAR, i. 413.

BELZONI, Mr., his description of the condition of poor cultivators in Upper Egypt, i. 62; royal tomb in the valley of Beban el Malook discovered by, 394.

BENJAMIN, birth of, i. 36; destruction of the tribe of, 243.

BENJAMIN of Tudela, his travels, iii. 157; his account of the sights of Rome, 311, note.

BERENICE, sister of Agrippa, ii. 183; interposes with Florus in behalf of her countrymen, 184; loved by Titus, 194; her death, 195.

BERNARD, St., protects the Jews, iii. 181; denounces the Lombard money-lenders, 188.

BERNARDINO di Feltre, iii. 340; founds the banks called "Monti della Pieth," 341.

BETHEL, i. 36.

BEZIERS, stoning of Jews in, iii. 169.

BITHER, siege and fall of, ii. 434; massacre at, 435.

BLEEK, Dr., on the antiquity of the Mosaic Law, referred to, i. 131, note.

BONAPARTE, Napoleon, summons a Sanhedrin at Paris, iii. 407; his twelve questions to Jewish deputation, 408; answers of the deputation, 409; his edict concerning the Jews, 411.

BRITTANY, Anuise of, its fanaticism against the Jews, iii. 196.

BRUGSCH.

BRUGSCH, M., on Egyptian antiquities, referred to, i. 102; on the date of the Exodus, 120.

BRUSSELS, story of the Host at, iii. 227.

BUNSEN, Baron de, his review of the Elohistic and Jehovistic controversy, i. 75, note; his explanation of the plagues of Egypt, 80, note; his chronology of Egyptian history, 102; his opinion as to extent of Egyptian conquests during Rameseid period, 113; on the date of the Exodus, 120; on the age of the Law of Moses, 131, note.

BURCKHARDT, Mr., quoted, i. 94; inaugurated a new era of Eastern travel, 121, note; referred to for the march through the desert, 124; his description of Petra, 200.

BURGON, Mr., his letters from Rome referred to, ii. 454, note.

BYZANTINE Empire, state of the Jews under, iii. 61.

C.

CABALA, the, ii. 414; dissertation of M. Ad. Franck upon, iii. 411; compared with the Zendavesta, 412; analysed, 413; its science and philosophy, 415; its purely Jewish character, 417.

CÆSAREA, foundation of, by Herod, ii. 74; disturbances in, 173; conflict between Jews and Greeks in, 181.

CALIGULA, accession of, ii. 136; exacts divine honours, 132; his irritation with the Jews, 142; he designs to profane the Temple, 143; his reception of the Alexandrian Jews, 144; orders his statue to be placed in the Temple, 145; suspends the decree, 149; his assassination, 155.

CALIPHS, Empire of the, iii. 98; Jews under the, 118; Jews as teachers of, 121; entrust the coinage to Jews, 122; decline of, 155.

CANAAN, land of, described, i. 194.

CAORSINI, the Italian bankers, iii. 246;

CROSROES.

ruin Jewish trade, 248; Jews mortgaged to, in England, 252.

CAPTIVITY of the ten tribes, i. 175; Babylonian, 407.

CARACALLA, ii. 476.

CASIMIR, the Great, favours the Jews in Poland, iii. 387.

CATACOMBS, Jewish, in Rome, ii. 454, note; inscriptions from, 456.

CESTIUS Gallus, Prefect of Syria, ii. 177; visits Jerusalem, 178; advances with an army against the Jews, 203; attacks the Temple, 206; his retreat, 207; his disgraceful defeat, 209.

CHAMPOLLION, Mr., his investigation of hieroglyphic monuments, i. 66; key to discovered by, 100.

CHASINA, Rabbi, iii. 77; legend of, 78.

CHARLEMAGNE, state of the Jews under, iii. 133; sends Isaac, a Jew, as ambassador to Haroun al Raschid, 135.

CHARLES V., King of France, his treaty when regent with the Jews, iii. 216; forbids compulsion against them, 218; his dealings with them, 219.

CHASIDIM, the sect of, ii. 2, 8, 11; greatly contributed to success of the Maccabees, 29.

CHAUCER, his tale of "The Lost Child," iii. 235.

CHEREM, solemn curse of, i. 22, note; proclamation of in the synagogue, ii. 465.

CHERUBIM, the, i. 145.

CHIARINI, the Abbé, his 'Talmud de Babylone,' iii. 4, note.

CHIEF Priests, the, ii. 293, note.

CHILPERIC, compels the Jews to be baptised, iii. 57.

CHINA, Jews in, ii. 487; their temple, 488; their chief priest, 489.

CHIVALRY, its effect upon the Jews, iii. 165.

CHOSROES, the Just, his "Everlasting Peace" with Justinian, iii. 79.

INDEX.

CHOSROES.

CHOSROES, the Second, iii. 80; takes Antioch, 81.
CHRISTIANITY, establishment of, by Constantine, iii. 8.
CHRISTIANS, persecutions of the early, by the Jews, ii. 462; Judaising, iii. 428.
CHRISTIANS, the "New," in Spain, iii. 300; persecuted by the Inquisition, 303; their sufferings, 304.
CHRONICLES, the Book of, I. 328, note; discrepancies between, and Book of Kings, 331, note; its silence about the Prophet Elijah, 355, note.
CHRONOLOGY, scheme of, for period between the Exodus and the building of the Temple, I. 237.
CIRCUMCISION, rite of, common in the East, I. 15.
CITIES of the Plain, destruction of the, I. 15; site of, 16; described by modern travellers, 17.
CLAUDIUS, his treaty with Agrippa, ii. 156; his edict in favour of the Jews, 157; his death, 171.
CLEOPATRA, in Jerusalem, ii. 65.
CLERGY, power of the, its effect upon the Jews, iii. 166.
CLOTAIRE the Second, his decree against Jews, iii. 115.
CLOVIS, King of the Franks, III. 165.
COMMERCE, internal, among the Jews, I. 234.
CONSTANTINE, the Great, iii. 8; his laws relating to the Jews, 13.
CONSTANTIUS, his severe laws against the Jews, iii. 15.
CONSTITUTION, religious, of the Jews, I. 150; civil, of the Jews, 162.
COOK, Mr., his article on the Book of Job referred to, I. 418, note.
CRASSUS, plunders the Temple of Jerusalem, ii. 50.
CROMWELL, Oliver, negotiation of the Jews with, iii. 356; compared with Buonaparte, 407.
CRUSADERS, horrible massacre of the

DAVID.

Jews by, iii. 177; against the Turks, murder and plunder the Jews, 389
CRUSADES, the, iii. 174; expenditure caused by, 187.
CUNEIFORM inscriptions, I. 5, note; 10, note; 167, 172, note; 412, note; 415, note; 418, note.
CUSPIUS FADUS, Governor of Judæa, ii. 162.
CYPRUS, revolt of Jews in, ii. 431.
CYRENE, commotions in, ii. 391.
CYRIL, Archbishop of Alexandria, iii. 34; his feud with the Prefect Orestes, 35; his adherents murder Hypatia, 36.
CYRUS, permits the Jews to return to the Holy Land, I. 417.

D.

DANIEL, the prophet, I. 410; his eminence in Babylon, 411; refuses to worship the golden image—cast into the den of lions—age and authenticity of book of, 412, and note; interprets the handwriting on the wall—promoted by Darius, 413; and Cyrus, 416.
DAVID, youth of, I. 277; anointed by Samuel—slays Goliath of Gath—his friendship for Jonathan—envied by Saul, 278; his advancement, 279; his flight to Nob, 280; in the cave of Adullam, 281; his hair-breadth escapes and magnanimity, 282; his embarrassment, 283; his elegy on the death of Saul and Jonathan, 286; declared king, 287; his qualifications for the office, 289; makes Jerusalem his capital, 290; dances before the Ark, 292; designs to build a temple, 293; his conquests, 294; his kindness to Mephibo-beth, 295; his adultery with Bathsheba, 296; his flight from Jerusalem, 299; his lamentation for Absalom—returns to Jerusalem, 301; takes a census of his dominions, 303; designates Solomon as his successor, 304; his death—

DEBORAH.

survey of his reign, 105; his character, 106; his hymns, 107.

DEBORAH, L. 246; her hymn of triumph—its historic value, 247.

DECALOGUE, the, delivered to Moses from Sinai, L. 117.

DEMETRIUS, King of Syria, ii. 9, 11, 12, 14, 16.

DESERT, the, march of the Israelites through, L. 121; means of subsistence in, 198, note.

DEUTERONOMY, antiquity of the book of, L. 207, note; variations of the Law in, 215, note.

DIAL of Ahaz, L. 174.

DIODORUS Siculus, quoted, L. 96; on the history of Egypt, 101.

DION Cassius, referred to, ii. 419; on the number of Jews who perished in war of pretended Messiah, 415.

DIVORCE, Jewish law of, L. 175.

DOMESTIC Law of the Jews, L. 171.

DOMITIAN, reign of, ii. 416.

DUNAAN, king of Homeritis, iii. 87.

E.

EBAL, Mount, L. 210; solemn recognition of the Law on, 225.

ECCLESIASTES, book of, its date, i. 325.

ECCLESIASTICUS, book of, the work of a Sadducee, ii. 12, note; on the office of a Scribe, 412.

EDOMITES, L. 29; oppose advance of Israelites into the Holy Land, 200.

EGYPT, state of, before the Israelitish settlement, L. 52; castes in, 53; shepherd kings of, 55; famine in—Joseph's administration of, 56; its prolific soil, 62; plagues of, 79; on rain in, 83; antiquity of its civilization discussed, 98; chronological systems on history of doubtful, 102; architecture of, 104; the horse unknown in early monuments of, 111.

EGYPTIANS, their hatred of the profession of a shepherd, L. 54; their

ENGLAND.

army drowned in the Red Sea, 93; the history of the Jewish Exodus preserved in their records, 96; their account of it contradictory—their traditions confirm the Mosaic narrative, 97.

EHUD, L. 245.

EISENMENGER, his 'Judaism exposed,' iii. 40; the merits and defects of this work, 41.

ELEAZAR, of the family of Judas the Galilean, ii. 186; his lofty tenets, 187; his speech to the garrison of Masada, 188, note.

ELEAZAR the scribe, martyrdom of, L. 464.

ELEAZAR, son of Simon, ii. 189; head of the war faction in Jerusalem, 191; excites the populace against Manahem—his followers massacre Roman garrison, 195; master of the public treasures, 217; his jealousy of John of Gischala, 115; strength of his faction in Jerusalem, 219.

ELI, judge and high-priest, L. 260.

ELIJAH, the prophet, L. 143; his outward appearance, 144; before Ahab, 345; his contest with priests of Baal on Mount Carmel, 346; divine communication to, 348; denounces God's vengeance on Ahab, 350; his marvellous departure, 355.

ELISHA, the prophet, L. 353; receives the mantle of Elijah, 355; miracles performed by, 356; contrasted with Elijah, 357.

ELOHIM, appellation of the Godhead, L. 75.

ELVIRA, council of, iii. 14; decree of against the Jews, 15.

ENGLAND, Jews in; their first settlement under the Saxons, iii. 229; their condition under William Rufus, 230; under Stephen and Henry the Second, 231; at the coronation of Richard the First, 233; attacked in London, 234; massacred at York,

ENRIQUEZ.

215; statute of Richard concerning, 238; persecution of, by John, 241; their treatment under Henry the Third, 242; hostility of the church to, 243; parliament of, summoned, 245; sold to Richard of Cornwall, 249; laws respecting, 251; their improved condition after battle of Lewes, 254; last statute of Henry III. against, 256; celebrated statute of Edward I. concerning, 258; their expulsion, 262; under the Tudors, 355; their negotiation with Cromwell, 356; readmitted by Charles II., 358; offer to buy St. Paul's, 397; propose to purchase Brentford, 398; bill for naturalization of, 399; number of, 400.

ENRIQUEZ de Paz, poetry of, iii. 448.
ERATOSTHENES, I. 101.
ESARHADDON, I. 387.
ESAU, birth of—sells his birthright, I. 29; his meeting with Jacob, 33.
ESDRAS, apocryphal book of, I. 375, note.
ESSENES, the, ii. 76; are the monks of Judaism, 110; their tenets and habits described, 111; persecuted by the Romans, 114; obscurity of their origin, 115.
ESTHER, history of, I. 428.
EWALD, his view of the sanction on which the Hebrew law was founded, I. 186, note; his theory on the date of the books of Job, Proverbs, and Deuteronomy, 388, note; on the last editor of the Pentateuch, 417, note; on the foundation of the Sanhedrim, ii. 105, note.
EXCOMMUNICATION, among the Jews, ii. 465.
EXODUS, date of the, discussed, I. 110.
EZEKIEL, the prophet; his splendid visions, I. 410.
EZRA, I. 411; compiles the sacred books, 417.

F.

FABER, Mr., his theory as to the building of the Pyramids is exploded, I. 66.
FEASTS, Jewish: the Sabbath — of Trumpets, I. 157; of the Passover, 158; of Pentecost—of Tabernacles, 159.
FELIX, governor of Judæa, ii. 168; his profligacy, 169; murders the high priest, 170; recalled, 171.
FERDINAND and Isabella, iii. 298; establishment of Inquisition by, 302; their edict against the Jews, 307; described by Rabbi Joshua, 317; impolicy of their expulsion of the Jews, 320.
FERDINAND Martinez, archdeacon of Ecija, iii. 284; excites the populace of Seville against Jews, 285; is not punished, 286
FERGUSSON, Mr., his description of Solomon's Temple, I. 311, note.
FEUDAL system, its effect upon the Jews, iii. 160.
FLACCUS Aquilius, Roman prefect of Egypt, ii. 134; he persecutes the Alexandrian Jews, 136; his cruelty, 138; his arrest and banishment, 140.
FLAGELLANTS, march of the, iii. 222.
FLAVIAN dynasty, accession of the, ii. 313.
FRANCK, M. Ad., quoted on the Mosaic conception of God, I. 75, note; his dissertation on the Cabala, iii. 431.
FRANK, Jacob, organises the sect of Zoharites, iii. 370; his oriental magnificence, 371; nature of his creed, 372; his wealth and splendid burial, 373.
FREDERICK II. protects the Jews, iii. 198; his patronage of learning, 200.
FREDERICK the Great; his edict respecting the Jews, iii. 196; mitigated by Frederick William II., 404.
FRENCH Revolution, Jews in France before and at the time of, iii. 405.

G.

GABARA, city of, destroyed by Vespasian, ii. 241.
GABINIUS, in Judæa, ii. 48; Sanhedrims established by, 49; his fate, 50.
GALILEE, province of, described, ii. 221; factions in, 224.
GAMALA, situation of, ii. 280; siege of, by Vespasian, 281; repulse of Romans before, 282; fall of, 286.
GAMALIEL, son of Judah, ii. 405.
GAMALIEL, son of Simon, escape of, ii. 403; school of, 404.
GENNESARET, description of the lake of, ii. 275; massacre on, 278.
GERIZIM, Mt., i. 210; solemn recognition of the Law on, 225; temple on, 442; temple on, destroyed by Hyrcanus, ii. 21; slaughter of Samaritans on, 261.
GESSIUS FLORUS, governor of Judæa —his oppression, ii. 177; drives the Jews to insurrection, 182; his massacre of the Jews, 183; retires to Cæsarea, 186.
GIBBON, Mr., his prejudices against the Jews, ii. 417, note; his account of the privileges granted to them by Antoninus Pius, 440.
GIDEON, the deliverer of his country, i. 250; destroys the altars of Baal —sign from heaven granted to—his victory over the Midianites, 251; refuses to be king—his death, 252.
GILBOA, battle of, i. 285.
GILGAL, encampment of Israelites in, i. 219, 222.
GISCHALA, siege and capture of, by Titus, ii. 287.
GOLDEN Age of the modern Jews, iii. 117; under the Caliphs, 118; under the Byzantine Empire, 130; in Italy, 131; under Charlemagne, 132; their trade with the East, 133; the Jews as financiers and physicians, 134; under Louis the Debonnaire, 135; privileges granted

HEROD.

to them, 137; edict of Agobard, Archbishop of Lyons, against, 139; under Charles the Bald, 142; in Spain, 146.
GOSHEN, family of Israel in, i. 59.
GRAHAM, Mr. Cyril, his description of Bashan, i. 228, note.
GRÉGOIRE, Abbé, his prize dissertation on the Jews, iii. 40.
GREGORY, the First, denounces the slave-trade, iii. 51; distinguishes between trade in and possession of slaves, 52; writes against slavery, 54; his tolerance towards the Jews, 55; prohibits forcible measures against, 58.
GUILLANY, Professor, his work 'Die Menschen-Opfer der alten Hebräer' referred to, i. 22, note.

H.

HADRIAN, accession of, ii. 423; his edict against the Jews, 424; his law prohibiting the Jews from entering Ælia Capitolina, 438; re-enacted, iii. 84.
HAMAN, i. 430.
HARRINGTON, his proposition to sell Ireland to the Jews, iii. 158.
HASSIDIN, sect of the, iii. 370.
HEBREW law, character of the, i. 130; sanction on which it was founded, 186.
HEBREW, poetry of the Bible, iii. 419; modern poetry, 441; a dead language, 443; Spanish poets, 446.
HEINRICH Heine, poetry of, iii. 449.
HELIODORUS, i. 456.
HELIOGABALUS, ii. 474.
HERACLIUS, retakes Syria and Egypt, iii. 83; is said to have excited the King of Spain to persecute the Jews, 102.
HEROD, the Great, governor of Galilee, ii. 52; made King of Judæa by the Romans, 57; besieges and takes Jerusalem, 58; his visit to Mark Antony, 64; his visit to Octavius,

INDEX

HEROD.

67; dissension in his family, 68; puts to death his wife Mariamne, 69; his remorse, 70; builds a theatre in Jerusalem, 71; conspiracy to assassinate, 72; rebuilds Samaria, 73; founds the city of Cæsarea, 74; his friendship with Augustus and Agrippa, 75; murmurs of the Jews against, 76; he rebuilds the Temple, 77; accuses his sons by Mariamne before Augustus, 79; dark intrigues in his family, 81; he brings his sons to trial, 84; his last illness and will, 87; his massacre of the Innocents, 88; his death, 89; his funeral, 93.

HEROD Antipas, tetrarch of Galilee, ii. 93; in Rome, 97; his government — puts to death John the Baptist, 125; visits Rome — is accused by Agrippa — banished by Caligula, 131.

HERODIAN family, the, ii. 90.

HERODION, fall of, ii. 383.

HERODOTUS, on the history of Egypt, i. 101; ruin of Sennacherib's army related by, 184.

HEZEKIAH, on the throne of Judah, i. 177; throws off the Assyrian yoke, 179; is attacked by Sennacherib, 180; his submission, 181; his sublime prayer, 183; his illness, 184; is cured by Isaiah, 185; his death, 186.

HIGH Priest, the, i. 145; government falls into the hands of, after Nehemiah, 446; before Alexander the Great, 447.

HILARY, Bishop of Poitiers, iii. 37.

HILKIAH, the high priest, original copy of the Law discovered by, i. 389, 437.

HILLEL, Patriarch of Tiberias, his baptism, iii. 11.

HOLLAND, state of Jews in, iii. 354.

HOLY of Holies, i. 145.

HOMERITES, Jewish kingdom in, iii. 86; fall of the, 89.

HONORIUS IV., rebukes the clergy of

IRON.

England, iii. 260; his bull condemning usury, and complaining of progress of Jews, 261.

HOSEA, the prophet, i. 170.

HUGH of Lincoln, story of, iii. 249; canonised, 250.

HYPATIA, barbarous murder of, iii. 37.

HYRCANUS builds a fortress beyond Jordan, i. 454; slays himself, 455.

HYRCANUS, the Second, ii. 39; resigns the sovereignty, 41; flies to Arabia, 43; nominated by Pompey to the priesthood, 48; put to death by Herod, 67.

I.

IDOLATRY, Mosaic law against, i. 151; of the Jews during the period of the Judges, 242.

IDUMEANS, the, march to Jerusalem, ii. 298; excluded the city, 299; enter Jerusalem, 300; massacre the people, 301; leave Jerusalem, 304.

IMAGES, the Jews breakers of, iii. 130.

IMMORTALITY of the soul, Jewish belief in, i. 435.

INNOCENT, the Third, iii. 166; his treatment of the Jews, 167; council of Lateran under, compels them to wear a peculiar dress, 198.

INNOCENT, the Fourth, his bull in favour of the Jews, iii. 167; quoted at length, 199, note.

INNOCENTS, massacre of the, ii. 88.

INQUISITION, the, in Spain, iii. 302; conspiracy against, 307; cruelties of, 324.

IRON Age of the modern Jews, iii. 152; their persecution in the East, 154; diminution of their number in Palestine, 157; and in the Byzantine Empire, 159; effect of the feudal system upon, 160; of chivalry upon, 165; of the power of the clergy upon, 166; of usury upon, 170; persecution of, in Granada, 171; horrible massacres of, by

VOL. III.   2 H

ISAAC.

the Crusaders, 177; their wealth and establishments in France, 185; spoiled and expelled by Philip Augustus, 189; re-admitted into France, 191; persecuted by St. Louis, 197; compelled to wear a peculiar dress, 198; calumnies against, 201; their condition in Spain, 201; expelled from France by Philip the Fair, 207; re-admitted by Louis X., 209; state of, under Philip the Long, 210; rising of the shepherds against, 211; accused as authors of the pestilence, 214, and note; their treaty with French Government, 217; their final expulsion from France, 221; in Germany, 222; plunder and massacre of in Frankfort, Prague, and other cities, 223.

ISAAC, birth of, i. 19; offering of, 20; marries Rebekah, 26; his death, 37.

ISAIAH, the prophet, i. 371; encourages Hezekiah to resist Sennacherib, 383; makes the shadow retrograde on the dial of Ahaz, 385; his martyrdom, 387; authorship of the later chapters of the book of, 418, note.

ISHMAEL, son of Abraham and Hagar, i. 14.

ISIDORE, of Seville, his protest against religious persecution, iii. 104.

ISRAEL, 'the prevailing,' Jacob commanded to assume the name of, i. 34; the twelve sons of, 47; his migration into Egypt—his establishment in Goshen, 59; list of the kings of, 330.

ISRAELITES, duration of their sojourn in Egypt, i. 64; number of, in Egypt, 65; persecutions of, 67; their march to the Red Sea, 89; pursued by the Egyptian army, 91; passage of the Red Sea, 92; multiplication of in Goshen, 117; their march through the desert, 124; arrive at the foot of Mt. Sinai—attacked by the Amalekites, 128;

JAMNIA

organization of, 129; receive the law from Moses, 130; advance to the Holy Land, 188; their number —accuracy of, as contained in the census, questioned, 189, note; arrive at Kadesh Barnea, 193; condemned to wander forty years, 195; second advance of, 199; invade Moab, 201; invade and extirpate the Midianites, 206; pass the Jordan, 218; capture Jericho, 220; the promised land divided among the twelve tribes of, 227; want of union among, 240; servitude to the King of Mesopotamia, 244; subdued by the Moabites—delivered by Ehud, 245; oppressed by the Canaanites, 246; and by the Midianites, 250; delivered by Gideon, 251; oppressed by the Philistines and Ammonites, 254; desire a king, 268; captivity of, 375 (see Jews).

ITALY, Jews of, iii. 325; their condition, 329; Roman Jews exempt from tribute, 331; riot at Trani, 331; bull of Martin V. in favour of, 335; bankers and money-lenders, 339; varying policy of the popes towards, 341; harsh edict of Paul IV. against, 344; toleration of proclaimed by Sixtus V., 345; in the Two Sicilies, 400.

IZATES, King of Adiabene, is converted to the Jewish religion, ii. 163; undergoes the rite of circumcision, 164; is buried at Jerusalem, 165.

J.

JACOB, birth of, he buys the right of primogeniture, i. 29; his vision of the ladder, 30; his contest with Laban, 31; marries Rachel—in Mesopotamia, 32; his vision—is commanded to assume the name of Israel—his meeting with Esau, 34; his family, 47; his migration into Egypt—is settled in Goshen, 59; his death and splendid prophecy, 62.

JAMNIA, school of, ii. 404; re-opened, 443; fall of, 444.

JAPHA.

JAPHA, fortress of, II. 259; fall of, 260.
JASHER, the book of, I. 221.
JASON, I. 458, 461; his death, 462.
JEHOIAKIM, King of Judah, I. 394; carried prisoner to Babylon, 397; buried with the burial of an ass, 398.
JEHOSHAPHAT, King of Judah, I. 350; organizes a judicial system, 351; his death, 351.
JEHOVAH, revelation of the name to Moses, i. 75; its full signification, 77, note.
JEHU, king of Israel, I. 358; his bloody but successful career, 360.
JEHUDA, the Holy, patriarch of Tiberias, II. 477; author of the Mischna, 478.
JEPHTHAH, chief of the Gileadites; his rash vow—defeats the Ammonites, I. 354; and the Ephraimites, 355.
JEREMIAH, the prophet, I. 393; his solemn warnings and denunciations, 395; foretells the captivity of the Jews, 396; thrown into a dungeon, 399; his predictions fulfilled, 400; his Lamentations, 401; his death in Egypt, 401.
JERICHO, capture of, I. 220; surrenders to the Romans, II. 308.
JEROBOAM, king of Israel, I. 333; his idolatry, 335; defeated by Abijah, 337; consults the prophet Abijah, 339; his family put to the sword, 340.
JERUSALEM, Jews not in possession of, till reign of David, I. 97; the seat of the Hebrew government, 290; its situation described, 291; besieged by Rabshakeh, 382; first capture by Necho, 393; second capture by Nebuchadnezzar, 398; rebuilding of, 436; its walls rebuilt by Nehemiah, 436; taken by Ptolemy, 449; its desolate condition after the persecution of Antiochus Epiphanes, II. 6; taken by Pompey, 47; taken by Herod, 59; seditious

JEWISH.

meetings in after death of Herod, 95; tumults in, 167; abandoned by the Christians, 180; surrender of Roman garrison in, 195; preparations for war in, 336; John of Gischala in, 289; hostile factions in, 290; infested by robbers, 291, civil war in, 293; state of, at the commencement of the siege (A.C. 69), 315; conflicts of the three factions in, 317; advance of Titus against, 319; the siege formed, 321; its walls described, 326; its magnificence, 330; the battering rams advanced, 336; first wall abandoned, 338; stratagem of Castor, 339; second wall lost and retaken, 341; second wall taken, 343; famine, 345; horrors of the siege, 347; effects of the famine, 351; the Antonia taken, 357; and razed, 358; the Temple besieged, 359; outer cloisters destroyed, 362; fearful ravages of the famine, 363; the Temple set on fire, 365; burning of the Temple, 367; the Romans enter the Temple, 368; indiscriminate carnage, 370; the upper city attacked, 371; "Fall of Jerusalem," 377; number killed and taken at the siege, 379; its ruins occupied by a Roman garrison, 415; a new city founded by Hadrian on its site, 424; its ruins taken by the pretended Messiah, 431; razed to the ground, 433; Constantine adorns the new city, III. 11; splendour of the new city, 16; conquest of, by the Persians, 82.
JETHRO, father-in-law of Moses; he joins the camp in the desert—his advice to Moses, I. 129.
JEWISH empire under Solomon, I. 328; dissolved by revolt of the ten tribes, 332; communities, re-establishment of, II. 199; mission to Antoninus at Rome, 443; impostors and enthusiasts, 459; education, 467, note; civilization of Spain, iii. 271; trade in the Levant, 338;

JEWS.

schools, intolerance of the, 439; modern poetry, 443; literature barren of history, 450.

JEWS. Prefatory remarks on their civil and religious history, L 1; influence of Egyptian civilization on the, 144, note; their religious constitution, 150; civil constitution, 161; domestic laws, 171; military laws, 176; close of the first period of their history, 403; their nationality, 405; number of carried away to Babylon, 409; their return from the Babylonian captivity, 419; national character on their return to the Holy Land, 422; edict for the massacre of, by Ahasuerus, 433; migration of, under Ezra, 433; number of, taken by Nehemiah, 436; their constitution re-established, 439; blank in their history, 441; tributary to Egypt, 451; persecuted by Antiochus Epiphanes, 461; victories of, under the Maccabees, II. 5; census of, taken when they became subjects of Rome, 116; expelled from Rome by Tiberius Cæsar, 119; number of, in Jerusalem (A.C. 65), 180; massacre of, in Jerusalem by Florus, 181; reject the imperial offerings to the Temple, 189; revolt of, in Jerusalem, 191; massacre of, in Cæsarea, 196; in Syria, 197; and in Scythopolis, 198; defeat the Romans under Cestius Gallus, 209; their preparations for war, 211; defeated near Ascalon, 218; advance of Vespasian against the, 240; their desperate defence of Jerusalem, 361; their political existence annihilated, 396; history of the modern, 397; their treatment during the reigns of Vespasian, Domitian, Nero, and Trajan, 416; insurrections of, in Babylonia, Egypt, Cyrene, and Judæa, 417; their sufferings, 418; their atrocities in Egypt, 420; dispersion of the, in Egypt—in Asia Minor, 449; in Greece, 450; in Rome, 451; in Spain, 455; their persecution of

JEZEBEL.

the early Christians, 463; their relations with Rome, 474; colony of, in China, at the Christian era, 487; their seclusion from the rest of mankind, 490; attempt under Constantine to convert, iii. 9; laws of Constantine respecting, 12; excesses of the, 15; interdicted from entering Jerusalem, 16; edict of Julian the Apostate for restoring their worship, 17; attempt to rebuild the Temple, 18; their treatment by Theodosius the Great, 24; conflict between Christians and— their treatment by Theodosius II., 28; conversion of, in Minorca, 29; and in Crete, 32; their condition under the barbarian kings, 45; trade carried on by, 47; state of, in Africa, 55; effect of Mohammedanism upon, 60; their condition under the Byzantine empire, 61; laws of Justinian against, 66; state of, in Persia, 77; assist the Persians to take Jerusalem, 82; in Arabia, 85; their treatment by Mohammed, 93; under the empire of the Caliphs, 98; persecuted in Spain, 99; and in France, 114; effect of the invention of printing on, 145; of the Reformation on—Imperial taxation of, 347; their treatment in Germany, 348; local persecutions of, 349; conflagrations laid to the charge of, 351; serve in the "Thirty Years' War," 354; change in their relative condition, 385; in western Europe, 395; Edict of Frederick the Great concerning, 396; in England since time of Charles II., 397; in Italy, 400; in Germany, 401; in France, 405; general improvement in their condition, 413; estimate of the number of, throughout the world, 414; survey of their influence in philosophy, poetry, history, &c., 426; their contributions to music, 455 (and see Golden and Iron Ages of the Modern Jews, Jews in England, Spain, &c.)

JEZEBEL, death of, L 359.

JOAB.

JOAB, i. 291, 297, 298; slays Absalom, 300; Solomon warned against by David, 304; slain by order of Solomon, 308.
JOASH, reign of, i. 161.
JOB, date and authorship of the book of, i. 438.
JOCHANAN Ben-Zaccai, ii. 401.
JOEL, the prophet, i. 370.
JOHN of Gischala, ii. 221; his escape from Gischala, 287; in Jerusalem, 289; his intrigues, 296; his ambitious projects, 306; strength of his faction, 319; he surprises the Inner Temple, 333; destroys the Roman embankments, 349; melts the Temple treasures, 354; surrenders to the Romans, 376.
JOHN Hyrcanus, the Maccabee, high priest, ii. 21; besieged in Jerusalem, 22; throws off the Syrian yoke, 23; his successful foreign policy, 28; joins the Sadducees, 33.
JONAH, the prophet, i. 369.
JONATHAN, the son of Saul, i. 273; overthrows the Philistines, 275; his friendship for David, 278; intervenes in behalf of David, 280; his death, 285.
JONATHAN, the high priest, ii. 168; murdered in the Temple by order of Felix, 170.
JONATHAN, the Maccabee, ii. 14; maintains a desultory war—becomes master of Judæa, 15; high priest, 16; is taken prisoner, 18; murdered by Tryphon, 19.
JOPPA, taken by the Romans under Vespasian, ii. 272; extermination of its inhabitants, 273.
JORDAN, passage of the, i. 218.
JOSEPH, birth of, i. 47; his coat of many colours—his two dreams—is sold by his brothers, 49; is carried into Egypt and bought by Potiphar—his rapid advancement—accused by Potiphar's wife—thrown into prison, 50; interprets the king's

JOSEPHUS.

dreams—made chief minister, 51; his brethren come to buy corn in Egypt, 57; makes himself known to them, 59; his administration in Egypt, 60; death of, 63; the Pharaoh whose minister he was sprung from the native race, 110.
JOSEPH ben Gorion, his audacious romances, iii. 451.
JOSEPH ben Joshua ben Meir, the chronicle of, iii. 454.
JOSEPH Pichon, iii. 282.
JOSEPH, the physician, iii. 11; converted to Christianity—promoted by Constantine—builds Christian churches in Jewish cities, 12.
JOSEPH, the Second, of Germany, ameliorates the condition of the Jews, iii. 401.
JOSEPH, son of Tobias, i. 451; farmer of the royal revenue, 452; father of Hyrcanus, 454.
JOSEPHUS, his contradictory statements as to duration of Egyptian captivity, i. 64; his comparison between marches of Alexander and Israelites, 94; has extracted the contradictory accounts of his ancestors from three Egyptian historians, 96; his attempt to identify the shepherd kings with his ancestors, 105; his description of Solomon's Temple, 333; number of the Essenes, according to, ii. 110; his account of Caligula compared with that of Philo, 148; his history the only trustworthy authority for war between Jews and Romans, 211; his history characterized, 214; appointed to the command in Galilee, 217; his early life and character, 218; his measures for the defence of Galilee, 221; interview with John of Gischala, 226; in Tarichea, 227; in Tiberias, 228; opposes the Romans, 230; intrigues against him, 231; his activity, 233; discrepancies between his 'Jewish War' and 'Life,' 235; his flight at the approach of Vespasian, 241; throws

JOSEPHUS.

himself into Jotapata, 244; directs defence of Jotapata, 246; attacks the Roman camp, 251; concealed in a well, 264; his speeches to his comrades, 266; his stratagem, 268; his conference with Vespasian, 269; his character, 270; with Titus at the siege of Jerusalem, 340; recommends the Jews to surrender, 343; his narrow escape, 353; his conduct and fate after the fall of Jerusalem, 393; Titus and Agrippa testify to the accuracy of his history, 393; his "Antiquities of the Jews," 394.

JOSEPHUS, the False, ii. 441, note.

JOSHUA, appointed to succeed Moses, i. 212; assumes the command, 217; commands the sun and moon to stand still, 222; conquers the North, 224; divides out the land, 227; his death, 216.

JOSHUA, Rabbi, his account of Ferdinand and Isabella, iii. 317; of the Reformation, 353.

JOSIAH, ascends the throne of Judah, i. 189; destroys idolatrous places—celebrates the Passover, 390; his death in battle, 392.

JOST, high value of his 'Geschichte der Israeliten seit der Zeit der Maccabäer,' and of his 'Geschichte des Judenthums,' ii. 476, note.

JOTAPATA, city of, ii. 244; siege of, by Vespasian, 245; description of, 246; blockade of, 249; siege of, resumed, 250; storming and magnificent defence of, 257; capture of, 262; massacre of the whole male population, 263; razed to the ground, 264.

JOTHAM, his parable, i. 251.

JUBILEE, the, i. 160, and note; its effect on the law of property, 231.

JUDÆA, earthquake in, ii. 66; becomes part of a Roman province, 104; famines in, 163; in rebellion against Rome, 211; final subjugation of, 389; insurrection in, led by the pretended Messiah, 430.

KARAITES.

JUDAH, silence of Deborah's hymn as to tribe of, i. 248; list of the kings of, 330; invaded by Sennacherib, 380; becomes a vassal state, 394.

JUDAISM, golden age of, iii. 117; iron age of, 154; in England, 229; statute of Edward I., 258; modern, 384; extent of, in the United States of America, 423.

JUDAS, the Galilean, ii. 116.

JUDAS, the Maccabee, ii. 1; unfolds their banner, 3; his victories over the Syrians, 5; his entry into Jerusalem, 6; subdues the country beyond Jordan, 8; defends Jerusalem against Lysias, 10; his victory over Nicanor—enters into alliance with Rome, 13; his noble death in battle, 14.

JUDGES, period of the, the heroic age of Hebrew history, i. 238; their authority and functions, 239; survey of the period of, 271.

JULIAN, the Apostate, accession of—his edict for rebuilding the Temple, iii. 17; his death, 22.

JULIUS Cæsar, mourned by the Jews, ii. 452.

JULIUS Severus, fl. 432.

JUSTIN, his penal laws against the Samaritans, iii. 70; and Jews, 71.

JUSTINIAN, his severe laws against the Jews and Samaritans, iii. 66; permissive enactment by, for use of the Greek Scriptures in the Synagogue, 75.

JUSTUS, of Tiberias, the historian, ii. 211, note; head of a faction in Tiberias, 234; his calumnies against Josephus, 235, note.

JUVENAL, his complaint against the Jews, ii. 454.

K.

KADESH Barnea, arrival of Israelites at, i. 193; site of, 197, note.

KARAITES, the Protestants of Judaism, iii. 125; revival of, 126; articles of

KHAIBAR.
their belief, 137; their later settlements, 138; orderly congregations of, 186; their hymns, 418; in the Crimea, 419.
KHAIBAR, Mohammed attacks the Jews in, iii. 95; capitulation of, 97.
KHAZAR, Jewish kingdom of, iii. 128.
KIBROTH Hattaavah, mutiny at, i. 191.
KINGS, the Book of, i. 328, note; discrepancies between, and Book of Chronicles, 331, note.
KORAH, rebellion of, i. 196.
KORAIDHITES, extirpation of the, by Mohammed, iii. 94.
KORAN, description of Abraham's iconoclasm in, i. 4, note.
KOSCIUSKO, Jews in the army of, iii. 394.

L.

LATERAN Council, acts of the, iii. 332.
LAW, the Mosaic, its antiquity discussed, i. 131, note; 437, note; reverence of the Jews for; ii. 409.
LE CLERC, his dissertations referred to, i. 18.
LEPERS, the, accused of poisoning rivers in France, iii. 233.
LEPROSY, the Hebrews in Egypt may have been subject to, i. 119; described, 178; Mosaic provisions against, 179.
LEPSIUS, Book of Kings of, i. 102; on the date of the Exodus, 110; "Todtenbuch" published by, 186, note.
LEVI, tribe of, its position and duties under Mosaic constitution, i. 161.
LEVIRATE Law, i. 48; treated in the Mischna as of perpetual obligation, ii. 478.
LEVITES, the, after the Babylonian captivity, ii. 408.
LEWES battle of, iii. 253.

MALTE.
LEWIS, Sir George, on the warlike character of the early Egyptian kings, i. 99, note; on the navigation of the Phoenicians, 223, note.
LOANS, law relating to in France, iii. 193; in Spain, 272.
LOCUSTS, i. 85.
LOMBARDS, the, iii. 170.
LOT, son of Haran, the brother of Abram, i. 4; migrates with Abram, 6; inhabits an independent settlement in Canaan, 9; attacked by neighbouring tribes, 10; rescued by Abram, 11; his flight, 12.
LOUIS, Saint, his accession, iii. 194; he represses usury, 195; his intolerance and piety, 196; he persecutes the Jews, 197.
LUTHER, the tone in which he speaks of the Jews, iii. 351.
LYNCH, Mr., his account of the Dead Sea referred to, i. 17, note.

M.

MACCABEES, the, derivation of the word uncertain, ii. 3; their first triumphal campaign, 6; re-establish a powerful state in Judæa, 7.
MACCABEES, the Books of, death of Antiochus Epiphanes as described in, ii. 9, note.
MACHÆRUS, surrender of, ii. 194.
MACHPELAH, i. 26.
MAGIAN religion, re-establishment of the, iii. 2.
MAIMONIDES, Moses, his explanation of the story of Balaam, i. 204, note; his birth at Cordova, iii. 149; his education, 150; his "More Nevochim" — is the founder of Rationalism, 151; called by his admirers the "Second Moses," 152.
MALACHI, the prophet, i. 440.
MALTE BRUN, his description of the valley of Jordan, i. 17; of Galilee, 226.

MANAHEM.

MANAHEM, son of Judas the Galilean, ii. 193; his exploits and insolence, 194; his death, 195.

MANASSEH, ascends the throne of Judah—his cruelties and idolatry, i. 386; sent captive to Babylon, 387; his restoration and repentance, 388.

MANASSEH ben Israel, iii. 356; his petition to Cromwell—and to the Commonwealth, 357.

MANES, iii. 2.

MANETHO, i. 101.

MANUFACTURES, Jewish, i. 235.

MANNA, i. 127.

MARAH, bitter waters of, i. 124; analysis of, 125, note.

MARCUS Aurelius, reign of, ii. 446.

MARIAMNE, the wife of Herod, ii. 56; her irresistible beauty, 64; and death, 69; her sons, 78.

MARRIAGE, Jewish law of, i. 175.

MARTIAL, his description of the Jews, ii. 454.

MASSADA, fortress of, ii. 189; its situation, 185; siege of, 186; self-destruction of the garrison of, 188.

MATTATHIAS, ii. 1.

MAXIMUS, reign of, iii. 23.

MELCHIZEDECH, i. 11.

MEMPHIS, city of, i. 100; priests of, 101; the capital of a kingdom far advanced in civilization, 103.

MENELAUS, i. 459, 461; ii. 11.

MENES, the first mythic or real king of Egypt, i. 100.

MESOPOTAMIA, insurrection of Jews in, ii. 422; abandoned by Hadrian, 423; condition of Jews in, iii. 1.

MESSIAH, the, foretold by Isaiah, i. 171; belief in the coming of after Babylonian captivity, 425; belief in his triumphant coming at the time of the Roman war, ii. 302; appearance of the pretended, 438.

MESSIAHS, account of the false, iii. 359.

MOSES.

MICHAEL Cardoso, his strange doctrine, iii. 369.

MICHAEL Silveyra, his epic poems, iii. 448.

MICHAELIS, quoted on the explanations of Jephthah's vow, i. 255.

MILAN, ballad of the Jew's daughter of, iii. 226.

MIRIAM, sister of Moses; her mutiny and punishment, i. 193; her death, 199.

MISCHNA, the, or code of traditional law described—sources whence derived, ii. 478; distribution of, 479; provisions of, 480; the treatise Sanhedrin in, 481.

MOHAMMED, his religious doctrine, iii. 85; rise of, 91; he persecutes the Jews, 93; his victories, 96.

MOHAMMEDANISM, iii. 59.

MOORS, conquest of Spain by the, iii. 111.

MORDECAI, i. 430.

MOROCCO, sufferings of Jews in, iii. 314.

MOSAIC constitution, the, i. 148.

MOSES ('drawn from the Waters'), his birth—preservation in a cradle of rushes, i. 68; his education—romantic fictions of later writers respecting, 69; his flight to Arabia, 72; return to Egypt—undertakes deliverance of the Israelites, 73; his qualifications for the undertaking—his credentials—the burning bush, 74; transformation of his rod—withering of his hand, 76; before Pharaoh—demands the release of the Israelites, 77; his contest with Egyptian magicians, 79; divides the Red Sea, 92; his hymn on crossing the Red Sea, 95; leads the Israelites through the desert, 111; sweetens the waters of Marah, 115; feeds the Israelites with manna, 127; smites the rock and draws water from it, 128; delivery of the Law by, 110; on Sinai, 136; his punishment of the idolaters,

MOSES.

119; revelation of the Godhead to, 140; quells the mutiny at Kibroth-Hattaavah, 193; lifts up the brazen serpent, 201; his last acts, 207; his last words, 211; views the promised land from Mount Nebo, 212; his death and character, 211.

MOSES ('clad in Sackcloth'), iii. 147; in the synagogue of Cordova, 148.
MOSES of Crete, the Impostor, iii. 32.
MOSES Mendelsohn, iii. 401; his influence in Germany, 402.
MUIR, Mr.; his Life of Mohammed referred to, iii. 91, note.
MURDER, Jewish law against, I. 180.

N.

NAHUM, the prophet, i. 369; inroad of the Scythians described by, 391.
NATHAN, the prophet, i. 193.
NATURALIZATION Bill in England, iii. 199.
NEBUCHADNEZZAR commands the armies of Assyria, i. 195; takes Jerusalem, 198.
NEHEMIAH, i. 434; rebuilds the walls of Jerusalem, 435; his reforms, 440; expels Manasseh from Jerusalem, 441; his death, 443.
NERO, decree of, ii. 181; sends Vespasian to Syria, 216; his death, 310.
NERVA, reign of, ii. 416.
NICOLAUS of Damascus, the historian, ii. 83; his speech on the trial of Antipater, 86; accompanies Archelaus to Rome, 96.
NIEBUHR, the Danish traveller; his hypothesis as to the passage of the Red Sea, I. 93.
NIGER of Perea, at the battle of Ascalon, ii. 238; his wonderful escape, 239; murdered by the Zealots in Jerusalem, 305.
NILE, the, i. 80.
NOTATION, Hebrew system of, i. 189.

PETER.

O.

OG, king of Bashan, i. 202.
OMAR II., anecdote of, iii. 124.
ONIAS, founds a Jewish temple in Alexandria, ii. 25.
ORESTES, prefect of Alexandria, iii. 14; his feud with Cyril, 15; defended by the Alexandrians, 16.
OTHNIEL, i. 244.
OXFORD, three halls opened for Jews in, iii. 230; outbreak of scholars against Jews in, 255; the cross insulted by the Jews in, 256.

P.

PALESTINE, character of its population and government, i. 119; described, 225; divided among the twelve tribes, 217; state of, after the fall of Jerusalem, ii. 400.
PARIS, Jewish synagogues in, iii. 191, note.
PARLIAMENT of Jews, in England, iii. 245.
PARTHIANS, the, ii. 54.
PASSOVER, feast of the; its institution, i. 88; schism between the schools of Babylonia and Palestine as to calculation of the day for, ii. 471.
PATRIARCH, Jewish, of the West, ii. 199; his power and dominions, 447; his apostles, 461; decline of his authority, iii. 7; fall of, 38.
PATRIARCHAL history, state of society in, i. 36.
PATRIARCHS, character of the, i. 41.
PENTATEUCH, books of the; their age and authorship, i. 111, note.
PETER Leonis, remarkable family of the, iii. 129.
PETER of Luna (Benedict XIII.); disputation at Tortosa in his presence, iii. 293; his severe bull against the Jews, 294.

PETER.

PETER, the Venerable, denounces the Jews, iii. 182; urges the plunder of them, 184.
PETRA, city of, i. 200.
PETRONIUS, governor of Syria, is ordered to place the statue of Caligula in the Temple, ii. 145; his hesitation, 147; his danger, 150.
PHARISEES, the, i. 415; growth and origin of the sect of, obscure, ii. 29; their tenets, 31; their popularity and pretensions, 108.
PHERORAS, brother of Herod, ii. 80; his intrigues, 81; his death, 85.
PHILIP Augustus, accession of, iii. 188; confiscates all debts due to Jews, 189; and all their unmoveable property, 190; his law relating to loans, 192; and interest, 193.
PHILIP the Fair; his rapacity and cruelty, iii. 206; expels and pillages the Jews, 207.
PHILIP the Long, favours the Jews, iii. 209.
PHILISTINES, the; their connexion with Crete, i. 256, note; defeat of, by Israelites, 267.
PHILO; his description of the persecution of the Alexandrian Jews by Flaccus, ii. 141; his account of Caligula's intended profanation of the Temple, 148.
PHŒNICIANS, naval discoveries of the, i. 122.
PILGRIMS, Christian, to the Holy City, iii. 16.
PINTO Delgado, his poems, iii. 447.
PLACIDUS, ii. 240; repulsed before Jotapata, 242; takes Stabyrium, 284; his victory by Jericho, 308.
PLAGUE, the Black; striking description of, by Rabbi Joshua, iii. 213, note; in Germany, 222.
PLINY, referred to, ii. 417.
POLAND, settlement of Jews in, iii. 386; their condition, 390; the seat of the Rabbinical papacy, 394; estimate of Polish Jews, 420.

QUIRINIUS.

POLYCARP, death of, ii. 462.
POLYGAMY permitted by Jewish law, i. 175.
POMPEY in Syria, ii. 43; approaches Jerusalem, 45; besieges it, 46; in the Temple, 47; respects the Temple treasures, 48.
PONTIUS Pilate, governor of Judæa, ii. 120; Jesus Christ before, 121; his disgrace, 124.
POPES, the, protectors of the Jews, iii. 166; taxes levied by, 227.
PORCIUS Festus, governor of Judæa, ii. 174.
PORTUGAL, cruel persecution of Jews in, iii. 314.
PRAGUE, massacre of Jews at, iii. 224; history of the Jews in, 350.
PRIESTHOOD, Egyptian, i. 53; schism in the Jewish, ii. 172.
PRINCE, of the Captivity in Mesopotamia; origin of the dignity, ii. 399; his state and splendour, 483; court of, 485; last prince of, iii. 156.
PRODIGIES, ii. 178.
PROPERTY, Jewish law of, i. 210.
PROPHETISM, confusion in the conception of, i. 365.
PROPHETS, the, i. 341; sacred writings of, 369.
PROSELYTES, law against pretended Jewish to Christianity, iii. 26.
PTOLEMY, takes Jerusalem, i. 449.
PTOLEMY (Philopator) repelled from the sanctuary of the Temple, i. 452.
PURIM, festival of, i. 432; tumultuous celebrations of, iii. 27; harlequinade for, 443.
PYRAMIDS, constructive skill of builders of, i. 103; hieroglyphical names and titles of kings on, 104.

Q.

QUIRINIUS, præfecture of, in Syria, ii. 116.

RABBINICAL.

R.

RABBINICAL rule, strictness of the, ii. 468.
RABBINISM, origin and growth of, ii. 407; domination of, iii. 386.
RABBINS, the, ii. 411; superintend the education of the Jews, 467; their jealousy of Greek letters, iii. 74; subtlety of their lore, 410.
RAHAB, i. 117, 121.
RAMESEID dynasties, wars of the—date of, i. 111; architectural magnificence of, 115; period of obscuration at the close of the nineteenth, 118.
RAWLINSON, Sir H.; his faith in cuneiform inscriptions, i. 5, note; his list of kings doubtful, 10, note; inscription relating to the insanity of Nebuchadnezzar translated by, 412.
RECORDS, earliest Hebrew; internal evidence of their authority, i. 44; of their antiquity, 46; synchronism of their dates with those of monumental history of Egypt—of their facts, 98; discussion as to how far they conform to Egyptian history, 108; general correspondence between Mosaic and monumental history of Egypt, 122; difficulties and discrepancies in the numbers occurring in, 189, note.
RED SEA, passage of, by the Israelites, i. 93; local traditions respecting, 95; maritime trade by, 131.
REFUGE, cities of, appointed by Moses, i. 180.
REHOBOAM, accession of—ten tribes of Israel revolt from, i. 312; death of, 337.
REVENUE of the Hebrew Commonwealth, i. 214.
RHAMSES the Great, i. 115; employed captives in his works, 116.
RHODES, Colossus of, sold to a Jew, iii. 119.
RIZPAH, i. 202.

SALOME.

ROBINSON, Dr.; his Travels in Palestine referred to, i. 123; on the geography of Sinai, 130.
ROME, alliance of, with the Jews under the Maccabees, ii. 13; account of the Jews in, 451; Jewish quarter in, iii. 168.
RUSSIA, hatred of Jews in, iii. 391; crypto-Judaic heresy in, 192; number of Jews in, 394; present condition of Jews in, 414; estimate of the Jews in Russian dominions, 420.
RUTH, story of, i. 272.

S.

SABBATHAI Sevi, a false Messiah, iii. 362; his proselyte Nathan Benjamin, 363; his progress, 364; is acknowledged by many, 365; excitement among Persian Jews, 366; he surrenders to the Sultan, 367; becomes a Mussulman, 368; his death, 369.
SABBATIC year, the, i. 160, and note.
SABINUS, procurator of Syria, ii. 96; his rapacity and insolence in Jerusalem, 97; attacked by the Jews—sends to Varus for relief, 98; retires to Rome, 101.
SACRIFICE, of human victims common among many early nations, i. 20; abhorred by Hebrew religion, 21, and note; Jewish sacrificial law, 154.
SACY, Baron de, on the sacred writings of the Chinese Jews, ii. 488, note.
SADDUCEES, the, i. 425; growth and origin of the sect of obscure, ii. 29; their tenets, 31; less numerous and influential than the Pharisees, 109.
SALOME, sister of Herod, accuses Mariamne of infidelity, ii. 65; inflames the resentment of Herod, 69; divorces and obtains the death of her husband Costobarus, 71; her hatred

SAMARIA.

of the sons of Mariamne, 78; accompanies Archelaus to Rome, 96; her death, 118.

SAMARIA, siege of, I. 156; razed by John Hyrcanus, ii. 28; rebuilt by Herod, 71; rebellion in, iii. 64.

SAMARITANS, the, I. 420; hated by the Jews, 422; build a rival temple on Mount Gerizim, 441; their retreat to Shechem, 448; join the Jews in their revolt against the Romans, II. 261; importance of, in the reigns of Justin and Justinian, iii. 62; their expulsion from Mount Gerizim, 63; their rebellion suppressed, 65; laws of Justinian against, 66; close of their history, 70.

SAMSON, birth of, I. 257; his riddle—slays the Philistines, 258; carries off the gates of Gaza—betrayed by Dalilah, 359; his death, 260.

SAMUEL, birth of, I. 260; call of, 262; judge, prophet, and priest, 265; his civil administration, 367; anoints David to succeed Saul, 278.

SANHEDRIN, established by Gabinius, ii. 49; origin of the, 104; constitution of the court described, 105; its jurisdiction, 106; escapes the general wreck after fall of Jerusalem, 401; its ten flittings, 403, note; of Tiberias, its haughty edicts, 469.

SANITARY Law of the Jews, I. 176.

SARAH, wife of Abraham, I. 8; burial of, 25.

SAUL, anointed king by Samuel—declared king at Mizpeh, I. 270; defeats the Ammonites—his inauguration, 271; usurps the priestly function, 274; overthrows the Amalekites, 276; seized with insanity, 277; seeks to kill David, 279; his vengeance on the priesthood, 281; consults the witch of Endor, 284; his death, 285.

SCAPE-GOAT, the, I. 155, and note.

SCRIBES, the, ii. 412.

SIMON.

SCRIPTURE, canon of Jewish, I. 437; perfected, 444; demand for Greek translations of, iii. 74.

SENNACHERIB, invades Judah, I. 380; destruction of the army of, 383.

SEPTUAGINT, the; legend of its origin, ii. 26; use of, by the Jews enjoined by Justinian, iii. 75.

SEPULCHRE, church of the Holy, III. 16; destroyed during Persian conquest, 83.

SEVERUS, laws of, favourable to the Jews, ii. 475.

SEVERUS, bishop of Minorca, iii. 29.

SHAMGAR, I. 245.

SHAMMATA, the, "excommunication," ii. 465; irrevocable—its fearful nature, 466.

SHECHEM, I. 7.

SHEPHERD Kings of Egypt, I. 55; invasion and conquest of Egypt by, 105; hostile to manners and religion of the Egyptians—their expulsion, 106.

SHEPHERDS, rising of the, III. 211; atrocities perpetrated by, against the Jews, 212.

SICARII, the, ii. 170, 174; surprise Engaddi, 307; delivered up to the Romans, 390.

SIMON, son of Gamaliel, Patriarch of Tiberias, ii. 470; asserts supremacy over the Prince of the Captivity, 471; his mission to Babylonia, 472.

SIMON, son of Gioras, ii. 205; his lawless warfare, 237; his invasion of Idumea, 310; before Jerusalem, 311; invited into the city, 311; strength of his faction, 319; his valour during the siege, 349; he murders Matthias the high priest, 352; surrenders to the Romans, 377; executed in Rome, 381.

SIMON, the Just, I. 450.

SIMON, the Maccabee, II. 18; recognised by the Romans as Prince of Judæa, 20; assassinated, 21.

SIMON Stylites, iii. 29.

INDEX. 477

SINAI.

SINAI, Mt., the Law delivered to Moses on, i. 116.
SIPPURIM, the, of Dr. Wolff Pascheles referred to, lii. 150.
SISEBUT, King of Spain, lii. 100; his law against the Jews, 101; his persecution of, 102; his conference with, 103.
SLAVE trade of Europe, in the hands of the Jews, iii. 48; opposed by Pope Gregory the First, 53; prevalence of, 144.
SLAVERY, Jewish law of, i. 166; edicts concerning, iii. 49; decrees of councils concerning, 50.
SLAVONIA, Jews of, iii. 188.
SOLOMON, birth of, i. 297; anointed and proclaimed successor of David, 304; his accession, 307; his justice, 308; his wisdom — his internal government — his foreign treaties, 309; begins to build the Temple, 310; his temple described, 311; his palaces, 318; his useful works — his "Song," 319; his splendour and riches, 320; his treaty with Tyre, 321; commerce of, 322; his writings, 325; his seraglio, 326; his old age, 327; his death, 328.
SOLOMON ben Virga, his so-called history, iii. 452.
SPAIN, Jews in, iii. 264; their superiority, 265; their condition under Alfonso VIII., 266; under Alfonso the Wise, 267; the "Siete Partidas," 268; privileges granted to, 269; their civilization of Spain, 271; their wealth, 272; protected by Spanish kings, 274; edict of Maria de Molina, 275; under Pedro the Cruel, 277; during the war of Arragon and Castile, 279; under Henry of Transtamare, 282; oppressed by the Cortes, 283; and by the clergy, 284; massacred in Seville, 286; and Barcelona, 287; persecuted in Navarre, 288; ordinance of Queen Catherine, 295; under John II., 297; assessment of, 299; expelled

TALMUD.

by Ferdinand and Isabella, 309; their sufferings, 311; secret, 321; persecuted by Charles II., 323.
SPINOSA, Benedict, iii. 374; his character, 375; his religion and philosophy, 377; his system analysed, 378; his theologico-political treatise, 379; Bayle's Life of, 381; his influence upon Goethe, 382; M. de Saisset's introduction to the French translation of, 383.
STANLEY, Dr., on the history of Bethel, i. 16, note; on the passage of the Red Sea, 91, note; his account of the Peninsula of Sinai, 171, note; on the geography of Sinai, 130; on the stations of the Israelites in the Wilderness, 197, note; his description of the battle of Jezreel, 252; on the Philistine territory, 356, note.
SUETONIUS, the belief of the Jews in the triumphant coming of Messiah mentioned by, ii. 202.
SYLVESTER, Pope, conference of Jews and Christians before, iii. 10.
SYNAGOGUE, the, ii. 410; worship of, 462; arrangement of, 463; service of, 464; disputes as to language to be used in, iii. 73.
SYNAGOGAL poetry, iii. 444; specimen of, 445.
SYNCELLUS, of Constantinople, i. 101.
SYRO-GRECIAN kingdom, foundation of, by Seleucus, i. 45 L.

T.

TABERNACLE, construction of the, i. 142.
TACITUS, his account of Felix referred to, ii. 168; belief of the Jews in the coming Messiah mentioned by, 202; on the Jewish war, 313, note.
TALMUD, the Babylonian, iii. 4; characterised, 5; its influence on European opinions, 6; modern translators of, 40.

INDEX.

TANAIM.

TANAIM, the, interpreters of the Mischna, ii. 481.

TARICHEA, siege of, ii. 276; surrender of, 277; treacherous massacre after the surrender, 279.

TAXES, Jewish, i. 233.

TEMPLE, the, of Solomon described, i. 110; the accounts of it contradictory, 112; dedication of, 115; foundation of the second after Babylonian captivity, 419; dedication of the second, 427; desecrated by Antiochus Epiphanes, 461; rebuilt by Herod, ii. 77; Caligula's design to profane, 141; description of at the time of the siege of Jerusalem, 331; besieged by Titus, 359; burning of, 367; entered by the Romans, 368; demolition of, 369; spoils taken from by Titus, 381; attempt of Julian to rebuild, iii. 18; supposed preternatural interruptions to the work, 19; explanation of, 20.

TENURES, Jewish law of, i. 233.

TERAH, the father of Abraham, i. 4.

TERTULLIAN, condition of the Jews described by, ii. 471.

THEBES, city of, i. 101; its magnificence, 107; its monuments instinct with history, 108; its unrivalled grandeur due to the Rameseid dynasty, 111.

THEFT, Jewish law of, i. 182.

THEODORIC, King of Italy, protects the Jews, iii. 56.

THEODORUS, Rabbi, iii. 30; his conversion, 32.

THEODOSIUS, the Great, iii. 23; his treatment of the Jews, 24.

THEUDAS, the Impostor, ii. 165.

THOMAS de Torquemada, iii. 306; number of victims put to death by the Inquisition under, 331, note.

TIBERIAS, city of, ii. 221; factions in, 224; surrenders to Vespasian, 275; becomes the seat of the Jewish Patriarch, 447.

TIBERIAS, Patriarch of, ii. 440; his

VESPASIAN.

office, 441; growth of his authority 443; survey of his dominions, 448

TIBERIUS Alexander, governor of Judæa, ii. 165; holds a high command in army of Titus, 319.

TIBERIUS Cæsar, policy of, ii. 118.

TITUS, son of Vespasian, ii. 216; joins his father at Ptolemais, 241; takes Japha, 260; his victory before Tarichea, 277; besieges and captures Gischala, 287; sent against Jerusalem, 314; forms the siege, 321; his critical situation, 322; advances his approaches, 324; reviews his troops, 342; his barbarity, 347; he begins a trench and a wall, 350; addresses his officers, 356; endeavours to save the Temple, 368; attacks and takes the upper city, 371; his solitary act of mercy, 378; his triumph, 381; arch of, in Rome, 382; his gift to Josephus, 392.

TOLEDO, councils of, iii. 104; their decrees respecting the Jews, 105; massacres at, 204.

TORTOSA, public disputation at, iii. 291.

TRADITION, ii. 413; authority of, 414.

TRAJAN, reign of, ii. 417.

TURKEY, Jews in, iii. 337.

U.

UR, description of, i. 5.

URIM and Thummim, the, i. 147.

USURY, Jewish law of, i. 232; effect o. upon the modern Jews, iii. 170.

V

VARUS, Prefect of Syria, ii. 96; in Jerusalem, 101.

VENTIDIUS Cumanus, governor of Judæa, ii. 166; is bribed by the Samaritans, 167; summoned to Rome and banished, 168.

VESPASIAN, appointed to the command in Syria, ii. 216; opens the

VIENNA.
campaign against the Jews, 240;
advances with his army, 242;
besieges Jotapata, 245; is wounded,
254; takes Jotapata, 263; marches
to Cesarea, 271; takes Tiberias,
275; and Tarichea, 276; treacherous massacre of captives by, 279;
takes Gamala, 286; marches against
Gadara, 307; his successes, 309;
assumes the purple, 313; his
triumph, 381; reign of, 415.
VIENNA, council of, its laws, iii. 202.
VINCENT Ferrer, his mission to convert the Jews, iii. 290; its success, 291.
VISIGOTHIC kings, fall of the, iii. 114.
VITELLIUS, at Jerusalem, ii. 124.
VOLTAIRE, his antipathy against the Jews, iii. 395.

W.

WAR, Jewish laws of, i. 183.
WARBURTON, Dr., his opinion on the sanction of the Hebrew law, i. 186, note.
WEIGHTS, Hebrew, imperfect knowledge of, i. 120.
WILKINSON, Sir Gardner, on Egyptian antiquities, i. 98, 102, note; on date of the Exodus, 120.

XUNZ.

X.

XERXES, i. 428.

Y.

YEMEN, Jewish kingdom in, iii. 87; massacre of Christians in, 88.
YOUNG, Dr., key to hieroglyphics discovered by, i. 100.

Z.

ZACHARIAS, the son of Baruch, ii. 303; murdered by the Zealots, 304.
ZACHARIAS of Novgorod, heresy of, iii. 391.
ZADIKIM, sect of the, ii. 2.
ZAMORA, council of, iii. 296.
ZEALOTS, the, ii. 191; faction of robber Zealots in Jerusalem, 292; bloody massacre by, 302.
ZEDEKIAH, King of Judah, i. 398.
ZENDAVESTA, the, compared with the Cabala, iii. 432.
ZENOBIA, Queen of Palmyra, iii. 8.
ZERUBBABEL, his royal descent, i. 418.
ZOHARITES, sect of the, iii. 371.
ZUNZ, Dr., his history of synagogal poetry referred to, iii. 445.

THE END.